Citroën Berlingo/ Peugeot Partner
Owners Workshop Manual

Peter T Gill

Models covered

(6341 - 6BA1 - 304)

Citroën Berlingo Multispace & Van and Peugeot Partner Teepee & Van ('B9' or 'II' model range) with 1.6 litre (1560cc) turbo-diesel engines

Does NOT cover petrol engined models
Does NOT cover Berlingo 'First' or Partner 'Origin' models

ABCDE
FGHIJ
KLMN

© Haynes Group Limited 2016

A book in the **Haynes Owners Workshop Manual Series**

ISBN **978 1 78521 341 0**

British Library Cataloguing in Publication Data
A catalogue record for this book is available from the British Library.

Printed in India

Haynes Group Limited
Sparkford, Yeovil, Somerset BA22 7JJ, England

Haynes North America, Inc
2801 Townsgate Road, Suite 340, Thousand Oaks, CA 91361

Contents

LIVING WITH YOUR CITROËN BERLINGO/ PEUGEOT PARTNER

Contents

REPAIRS AND OVERHAUL

Engine and Associated Systems

Transmission

Brakes and suspension

Body equipment

REFERENCE

Designed as a joint venture between Citroën and Peugeot, the Berlingo and Partner were introduced into the UK in 1996 as purpose-built Vans available in 600kg or 800kg payloads. To increase the appeal of the range, the Berlingo Multispace MPV was introduced in mid-1998. The Multispace is mechanically identical to the Van version but with the addition of rear seats, side windows and additional interior trim. Initially, all models were available only in three-door format, but in mid-1999, the option of a sliding side door on the right-hand side was added. The Peugeot MPV version, known as the Partner Combi, joined the model line-up for the 2001 model year, which also saw the introduction, on all models, of a second sliding side door for the left-hand side. In the autumn of 2002, the entire range underwent a major facelift, with significant styling changes to the front bumpers, headlights, bonnet and front wings, together with numerous mechanical and electrical revisions.

During the production run a variety of petrol and diesels engines have been offered according to model and year of production. These include 1.4 litre (1360cc) and 1.6 litre (1587cc) petrol engines, and 1.6 litre (1560cc), 1.8 litre (1769cc), 1.9 litre (1868cc &1905cc) and 2.0 litre (1997cc), including turbo diesel engines.

This manual will be covering models from 2008, which are new "B9" versions, launched and renamed as "Berlingo II" and "Partner II". These models where introduced with 1.6 litre petrol and diesel engines. The petrol engine models where only sold in small numbers, so this manual only covers the 1.6 litre diesel engines. The engine is mounted transversely at the front of vehicle, with the transmission mounted on its left-hand end. All engines are fitted with a manual transmission as standard (an automatic transmission is available on certain engines).

All models have fully independent front suspension, incorporating shock absorbers, coil springs and an anti-roll bar. The rear beam axle has a built-in anti-roll bar, with separate shock absorbers and coil spring. Rack-and-pinion steering gear is used with power assistance.

A wide range of standard and optional equipment is available within the range to suit most tastes, including power steering, central locking, engine immobiliser, electric windows, electric sunroof and airbags. An anti-lock braking system and air conditioning system are also available as options, or standard equipment on certain models.

Provided that regular servicing is carried out in accordance with the manufacturer's recommendations, the vehicle should prove reliable and very economical. The engine compartment is well-designed, and most of the items requiring frequent attention are easily accessible.

Your Owner's Manual

The aim of this manual is to help you get the best value from your vehicle. It can do so in several ways. It can help you decide what work must be done (even should you choose to get it done by a garage), provide information on routine maintenance and servicing, and give a logical course of action and diagnosis when random faults occur. However, it is hoped that you will use the manual by tackling the work yourself. On simpler jobs it may even be quicker than booking the vehicle into a garage and going there twice, to leave and collect it. Perhaps most important, a lot of money can be saved by avoiding the costs a garage must charge to cover its labour and overheads.

The manual has drawings and descriptions to show the function of the various components so that their layout can be understood. Tasks are described and photographed in a clear step-by-step sequence.

References to the 'left-hand' and 'right-hand' sides of the vehicle are always in the sense of when viewed by a person sat in the driver's seat, facing forwards.

Acknowledgements

Thanks are due to Draper Tools Limited, who provided some of the workshop tools, and to all those people at Sparkford who helped in the production of this Manual.

We take great pride in the accuracy of information given in this manual, but vehicle manufacturers make alterations and design changes during the production run of a particular vehicle of which they do not inform us. No liability can be accepted by the authors or publishers for loss, damage or injury caused by errors in, or omissions from, the information given.

Citroën Berlingo

Working on your car can be dangerous. This page shows just some of the potential risks and hazards, with the aim of creating a safety-conscious attitude.

General hazards

Scalding

• Don't remove the radiator or expansion tank cap while the engine is hot.

• Engine oil, transmission fluid or power steering fluid may also be dangerously hot if the engine has recently been running.

Burning

• Beware of burns from the exhaust system and from any part of the engine. Brake discs and drums can also be extremely hot immediately after use.

Crushing

• When working under or near a raised vehicle, always supplement the jack with axle stands, or use drive-on ramps. *Never venture under a car which is only supported by a jack*.

• Take care if loosening or tightening high-torque nuts when the vehicle is on stands. Initial loosening and final tightening should be done with the wheels on the ground.

Fire

• Fuel is highly flammable; fuel vapour is explosive.

• Don't let fuel spill onto a hot engine.

• Do not smoke or allow naked lights (including pilot lights) anywhere near a vehicle being worked on. Also beware of creating sparks (electrically or by use of tools).

• Fuel vapour is heavier than air, so don't work on the fuel system with the vehicle over an inspection pit.

• Another cause of fire is an electrical overload or short-circuit. Take care when repairing or modifying the vehicle wiring.

• Keep a fire extinguisher handy, of a type suitable for use on fuel and electrical fires.

Electric shock

• Ignition HT and Xenon headlight voltages can be dangerous, especially to people with heart problems or a pacemaker. Don't work on or near these systems with the engine running or the ignition switched on.

• Mains voltage is also dangerous. Make sure that any mains-operated equipment is correctly earthed. Mains power points should be protected by a residual current device (RCD) circuit breaker.

Fume or gas intoxication

• Exhaust fumes are poisonous; they can contain carbon monoxide, which is rapidly fatal if inhaled. Never run the engine in a confined space such as a garage with the doors shut.

• Fuel vapour is also poisonous, as are the vapours from some cleaning solvents and paint thinners.

Poisonous or irritant substances

• Avoid skin contact with battery acid and with any fuel, fluid or lubricant, especially antifreeze, brake hydraulic fluid and Diesel fuel. Don't syphon them by mouth. If such a substance is swallowed or gets into the eyes, seek medical advice.

• Prolonged contact with used engine oil can cause skin cancer. Wear gloves or use a barrier cream if necessary. Change out of oil-soaked clothes and do not keep oily rags in your pocket.

• Air conditioning refrigerant forms a poisonous gas if exposed to a naked flame (including a cigarette). It can also cause skin burns on contact.

Asbestos

• Asbestos dust can cause cancer if inhaled or swallowed. Asbestos may be found in gaskets and in brake and clutch linings. When dealing with such components it is safest to assume that they contain asbestos.

Special hazards

Hydrofluoric acid

• This extremely corrosive acid is formed when certain types of synthetic rubber, found in some O-rings, oil seals, fuel hoses etc, are exposed to temperatures above 4000C. The rubber changes into a charred or sticky substance containing the acid. *Once formed, the acid remains dangerous for years. If it gets onto the skin, it may be necessary to amputate the limb concerned*.

• When dealing with a vehicle which has suffered a fire, or with components salvaged from such a vehicle, wear protective gloves and discard them after use.

The battery

• Batteries contain sulphuric acid, which attacks clothing, eyes and skin. Take care when topping-up or carrying the battery.

• The hydrogen gas given off by the battery is highly explosive. Never cause a spark or allow a naked light nearby. Be careful when connecting and disconnecting battery chargers or jump leads.

Air bags

• Air bags can cause injury if they go off accidentally. Take care when removing the steering wheel and trim panels. Special storage instructions may apply.

Diesel injection equipment

• Diesel injection pumps supply fuel at very high pressure. Take care when working on the fuel injectors and fuel pipes.

⚠ *Warning: Never expose the hands, face or any other part of the body to injector spray; the fuel can penetrate the skin with potentially fatal results.*

Remember...

DO

• Do use eye protection when using power tools, and when working under the vehicle.

• Do wear gloves or use barrier cream to protect your hands when necessary.

• Do get someone to check periodically that all is well when working alone on the vehicle.

• Do keep loose clothing and long hair well out of the way of moving mechanical parts.

• Do remove rings, wristwatch etc, before working on the vehicle – especially the electrical system.

• Do ensure that any lifting or jacking equipment has a safe working load rating adequate for the job.

DON'T

• Don't attempt to lift a heavy component which may be beyond your capability – get assistance.

• Don't rush to finish a job, or take unverified short cuts.

• Don't use ill-fitting tools which may slip and cause injury.

• Don't leave tools or parts lying around where someone can trip over them. Mop up oil and fuel spills at once.

• Don't allow children or pets to play in or near a vehicle being worked on.

The following pages are intended to help in dealing with common roadside emergencies and breakdowns. You will find more detailed fault finding information at the back of the manual, and repair information in the main chapters.

If your car won't start and the starter motor doesn't turn

☐ Open the bonnet and make sure that the battery terminals are clean and tight.
☐ Switch on the headlights and try to start the engine. If the headlights go very dim when you'r e trying to start, the battery is probably flat. Try jump starting using another car.

If your car won't start even though the starter motor turns as normal

☐ Is there fuel in the tank?
☐ Is there moisture on electrical components under the bonnet? Switch off the ignition, and then wipe off any obvious dampness with a dry cloth. Spray a water-repellent aerosol product (WD-40 or equivalent) on ignition and fuel system electrical connectors like those shown in the photos (Note that diesel engines do not normally suffer from damp).

A Remove the plastic cover and check the fused links and security of the battery connections.

B Check the crankshaft sensor wiring connector is secure.

C Check the camshaft sensor wiring connector is secure.

D Remove the cover and check that all fuses are still in good condition and none have blown.

Check that electrical connections are secure (with the ignition switched off) and spray them with a water dispersantspray like WD-40 if you suspect a problem due to damp.

Jump starting

 Jump starting will get you out of trouble, but you must correct whatever made the battery go flat in the first place. There are three possibilities:

1 *The battery has been drained by repeated attempts to start, or by leaving the lights on.*

2 *The charging system is not working properly (alternator drivebelt slack or broken, alternator wiring fault or alternator itself faulty).*

3 *The battery itself is at fault (electrolyte low, or battery worn out).*

When jump-starting a car, observe the following precautions:

Note: *Remove the key in case the central locking engages when the jump leads are connected*

✓ Before connecting the booster battery, make sure that the ignition is switched off.
✓ Ensure that all electrical equipment (lights, heater, wipers, etc) is switched off.
✓ Take note of any special precautions printed on the battery case.
✓ Make sure that the booster battery is the same voltage as the discharged one in the vehicle.

✓ If the battery is being jump-started from the battery in another vehicle, the two vehicles MUST NOT TOUCH each other.
✓ Make sure that the transmission is in neutral (or PARK, in the case of Multitronic transmission).

 Budget jump leads can be a false economy, as they often do not pass enough current to start large capacity or diesel engines. They can also get hot.

1 Unclip the plastic cover and connect the red jump lead to the positive (+) battery terminal.

2 Connect the other end of the red jump lead to the positive (+) terminal of the booster battery.

3 Connect one end of the black jump lead to the negative (-) terminal of the booster battery.

4 Connect the other end of the black jump lead negative (-) terminal to the metal earth point on the near side front inner wing panel.

5 Make sure that the jump leads will not come into contact with the fan, drive-belts or other moving parts of the engine.

6 Start the engine using the booster battery and run it at idle speed. Switch on the lights, rear window demister and heater blower motor, then disconnect the jump leads in the reverse order of connection. Turn off the lights etc.

Identifying leaks

Puddles on the garage floor or drive, or obvious wetness under the bonnet or underneath the car, suggest a leak that needs investigating. It can sometimes be difficult to decide where the leak is coming from, especially if an engine undershield is fitted. Leaking oil or fluid can also be blown rearwards by the passage of air under the car, giving a false impression of where the problem lies.

 Warning: Most automotive oils and fluids are poisonous. Wash them off skin, and change out of contaminated clothing, without delay.

 The smell of a fluid leaking from the car may provide a clue to what's leaking. Some fluids are distinctively coloured. It may help to remove the engine undershield, clean the car carefully and to park it over some clean paper overnight as an aid to locating the source of the leak.

Sump oil

Engine oil may leak from the drain plug...

Oil from filter

...or from the base of the oil filter.

Gearbox oil

Gearbox oil can leak from the seals at the inboard ends of the driveshafts.

Antifreeze

Leaking antifreeze often leaves a crystalline deposit like this.

Brake fluid

A leak occurring at a wheel is almost certainly brake fluid.

Power steering fluid

Power steering fluid may leak from the pipe connectors on the steering rack.

Towing

When all else fails, you may find yourself having to get a tow home – or of course you may be helping somebody else. Long-distance recovery should only be done by a garage or breakdown service. For shorter distances, DIY towing using another car is easy enough, but observe the following points:

Caution: When towing a vehicle which has automatic transmission, do not tow the car at speeds in excess of 30 mph or for a distance greater than 30 miles. If towing speeds/distances are to exceed these limits, then the car must be towed with its front wheels off the ground.

☐ Use a proper tow-rope – they are not expensive. The vehicle being towed must display an ON TOW sign in its rear window.

☐ Always turn the ignition key to the 'on' position when the vehicle is being towed, so that the steering lock is released, and that the direction indicator and brake lights work.

☐ The towing eye is kept inside the spare wheel (see Wheel changing). To fit the eye, unclip the access cover from the relevant bumper and screw the eye firmly into position (see illustrations)

☐ Before being towed, release the handbrake and select neutral on the transmission.

☐ Note that greater-than-usual pedal pressure will be required to operate the brakes, since the vacuum servo unit is only operational with the engine running.

☐ The driver of the car being towed must keep the tow-rope taut at all times to avoid snatching.

☐ Make sure that both drivers know the route before setting off.

☐ Only drive at moderate speeds and keep the distance towed to a minimum. Drive smoothly and allow plenty of time for slowing down at junctions.

Unclip the access cover from the rear bumper ...

... then screw the towing eye in securely (use wheel brace through eye to tighten)

Unclip the cover from the front bumper ...

... and then fit the towing eye to the front of the vehicle

Wheel changing

⚠️ *Warning: Do not change a wheel in a situation where you risk being hit by another vehicle. On busy roads, try to stop in a lay-by or a gateway. Be wary of passing traffic while changing the wheel – it is easy to become distracted by the job in hand.*

Preparation

☐ When a puncture occurs, stop as soon as it is safe to do so.
☐ Park on firm level ground, if possible, and well out of the way of other traffic.
☐ Use hazard warning lights if necessary.
☐ If you have one, use a warning triangle to alert other drivers of your presence.
☐ Apply the handbrake and engage first or reverse gear.
☐ If the ground is soft, use a flat piece of wood to spread the load under the foot of the jack.
☐ Place a chock against the wheel diagonally opposite the wheel to be removed, or use a large stone (or similar) to stop the car rolling.
☐ The jack and tool kit are kept in a storage compartment under the front passenger seat. On 5 and 7 seater models, slide the front passenger seat forwards to access the tools. On van models, hinge the outer passenger seat upwards from the front to access the tools.

Changing the wheel

1 Unclip the trim cover…

2 …to access the wheel changing tools.

3 At the rear of the load/luggage area, use the wheel brace to turn the securing bolt anti-clockwise, approx. five turns…

4 …then unhook the spare wheel carrier and lower the wheel down from under the rear floor panel.

5 Slide the spare wheel from under the rear of the vehicle.

6 Remove the wheel chock from the tool kit and place it against the wheel diagonally opposite the wheel to be removed.

7 On models with steel wheels, remove the wheel trim using the hooked tool from the wheel changing tool kit.

8 On models with alloy wheels, unclip the plastic wheel bolt covers, using the plastic tool provided in the tool kit.

9 Where anti-theft wheel bolts are fitted, unscrew the anti-theft bolt using the special tool provided – normally stored in the passenger glovebox or toolkit.

10 With the vehicle still on the ground, use the tool provided to slacken each wheel bolt by half a turn.

11 Make sure the jack is located on firm ground, and engage the jack head correctly with the sill. Then raise the jack until the wheel is raised clear of the ground.

12 Unscrew the wheel bolts and remove the wheel. Place the wheel under the vehicle sill in case the jack fails.

13 On alloy wheels, use the plastic tool provided in the tool kit to withdraw the wheel bolts.

14 Fit the spare wheel and screw in the bolts. Lightly tighten the bolts with the wheel brace then lower the car to the ground.

15 Securely tighten the wheel bolts in a diagonal sequence then refit the wheel trim/wheel bolt covers (as applicable). Stow the punctured wheel back under the rear of the vehicle and secure in position. Place the jack, wheel brace and tools back in the compartment under the front passenger seat.

Finally . . .

- ☐ Remove the wheel chock.
- ☐ Check the tyre pressure on the wheel just fitted. If it is low, or if you don't have a pressure gauge with you, drive slowly to the next garage and inflate the tyre to the correct pressure.
- ☐ The wheel bolts should be slackened and retightened to the specified torque at the earliest possible opportunity (see Chapter 1 Specifications).
- ☐ Have the damaged tyre or wheel repaired as soon as possible, or another puncture will leave you stranded.

Introduction

There are some very simple checks which need only take a few minutes to carry out, but which could save you a lot of inconvenience and expense.

These checks require no great skill or special tools, and the small amount of time they take to perform could prove to be very well spent, for example;

☐ Keeping an eye on tyre condition and pressures, will not only help to stop them wearing out prematurely, but could also save your life.

☐ Many breakdowns are caused by electrical problems. Battery-related faults are particularly common, and aw quick check on a regular basis will often prevent the majority of these.

☐ If your car develops a brake fluid leak, the first time you might know about it is when your brakes don't work properly. Checking the level regularly will give advance warning of this kind of problem.

☐ If the oil or coolant levels run low, the cost of repairing any engine damage will be far greater than fixing the leak, for example.

Underbonnet check points

◄ 1.6 litre SOHC engine

A *Engine oil level dipstick*

B *Engine oil filler cap*

C *Coolant expansion tank/reservoir*

D *Brake (and clutch) fluid reservoir*

E *Screen washer fluid reservoir*

F *Power steering fluid reservoir (electro-pump type)*

G *Battery*

◄ 1.6 litre DOHC engine

A *Engine oil level dipstick*

B *Engine oil filler cap*

C *Coolant expansion tank/reservoir*

D *Brake (and clutch) fluid reservoir*

E *Screen washer fluid reservoir*

F *Power steering fluid reservoir (belt driven pump type)*

G *Battery*

Engine oil level

Before you start

✔ Make sure that your car is on level ground.
✔ Check the oil level before the car is driven, or at least 5 minutes after the engine has been switched off.

 HAYNES HiNT *If the oil is checked immediately after driving the vehicle, some of the oil will remain in the upper engine components, resulting in an inaccurate reading on the dipstick.*

The correct oil

Modern engines place great demands on their oil. It is very important that the correct oil for your car is used (see *Lubricants and fluids*).

Car care

● If you have to add oil frequently, you should check whether you have any oil leaks. Place some clean paper under the car overnight, and check for stains in the morning. If there are no leaks, the engine may be burning oil.
● Always maintain the level between the upper and lower dipstick marks (see photo 3). If the level is too low severe engine damage may occur. Oil seal failure may result if the engine is overfilled by adding too much oil.

1 The dipstick is located at the front of the engine (see Underbonnet check points); the dipstick is often brightly coloured and/or has a picture of an oil-can on the top for identification. Withdraw the dipstick (1.6 litre SOHC engine shown).

2 Using a clean rag or paper towel, remove all oil from the dipstick. Insert the clean dipstick into the tube as far as it will go, then withdraw it again.

3 Note the oil level on the end of the dipstick, which should be between the upper (MAX) mark and lower (MIN) mark. Approximately 1.0 litre of oil will raise the level from the lower mark to the upper mark.

4 Oil is added through the filler cap aperture. Unscrew the cap and top-up the level; a funnel may help to reduce spillage. Add the oil slowly, checking the level on the dipstick often. **Don't overfill** (see *Car care*).

Coolant level

 Warning: DO NOT attempt to remove the expansion tank pressure cap when the engine is hot, as there is a very great risk of scalding.
Warning: Do not leave open containers of coolant about, as it is poisonous.

Car care

● Adding coolant should not be necessary on a regular basis. If frequent topping-up is required, it is likely there is a leak. Check the radiator, all hoses and joint faces for signs of staining or wetness, and rectify as necessary.

● It is important that antifreeze is used in the cooling system all year round, not just during the winter months. Don't top-up with water alone, as the antifreeze will become too diluted.

1 The coolant level must be checked with the engine cold; the coolant level should be between the MAX and MIN marks on the expansion tank.

2 If topping-up is necessary, remove the pressure cap (when engine is cold) from the expansion tank, which is located on the right-hand side of the engine compartment.

3 Add the pre-mixed coolant to the expansion tank until the level is between the MAX and MIN markings. Once the level is correct, securely refit the cap.

Brake (and clutch) fluid level

Warning: Brake fluid can harm your eyes and damage painted surfaces, so use extreme caution when handling and pouring it.

Warning: Do not use fluid that has been standing open for some time, as it absorbs moisture from the air, which can cause a dangerous loss of braking effectiveness.

Before you start
✔ Make sure that your car is on level ground.

Safety first!
● If the reservoir requires repeated topping-up this is an indication of a fluid leak somewhere in the system, which should be investigated immediately.

● If a leak is suspected, the car should not be driven until the braking system has been checked. Never take any risks where brakes are concerned.

1 The upper (MAX) fluid level marking is on the side of the upper reservoir, which is located at the rear of the engine compartment.

2 If topping-up is necessary, first wipe clean the area around the filler cap with a clean cloth, then unscrew the cap and remove it along with the rubber diaphragm.

3 Carefully add fluid, avoiding spilling it on the surrounding paintwork. Use only the specified hydraulic fluid. After filling to the correct level, refit the diaphragm and cap, and tighten it securely. Wipe off any spilt fluid.

Power steering fluid level

Before you start
✔ Park the vehicle on level ground.
✔ Set the steering wheel straight-ahead.
✔ The engine should be cold and turned off.

Safety first!
● The need for frequent topping-up indicates a leak, which should be investigated immediately.

1 On models with an electro-pump assembly, the fluid reservoir is on the right-hand side of the engine compartment, behind the headlight, below the coolant reservoir. Unscrew the cap complete with dipstick from the reservoir.

2 On models with a belt driven pump assembly, the fluid reservoir is on the right-hand side of the engine compartment, on a bracket above the engine mounting. Unscrew the cap from the reservoir.

3 On models with an electro-pump assembly, check the fluid level is up to the upper (MAX) level indicator on the dipstick.

4 On models with a belt driven pump assembly, check the fluid level is up to the upper (MX – MAX) level indicator inside the aperture of the reservoir.

5 Top-up the reservoir with the specified type of the fluid, using a funnel. Once the level is correct, securely refit the reservoir cap. Do not overfill the reservoir.

Screen washer fluid level

● Screenwash additives not only keep the windscreen clean during foul weather, they also prevent the washer system freezing in cold weather – which is when you are likely to need it most. Don't top-up using plain water as the screenwash will become too diluted, and will freeze during cold weather.

 Warning: On no account use coolant antifreeze in the washer system, as this may damage the paintwork.

1 The washer fluid reservoir is located in the right-hand front corner of the engine compartment. To check the fluid level, open the cap and look down the filler neck.

2 If topping-up is necessary, add water and a screenwash additive in the quantities recommended on the bottle.

Battery

Caution: Before carrying out any work on the vehicle battery, read the precautions given in 'Safety first!' at the start of this manual.

✔ Make sure that the battery tray is in good condition, and that the clamp is tight. Corrosion on the tray, retaining clamp and the battery itself can be removed with a solution of water and baking soda. Thoroughly rinse all cleaned areas with water. Any metal parts damaged by corrosion should be covered with a zinc-based primer, and then painted.

✔ Periodically (approximately every three months), check the charge condition of the battery, as described in Chapter 5A Section 3.

✔ If the battery is flat, and you need to jump start your vehicle, see Roadside repairs.

1 Lift the plastic cover to gain access to the battery positive terminal, which is located on the left-hand side of the engine compartment. The exterior of the battery should be inspected periodically for damage such as a cracked case or cover.

2 Check the battery lead clamps for tightness to ensure good electrical connections, and check the leads for signs of damage.

HAYNES HiNT

Battery corrosion can be kept to a minimum by applying a layer of petroleum jelly to the clamps and terminals after they are reconnected.

3 If corrosion (white, fluffy deposits) is evident, remove the cables from the battery terminals, clean them with a small wire brush, then refit them. Automotive stores sell a tool for cleaning the battery post ...

4 ... as well as the battery cable clamps.

Wiper blades

1 Check the condition of the wiper blades: if they are cracked or show signs of deterioration, or if the glass swept area is smeared, renew them. For maximum clarity of vision, wiper blades should be renewed annually.

2 To remove a windscreen wiper blade, lift the wiper from the screen and press down on the square retaining clip (arrowed)…

3 …then disengage the blade by sliding it from the end of the wiper arm, taking care not to allow the wiper arm to spring back and damage the windscreen.

4 To remove the rear wiper blade, tilt the wiper blade …

5 … and then pull the blade to unclip it from the arm, taking care not to allow the arm to spring back and damage the rear screen.

Bulbs and fuses

✔ Check all external lights and the horn. Refer to Chapter 12 Section 2 for details if any of the circuits are found to be inoperative.

✔ Visually check all accessible wiring connectors, harnesses and retaining clips for security, and for signs of chafing or damage.

HAYNES HiNT *If you need to check your brake lights and indicators unaided, back up to a wall or garage door and operate the lights. The reflected light should show if they are working properly.*

1 If a single indicator light, brake light, sidelight or headlight has failed, it is likely that a bulb has blown, and will need to be renewed. Refer to Chapter 12, Section 5 for details. If both brake lights have failed, it is possible that the switch has failed (see Chapter 9, Section 17).

2 If more than one indicator or tail light has failed, it is likely that either a fuse has blown or that there is a fault in the circuit. Fuses are located behind a cover in the glovebox. Open the glovebox, rotate the screw fastener to lower the cover.

3 Additional fuses and relays are located in the left-hand side of the engine compartment fusebox. To renew a blown fuse, simply pull it out and fit a new fuse of the correct rating (see Wiring diagrams). If the fuse blows again, it is important that you find out why – a complete checking procedure is given in Chapter 12, Section 2.

Tyre condition and pressure

It is very important that tyres are in good condition, and at the correct pressure – having a tyre failure at any speed is highly dangerous. Tyre wear is influenced by driving style – harsh braking and acceleration, or fast cornering, will all produce more rapid tyre wear. As a general rule, the front tyres wear out faster the the rears. Interchanging the tyres from front to rear ("rotating" the tyres) may result in more even wear. However, if this is completely effective, you may have the expense of replacing all four tyres at once!

Remove any nails or stones embedded in the tread before they penetrate the tyre to cause deflation. If removal of a nail does

reveal that the tyre has been punctured, refit the nail so that its point of penetration is marked. Then immediately change the wheel, and have the tyre repaired by a tyre dealer.

Regularly check the tyres for damage in the form of cuts or bulges, especially in the side walls. Periodically remove the wheels, and clean any dirt or mud from the inside and outside surfaces. Examine the wheel rims for signs of rusting, corrosion or other damage. Light alloy wheels are easily damaged by "kerbing" whilst parking; steel wheels may also become dented or buckled. A new wheel is very often the only way to overcome severe damage.

New tyres should be balanced when they are fitted, but it may become necessary to re-balance them as they ear, or if the balance weights fitted to the wheel rim should fall off. Unbalanced tyres will wear more quickly, as will the steering and suspension components. Wheel imbalance is normally signified by vibration, particularly at t certain speed (typically around 50 mph). If this vibration is felt only through the steering wheel, then it is likely that just the front wheels need balancing. If, however, the vibration is felt through the whole car, the rear wheels could be out of balance. Wheel balancing should be carried out by a tyre dealer or garage.

1 Tread Depth - visual check
The original tyres have tread wear safety bands (B), which will appear when the tread depth reaches approximately 1.6 mm. The band positions are indicated by a triangular mark on the tyre sidewall (A).

2 Tread Depth - manual check
Alternatively, tread wear can be monitored with a simple, inexpensive device known as a tread depth indicator gauge.

3 Tyre Pressure Check
Check the tyre pressures regularly with the tyres cold. Do not adjust the tyre pressures immediately after the vehicle has been used, or an inaccurate setting will result.

Tyre tread wear patterns

Shoulder Wear

Underinflation (wear on both sides)
Under-inflation will cause overheating of the tyre, because the tyre will flex too much, and the tread will not sit correctly on the road surface. This will cause a loss of grip and excessive wear, not to mention the danger of sudden tyre failure due to heat build-up.
Check and adjust pressures
Incorrect wheel camber (wear on one side)
Repair or renew suspension parts
Hard cornering
Reduce speed!

Centre Wear

Overinflation
Over-inflation will cause rapid wear of the centre part of the tyre tread, coupled with reduced grip, harsher ride, and the danger of shock damage occurring in the tyre casing.
Check and adjust pressures

If you sometimes have to inflate your car's tyres to the higher pressures specified for maximum load or sustained high speed, don't forget to reduce the pressures to normal afterwards.

Uneven Wear

Front tyres may wear unevenly as a result of wheel misalignment. Most tyre dealers and garages can check and adjust the wheel alignment (or "tracking") for a modest charge.
Incorrect camber or castor
Repair or renew suspension parts
Malfunctioning suspension
Repair or renew suspension parts
Unbalanced wheel
Balance tyres
Incorrect toe setting
Adjust front wheel alignment
Note: *The feathered edge of the tread which typifies toe wear is best checked by feel.*

Lubricants and fluids

Engine
Without particulate filter . . . .   Multigrade engine oil, viscosity SAE 10W/40, 5W/40, 5W/30 or 0W/30 to ACEA B3 and API CD/CF specification*

With particulate filter . . . .   Multigrade engine oil, viscosity SAE 10W/40, 5W/40 or 5W/30 to ACEA B3 and API CD/CF specification*

Cooling system
All models. . . . .   Glysantin G33 or RevkoGel 2000

Transmission
Manual transmission . . . .   ESSO EZL848 or TOTAL H6965 gear oil (SAE 75W-80W)

Braking and clutch system
All models. . . . .   Hydraulic fluid to DOT 4

Power steering system
Electro-pump assembly . . . .   Total Fluide DA

Belt driven pump assembly . . . .   Total AT42

Particulate filter additives (where applicable)
All models. . . . .   Eolys DPX42 or Eolys 176**

Models between RPO 12110 and 12166 – (third generation additive)*** . .   Rhodia Eolys Powerflex or Infineum F7995

Due to the extended service intervals Peugeot/Citroen specify, it is essential that semi-synthetic or fully-synthetic engine oil be used.

*** Eolys 176 will not be available from the manufacturer from 15/07/10 onwards.*

****The new third generation additive, Rhodia Eolys Powerflex and Infinium F7995, will replace the Eolys 176 additive.*

Tyre pressures

Note: *The make of tyres, the sizes and the pressures for each vehicle are given on a label attached to the driver's door B-pillar.*

Note: *Pressures on the label apply to original-equipment tyres listed, and may vary if any other makes or type of tyre is fitted; check with the tyre manufacturer or supplier for correct pressures if necessary.*

Note: *Tyre pressures must always be checked with the tyres cold to ensure accuracy.*

Chapter 1
Routine maintenance and servicing

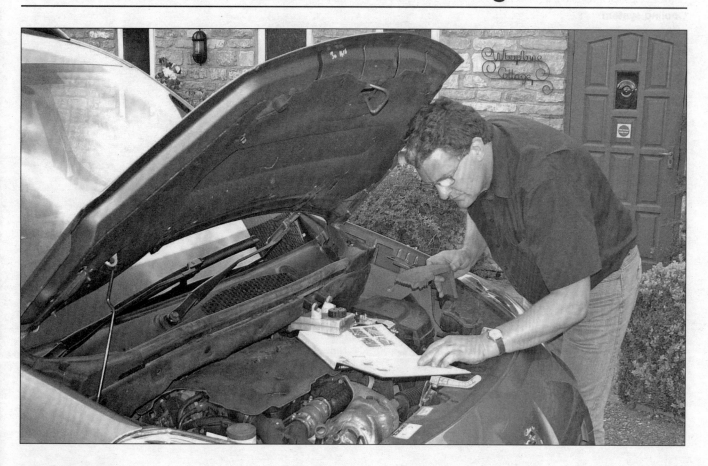

Contents

Degrees of difficulty

| Easy, suitable for novice with little experience | Fairly easy, suitable for beginner with some experience | Fairly difficult, suitable for competent DIY mechanic | Difficult, suitable for experienced DIY mechanic | Very difficult, suitable for expert DIY or professional |

1•2 Servicing specifications

Lubricants and fluids . . . . Refer to Lubricants and fluids

Capacities
Note: *All values are approximate.*

Engine oil
Drain and refill, with filter change . . . . 3.75 litres
Between dipstick MAX and MIN markings . . . . 1.5 litres

Cooling system
All engines . . . . 6.25 litres

Manual transmission:
Drain and refill: . . . . 1.9 litres

Power-assisted steering
Steering circuit capacity . . . . 1.8 litres

Fuel tank
All models (when full) . . . . 60 litres
Reserve (warning light on) . . . . 8 litres

Cooling system
Antifreeze mixture: *
    50% antifreeze . . . . Protection down to -37°C
    55% antifreeze . . . . Protection down to -45°C
Note: * *Refer to antifreeze manufacturer for latest recommendations.*

Brakes
Brake pad friction material minimum thickness . . . . 2.0 mm

Tyre pressures . . . . See *Lubricants, fluids and tyre pressures*

Remote control battery
Type CR1620
Volts 3V

Torque wrench settings

	Nm	lbf ft
Engine oil sump drain plug	25	18
Manual transmission:		
Filler/level plug	22	16
Drain plug	35	26
Oil filter cap	25	18
Wheel bolts	100	74

Note: *This maintenance schedule is a guide recommended by Haynes for servicing your own vehicle. Check with your local dealer for the manufacturer's maintenance schedule.*

1 The maintenance intervals in this manual are provided with the assumption that you will be carrying out the work yourself. These are the minimum maintenance intervals recommended by ourselves for vehicles driven daily, based on the schedule produced by the manufacturer. If you wish to keep your vehicle in peak condition at all times, you may wish to perform some of these procedures more often. We encourage frequent maintenance, because it enhances the efficiency, performance and resale value of your vehicle.

2 If the vehicle is driven in dusty areas, used to tow a trailer, or driven frequently at slow speeds (idling in traffic) or on short journeys, more frequent maintenance intervals are recommended.

3 When the vehicle is new, it should be serviced by a dealer service department (or other workshop recognised by the vehicle manufacturer as providing the same standard of service) in order to preserve the warranty. The vehicle manufacturer may reject warranty claims if you are unable to prove that servicing has been carried out as and when specified, using only original equipment parts or parts certified to be of equivalent quality.

4 All Citroën/Peugeot models are equipped with a service indicator function incorporated into the mileage recorder, which will indicate the mileage until the next service is due. However, Citroën/Peugeot point out that, 'due to the relationship between time and mileage, some operating conditions will make annual service more suitable'.

Every 250 miles or weekly

☐ Refer to *Weekly checks*

Every 10 000 miles or 12 months – whichever comes first

☐ Renew the engine oil and filter (Section 2)
☐ Check all underbonnet components for fluid leaks (Section 3)
☐ Check the steering and suspension components (Section 4)
☐ Check the condition of the driveshaft joints and rubber gaiters (Section 5)
☐ Lubricate all hinges and locks (Section 6)
☐ Drain the fuel filter (Section 7)
☐ Reset the service interval indicator (Section 8)

Every 20 000 miles or 2 years – whichever comes first

☐ Check the condition of the brake pads and discs (Section 9)
☐ Check the operation of the handbrake (Section 10)
☐ Check the seat belt condition (Section 11)
☐ Check the airbag system (Section 12)
☐ Carry out a road test (Section 13)
☐ Check the coolant antifreeze concentration (Section 14)
☐ Check the exhaust system (Section 15)
☐ Check the condition of the auxiliary drivebelt (Section 16)
☐ Check and renew the pollen filter (Section 17)

Every 40 000 miles or 4 years – whichever comes first

☐ Renew the brake fluid (Section 18)

Note: *The hydraulic clutch shares its fluid reservoir with the braking system, and will also need to be bled.*

☐ Renew the coolant (Section 19)
☐ Renew the air filter element (Section 20)
☐ Check the manual transmission oil level (Section 21)
☐ Renew the fuel filter (Section 7)
☐ Renew the remote control battery (Section 22)

Every 80 000 miles or 8 years – whichever comes first

☐ Check the particulate filter fluid (Section 23)
☐ Renew the particulate filter (Section 24)
☐ Timing belt renewal (Section 25)

Note: *The interval recommended by Peugeot/Citroën is 150 000 miles or 10 years. However, It is strongly recommended that the interval be reduced on vehicles that are subjected to intensive use, ie, mainly short journeys or a lot of stop-start driving. The actual belt renewal interval is very much up to the individual owner, but bear in mind that severe engine damage will result if the belt breaks.*

Every 15 years

☐ Renew the airbags and seat belt pretensioners (Section 26)

Front underbody view

1 Engine oil drain plug
2 Transmission drain plug
3 Driveshaft
4 Brake caliper
5 Track rod balljoint
6 Anti-roll bar
7 Air conditioning compressor
8 Radiator bottom hose
9 Catalytic converter/particle filter
   (depending on model)
10 Auxiliary belt

Rear underbody view

1 Fuel tank
2 Beam axle
3 Handbrake cable
4 Brake caliper
5 Coil spring
6 Shock absorber
7 Exhaust rear silencer
8 Fuel filler neck
9 Heat shields
10 Spare wheel/tyre

Underbonnet view

1 Engine oil filler cap
2 Engine oil level dipstick
3 Battery
4 Brake/clutch fluid reservoir
5 Coolant expansion tank
6 Air filter housing
7 Turbocharge
8 Power steering fluid reservoir
   (electro-pump type)
9 Washer fluid reservoir
10 Fuse/electrical box

1 This Chapter is designed to help the home mechanic maintain his/her vehicle for safety, economy, long life and peak performance.
2 The Chapter contains a master maintenance schedule, followed by Sections dealing specifically with each task in the schedule. Visual checks, adjustments, component renewal and other helpful items are included. Refer to the accompanying illustrations of the engine compartment and the underside of the vehicle for the locations of the various components.
3 Servicing your vehicle in accordance with the mileage/time maintenance schedule and the following Sections will provide a planned maintenance programme, which should result in a long and reliable service life. This is a comprehensive plan, so maintaining some items, but not others, at the specified service intervals will not produce the same results.
4 As you service your vehicle, you will discover that many of the procedures can – and should – be grouped together, because of the particular procedure being performed, or because of the close proximity of two otherwise-unrelated components to one another. For example, if the vehicle is raised for any reason, the exhaust system could be inspected at the same time as the suspension and steering components.
5 The first step in this maintenance programme is to prepare yourself before the actual work begins. Read through all the Sections relevant to the work to be carried out, then make a list and gather together all the parts and tools required. If a problem is encountered, seek advice from a parts specialist, or a dealer service department.

1 Routine Maintenance

1 If, from the time the vehicle is new, the routine maintenance schedule is followed closely, and frequent checks are made of fluid levels and high-wear items, as suggested throughout this manual, the engine will be kept in relatively good running condition, and the need for additional work will be minimised.
2 It is possible that there will be times when the engine is running poorly due to the lack of regular maintenance. This is even more likely if a used vehicle, which has not received regular and frequent maintenance checks, is purchased. In such cases, additional work may need to be carried out, outside of the regular maintenance intervals.
3 If engine wear is suspected, a compression test (Chapter 2A Section 2 or Chapter 2B Section 2) will provide valuable information regarding the overall performance of the main internal components. Such a test can be used as a basis to decide on the extent of the work to be carried out. If, for example, a compression test indicates serious internal engine wear, conventional maintenance as described in this Chapter will not greatly improve the performance of the engine, and may prove a waste of time and money, unless extensive overhaul work (Chapter 2C) is carried out first.
4 The following series of operations are those most often required to improve the performance of a generally poor-running engine:

Primary operations

a) Clean, inspect and test the battery (Weekly checks and Chapter 5A)
b) Check all the engine-related fluids (Weekly checks).
c) Check the condition and tension of the auxiliary drivebelt (Section 16).
d) Check the condition of the air filter element, and renew if necessary (Section 20).
e) Check the condition of all hoses, and check for fluid leaks (Section 3).

5 If the above operations do not prove fully effective, carry out the following secondary operations:

Secondary operations

a) Check the charging system (Chapter 5A Section 5).
b) Check the fuel system (Chapter 4A Section 1).

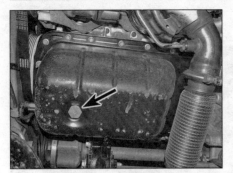

2.5 Engine oil drain plug

As the drain plug releases from the sump threads, move it away sharply, so the stream of oil issuing from the sump runs into the container, not up your sleeve.

2.7 Engine oil filter location

2 Engine oil and filter renewal

Note: *A suitable square-section wrench may be required to undo the sump drain plug on certain models. These wrenches can be obtained from most motor factors or your Peugeot/Citroën dealer.*

1 Frequent oil changes are the most important preventative maintenance the DIY home mechanic can give the engine, because ageing oil becomes diluted and contaminated, which leads to premature engine wear.

2 Before starting this procedure, gather together all the necessary tools and materials. Also make sure that you have plenty of clean rags and newspapers handy, to mop-up any spills. Ideally, the engine oil should be warm,

as it will drain better, and more built-up sludge will be removed with it. Take care, however, not to touch the exhaust or any other hot parts of the engine when working under the vehicle. To avoid any possibility of scalding, and to protect yourself from possible skin irritants and other harmful contaminants in used engine oils, it is advisable to wear gloves when carrying out this work.

3 Access to the filter and drain plug will be greatly improved if the front of the vehicle is raised and support securely on axle stands (see *Jacking and vehicle support*).

4 Undo the fasteners and remove the engine undershield.

5 Slacken the plug about half a turn **(see**

illustration). Position the draining container under the drain plug, then remove the plug completely – recover the sealing washer (see **Haynes Hint**).

6 Allow some time for the old oil to drain, noting that it may be necessary to reposition the container as the oil flow slows to a trickle.

7 The oil filter is of a separate disposable paper element contained under a plastic cap, which is screwed into a housing on the front of the cylinder block **(see illustration)**.

8 Remove the air intake hoses from the front left-hand corner of the engine compartment to make easier access the oil filter cap **(see illustrations)**.

9 Using a socket or spanner, slacken the oil filter plastic cap a couple of turns to allow the oil in the filter housing to drain into the sump **(see illustrations)**. Do not completely remove at this stage.

10 After all the oil has drained, wipe off the drain plug with a clean rag. Clean the area around the drain plug opening, and refit the plug with a new sealing washer. Tighten the plug to the specified torque.

11 The oil filter plastic cap can now be unscrewed the rest of the way by hand **(see illustration)**. Use a rag to catch any oil spillage as the filter is removed.

12 Lift the oil filter plastic cap away, depending on model the paper filter element may stay in the lower part of the housing or will stay in the cap as it is removed. Remove the paper element from the filter housing, if required.

2.8a Release the securing clips ...

2.8b ... and remove the air intake ducting

2.9a Slacken the engine oil filter cover ...

2.9b ... until the vent hole (arrowed) is uncovered

2.11 Unscrew the oil filter plastic cover

2.13 Renew the O-ring seal ...

2.14a ... insert the new filter into the cap ...

2.14b ... then apply a little clean oil to the seal

2.14c Ensure the filter locating peg (arrowed) locates into the corresponding hole in the housing (arrowed)

2.16a Remove the oil filler cap ...

2.16b ... and the oil level dipstick

13 Use a clean rag to remove all oil and dirt from inside the filter cap and housing, and then remove the O-ring seal from the cap **(see illustration)**. A new seal should be supplied with the new filter.
14 Fit a new O-ring seal to the cap, and fit the new paper element to the cap. Fit the element to the housing, ensuring the lug on the base of the element locates correctly in the corresponding hole in the housing. Lightly lubricate the O-ring seal with clean engine oil **(see illustrations)**.
15 Screw the cap into place by hand, and then tighten it to the specified torque.
16 Lower the vehicle to the ground, then remove the oil filler cap and withdraw the level dipstick from the tube **(see illustrations)**.
17 Fill the engine, using the correct oil (see Lubricants and fluids). An oil can spout or funnel may help to reduce spillage. Pour in

MIN

MAX

2.17 Upper and lower dipstick markings (arrowed)

half the specified quantity of oil first (see Specifications), and then wait a few minutes for the oil to run to the sump. Continue adding oil a small quantity at a time until the level is up to the lower mark on the dipstick. Adding a further 1.5 litres (approx.) will bring the level up to the upper mark on the dipstick **(see illustration)**. Insert the dipstick, and refit the filler cap when completed.
18 Start the engine and run it for a few minutes; check for leaks around the oil filter seal and the sump drain plug. Note that there may be a delay of a few seconds before the oil pressure warning light goes out when the engine is first started, as the oil circulates through the engine oil galleries and the new oil filter before the pressure builds-up.
19 Switch off the engine, and wait a few minutes for the oil to settle in the sump once

HAYNES HiNT

A leak in the cooling system will usually show up as white- or antifreezecoloured deposits on the area adjoining the leak.

more. With the new oil circulated and the filter completely full, recheck the level on the dipstick, and add more oil as necessary. When completed, jack up the vehicle and place it on axle stands, (see *Jacking and vehicle support*), then refit the engine undershield.
20 Dispose of the used engine oil safely, in accordance with the guidance given in *General repair procedures*.

3 Hose and fluid leak check

Cooling system

⚠️ *Warning: Refer to the safety information given in Safety first! and Chapter 3 Section 1 before disturbing any of the cooling system components.*

1 Carefully check the radiator and heater coolant hoses along their entire length. Renew any hose that is cracked, swollen or which shows signs of deterioration. Cracks will show up better if the hose is squeezed. Pay close attention to the clips that secure the hoses to the cooling system components. Hose clips that have been overtightened can pinch and puncture hoses, resulting in cooling system leaks.
2 Inspect all the cooling system components (hoses, joint faces, etc) for leaks. Where any problems of this nature are found on system components, renew the component or gasket with reference to Chapter 3 (see **Haynes hint**).

Fuel system

Warning: Refer to the safety information given in Safety first! and Chapter 4A Section 1 before disturbing any of the fuel system components.

3 Diesel leaks are easier to spot than petrol, but can be difficult to pinpoint unless the leakage is significant and hence easily visible. Fuel tends to spread, especially in a hot engine bay. Small drips can spread before you get a chance to identify the point of leakage. If you suspect that there is a fuel leak from the area of the engine bay, leave the vehicle overnight then start the engine from cold, with the bonnet open. Metal components tend to shrink when they are cold, and rubber seals and hoses tend to harden, so any leaks will be more apparent whilst the engine is warming-up from a cold start.

4 Check all fuel lines at their connections to the fuel rail, fuel pressure regulator, fuel filter, fuel cooler and especially the return hoses on top of the injectors. Examine each rubber fuel hose along its length for splits or cracks. Check for leakage from the crimped joints between rubber and metal fuel lines. Examine the unions between the metal fuel lines and the fuel filter housing. Also check the area around the fuel injectors for signs of O-ring leakage.

5 To identify fuel leaks between the fuel tank and the engine bay, the vehicle should be raised and securely supported on axle stands (see *Jacking and vehicle support*). Inspect the fuel tank and filler neck for punctures, cracks and other damage. The connection between the filler neck and tank is especially critical. Sometimes a rubber filler neck or connecting hose will leak due to loose retaining clamps or deteriorated rubber.

6 Carefully check all rubber hoses and metal fuel lines leading away from the fuel tank. Check for loose connections, deteriorated hoses, kinked lines, and other damage. Pay particular attention to the vent pipes and hoses, which often loop up around the filler neck and can become blocked or kinked, making tank filling difficult. Follow the fuel supply and return lines to the front of the vehicle, carefully inspecting them all the way for signs of damage or corrosion. Renew damaged sections as necessary.

Engine oil

7 Inspect the area around the camshaft cover, cylinder head, oil filter and sump joint faces. Bear in mind that, over a period of time, some very slight seepage from these areas is to be expected – what you are really looking for is any indication of a serious leak caused by gasket failure. Engine oil seeping from the base of the timing belt cover or the transmission bellhousing may be an indication of crankshaft or transmission input shaft oil seal failure. Should a leak be found, renew the failed gasket or oil seal by referring to the appropriate Chapters in this manual.

Air conditioning refrigerant

Warning: Refer to the safety information given in Safety first! and Chapter 3 Section 11 regarding the dangers of disturbing any of the air conditioning system components.

8 The air conditioning system is filled with a liquid refrigerant, which is retained under high pressure. If the air conditioning system is opened and depressurised without the aid of specialised equipment the refrigerant will immediately turn into gas and escape into the atmosphere. If the liquid comes into contact with your skin, it can cause severe frostbite. In addition, the refrigerant contains substances which are environmentally damaging; for this reason, it should not be allowed to escape into the atmosphere in an uncontrolled fashion.

9 Any suspected air conditioning system leaks should be immediately referred to a Citroën/Peugeot dealer or air conditioning specialist. Leakage will be shown up as a steady drop in the level of refrigerant in the system.

10 Note that water may drip from the condenser drain pipe, underneath the car, immediately after the air conditioning system has been in use. This is normal, and should not be cause for concern.

Brake (and clutch) fluid

Warning: Refer to the safety information given in Safety first! and Chapter 9 regarding the dangers of handling brake fluid.

11 With reference to Chapter 9, examine the area surrounding the brake/clutch pipe unions at the master cylinder for signs of leakage. Check the area around the base of fluid reservoir, for signs of leakage caused by seal failure. Also examine the brake pipe unions at the ABS hydraulic unit.

12 If fluid loss is evident, but the leak cannot be pinpointed in the engine bay, the brake calipers and underbody brake lines should be carefully checked with the vehicle raised and supported on axle stands (see *Jacking and vehicle support*). Leakage of fluid from the braking system is a serious fault that must be rectified immediately.

13 Brake/clutch hydraulic fluid is a toxic substance with a watery consistency. New fluid is almost colourless, but it becomes darker with age and use.

Unidentified fluid leaks

14 If there are signs that a fluid of some description is leaking from the vehicle, but you cannot identify the type of fluid or its exact origin, park the vehicle overnight and slide a large piece of card underneath it. Providing that the card is positioned in roughly the right location, even the smallest leak will show up on the card. Not only will this help you to pinpoint the exact location of the leak, it should be easier to identify the fluid from its colour. Bear in mind, though, that the leak may only be occurring when the engine is running!

Vacuum hoses

15 Although the braking system is hydraulically operated, the brake servo unit amplifies the effort applied at the brake pedal by making use of the vacuum supplied by the vacuum pump, driven by the engine. Vacuum is ported to the servo by means of a large-bore hose. Any leaks that develop in this hose will reduce the effectiveness of the braking system, and may affect the running of the engine.

16 In addition, a number of the underbonnet components, particularly the turbocharger control components, are driven by vacuum supplied from the vacuum pump via narrow-bore hoses. A leak in a vacuum hose means that air is being drawn into the hose (rather than escaping from it) and this makes leakage very difficult to detect. One method is to use an old length of vacuum hose as a kind of stethoscope – hold one end close to (but not in) your ear and use the other end to probe the area around the suspected leak. When the end of the hose is directly over a vacuum leak, a hissing sound will be heard clearly through the hose. Care must be taken to avoid contacting hot or moving components, as the engine must be running, when testing in this manner. Renew any vacuum hoses that are found to be defective.

4 Steering and suspension components check

Front suspension and steering

1 Raise the front of the vehicle, and securely support it on axle stands (see *Jacking and vehicle support*).

2 Visually inspect the balljoint dust covers and the steering rack-and-pinion gaiters for splits **(see illustration)**, chafing or deterioration. Any wear of these components will cause loss of lubricant, together with dirt and water entry, resulting in rapid deterioration of the balljoints or steering gear.

3 Check the power steering fluid hoses for chafing or deterioration, and the pipe and hose unions for fluid leaks. Also check for signs of fluid leakage under pressure from the steering gear rubber gaiters, which would indicate failed fluid seals within the steering gear.

4.2 Check the steering rack gaiters for signs of damage or deterioration

4.4 Check for wear in the hub bearings by grasping the wheel and trying to rock it …

4.5 … and checking for wear in the steering rack and balljoints

5.1 Check the driveshaft gaiters for signs of damage or deterioration

4 Grasp the roadwheel at the 12 o'clock and 6 o'clock positions, and try to rock it **(see illustration)**. Very slight free play may be felt, but if the movement is appreciable, further investigation is necessary to determine the source. Continue rocking the wheel while an assistant depresses the footbrake. If the movement is now eliminated or significantly reduced, it is likely that the hub bearings are at fault. If the free play is still evident with the footbrake depressed, then there is wear in the suspension joints or mountings.
5 Now grasp the wheel at the 9 o'clock and 3 o'clock positions, and try to rock it as before **(see illustration)**. Any movement felt now may again be caused by wear in the hub bearings or the steering track rod balljoints. If the outer balljoint is worn, the visual movement will be obvious. If the inner joint is suspect, it can be felt by placing a hand over the rack-and-pinion rubber gaiter and gripping the track rod. If the wheel is now rocked, movement will be felt at the inner joint if wear has taken place.
6 Using a large screwdriver or flat bar, check for wear in the suspension mounting bushes by levering between the relevant suspension component and its attachment point. Some movement is to be expected, as the mountings are made of rubber, but excessive wear should be obvious. Also check the condition of any visible rubber bushes, looking for splits, cracks or contamination of the rubber.
7 With the car standing on its wheels, have an assistant turn the steering wheel back-and-forth, about an eighth of a turn each way. There should be very little, if any, lost movement between the steering wheel and roadwheels. If this is not the case, closely observe the joints and mountings previously described. In addition, check the steering column universal joints for wear, and also check the rack-and-pinion steering gear itself.
8 The front suspension mountings should be checked for tightness.

Rear suspension

9 Chock the front wheels, then jack up the rear of the vehicle and support securely on axle stands (see *Jacking and vehicle support*).
10 Working as described previously for the front suspension, check the rear hub bearings,

the suspension bushes and the strut or shock absorber mountings (as applicable) for wear.
11 The rear suspension mountings should be checked for tightness.

Shock absorber

12 Check for any signs of fluid leakage around the shock absorber bodies, or from the rubber gaiters around the piston rods. Should any fluid be noticed, the shock absorber is defective internally, or the rubber gaiter is split, and may need renewing. **Note:** *Shock absorbers should always be renewed in pairs on the same axle.*

5 Driveshaft joints and gaiters check

1 With the front of the vehicle raised and securely supported on stands, turn the steering onto full lock then slowly rotate the roadwheel. Inspect the condition of the outer constant velocity (CV) joint rubber gaiters while squeezing the gaiters to open out the folds **(see illustration)**. Check for signs of cracking, splits or deterioration of the rubber, which may allow the grease to escape and lead to water and grit entry into the joint. Also check the security and condition of the retaining clips. Repeat these checks on the inner CV joints. If any damage or deterioration is found, the gaiters should be renewed as described in Chapter 8 Section 3 .
2 At the same time check the general condition of the CV joints themselves by first holding the driveshaft and attempting

7.2a Remove the engine cover…

to rotate the wheel. Repeat this check by holding the inner joint and attempting to rotate the driveshaft. Any appreciable movement indicates wear in the joints, wear in the driveshaft splines or a loose driveshaft retaining nut.

6 Hinges and locks lubrication

1 Work around the vehicle and lubricate the hinges of the bonnet, doors and tailgate with a light machine oil.
2 Lightly lubricate the two bonnet release locks with a smear of grease.
3 Check carefully the security and operation of all hinges, latches and locks. Check that the central locking system operates correctly.
4 Check the condition and operation of the bonnet and tailgate/boot lid struts, renewing them if either is leaking or no longer able to support the bonnet/tailgate/boot lid.

7 Fuel filter draining and renewal

Draining

1 The purpose of this operation is to purge the filter assembly of any accumulated water.
SOHC engines
2 Unclip the cover from the top of the engine to access the priming hand pump **(see illustrations)**.

7.2b …to access the priming pump (arrowed)

7.3a Drain hose (arrowed)

7.3b Turn drain/sensor clockwise

3 Place a container underneath the vehicle, directly below the fuel filter drain hose, then turn the fuel filter drain/sensor in the top centre of the filter head a quarter of a turn clockwise **(see illustrations)**.

4 Operate the hand priming pump a few times until all water or impurities cease to run out **(see illustration)**. Turn the drain screw/sensor anti-clockwise, back to its original position, making sure it is secure.

5 Start the engine and run it at a fast idle speed (less than 2000 rpm) for 30 seconds.

Refit the engine cover and brake/clutch fluid reservoir.

DOHC engines

6 Undo the two retaining screws and move the brake fluid upper reservoir to one side, do not disconnect any pipes/hoses. Remove the air intake hose from the air filter lower housing **(see illustrations)**.

7 Unclip the cover from the top of the engine to access the priming hand pump **(see illustrations)**.

8 Place a container underneath the filter, then

slacken the fuel filter drain screw, and operate the hand priming pump a few times until all water or impurities cease to run out **(see illustration)**. Tighten the drain screw.

9 Start the engine and run it at a fast idle speed (less than 2000 rpm) for 30 seconds.

10 Refit the engine cover and brake/clutch fluid reservoir.

Renewal

SOHC engines

11 Pull up on the rubber securing clips and

7.4 Operating the priming pump

7.6a Move the reservoir (arrowed) to one side to access the filter

7.6b Remove the air intake hose from above the filter

7.7a Remove the cover...

7.7b ...to access the priming pump

7.8 Vent screw and water drain hose (arrowed)

7.11 Unclip the securing clips to remove cover

7.13a Disconnect the fuel pipes...

7.13b ...by releasing the securing clip (on the one shown)...

7.13c ...and pressing down on the securing clips (arrowed) for the other two pipes

7.14a Undo the two retaining bolts (arrowed)...

7.14b ...and withdraw the filter houisng

remove the trim cover from the top of the engine **(see illustration)**.

12 Where applicable, disconnect the wiring connector(s) from the fuel sensor(s) on the top of the filter housing.

13 Disconnect the fuel pipes from the top of the fuel filter, noting their fitted positions **(see illustrations)**. Plug the openings to prevent contamination. Use a rag around the filter to soak up any spilt fuel from the pipes.

14 Undo the two retaining bolts at the rear of the filter housing, and then withdraw it upwards and out from the top of the engine **(see illustrations)**.

15 Undo the three retaining screws and remove the upper housing from the fuel filter element **(see illustrations)**. Take care as the old filter is removed as it will be full of fuel.

16 Fit the new seal to the filter, then fit the new filter (full of clean fuel) to the upper housing and tighten the securing screws **(see illustration)**.

17 Bolt the new filter into place, remove the plugs and reconnect the pipes, and the wiring plug(s), where applicable.

18 As described previously in this Section (Draining – SOHC engines), use the priming hand pump to bleed the fuel system and re-fill the filter with clean fuel.

7.15a Undo the retaining screws (arrowed)...

7.15b ...and remove the filter upper housing

7.16 Fit new seal between filter and upper housing

7.23a Release from the locating lug (arrowed) ...

7.23b ... and remove the air intake hose

7.24 Disconnect the wiring connector (arrowed)

DOHC engines

19 If required, to make access easier, remove the battery cover and battery as described in Chapter 5A Section 4 .

20 Unclip the plastic trim cover from the top of the engine **(see illustration 12.6a)**.

21 Undo the two retaining screws and move the brake fluid upper reservoir to one side **(see illustration 12.5a)**. Do not disconnect any pipes/hoses.

22 Remove the air intake hoses from the front left-hand corner of the engine compartment to access the fuel filter **(see illustrations 7.8b and 12.5b)**.

23 Remove the upper part of the air filter housing as described in Section 20. Also release the air intake hose from its locating peg and unclip it from the air filter lower housing **(see illustrations)**.

24 Disconnect the wiring connector from the fuel heater at the rear of the filter **(see illustration)**

25 Place rags beneath the filter housing, and then disconnect the fuel pipes from the fuel filter, noting their fitted positions **(see illustration)**. Plug the openings to prevent contamination.

26 Release the retaining clip and lift the filter from the bracket on the end of the cylinder head **(see illustrations)**. As the filter is withdrawn, disconnect the wiring connector from the base of the fuel filter and disconnect the drain tube.

27 Release the clip and detach the fuel heater from the side of the filter assembly **(see illustrations)**.

28 Clip the fuel heater into place on the new filter. Fit the new filter into place, remove the plugs and reconnect the pipes, and the wiring plug.

29 Refit the upper part of the filter housing, air intake hoses and battery (where removed).

30 Reconnect the battery negative lead (refer to precautions in Chapter 5A).

31 As described previously in this Section (Draining – DOHC engines), use the priming hand pump to bleed the fuel system and re-fill the filter with clean fuel.

7.25 Release the securing clips and disconnect the fuel lines (arrowed)

7.26a Release the clip (arrowed) ...

7.26b ... and slide the filter upwards from the mounting bracket

7.26c Disconnect the wiring connector and the drain tube (arrowed)

7.27a Release the clip (arrowed) ...

7.27b ... and slide the heater from the filter body

8.2 Service indicator trip/reset button (arrowed)

8 Resetting the service indicator

1 The instrument cluster mileage recorder incorporates a service interval indicator. When the vehicle is started, the unit displays the mileage until the next service, or the mileage covered since the service was due. The service indicator is manually reset to zero after the vehicle has been serviced. The indicator can also be reset at any time using the Citroën/Peugeot diagnostic tool.

2 To manually reset the mileage to zero, carry out the following procedure:

a) *Switch off the ignition and place the key in the steering lock "S" position.*
b) *Press and hold down the trip/reset button on the instrument panel (see illustration)*
c) *While the trip/reset button is held down, switch on the ignition.*
d) *Keep the trip/reset button pressed until zero appears and the maintenance symbol disappears.*
e) *Release the trip/reset button and switch off the ignition.*

3 Switch on the ignition – the distance remaining until (or covered since) the next service is due will flash in the display.

9 Brake pad wear and disc check

1 The work described in this Section should be carried out at the specified intervals, or whenever a defect is suspected in the braking system. Any of the following symptoms could indicate a potential brake system defect:

a) *The vehicle pulls to one side when the brake pedal is depressed.*
b) *The brakes make squealing, scraping or dragging noises when applied.*
c) *Brake pedal travel is excessive, or pedal feel is poor.*
d) *The brake fluid requires repeated topping-up. Note that, because the hydraulic clutch shares the same fluid as the braking system, this problem could be due to a leak in the clutch system.*

9.3 Checking brake pad thickness through alloy wheels

Front disc brakes

2 Chock the rear wheels then loosen the front wheel bolts. Jack up the front of the vehicle, and support it on axle stands (see *Jacking and vehicle support*).

3 For better access to the brake calipers, remove the wheels **(see illustration)**.

4 Look through the inspection window in the caliper, and check that the thickness of the friction lining material on each of the pads is not less than the recommended minimum thickness given in the Specifications (see **Haynes hint**). Bear in mind that the lining material is normally bonded to a metal backing plate. To differentiate between the metal and the lining material, it is helpful to turn the disc slowly at first – the edge of the disc can then be identified, with the lining material on each pad either side of it, and the backing plates behind.

5 If it is difficult to determine the exact thickness of the pad linings, or if you are at all concerned about the condition of the pads, then remove them from the calipers for further inspection (refer to Chapter 9 Section 4).

6 Check the other caliper in the same way.

7 If any one of the brake pads has worn down to, or below, the specified limit, all four pads at that end of the car must be renewed as a set **(see illustration)**. If the pads on one side are significantly more worn than the other, this may indicate that the caliper pistons have partially seized – refer to the brake pad renewal procedure in Chapter 9 Section 4, and push the pistons back into the caliper to free them.

8 Measure the thickness of the discs with a micrometer, if available, to make sure that they still have service life remaining. Do not be fooled by the lip of rust which often forms on the outer edge of the disc, which may make the disc appear thicker than it really is – scrape off the loose rust if necessary, without scoring the disc friction (shiny) surface.

9 If any disc is thinner than the specified minimum thickness, renew both (refer to Chapter 9 Section 6).

10 Check the general condition of the discs. Look for excessive scoring and discolouration caused by overheating. If these conditions exist, remove the relevant disc and have it resurfaced or renewed (refer to Chapter 9 Section 6).

For a quick check, the thickness of the friction material on each brake pad can be measured through the aperture in the caliper body.

11 Make sure that the transmission is in neutral. Spin the wheel, and check that the brake is not binding. Some drag is normal with a disc brake, but it should not require any great effort to turn the wheel – also, do not confuse brake drag with resistance from the transmission.

12 Before refitting the wheels, check all brake lines and hoses (refer to Chapter 9 Section 3). In particular, check the flexible hoses in the vicinity of the calipers, where they are subjected to most movement. Bend them between the fingers (but do not actually bend them double, or the casing may be damaged) and check that this does not reveal previously hidden cracks, cuts or splits.

13 On completion, refit the wheels and lower the car to the ground. Tighten the wheel bolts to the specified torque.

Rear disc brakes

14 Loosen the rear wheel bolts then chock the front wheels. Jack up the rear of the car, and support it on axle stands. Release the handbrake and remove the rear wheels.

15 The procedure for checking the rear brakes is much the same as described in paragraphs 2 to 13 above. Check that the rear brakes are not binding, noting that transmission resistance is not a factor on the rear wheels. Abnormal effort may indicate that the handbrake needs adjusting – see Chapter 9 Section 14 .

9.7 Check the thickness of the brake pad friction material

10 Handbrake check and adjustment

1 To check the handbrake adjustment, apply normal moderate pressure and pull the handbrake lever to the fully applied position, counting the number of clicks emitted from the handbrake ratchet mechanism. If adjustment is correct, there should be 2 clicks before the brakes begins to apply, and no more than 6 before the handbrake is fully applied. If this is not the case, adjust as described in Chapter 9 Section 14 .

11 Seat belt condition check

1 Working on each seat belt in turn, carefully examine the seat belt webbing for cuts, or for any signs of serious fraying or deterioration. Pull the belt all the way out, and examine the full extent of the webbing.
2 Fasten and unfasten the belt, ensuring that the locking mechanism holds securely, and releases properly when intended. Check also that the retracting mechanism operates correctly when the belt is released.
3 Check the security of all seat belt mountings and attachments, which are accessible from inside the vehicle without removing any trim or other components.
4 Check the function of the seat belt reminder lamp.

12 Airbag system check

1 The following work can be carried out by the home mechanic, however, if an electronic fault is apparent, it will be necessary to take the car to a Citroën/Peugeot dealer or specialist who will have the necessary diagnostic equipment to extract fault codes from the system.
2 Turn the ignition switch to the drive position (ignition warning lights on), and check that the airbag warning light is illuminated for approximately 6 seconds. After this period the light should go out, indicating that the system has been checked and is functioning correctly.
3 If the warning light remains on or refuses to light, have the system checked by a Citroën/ Peugeot dealer or specialist.
4 Visually examine the steering wheel centre pad, knee airbag and the passenger airbag modules for external damage. Also check the exterior of the front seats around the side airbag locations. If damage is evident, consult a Citroën/Peugeot dealer or specialist.
5 In the interests of safety, make sure that there are no loose items inside the car, which could be thrown onto the airbag modules in the event of an accident.

13 Road test

Instruments and electrical equipment

1 Check the operation of all instruments and electrical equipment.
2 Make sure that all instruments read correctly, and switch on all electrical equipment in turn to check that it functions properly. Check the function of the heating, air conditioning and automatic climate control systems.

Steering and suspension

3 Check for any abnormalities in the steering, suspension, handling or road 'feel'.
4 Drive the vehicle, and check that there are no unusual vibrations or noises.
5 Check that the steering feels positive, with no excessive 'sloppiness', or roughness, and check for any suspension noises when cornering, or when driving over bumps. Check that the power steering system operates correctly.

Drivetrain

6 Check the performance of the engine, clutch, transmission and driveshafts.
7 Listen for any unusual noises from the engine, clutch and transmission.
8 Make sure that the engine runs smoothly when idling, and that there is no hesitation when accelerating.
9 Check that the clutch action is smooth and progressive, that the drive is taken up smoothly, and that the pedal travel is not excessive. Also listen for any noises when the clutch pedal is depressed. Check that all gears can be engaged smoothly, without noise, and that the gear lever action is smooth and not abnormally vague or 'notchy'.
10 Listen for a metallic clicking sound from the front of the vehicle, as the vehicle is driven slowly in a circle with the steering on full lock. Carry out this check in both directions. If a clicking noise is heard, this indicates wear in a driveshaft joint, in which case, refer to Chapter 8 Section 2 .

Braking system

11 Make sure that the vehicle does not pull to one side when braking, and that the wheels do not lock when braking hard.
12 Check that there is no vibration through the steering when braking.
13 Check that the handbrake operates correctly, without excessive movement of the lever, and that it holds the vehicle stationary on a slope.
14 Test the operation of the brake servo unit as follows. With the engine off, depress the footbrake four or five times to exhaust the vacuum, and then start the engine while holding the brake pedal depressed. As the engine starts, there should be a noticeable 'give' in the brake pedal as vacuum builds-up. Allow the engine to run for at least two minutes, and then switch it off. If the brake pedal is now depressed again, it should be possible to detect a 'hiss' from the servo as the pedal is depressed. After about four or five applications, no further hissing should be heard, and the pedal should feel considerably harder.

14 Coolant antifreeze concentration check

1 The cooling system should be filled with the recommended antifreeze and corrosion protection fluid. Over a period of time, the concentration of fluid may be reduced due to topping-up (this can be avoided by topping-up with the correct antifreeze mixture) or fluid loss. If loss of coolant has been evident, it is important to make the necessary repair before adding fresh fluid. The exact mixture of antifreeze-to-water that you should use depends on the relative weather conditions. The mixture should contain at least 40% antifreeze, but not more than 70%. Consult the mixture ratio chart on the antifreeze container before adding coolant. Use antifreeze, which meets the vehicle manufacturer's specifications.
2 With the engine cold, carefully remove the cap from the expansion tank. If the engine is not completely cold, place a cloth rag over the cap before removing it, and remove it slowly to allow any pressure to escape.
3 Antifreeze checkers are available from car accessory shops. Draw some coolant from the expansion tank and observe how many plastic balls are floating in the checker **(see illustration)**. Usually, 2 or 3 balls must be floating for the correct concentration of antifreeze, but follow the manufacturer's instructions.
4 If the concentration is incorrect, it will be necessary to either withdraw some coolant and add antifreeze, or alternatively drain the old coolant and add fresh coolant of the correct concentration.

14.3 Check the antifreeze concentration with a hydrometer

15 Exhaust system check

1 With the engine cold, check the complete exhaust system, from its starting point at the engine to the end of the tailpipe. If necessary, raise the front and rear of the vehicle and support it on axle stands (see *Jacking and vehicle support*). Remove any engine undershields as necessary for full access to the exhaust system.
2 Check the exhaust pipes and connections for evidence of leaks, severe corrosion, and damage. Make sure that all brackets and mountings are in good condition and that all relevant nuts and bolts are tight **(see illustrations)**. Leakage at any of the joints or in other parts of the system will usually show up as a black sooty stain in the vicinity of the leak.
3 Rattles and other noises can often be traced to the exhaust system, especially the brackets and rubber mountings. Try to move the pipes and silencers. If the components are able to come into contact with the body or suspension parts, secure the system with new mountings. Otherwise separate the joints (if possible) and twist the pipes as necessary to provide additional clearance.

16 Auxiliary drivebelt check and renewal

1 On all engines, a single, multi-grooved auxiliary drivebelt is used to transmit drive from the crankshaft pulley to the alternator, power steering pump and the refrigerant compressor, depending on model. The drivebelt is tensioned automatically by a spring-loaded tensioner pulley. The layout of the belt routing will depend on whether there is air-conditioning and/or a belt driven power steering pump fitted. The following procedures show two different types of tensioner depending on model/engine type.
2 Due to their function and material make-up, drivebelts are prone to failure after a long period of time, and should therefore be inspected regularly.

15.2a Check the condition of the exhaust rubber mountings at the front ...

15.2b ... and the mountings along the length of the exhaust system

Check

3 For better access to the drivebelt, chock the rear wheels then jack up the front of the car and support it on axle stands (see *Jacking and vehicle support*). Remove the right-hand front roadwheel, and then remove the plastic liner from under the right-hand wheel arch to expose the crankshaft pulley.
4 Using a suitable socket and extension bar fitted to the crankshaft pulley bolt, rotate the crankshaft so that the entire length of the drivebelt(s) can be examined. Examine the drivebelt for cracks, splitting, fraying, or other damage **(see illustration)**. Check also for signs of glazing (shiny patches) and for separation of the belt plies.
5 To check whether the belt tension is serviceable, check the markings on the side of the automatic tensioner. On both types of

tensioner, there are two lines on the housing and the flat side of the lug on the side of the casting must align between these two lines **(see illustrations)**. If it goes beyond these lines, then the belt will need to be renewed.
6 If at any point the belt is to be removed and then refitted, mark its direction of normal rotation **(see illustration)**.

Renewal

Type 1 tensioner

7 If not already done, proceed as described in paragraphs 3 and 4.
8 Working from under the right-hand wheel arch, use a spanner to rotate the tensioner clockwise. When aligned, insert a locking peg/drill bit through the hole in the tensioner housing to lock the tensioner in the released position **(see illustration)**.

16.4 Check the condition of the auxiliary belt

16.5a Lug (arrowed) must align between the two markings, when belt is fitted

16.5b Lug (arrowed) aligned between the two markings on the housing

16.6 Direction of rotation marked with an arrow

16.8 Using a drill bit (arrowed) to lock the tensioner in position

16.9a Remove the auxiliary belt from the crankshaft pulley

16.9b Auxiliary belt routing (DOHC with belt driven PAS pump and without A/C)

16.14 Rotate the tensioner arm clockwise, then lock it in place by inserting a 4 mm drill into the hole (hidden behind spanner) in the tensioner body (arrowed)

16.15 Auxiliary belt routing and adjustment (with air conditioning)

A Automatic tensioner
B Alternator pulley
C Air conditioning compressor pulley
D Crankshaft pulley

9 Note how the auxiliary belt is routed around all the pulleys, and then remove it from the engine compartment (see illustrations).

10 Fit the new drivebelt onto the crankshaft, air conditioning compressor (where fitted), power steering pump (where fitted), alternator and tensioner/idler pulleys. Fit the spanner to the tensioner pulley bolt, hold the tensioner stationary and remove the locking peg/drill bit. Slowly allow the tensioner to rotate anti-clockwise and tension the belt, and then remove the spanner.

Caution: Do not allow the tensioner pulley to spring forcefully onto the belt as this could result in damage.

11 Using a socket on the crankshaft pulley, rotate the engine twice in the normal (clockwise) direction of rotation, checking that the belt is correctly located on all of the pulleys, as the engine is rotated

12 Refit the wheel arch liner and road wheel, then lower the car to the ground. Tighten the roadwheel bolts to the specified torque.

Type 2 tensioner

13 If not already done, proceed as described in paragraphs 3 and 4.

14 Using an open-ended spanner, reach down and rotate the tensioner arm clockwise to release the belt tension. Insert a 4 mm drill bit or peg into the hole in the tensioner body, so that the tensioner arm rests against it, and locks it in this position (see illustration). It is useful to have a small mirror available to enable the alignment of the locking holes to be more easily seen in the limited space available.

15 Manoeuvre the belt from the pulleys (see illustration). Take the opportunity to check the tensioner and idler pulleys spin freely, with no signs of roughness or slack.

16 Refit the belt around the pulleys, ensuring that the ribs on the belt are correctly engaged with the grooves in the pulleys, and the drivebelt is correctly routed. If refitting a used belt, use the marks made on removal to ensure it is fitted the correct way around.

Caution: Do not allow the tensioner pulley to spring forcefully onto the belt as this could result in damage.

17 Using an open-ended spanner, hold the tensioner arm so that the locking drill bit/peg can be removed, then release the pressure on the spanner so that the automatic tensioner takes up the slack in the drivebelt.

18 Refit the wheel arch liner and roadwheel, then lower the vehicle to the ground. Tighten the roadwheel bolts to the specified torque.

17 Pollen filter check and renewal

Note: *There are two pollen filter elements fitted to the heater housing on these models. They are both the same size, and are fitted one on top of the other.*

1 Open the driver's front door, remove the securing clips and withdraw the trim panel from under the facia panel, above the pedal assembly (see illustration).

2 Reach up the side of the heater housing assembly, to the left-hand side of the clutch pedal, and unclip the pollen filter cover (see illustration).

3 Grasp the tab on the end of the upper pollen filter and withdraw it from it's position inside the heater housing unit (see illustration).

4 Reach back up to the heater housing and grasp the tab on the end of the lower pollen

17.1 Remove trim panel (arrowed)

17.2 Pollen filter location (arrowed)

17.3 Withdraw the upper filter

filter and slide the filter upwards inside the heater housing. Once the lower filter is in line with the opening, slide it out from the heater housing, the same way as the upper one.

5 Note the fitted position of the filter elements, with the Air Flow arrows pointing towards the passenger compartment **(see illustration)**.

6 Check the condition of the filter, and renew it if dirty.

7 If possible, wipe clean the inside of the housing and then fit both upper and lower pollen filter elements **(see illustration)**, making sure that they are correctly seated. As there is not much room between the clutch pedal and heater housing, the filter elements will need to be compressed slightly to get them into place. Take care not to damage them as they are fitted.

8 Refit the pollen filter cover to the heater housing.

9 Refit the trim panel under the facia, making sure it is secured in place with the plastic rivets.

18 Brake fluid renewal

⚠️ **Warning: Brake hydraulic fluid can harm your eyes and damage painted surfaces, so use extreme caution when handling and pouring it. Do not use fluid that has been standing open for some time, as it absorbs moisture from the air. Excess moisture can cause a dangerous loss of braking effectiveness.**

Note: *A hydraulic clutch shares its fluid reservoir with the braking system, and will also need to be bled (see Chapter 6 Section 2).*

1 The procedure is similar to that for the bleeding of the hydraulic system as described in Chapter 9 Section 2, except that the brake fluid reservoir should be emptied by siphoning, using a clean ladle or similar before starting, and allowance should be made for the old fluid to be expelled when bleeding a section of the circuit.

2 Working as described in Chapter 9 Section 2, open the first bleed screw in the sequence, and pump the brake pedal gently until nearly

17.5 Direction of Air Flow arrows

all the old fluid has been emptied from the master cylinder reservoir.

3 Top-up to the MAX level with new fluid **(see illustration)**, and continue pumping until only the new fluid remains in the reservoir, and new fluid can be seen emerging from the bleed screw. Tighten the screw, and top the reservoir level up to the MAX level line.

4 Work through all the remaining bleed screws in the sequence until new fluid can be seen at all of them. Be careful to keep the master cylinder reservoir topped-up to above the DANGER level marking at all times, or air may enter the system and increase the length of the task.

5 When the operation is complete, check that all bleed screws are securely tightened, and that their dust caps are refitted **(see illustration)**. Wash off all traces of spilt fluid, and recheck the master cylinder reservoir fluid level.

6 Check the operation of the brakes before taking the car on the road.

19 Coolant renewal

⚠️ **Warning: Do not allow antifreeze to come in contact with your skin or painted surfaces of the vehicle. Flush contaminated areas immediately with plenty of water. Don't store new coolant, or leave old coolant lying around, where it's accessible**

17.7 Slide the filter elements back up into place

to children or pets – they're attracted by its sweet smell. Ingestion of even a small amount of coolant can be fatal. Wipe up garage-floor and drip pan spills immediately. Keep antifreeze containers covered, and repair cooling system leaks as soon as they're noticed.

⚠️ **Warning: Never remove the expansion tank filler cap when the engine is running, or has just been switched off, as the cooling system will be hot, and the consequent escaping steam and scalding coolant could cause serious injury.**

⚠️ **Warning: Wait until the engine is cold before starting these procedures.**

Cooling system draining

1 With the engine completely cold, remove the expansion tank filler cap. Turn the cap anti-clockwise, wait until any pressure remaining in the system is released, then unscrew it and lift it off.

2 Chock the rear wheels, and then raise the front of the vehicle and support it on axle stands (see *Jacking and vehicle support*). Undo the retaining bolts/nuts and remove the engine undershield.

3 Position a suitable container beneath the radiator lower hose outlet at the lower centre of the radiator.

4 Release the retaining clip and disconnect the radiator lower hose **(see illustration)**. Be prepared for coolant spillage.

5 Open the bleed screws; there are two

18.3 Brake/clutch fluid level markings

18.5 Make sure dust cap (arrowed) is refitted to bleed screw

19.4 Squeeze together the tabs to release the hose clamp

19.5a Undo the bleed screw from the heater hose union (arrowed) …

19.5b … and the bleed screw (arrowed) on the coolant housing

19.5c …some models have a return pipe (arrowed) to the reservoir

bleed screws, one on the heater hose at the bulkhead connection and one on the top of the thermostat housing at the left-hand side of the cylinder head **(see illustrations)**. **Note:** *On some models there is no bleed screw on the thermostat housing; the return pipe to the reservoir fits in its place.*

6 To drain the cylinder block, pull out the clip and remove the plug located in the coolant housing at the rear of the engine **(see illustration)**. The plug must be refitted with a new clip and O-ring. **Note:** *A cylinder block drain plug may not be fitted to all models.*

7 Once the coolant has finished draining, refit the plug, and reconnect the bottom hose. If the coolant has been drained for a reason other than renewal, then provided it is clean and less than two years old, it can be re-used, though this is not always recommended.

8 Refit the engine undershield, and then lower the vehicle to the ground.

Cooling system flushing

9 If coolant renewal has been neglected, or if the antifreeze mixture has become diluted, then in time, the cooling system may gradually lose efficiency, as the coolant passages become restricted due to rust, scale deposits, and other sediment. The cooling system efficiency can be restored by flushing the system clean.

10 The radiator should be flushed separately from the engine, to avoid excess contamination.

Radiator flushing

11 Disconnect the top and bottom hoses and any other relevant hoses from the radiator (see Chapter 3 Section 4).

12 Insert a garden hose into the radiator top inlet. Direct a flow of clean water through the radiator, and continue flushing until clean water emerges from the radiator bottom outlet.

13 If after a reasonable period, the water still does not run clear, the radiator can be flushed with a good proprietary cleaning agent. It is important that their manufacturer's instructions are followed carefully. If the contamination is particularly bad, insert the hose in the radiator bottom outlet, and reverse-flush the radiator.

Engine flushing

14 To flush the engine, remove the thermostat (see Chapter 3 Section 5). If the radiator top hose has been disconnected, temporarily reconnect the hose. **Note:** *This may not be possible on some models, as the thermostat may be part of the coolant housing on the end of the cylinder head.*

15 With the bottom hose disconnected from the radiator, insert a garden hose into the coolant housing. Direct a clean flow of water through the engine, and continue flushing until clean water emerges from the radiator bottom hose.

16 When flushing is complete, refit the thermostat and reconnect the hoses.

Cooling system filling

17 Before attempting to fill the cooling system, make sure that all hoses and clips are in good condition, and that the clips are tight. Note that an antifreeze mixture must be used all year round, to prevent corrosion of the engine components (see following sub-Section).

18 Make sure that the air conditioning (A/C) or automatic climate control (ACC) is switched off. This is to prevent the air conditioning system starting the radiator cooling fan before the engine is at normal temperature when refilling the system.

19 Remove the expansion bottle filler cap and remove the cooling system bleed screws (see paragraph 5).

20 Citroën/Peugeot recommend the use of a 'header tank' when refilling the cooling

19.6 Prise out the retaining clip (arrowed) and pull out the coolant drain plug

system, to reduce the possibility of air being trapped in the system. This brings the level of the coolant above all other cooling system components. Although Citroën/Peugeot dealers use a special header tank which screws onto the expansion bottle, the same effect can be achieved by using a suitable 1.0 litre bottle, with a seal between the bottle and the expansion tank **(see illustration)**. This can also be achieved by removing the securing bolts and holding the expansion bottle up higher than the level of the engine, taking care not to damage the hoses.

21 Fit the header tank to the expansion bottle and slowly fill the system whilst observing the bleed holes. Coolant will emerge from each of the bleed holes in turn, starting with the heater matrix hose. As soon as coolant free from air bubbles emerges from the heater matrix hose outlet, securely refit the cap/screw (as applicable) then watch the bleed hole on the coolant housing. Once coolant free from air bubbles emerges from the housing hole, refit the bleed screw and sealing washer and tighten securely.

22 Continue to fill the cooling system until bubbles stop appearing in the expansion bottle. Help to bleed the air from the system by repeatedly squeezing the radiator bottom hose.

23 When no more bubbles appear, ensure the header tank is full (at least 1.0 litre of coolant) then start the engine. Run the engine at a fast idle speed (do not exceed 2000 rpm) until the cooling fan cuts in and out TWICE, then when the fan has stopped for the second time, switch the engine off.

19.20 Using a 1.0 litre plastic bottle as a header tank

Caution: The coolant will be hot. Take great care not to scald yourself.

24 Allow the engine to cool, and then remove the 'header tank' from the reservoir. Wash off any spilt coolant with cold water.

25 When the engine has cooled, check the coolant level with reference to *Weekly checks*. Top-up the level if necessary, and refit the expansion bottle cap.

Antifreeze mixture

26 The antifreeze should always be renewed at the specified intervals. This is necessary not only to maintain the antifreeze properties, but also to prevent corrosion, which would otherwise occur as the corrosion inhibitors become progressively less effective.

27 Always use an ethylene glycol based antifreeze, which is suitable for use in mixed-metal cooling systems.

28 Before adding antifreeze, the cooling system should be completely drained, preferably flushed, and all hoses checked for condition and security.

29 After filling with antifreeze, a label should be attached to the expansion tank, stating the type and concentration of antifreeze used, and the date installed. Any subsequent topping-up should be made with the same type and concentration of antifreeze.

Caution: Do not use engine antifreeze in the windscreen/tailgate washer system, as it will cause damage to the vehicle paintwork. A screen wash additive should be added to the washer system in the quantities stated on the bottle.

20 Air filter element renewal

SOHC engines

1 Release the securing clips and remove

20.1 Remove the engine cover

20.2a Undo the retaining screws (arrowed)…

20.2b …release the retaining clip (arrowed)…

20.2c …then withdraw the upper housing

the cover from the top of the engine **(see illustration)**.

2 Undo the three retaining screws, release the retaining clip to the side of the housing, and then withdraw the upper housing from the air filter element **(see illustrations)**.

3 Lift and remove the air filter element from the lower housing **(see illustration)**.

4 Wipe clean the inner surfaces of the cover and main housing, then locate the new element in the housing, making sure that the sealing lip is correctly engaged around the edge of the housing.

5 Refit the filter cover, ensuring the rear edge of the cover engages correctly with the rear of the filter housing. Tighten the securing screws and secure the retaining clip on the side of the filter housing.

6 When completed, refit the trim cover to the top of the engine.

DOHC engines

7 Pull the plastic cover upwards from the top of the engine **(see illustration)**.

8 Slacken the securing clips from each end

20.3 Remove the air filter element

20.7 Unclip the plastic engine cover

20.8a Slacken the air cleaner retaining clip (arrowed) ...

20.8b ... and the retaining clip (arrowed) on the turbo ...

20.8c ... release the securing clip ...

20.8d ... and remove the air intake hose

20.9 Disconnect the wiring connector

screws, and lift the cover from air filter housing **(see illustrations)**.

12 Note which way round the air filter element is fitted, and then lift it out from the housing **(see illustration)**.

13 Wipe clean the inner surfaces of the cover and main housing, then locate the new element in the housing, making sure that the sealing lip is correctly engaged with the edge of the housing.

14 Refit the filter cover/intake ducting assembly, ensuring the rear edge of the cover engages correctly with the rear of the filter housing.

15 Connect the wiring plug to the airflow sensor, and then refit the plastic cover to the top of the engine.

21 Manual transmission oil level check

Note: *Some transmissions are described as 'Lubricated for life'. However, we consider it prudent to check the oil level, as a leak from the driveshaft oil seal or sealing washer could cause expensive damage. On these transmissions, there is also no level plug. If it is suspected the oil level is low, drain and refill the transmission as described in Chapter 7 Section 2 .*

Note: *A suitable square-section wrench may be required to undo the transmission filler/ level plug on some models. These wrenches can be obtained from most motor factors or*

of the air intake ducting to the turbocharger, release the breather tube clips and remove the air ducting **(see illustrations)**.

9 Disconnect the wiring plug connector from the mass airflow sensor **(see illustration)**.

10 Release the retaining clips and move the fuel priming pump to one side to access the air filter cover retaining screws **(see illustrations)**.

11 Undo the air filter cleaner cover retaining

20.10a Release the two locking clips (arrowed) ...

20.10b ... and move the priming pump to one side

20.11a Undo the retaining screws (arrowed) ...

20.11b ... and remove the upper housing

20.12 Remove the air filter element

21.4 Fluid level/filler plug (arrowed)

21.5 Add oil until a continuous trickle emerges from the plug hole

23.1 Particle filter additive fluid tank

your Peugeot/Citroën dealer. A new sealing washer will be required for the transmission filler/level plug when refitting.

Transmissions with level/filler plugs

1 Take the car on a short journey to warm the transmission up to normal operating temperature. Position the car over an inspection pit, or alternatively jack up the front and rear of the car and support on axle stands (see Jacking and vehicle support). Whichever method is used, make sure that the car is level for checking the fluid level later.

2 The oil level must be checked at least 5 minutes after the engine has been switched off. If the oil is checked immediately after driving the car, some of the oil will remain distributed around the transmission, resulting in an inaccurate level reading.

3 Remove the left-hand front wheel, and then release the fasteners and remove the wheel arch liner.

4 Wipe clean the area around the filler/level plug, which is on the left-hand end of the transmission. Unscrew the plug and clean it; discard the sealing washer (see illustration).

5 The oil level should reach the lower edge of the filler/level hole. A certain amount of oil will have gathered behind the filler/level plug, and will trickle out when it is removed; this does not necessarily indicate that the level is correct. To ensure that a true level is established, wait until the initial trickle has stopped, then add oil as necessary until a trickle of new oil can be seen emerging (see illustration). The level will be correct when the flow ceases; use only good-quality oil of the specified type (see Lubricants and fluids).

6 Filling the transmission with oil is an extremely awkward operation; above all, allow plenty of time for the oil level to settle properly before checking it. If a large amount is added to the transmission, and a large amount flows out on checking the level, refit the filler/level plug and take the vehicle on a short journey

so that the new oil is distributed fully around the transmission components, then recheck the level when it has settled again.

7 If the transmission has been overfilled so that oil flows out as soon as the filler/level plug is removed, Check that the car is completely level (front-to-rear and side-to-side), allow the surplus to drain off into a container.

8 When the level is correct, fit a new sealing washer to the filler/level plug. Refit the plug, tightening it to the specified torque setting. Wash off any spilt oil then refit the wheel arch liner, securing it in position with the fasteners. Refit the roadwheel and tighten to the specified torque setting.

9 Frequent need for topping-up indicates a leak, which should be found and corrected before it becomes serious.

22 Remote control battery renewal

1 Refer to Chapter 11 Section 18, for the renewal of the remote control battery.

23 Particle filter fluid check

1 Eolys 176 and DPX42 fluid is an additive used on vehicles equipped with a particulate filter incorporated into the exhaust system. Over a period of time, the soot produced by the engine will clog the filter. When the filter requires cleaning, the engine management system injects a small quantity of fuel into the combustion chamber after combustion has taken place. The unburnt fuel enters the exhaust system, where it ignites, and burns the soot deposits from the particulate filter. In order to lower the temperature at which the soot is burnt, Eolys fluid is added to the fuel in the tank. The fluid is stored in a separate

tank to the right-hand side of the fuel tank (see illustration), and added to the main fuel tank. Every time the fuel tank is filled, the system computes how much Eolys fluid to add. Eventually the level of fluid will fall below a minimum level and a warning light will illuminate on the instrument cluster.

2 If the system runs out of fluid, the particulate filter will be unable to purge, causing its blockage, and premature failure. Unfortunately, the process of checking the level, replenishing the Eolys fluid tank and resetting the engine management values requires access to special diagnostic equipment, and therefore must be entrusted to a Peugeot/Citroën dealer or suitably-equipped specialist. Failure to reset the ECM values will prevent the filter cleaning process from occurring.

24 Particulate filter renewal

1 Renewal of the particulate filter is described in Chapter 4A Section 18 .

25 Timing belt renewal

1 Refer to Chapter 2A Section 7 and Chapter 2B Section 7 for timing belt renewal.

26 Airbags and seat belt pretensioners renewal

1 Peugeot/Citroën recommends that the airbags and seat belt pretensioners be renewed regardless of their condition within fifteen years. Refer to Chapter 12 Section 22 for airbag renewal, and Chapter 11 Section 25 for seat belt pretensioner renewal.

Chapter 2 Part A
1.6 litre SOHC engine in-car repair procedures

Contents

Degrees of difficulty

| Easy, suitable for novice with little experience | | Fairly easy, suitable for beginner with some experience | | Fairly difficult, suitable for competent DIY mechanic | | Difficult, suitable for experienced DIY mechanic | | Very difficult, suitable for expert DIY or professional | |

Specifications

General

Designation	DV6C, DV6CM, DV6CTED, DV6DTED, DV6DTEDM and DV6ETED
Engine codes*	
DV6C	9HL and 9HR
DV6CM	9HG
DV6CTED	9HC, 9HD and 9HR
DV6DTED	9HF, 9HJ and 9HP
DV6DTEDM.	9HE
DV6ETED	9HK and 9HL
Capacity	1560 cc
Bore	75.0 mm
Stroke	88.3 mm
Direction of crankshaft rotation	Clockwise (viewed from the right-hand side of vehicle)
No 1 cylinder location.	At the transmission end of block
Maximum power output	
9HK and 9HN	55 kW (75 PS) @ 4000 rpm
9HF and 9HE	66 kW (90 PS) @ 4000 rpm
9HJ and 9HP	68 kW (92 PS) @ 4000 rpm
9HL and 9HR	82 kW (111 PS) @ 4000 rpm
9HC, 9HD and 9HG	85 kW (116 PS) @ 4000 rpm
Maximum torque output	
9HK and 9HN	185 Nm @ 1500 rpm
9HF and 9HE	215 Nm @ 1500 rpm
9HJ and 9HP	230 Nm @ 1750 rpm
9HL	240 Nm @ 1500 rpm
9HC, 9HD and 9HG	254 Nm @ 1750 rpm
9HR	270 Nm @ 1750 rpm
Compression ratio	16 : 1

* The engine code is stamped on a plate attached to the front of the cylinder block, next to the oil filter

Compression pressures (engine hot, at cranking speed)

Normal	20 ± 5 bar
Minimum	15 bar
Maximum difference between any two cylinders.	5 bar

Cylinder head gasket

Gasket thickness:
1 notch	1.35 mm
2 notch	1.25 mm
3 notch	1.30 mm
4 notch	1.40 mm
5 notch	1.45 mm

Piston protrusion (gasket required):
0.685 to 0.734 mm	1 notch
0.533 to 0.634 mm	2 notch
0.635 to 0.684 mm	3 notch
0.735 to 0.784 mm	4 notch
0.785 to 0.886 mm	5 notch

Cylinder head bolts

Maximum length (measured under head)	149 mm

Camshaft

Drive	Toothed belt from crankshaft
Length	410.10 ± 0.25 mm
Endfloat	0.195 to 0.300 mm

Lubrication system

Oil pump type	Gear-type, driven directly by the right-hand end of the crankshaft, by two flats machined along the crankshaft journal.

Oil pressure at 110°C:
1000 rpm	1.3 bar
4000 rpm	3.5 bar

Torque wrench settings

	Nm	lbf ft
Ancillary drivebelt tensioner roller	20	15
Big-end bolts: *		
Stage 1	10	7
Stage 2	Slacken 180°	
Stage 3	10	7
Stage 4	Angle-tighten a further 130°	
Camshaft bearing caps	10	7
Camshaft cover/bearing ladder:		
Studs	10	7
Bolts	10	7
Camshaft position sensor bolt	5	4
Camshaft sprocket bolt		
Stage 1	20	15
Stage 2	Angle-tighten a further 50°	
Coolant outlet housing bolts	8	6
Crankshaft position/speed sensor bolt	10	7
Crankshaft pulley/sprocket bolt: *		
Stage 1	35	26
Stage 2	Angle-tighten a further 190°	
Cylinder head bolts: *		
Stage 1	20	15
Stage 2	40	30
Stage 3	Angle-tighten a further 260°	
Cylinder head cover/manifold	13	10
EGR valve	10	7
Engine-to-transmission fixing bolts	47	35
Flywheel bolts: *		
Stage 1	30	22
Stage 2	Angle-tighten a further 90°	
Fuel pump sprocket	50	37
Left-hand engine/transmission mounting:		
Mounting-to-bracket centre nut	65	48
Mounting-to-bracket outer		
Nuts	30	22
Bolts	20	15
Mounting bracket-to-transmission:		
Large bolt	60	44
Small bolt	30	22

Torque wrench settings (continued)

	Nm	lbf ft
Main bearing ladder outer seam bolts:		
Stage 1	5	4
Stage 2	10	7
Main bearing ladder to cylinder block:		
Stage 1	10	7
Stage 2	Slacken 180°	
Stage 3	30	22
Stage 4	Angle-tighten a further 140°	
Piston oil jet spray tube bolt..........................	20	15
Oil cooler retaining bolts..............................	10	7
Oil filter cover......................................	25	18
Oil pick-up pipe	10	7
Oil pressure switch..................................	30	22
Oil pump to cylinder block:		
Stage 1	5	4
Stage 2	9	7
Rear engine/transmission mounting......................	25	18
Right-hand engine mounting:		
Mounting to Inner wing (nuts/bolts)	48	35
Mounting bracket to engine block	55	41
Sump drain plug....................................	35	26
Sump bolts/nuts....................................	10	7
Timing belt idler pulley	37	27
Timing belt tensioner pulley	30	22
Vacuum pump bolts..................................	20	15

* Do not re-use

1 General Information

How to use this Chapter

1 This Part of Chapter 2 describes the repair procedures that can reasonably be carried out on the engine while it remains in the vehicle. If the engine has been removed from the vehicle and is being dismantled as described in Part C, any preliminary dismantling procedures can be ignored.

2 Note that, while it may be possible physically to overhaul items such as the piston/connecting rod assemblies while the engine is in the car, such tasks are not usually carried out as separate operations. Usually, several additional procedures are required (not to mention the cleaning of components and oilways); for this reason, all such tasks are classed as major overhaul procedures, and are described in Part C of this Chapter.

3 Part C describes the removal of the engine/transmission from the car, and the full overhaul procedures that can then be carried out.

DV series engines

4 The 1.6 litre DV series of engines are the result of development collaboration between Peugeot/Citroën and Ford. Originally specified as a double overhead camshaft (DOHC) 16-valve design, the latest version covered by this Chapter is a single overhead cam (SOHC), 8 valve variant. The direct injection, turbocharged, four-cylinder engine is mounted transversely, with the transmission mounted on the left-hand side.

5 A toothed timing belt drives the camshaft, high-pressure fuel pump and coolant pump. The camshaft operates the inlet and exhaust valves via rocker arms which are supported at their pivot ends by hydraulic self-adjusting tappets. The camshaft Is supported by bearings machined directly in the cylinder head and camshaft bearing housing.

6 The high-pressure fuel pump supplies fuel to the fuel rail, and subsequently to the electronically-controlled injectors which inject the fuel direct into the combustion chambers. This design differs from the previous type where an injection pump supplies the fuel at high pressure to each injector. The earlier, conventional type injection pump required fine calibration and timing, and these functions are now completed by the high-pressure pump, electronic injectors and engine management ECM (Electronic Control Module).

7 The crankshaft runs in five main bearings of the usual shell type. Endfloat is controlled by thrustwashers either side of No 2 main bearing.

8 The pistons are selected to be of matching weight, and incorporate fully-floating gudgeon pins retained by circlips.

Repair operations precaution

9 The engine is a complex unit with numerous accessories and ancillary components. The design of the engine compartment is such that every conceivable space has been utilised, and access to virtually all of the engine components is extremely limited. In many cases, ancillary components will have to be removed, or moved to one side, and wiring, pipes and hoses will have to be disconnected or removed from various cable clips and support brackets.

10 When working on this engine, read through the entire procedure first, look at the car and engine at the same time, and establish whether you have the necessary tools, equipment, skill and patience to proceed. Allow considerable time for any operation, and be prepared for the unexpected.

11 Because of the limited access, many of the engine photographs appearing in this Chapter were, by necessity, taken with the engine removed from the vehicle.

⚠ *Warning: It is essential to observe strict precautions when working on the fuel system components of the engine, particularly the high-pressure side of the system. Before carrying out any engine operations that entail working on, or near, any part of the fuel system, refer to the special information given in Chapter 4A Section 1.*

12 Operations with engine in vehicle

a) Compression pressure – testing.
b) Cylinder head cover – removal and refitting.
c) Crankshaft pulley – removal and refitting.
d) Timing belt covers – removal and refitting.
e) Timing belt – removal, refitting and adjustment.
f) Timing belt tensioner and sprockets – removal and refitting.
g) Camshaft oil seal – renewal.
h) Camshaft, rocker arms and hydraulic tappets – removal, inspection and refitting.
i) Sump – removal and refitting.
j) Oil pump – removal and refitting.
k) Crankshaft oil seals – renewal.
l) Engine/transmission mountings – inspection and renewal.
m) Flywheel – removal, inspection and refitting.

2 Compression and leakdown tests – description and interpretation

Compression test

Note: *A compression tester specifically designed for diesel engines must be used for this test.*

1 When engine performance is down, or if misfiring occurs which cannot be attributed to the fuel system, a compression test can provide diagnostic clues as to the engine's condition. If the test is performed regularly, it can give warning of trouble before any other symptoms become apparent.

2 A compression tester specifically intended for diesel engines must be used, because of the higher pressures involved. The tester is connected to an adapter which screws into the glow plug or injector hole. On this engine, an adapter suitable for use in the glow plug holes will be required, so as not to disturb the fuel system components. It is unlikely to be worthwhile buying such a tester for occasional use, but it may be possible to borrow or hire one – if not, have the test performed by a garage.

3 Unless specific instructions to the contrary are supplied with the tester, observe the following points:

a) *The battery must be in a good state of charge, the air filter must be clean, and the engine should be at normal operating temperature.*

b) *All the glow plugs should be removed as described in Chapter 5B Section 2 before starting the test.*

c) *Disconnect the fuel injector wiring plugs.*

4 The compression pressures measured are not so important as the balance between cylinders. Values are given in the Specifications.

5 The cause of poor compression is less easy to establish on a diesel engine than on a petrol one. The effect of introducing oil into the cylinders ('wet' testing) is not conclusive, because there is a risk that the oil will sit in the swirl chamber or in the recess on the piston crown instead of passing to the rings. However, the following can be used as a rough guide to diagnosis.

6 All cylinders should produce very similar pressures; any difference greater than that specified indicates the existence of a fault. Note that the compression should build-up quickly in a healthy engine; low compression on the first stroke, followed by gradually-increasing pressure on successive strokes, indicates worn piston rings. A low compression reading on the first stroke, which does not build-up during successive strokes, indicates leaking valves or a blown head gasket (a cracked head could also be the cause). Deposits on the undersides of the valve heads can also cause low compression.

7 A low reading from two adjacent cylinders is almost certainly due to the head gasket having blown between them; the presence of coolant in the engine oil will confirm this.

8 If the compression reading is unusually high, the cylinder head surfaces, valves and pistons are probably coated with carbon deposits. If this is the case, the cylinder head should be removed and decarbonised.

Note: *After performing this test, a fault code may be generated and stored in the ECM memory. Have the ECM self-diagnosis facility interrogated by a Peugeot/Citroen dealer or suitably-equipped specialist, and the fault code erased.*

Leakdown test

9 A leakdown test measures the rate at which compressed air fed into the cylinder is lost. It is an alternative to a compression test, and in many ways it is better, since the escaping air provides easy identification of where pressure loss is occurring (piston rings, valves or head gasket).

10 The equipment needed for leakdown testing is unlikely to be available to the home mechanic. If poor compression is suspected, have the test performed by a suitably-equipped garage.

3 Engine assembly/valve timing holes – general information and usage

Note: *Do not attempt to rotate the engine whilst the crankshaft and camshaft are locked in position. If the engine is to be left in this state for a long period of time, it is a good idea to place suitable warning notices inside the vehicle, and in the engine compartment. This will reduce the possibility of the engine being accidentally cranked on the starter motor, which is likely to cause damage with the locking pins in place.*

1 Timing holes or slots are located only in the crankshaft pulley flange and camshaft sprocket hub. The holes/slots are used to position the pistons halfway up the cylinder bores. This will ensure that the valve timing is maintained during operations that require removal and refitting of the timing belt. When the holes/slots are aligned with their corresponding holes in the cylinder block and cylinder head, suitable diameter bolts/pins can be inserted to lock the crankshaft and camshaft in position, preventing rotation.

2 Note that the fuel system used on these engines does not have a conventional diesel injection pump, but instead uses a high-pressure fuel pump. However, the fuel pump sprocket must be pegged in position in a similar fashion to the camshaft sprocket.

3 To align the engine assembly/valve timing holes, proceed as follows.

4 Apply the handbrake, then jack up the front of the vehicle and support it on axle stands (see *Jacking and vehicle support*). Remove the right-hand front roadwheel.

5 To gain access to the crankshaft pulley, to enable the engine to be turned, the wheel arch plastic liner must be removed. The liner is secured by several plastic expanding rivets/ nut/bolts. To remove the rivets, push in the centre pins a little, then prise the clips from place. Remove the liner from under the front wing.

6 Remove the starter motor and remove the crankshaft pulley as described in Section 5.

7 Remove the upper and lower timing belt covers as described in Section 6.

8 Temporarily refit the crankshaft pulley bolt (without the crankshaft pulley) and then remove the crankshaft locking tool.

9 Turn the crankshaft until the timing hole in the crankshaft sprocket aligns with the hole in the oil pump casing (this is at the 12 o'clock position). Fit the special tool (No.303-732), or a suitable alternative and lock the crankshaft in position **(see illustration)**.

10 With the crankshaft locked in position fit the camshaft locking tool (No.303-735 or similar). The hole in the camshaft sprocket should be at approximately the 1 o'clock position **(see illustration)**. If this is not the case remove the crankshaft locking pin and rotate the engine one revolution. Note that the crankshaft must always be turned

3.9 Insert a 5.0 mm drill bit/bolt through the round hole in the sprocket flange into the hole in the oil pump housing (lower timing belt removed for clarity)

3.10 Insert an 8.0 mm bolt through the hole in the camshaft sprocket into the corresponding hole in the cylinder head

4.4 Remove the hose from the throttle body

4.5a Disconnect the wiring plug and...

4.5b ...remove the hose complete with the throttle body

in a clockwise direction (viewed from the right-hand side of vehicle).

11 When refitting the timing belt, insert special tool (No.303-732) through the slot in the fuel pump sprocket and into the corresponding hole in the fuel pump mounting bracket. In the absence of this tool use a 5 mm bolt or drill bit.

12 The crankshaft and camshaft are now locked in position, preventing unnecessary rotation.

4.6a Remove the hose clamps and mounting bolt...

4.6b ... and then remove the hose

4 Cylinder head cover – removal and refitting

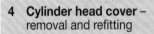

Removal

1 Disconnect the battery negative lead as described in Chapter 5A Section 4.

2 Pull the plastic cover upwards from the top of the engine.

3 Unbolt the fuel filter housing and move it to one side.

4 Release the hose clamp and remove the hose from the throttle body **(see illustration)**.

5 Unclip the fuel lines from the inlet manifold hose on top of the engine. Disconnect the wiring plug from the throttle body and then unbolt and remove the throttle body complete with the hose **(see illustrations)**. Plug the openings to prevent contamination.

6 Unbolt and then remove the turbocharger

to intercooler hose **(see illustrations)**. Seal the opening to the turbocharger.

7 Remove the sound insulation from the top of the engine **(see illustration)**.

8 Disconnect the wiring plugs from the fuel injectors and camshaft position sensor and then remove the breather hose from the valve cover.

9 Unbolt and then remove the timing belt upper cover.

10 Remove the 9 bolts and then remove the valve cover **(see illustration)**. Recover the rubber seal.

Refitting

11 Refitting is a reversal of removal, but ensure that the valve cover seal is correctly located in the valve cover **(see illustration)**.

5 Crankshaft pulley – removal and refitting

Removal

1 Jack up and support the front of the vehicle (see *Jacking and vehicle support*).

2 Disconnect the battery and remove the engine undershield.

3 Remove the starter motor as described in Chapter 5A Section 10.

4 Remove wing liner and then remove the auxiliary drivebelt as described in Chapter 1 Section 16.

5 To lock the crankshaft, fit the manufacturers

4.7 Remove the insulation

4.10 Remove the valve cover

4.11 Fit the seal correctly

5.5 Install the flywheel locking tool (arrowed)

5.6a Where fitted remove the cover

5.6b Remove the bolt and...

5.6c ...then the pulley

special tool (No.303-393) or suitable equivalent, to the flywheel ring gear **(see illustration)**.

6 Using a suitable socket and extension bar, unscrew the retaining bolt, remove the washer, then slide the pulley off the end of the crankshaft **(see illustrations)**. If the pulley is tight fit, it can be drawn off the crankshaft

using a suitable puller. If a puller is being used, refit the pulley retaining bolt without the washer, to avoid damaging the crankshaft as the puller is tightened.

Caution: Do not touch the outer magnetic sensor ring of the sprocket with your fingers, or allow metallic particles to come into contact with it.

Refitting

7 Refit the pulley to the end of the crankshaft

8 Refit the crankshaft pulley. Fit a new bolt and retaining washer. Tighten the bolt to the specified torque, then through the specified angle.

9 Remove the locking tool and refit the starter motor

10 Refit and tension the auxiliary drivebelt as described in Chapter 1 Section 16.

11 Refit the remaining components in reverse order of removal.

6 Timing belt covers – removal and refitting

> ⚠ *Warning: Refer to the precautionary information contained in Section 1 before proceeding.*

Removal

Upper cover

1 Remove the engine cover from the top of the engine.

2 Remove the fuel lines and wiring loom from the support bracket next to the cover and then work the bracket free **(see illustrations)**.

3 Undo the 4 bolts and remove the timing belt upper cover **(see illustration)**.

Lower cover

4 Remove the crankshaft pulley as described in Section 5.

5 Position a trolley/workshop jack under the engine. Place a block of wood on the jack head (to help spread the load on the sump), then take the weight of the engine.

6 Undo the nuts/bolts, and remove the right-hand engine mounting as described in Section 17.

7 Whilst not strictly necessary access is greatly improved if the mounting bracket is removed from the engine.

8 Undo the 4 bolts and remove the lower cover **(see illustration)**.

Refitting

9 Refitting of all the covers is a reversal of the relevant removal procedure, ensuring that each cover section is correctly located, and that the cover retaining bolts are securely tightened. Ensure that all disturbed hoses are reconnected and retained by their relevant clips.

6.2a Release the fuel lines and...

6.2b ...remove the bracket

6.3 Remove the upper cover

6.8 Remove the lower timing belt cover from below

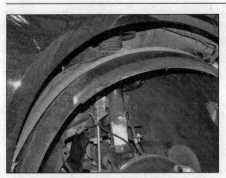

7.4 Remove the wing liner

7.6 Undo the bolt (arrowed) and remove the crankshaft position sensor

7.7 Remove the timing belt protection bracket

7 Timing belt – removal, inspection, refitting and tensioning

General

1 The timing belt drives the camshaft, high-pressure fuel pump, and coolant pump from a toothed sprocket on the end of the crankshaft. If the belt breaks or slips in service, the pistons are likely to hit the valve heads, resulting in expensive damage.

2 The timing belt should be renewed at the specified intervals, or earlier if it is contaminated with oil, or at all noisy in operation (a 'scraping' noise due to uneven wear).

3 If the timing belt is being removed, it is a wise precaution to renew the coolant pump at the same time. This may avoid the need to remove the timing belt again at a later stage, should the coolant pump fail. The timing belt tensioner should always be replaced when a new timing belt is fitted.

Removal

4 Apply the handbrake, then jack up the front of the vehicle and support it on axle stands (see *Jacking and vehicle support*). Remove the front right-hand roadwheel, wing liner **(see illustration)** and the engine undershield.

5 Remove the upper and lower timing belt covers, as described in Section 6.

6 Undo the bolt and remove the crankshaft position sensor adjacent to the crankshaft sprocket flange, and move it to one side **(see illustration)**.

7 Undo the retaining bolt and remove the timing belt protection bracket, again, adjacent to the crankshaft sprocket flange **(see illustration)**.

8 Lock the crankshaft and camshaft in the correct position as described in Section 3. If necessary, temporarily refit the crankshaft pulley bolt to enable the crankshaft to be rotated.

9 Insert a hexagon key into the belt tensioner pulley centre, slacken the pulley bolt, and allow the tensioner to rotate, relieving the belt tension **(see illustration)**. With belt slack, temporarily tighten the pulley bolt.

10 Note its routing, then remove the timing belt from the sprockets **(see illustration)**.

Inspection

11 Renew the belt as a matter of course, regardless of its apparent condition. The cost of a new belt is nothing compared with the cost of repairs should the belt break in service. If signs of oil contamination are found, trace the source of the oil leak and rectify it. Wash down the engine timing belt area and all related components, to remove all traces of oil. The tensioner must always be replaced. Check that the idler pulleys rotate freely without any sign of roughness, and also check that the coolant pump pulley rotates freely. It

is highly recommended that both the coolant pump and the idler pulley are replaced at the same time as the timing belt and tensioner.

Refitting and tensioning

12 Commence refitting by ensuring that the crankshaft, camshaft and fuel pump sprocket timing pins are in position as described in Section 3.

13 Locate the timing belt on the crankshaft sprocket, then keeping it taut, locate it around the idler pulley, camshaft sprocket, high-pressure pump sprocket, coolant pump sprocket, and the tensioner roller **(see illustration)**.

14 Refit the timing belt protection bracket and tighten the retaining bolt securely.

7.13 Timing belt routing

1 Crankshaft 4 Tensioner
2 Waterpump 5 Fuel pump
3 Idler 6 Camshaft

7.9 Slacken the bolt and allow the tensioner to rotate, relieving the tension on the belt

7.10 Remove the timing belt

7.15 The index arm must align with the lug (arrowed)

15 Slacken the tensioner pulley bolt, and using a hexagonal key, rotate the tensioner anti-clockwise, which moves the index arm clockwise, until the index arm is aligned as shown **(see illustration)**.

16 Remove the camshaft, crankshaft and fuel pump sprocket (where applicable) timing pins and, using a socket on the crankshaft pulley bolt, rotate the crankshaft clockwise 10 complete revolutions. Refit the crankshaft and camshaft locking pins.

17 Check that the tensioner index arm is still aligned between the edges of the area shown **(see illustration 7.15)**. If it is not, remove the belt and begin the refitting process again, starting at Paragraph 12.

18 The remainder of refitting is a reversal of removal. Tighten all fasteners to the specified torque where given.

8 Timing belt sprockets and tensioner – removal and refitting

Camshaft sprocket

Removal

1 Remove the timing belt as described in Section 7.

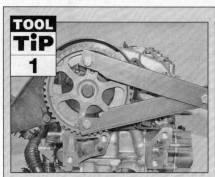

A sprocket holding tool can be made from two lengths of steel strip bolted together to form a forked end. Drill holes and insert bolts in the ends of the fork to engage with the sprocket spokes.

2 Remove the locking tool from the camshaft sprocket/hub. Slacken the sprocket hub retaining bolt. To prevent the camshaft rotating as the bolt is slackened, a sprocket holding tool will be required. In the absence of the special manufacturers tool, an acceptable substitute can be fabricated at home (see **Tool Tip 1**). Do not attempt to use the engine assembly/valve timing locking tool to prevent the sprocket from rotating whilst the bolt is slackened.

3 Remove the sprocket hub retaining bolt, and slide the sprocket and hub off the end of the camshaft.

4 Clean the camshaft sprocket thoroughly, and renew it if there are any signs of wear, damage or cracks.

Refitting

5 Refit the camshaft sprocket to the camshaft **(see illustration)**.

6 Refit the sprocket hub retaining bolt. Tighten the bolt to the specified torque, preventing the camshaft from turning as during removal.

7 Align the engine assembly/valve timing slot

8.5 Ensure the lug on the sprocket hub engages with the slot on the end of the camshaft (arrowed)

in the camshaft sprocket hub with the hole in the cylinder head and refit the timing pin to lock the camshaft in position.

8 Fit the timing belt around the pump sprocket and camshaft sprocket, and tension the timing belt as described in Section 7.

Crankshaft sprocket

Removal

9 Remove the timing belt as described in Section 7.

10 Check that the engine assembly/valve timing holes are still aligned as described in Section 3, and the camshaft sprocket and flywheel are locked in position.

11 Slide the sprocket off the end of the crankshaft and collect the Woodruff key **(see illustrations)**.

12 Examine the crankshaft oil seal for signs of oil leakage and, if necessary, renew it as described in Section 14.

13 Clean the crankshaft sprocket thoroughly, and renew it if there are any signs of wear, damage or cracks. Recover the crankshaft locating key.

Refitting

14 Refit the key to the end of the crankshaft, then refit the crankshaft sprocket (with the flange facing the crankshaft pulley).

8.11a Slide the sprocket from the crankshaft...

8.11b ...and recover the Woodruff key

Make a sprocket releasing tool from a short strip of steel. Drill two holes in the strip to correspond with the two holes in the sprocket. Drill a third hole just large enough to accept the flats of the sprocket retaining nut.

15 Fit the timing belt around the crankshaft sprocket, and tension the timing belt as described in Section 7.

Fuel pump sprocket

Removal

16 Remove the timing belt as described in Section 7.
17 Using a socket, undo the pump sprocket retaining nut. The sprocket can be held stationary by inserting a locking pin, drill or rod through the slot in the sprocket, and into the corresponding hole in the backplate, or by using a forked tool engaged with the holes in the sprocket (see **Tool Tip 1**).
18 The pump sprocket is a taper fit on the pump shaft and it will be necessary to make up another tool to release it from the taper (see **Tool Tip 2**).
19 Partially unscrew the sprocket retaining nut, fit the home-made tool, and secure it to the sprocket with two bolts. Prevent the sprocket from rotating as before, and unscrew the sprocket retaining nut. The nut will bear against the tool as it is undone, forcing the sprocket off the shaft taper. Once the taper is released, remove the tool, unscrew the nut fully, and remove the sprocket from the pump shaft.

9.4 Remove the vacuum pump

8.25 Remove the tensioner

20 Clean the sprocket thoroughly, and renew it if there are any signs of wear, damage or cracks.

Refitting

21 Refit the pump sprocket and retaining nut, and tighten the nut to the specified torque. Prevent the sprocket rotating as the nut is tightened using the sprocket holding tool.
22 Refit the timing belt as described in Section 7.

Coolant pump sprocket

23 The coolant pump sprocket is integral with the pump, and cannot be removed. Coolant pump removal is described in Chapter 3 Section 8.

Tensioner pulley

Removal

24 Remove the timing belt as described in Section 7.
25 Remove the tensioner pulley retaining bolt, and then remove the tensioner (see **illustration**).
26 Clean the tensioner pulley, but do not use any strong solvent which may enter the pulley bearings. Check that the pulley rotates freely, with no sign of stiffness or free play. The pulley should always be replaced when the timing belt is replaced.
27 Examine the pulley mounting stud for signs of damage and if necessary, renew it.

Refitting

28 Refitting is a reversal of removal.

9.6 Remove the camshaft position sensor (arrowed)

8.31 Timing belt idler pulley retaining nut (arrowed)

29 Refit the timing belt as described in Section 7.

Idler pulley

Removal

30 Remove the timing belt as described in Section 7.
31 Undo the retaining bolt/nut and withdraw the idler pulley from the engine (see **illustration**).
32 Clean the idler pulley, but do not use any strong solvent which may enter the bearings. Check that the pulley rotates freely, with no sign of stiffness or free play. Renew the idler pulley if there is any doubt about its condition, or if there are any obvious signs of wear or damage.

Refitting

33 Locate the idler pulley on the engine, and fit the retaining bolt/nut. Tighten the bolt/nut to the specified torque.
34 Refit the timing belt as described in Section 7.

9 Camshafts, rocker arms and hydraulic tappets – removal, inspection and refitting

Removal

1 Remove the cylinder head cover/manifold as described in Section 4.
2 Remove the timing belt (Section 7) and the camshaft sprocket as described in Section 8.
3 Refit the right-hand engine mounting, but only tighten the bolts moderately; this will keep the engine supported during the camshaft removal.
4 Undo the bolts and remove the vacuum pump (see Chapter 9 Section 20). Recover the pump O-ring seals (see **illustration**).
5 Unbolt the fuel filter (see Chapter 1 Section 12) and move it to one side.
6 Disconnect the wiring plug from the camshaft position sensor (see **illustration**). Unbolt and remove the sensor from the bearing ladder.
7 Working in reverse order to that shown (see **illustration 9.22**) remove the retaining bolts

9.7 Remove the bearing ladder

9.8 Remove the camshaft

9.10 Remove the rocker arms (cam followers)

and then remove camshaft bearing cap ladder **(see illustration)**.

8 Lift out the camshaft **(see illustration)** and dispose of the oil seal. A new one will be required.

9 Obtain 8 small, clean plastic containers, and number them 1 to 4 inlet and 1 to 4 exhaust; alternatively, divide a larger container into 8 compartments.

10 Lift out each rocker arm. Place the rocker arms in their respective positions in the box or containers **(see illustration)**.

11 A compartmentalised container filled with engine oil is now required to retain the hydraulic tappets while they are removed from the cylinder head. Withdraw each hydraulic follower **(see illustration)** and place it in the container, keeping them each identified for correct refitting. The tappets must be totally submerged in the oil to prevent air entering them.

Inspection

12 Inspect the cam lobes and the camshaft bearing journals for scoring or other visible evidence of wear. Once the surface hardening of the cam lobes has been eroded, wear will occur at an accelerated rate. **Note:** *If these symptoms are visible on the tips of the camshaft lobes, check the corresponding rocker arm, as it will probably be worn as well.*

13 Examine the condition of the bearing surfaces in the cylinder head and camshaft bearing housing. If wear is evident, the cylinder head and bearing housing will both have to be renewed, as they are a matched assembly.

14 Inspect the rocker arms and tappets for scuffing, cracking or other damage and renew any components as necessary. Also check the condition of the tappet bores in the cylinder head. As with the camshafts, any wear in this area will necessitate cylinder head renewal.

Refitting

15 Thoroughly clean the sealant from the mating surfaces of the cylinder head and camshaft bearing housing. Use a suitable liquid gasket dissolving agent (available from the manufacturer) together with a soft putty knife; do not use a metal scraper or the faces will be damaged. As there is no conventional gasket used, the cleanliness of the mating faces is of the utmost importance.

16 Clean off any oil, dirt or grease from both components and dry with a clean lint-free cloth. Ensure that all the oilways are completely clean.

17 Liberally lubricate the hydraulic tappet bores in the cylinder head with clean engine oil.

18 Insert the hydraulic tappets into their original bores in the cylinder head unless they have been renewed.

19 Lubricate the rocker arms and place them over their respective tappets and valve stems. Lubricate the bearing surfaces **(see illustration)** and then refit the camshaft.

20 Apply a thin bead of silicone sealant (part No WSE-M4G323-A4) to the mating surface of the camshaft cover/bearing ladder as shown **(see illustration)**.

21 Assembly the bearing ladder within 10 minutes of applying the sealant **(see illustration)**. A special tool (No.303-245) to align the bearing ladder is used, however 2 suitable bolts (with their heads and threads cut off) can be used if the tool is not available.

22 Tighten the bolts to the specified torque in sequence **(see illustration)**.

9.11 Use long nose pliers to remove the hydraulic tappets

9.19 Lubricate the bearing surfaces

9.20 Apply sealant to the camshaft housing

9.21 Refit the bearing ladder

9.22 Tighten the bolts to the specified torque in the order shown

23 Fit a new camshaft oil seal as described in Section 14.
24 Refit the camshaft sprocket, and tighten the retaining bolt.
25 Refit the timing belt and temporarily refit the crankshaft pulley bolt – use the old bolt. Rotate the engine at least 20 revolutions to allow the oil pump to deliver oil to the camshaft and associated components. Refit the timing belt cover.
26 Refit the remainder of the components in the reverse order of removal.

10 Cylinder head – removal and refitting

Removal

1 Apply the handbrake, then jack up the front of the vehicle and support it on axle stands (see *Jacking and vehicle support*). Remove the front right-hand roadwheel, the engine undershield, and the right-hand front wheel arch liner.
2 Remove the engine cover and then disconnect the battery negative lead as described in Chapter 5A Section 4. With reference to Chapter 12 remove the wiper arms and screen cowl panel.
3 Drain the cooling system as described in Chapter 1 Section 19.
4 Remove the timing belt, camshaft, rocker arms and hydraulic tappets as described in Section 9.

5 Remove the turbocharger and exhaust manifold as described in Chapter 4A Section 14 and 16.
6 Unbolt the fuel filter assembly (and move it to one side) and the remove the glow plugs as described in Chapter 5B Section 2.
7 Undo the upper mounting bolts, and pivot the alternator away from the engine, undo the oil dipstick guide tube bolt, then undo the bolts securing the alternator mounting bracket to the cylinder head/block **(see illustration)**.
8 Undo the coolant outlet housing (left-hand end of the cylinder head) retaining bolts, slacken the two bolts securing the housing support bracket to the top of the transmission bellhousing, and move the outlet housing away from the cylinder head a little **(see illustration)**. There is no need to disconnect the hoses.
9 Remove the brake vacuum pump as described in Chapter 9 Section 20.
10 Disconnect the high-pressure fuel pipe from the common rail to the pump, and disconnect the fuel supply and return hoses. Where fitted, remove the bracket at the rear of the pump, then undo the bolt/nut and remove the pump and mounting bracket as an assembly **(see illustrations)**. Immediately seal all the openings in the fuel system. Note that a new high-pressure pipe must be fitted – see Chapter 4A Section 2.
11 Unbolt the EGR pipe and inlet duct from the rear of the cylinder head.
12 Check that no components or electrical connectors are still fitted to the cylinder head.

13 Working in the reverse of the sequence shown **(see illustration 10.33)** undo the cylinder head bolts. Discard the bolts – new ones must be fitted.
14 Release the cylinder head from the cylinder block and location dowels by rocking it. The special manufacturers tool for doing this consists simply of two metal rods with 90-degree angled ends **(see illustration)**. Do not prise between the mating faces of the cylinder head and block, as this may damage the gasket faces.
15 Lift the cylinder head from the block, and recover the gasket.

Preparation for refitting

16 The mating faces of the cylinder head and cylinder block must be perfectly clean before refitting the head. The manufacturer recommends that a scouring agent is used for this purpose, but acceptable results can be achieved by using a hard plastic or wood scraper to remove all traces of gasket and carbon. The same method can be used to clean the piston crowns. Take particular care to avoid scoring or gouging the cylinder head/ cylinder block mating surfaces during the cleaning operations, as aluminium alloy is easily damaged. Make sure that the carbon is not allowed to enter the oil and water passages – this is particularly important for the lubrication system, as carbon could block the oil supply to the engine's components. Using adhesive tape and paper, seal the water, oil and bolt holes in the cylinder block.

10.7 The engine oil level dipstick guide tube is secured to the alternator bracket by a Torx bolt (arrowed)

10.8 Access to the coolant outlet housing will be improved if the vacuum pump is removed first

10.10a Remove the high-pressure pipe (arrowed)

10.10b Compress the collars and...

10.10c ...remove the fuel bleed hoses from the injectors

10.14 Free the cylinder head using angled rods

10.18a Pull the non-return valve from the cylinder head...

10.18b ...and push a new one into place

10.23 Measure the piston protrusion using a DTI gauge

To prevent carbon entering the gap between the pistons and bores, smear a little grease in the gap. After cleaning each piston, use a small brush to remove all traces of grease and carbon from the gap, then wipe away the remainder with a clean rag.

17 Check the mating surfaces of the cylinder block and the cylinder head for nicks, deep scratches and other damage. If slight, they may be removed carefully with a file, but if excessive, machining may be the only alternative to renewal. If warpage of the cylinder head gasket surface is suspected, use a straight-edge to check it for distortion. Refer to Part C of this Chapter if necessary.

18 Thoroughly clean the threads of the cylinder head bolt holes in the cylinder block. Ensure that the bolts run freely in their threads, and that all traces of oil and water are removed from each bolt hole. If required, pull the oil feed non-return valve from the cylinder head, and check the ball moves freely. Push a new valve into place if necessary **(see illustrations)**.

Gasket selection

19 The gasket thickness is indicated by notches/holes on the front edge of the gasket. If the crankshaft or pistons/connecting rods have not been disturbed, fit a new gasket with the same number of notches/holes as the previous one. If the crankshaft/piston or connecting rods have been disturbed, it's necessary to work out the piston protrusion as follows:

20 Remove the crankshaft timing pin, then turn the crankshaft until pistons 1 and 4 are at TDC (Top Dead Centre). Position a dial test indicator (dial gauge) on the cylinder block adjacent to the rear of No 1 piston, and zero it on the block face. Transfer the probe to the crown of No 1 piston (10.0 mm in from the rear edge), then slowly turn the crankshaft back-and-forth past TDC, noting the highest reading on the indicator. Record this reading as protrusion A.

21 Repeat the check described in paragraph 18, this time 10.0 mm in from the front edge of the No 1 piston crown. Record this reading as protrusion B.

22 Add protrusion A to protrusion B, then divide the result by 2 to obtain an average reading for piston No 1.

23 Repeat the procedure described in paragraphs 20 to 22 on piston 4, then turn the crankshaft through 180° and carry out the procedure on the piston Nos 2 and 3 **(see illustration)**. Check that there is a maximum difference of 0.07 mm protrusion between any two pistons.

24 If a dial test indicator is not available, piston protrusion may be measured using a straight-edge and feeler blades or Vernier calipers. However, this is much less accurate, and cannot therefore be wrecommended.

25 Note the greatest piston protrusion measurement, and use this to determine the correct cylinder head gasket from the table below. The series of notches/holes on the

side of the gasket are used for thickness identification **(see illustration)**.

Head bolt examination

26 Carefully examine the cylinder head bolts for signs of damage to the threads or head, and for any sign of corrosion. If the bolts are in a satisfactory condition, measure the length of each bolt from the underside of the head to the end of the shank. The bolts may be re-used providing that the measured length does not exceed 149.0 mm **(see illustration)**. **Note:** *Considering the stress to which the cylinder head bolts are subjected, it is highly recommended that they be all renewed, regardless of their apparent condition.*

Refitting

27 Turn the crankshaft and position Nos 1 and 4 pistons at TDC, then turn the crankshaft a quarter turn (90°) anti-clockwise.

28 Thoroughly clean the surfaces of the cylinder head and block.

29 Make sure that the locating dowels are in place, then fit the correct gasket the right way round on the cylinder block **(see illustration)**.

30 Carefully lower the cylinder head onto the gasket and block, making sure that it locates correctly onto the dowels.

31 Apply a smear of grease to the threads, and to the underside of the heads of the new cylinder head bolts.

32 Carefully insert the cylinder head bolts into their holes (do not drop them in) and initially finger-tighten them.

10.25 Cylinder head gasket thickness identification notches (arrowed)

10.26 Measure the length from under the bolt head to its end

10.29 Ensure the gasket locates over the dowels (arrowed)

10.33 Cylinder head bolt tightening sequence

33 Working progressively and in sequence, tighten the cylinder head bolts to their Stage 1 torque setting, using a torque wrench and suitable socket **(see illustration)**.

34 Once all the bolts have been tightened to their Stage 1 torque setting, working again in the specified sequence, tighten each bolt to the specified Stage 2 setting. Finally, angle-tighten the bolts through the specified Stage 3 angle. It is recommended that an angle-measuring gauge is used during this stage of tightening, to ensure accuracy. **Note:** *Retightening of the cylinder head bolts after running the engine is not required.*

35 Refit the hydraulic tappets, rocker arms, and camshaft housing (complete with camshafts) as described in Section 9.

36 Refit the timing belt as described in Section 7.

37 The remainder of refitting is a reversal of removal, noting the following points.

a) *Use a new seal when refitting the coolant outlet housing.*

b) *When refitting a cylinder head, it is good practice to renew the thermostat.*

c) *Refit the camshaft position sensor and set the air gap with reference to Chapter 4A Section 12.*

d) *Tighten all fasteners to the specified torque where given.*

e) *Refill the cooling system as described in Chapter 1 Section 19.*

f) *The engine may run erratically for the first few miles, until the engine management ECM relearns its stored values.*

11 Sump – removal and refitting

Removal

1 Drain the engine oil, then clean and refit the engine oil drain plug, tightening it securely. If the engine is nearing its service interval when the oil and filter are due for renewal, it is recommended that the filter is also removed, and a new one fitted. After reassembly, the engine can then be refilled with fresh oil. Refer to Chapter 1 Section 2 for further information.

2 Apply the handbrake, then jack up the front of the vehicle and support it on axle stands (see *Jacking and vehicle support*). Undo the bolts and remove the engine undershield.

3 Remove the exhaust front pipe as described in Chapter 4A Section 18.

4 Where necessary, disconnect the wiring connector from the oil temperature sender unit, which is screwed into the sump.

5 Progressively slacken and remove all the sump retaining bolts/nuts. Since the sump bolts vary in length, remove each bolt in turn, and store it in its correct fitted order by pushing it through a clearly-marked cardboard template. This will avoid the possibility of installing the bolts in the wrong locations on refitting.

6 Try to break the joint by striking the sump with the palm of your hand, then lower and withdraw the sump from under the car. If the sump is stuck (which is quite likely) use a putty knife or similar, carefully inserted between the sump and block. Ease the knife along the joint until the sump is released. While the sump is removed, take the opportunity to check the oil

pump pick-up/strainer for signs of clogging or splitting. If necessary, remove the pump as described in Section 12, and clean or renew the strainer.

Refitting

7 Clean all traces of sealant from the mating surfaces of the cylinder block/crankcase and sump, then use a clean rag to wipe out the sump and the engine's interior.

8 Ensure that the sump mating surfaces are clean and dry, then apply a 3mm diameter bead of sealant (part No WSE-M4G323-A4) to the sump mating surface **(see illustration)**. The sealant must be applied to the Inside of the bolt holes. Note that the sump must be installed within 10 minutes of applying the sealant, and the bolts tightened within a further 5 minutes.

9 Offer up the sump to the cylinder block/crankcase. Refit its retaining bolts/nuts, ensuring that each bolt is screwed into its original location. Tighten the bolts evenly and progressively to the specified torque setting **(see illustration)**.

10 Reconnect the wiring connector to the oil temperature sensor (where fitted).

11 Lower the vehicle to the ground, wait at least 30 minutes and then refill the engine with oil as described in Chapter 1 Section 2.

12 Oil pump – removal, inspection and refitting

Removal

1 Remove the sump as described in Section 11.

2 Remove the crankshaft sprocket as described in Section 8. Recover the locating key from the crankshaft.

3 Disconnect the wiring plug, undo the bolts and remove the crankshaft position sensor, located on the right-hand end of the cylinder block.

11.8 Apply a bead of sealant to the sump or crankcase mating surface. Ensure the sealant is applied to the inside of the retaining bolt holes

11.9 Refit the sump and tighten the bolts

12.4 Oil pick-up tube bolts (arrowed)

12.5 Oil pump retaining bolts (arrowed)

4 Undo the three bolts and remove the oil pump pick-up tube from the pump/block **(see illustration)**. Discard the oil seal, a new one must be fitted.
5 Undo the 8 bolts, and remove the oil pump **(see illustration)**.

Inspection

6 Undo and remove the Torx bolts securing the cover to the oil pump **(see illustration)**. Examine the pump rotors and body for signs of wear and damage. If worn, the complete pump must be renewed.
7 Remove the circlip, and extract the cap, valve piston and spring, noting which way around they are fitted **(see illustrations)**. The condition of the relief valve spring can only be measured by comparing it with a new one; if there is any doubt about its condition, it should also be renewed.
8 Refit the relief valve piston and spring, then secure them in place with the circlip.

9 Refit the cover to the oil pump, and tighten the Torx bolts securely.

Refitting

10 Remove all traces of sealant, and thoroughly clean the mating surfaces of the oil pump and cylinder block.
11 Apply a 4 mm diameter bead of silicone sealant to the mating face of the cylinder block **(see illustration)**. Ensure that no sealant enters any of the holes in the block.

12.6 Undo the Torx bolts and remove the pump cover

12.7a Remove the circlip...

12.7b ...cap...

12.7c ...spring...

12.7d ...and piston

12.11 Apply a bead of sealant to the cylinder block mating surface

12.12a Fit a new seal...

12.12b ...align the pump gear flats
(arrowed)...

12.12c ...with those of the crankshaft
(arrowed)

12 With a new oil seal fitted, refit the oil pump over the end of the crankshaft, aligning the flats in the pump drive gear with the flats machined in the crankshaft **(see illustrations)**. Note that new oil pumps are supplied with the oil seal already fitted, and a seal protector sleeve. The sleeve fits over the end of the crankshaft to protect the seal as the pump is fitted.

13 Install the oil pump bolts and tighten them to the specified torque.

14 Refit the oil pick-up tube to the pump/cylinder block using a new O-ring seal. Ensure the oil dipstick guide tube is correctly refitted.

15 Refit the woodruff key to the crankshaft, and slide the crankshaft sprocket into place.

16 The remainder of refitting is a reversal of removal.

13 Oil cooler – removal and refitting

Removal

1 Apply the handbrake, then jack up the front of the vehicle and support it on axle stands (see *Jacking and vehicle support*). Undo the fasteners and remove the engine undershield.

2 The oil cooler is fitted to the front of the oil filter housing. Drain the coolant as described in Chapter 1 Section 19.

3 Drain the engine oil as described in Chapter 1 Section 2, or be prepared for fluid spillage.

4 Undo the bolts/stud and remove the oil cooler **(see illustration)**. Recover the gasket.

Refitting

5 Fit a new gasket into the recesses in the oil filter housing, and refit the cooler. Tighten the bolts securely.

6 Refill or top-up the cooling system and engine oil level as described in Chapter 1 or *Weekly checks* (as applicable). Start the engine, and check the oil cooler for signs of leakage.

14 Oil seals – renewal

Crankshaft

Right-hand oil seal

1 Remove the crankshaft sprocket and Woodruff key as described in Section 8.

2 Measure and note the fitted depth of the oil seal.

3 Pull the oil seal from the housing using a screwdriver **(see illustration)**. Alternatively, drill a small hole in the oil seal, and use a self-tapping screw and a pair of pliers to remove it.

4 Clean the oil seal housing and the crankshaft sealing surface.

5 The new seal should be supplied with a protective sleeve, which fits over the end

13.4 Undo the oil cooler bolts/stud
(arrowed)

of the crankshaft to prevent any damage to the seal lip. With the sleeve in place, press the seal (open end first) into the pump to the previously-noted depth, using a suitable tube or socket **(see illustrations)**.

6 Where applicable, remove the plastic sleeve from the end of the crankshaft.

7 Refit the crankshaft sprocket as described in Section 8.

Left-hand oil seal

8 Remove the flywheel, as described in Section 16.

9 Measure and note the fitted depth of the oil seal.

10 Pull the oil seal from the housing using a screwdriver. Alternatively, drill a small hole in the oil seal, and use a self-tapping screw and a pair of pliers to remove it **(see illustration 14.3)**.

14.3 Take great care not to mark the
crankshaft whilst levering out the oil seal

14.5a Slide the seal and protective sleeve
over the end of the crankshaft...

14.5b ...and press the seal into place

14.12 Slide the seal and protective sleeve over the left-hand end of the crankshaft

14.16 Drill a hole, insert a self-tapping screw, and pull the seal from place using pliers

14.18a Use the correct tool to fit the seal...

14.18b ...or a suitable socket

11 Clean the oil seal housing and the crankshaft sealing surface.
12 The new seal should be supplied with a protective sleeve, which fits over the end of the crankshaft to prevent any damage to the seal lip **(see illustration)**. With the sleeve in place, press the seal (open end first) into the housing to the previously-noted depth, using a suitable tube or socket.
13 Where applicable, remove the plastic sleeve from the end of the crankshaft.
14 Refit the flywheel, as described in Section 16.

Camshaft

15 Remove the camshaft sprocket as described in Section 8. In principle there is no need to remove the timing belt completely, but remember that if the belt

has been contaminated with oil, it must be renewed.
16 Pull the oil seal from the housing using a hooked instrument. Alternatively, drill a small hole in the oil seal and use a self-tapping screw and a pair of pliers to remove it **(see illustration)**.
17 Clean the oil seal housing and the camshaft sealing surface.
18 Press the seal (open end first) into the housing to the previously-noted depth, using either the correct tool (No.303-684), a suitable tube or a socket which bears only of the outer edge of the seal **(see illustrations)**. If the seal was supplied with a protective sleeve, remove it.
19 Refit the camshaft sprocket as described in Section 8.
20 Where necessary, fit a new timing belt with reference to Section 7.

15.3 The oil pressure switch is located on the front face of the cylinder block (arrowed)

15.5 The oil level sensor is located on the rear face of the cylinder block (arrowed)

15 Oil pressure switch and level sensor – removal and refitting

Removal

Oil pressure switch

1 The oil pressure switch is located at the front of the cylinder block, adjacent to the oil dipstick guide tube. Note that on some models, access to the switch may be improved if the vehicle is jacked up and supported on axle stands, then undo the bolts and remove the engine undershield so that the switch can be reached from underneath (see *Jacking and vehicle support*).
2 Remove the protective sleeve from the wiring plug (where applicable), then disconnect the wiring from the switch.
3 Unscrew the switch from the cylinder block, and recover the sealing washer **(see illustration)**. Be prepared for oil spillage, and if the switch is to be left removed from the engine for any length of time, plug the hole in the cylinder block.

Oil level sensor

4 The oil level sensor is located at the rear of the cylinder block. Jack up the front of the vehicle and support it securely on axle stands (see *Jacking and vehicle support*). Undo the bolts and remove the engine undershield.
5 Reach up between the driveshaft and the cylinder block, and disconnect the sensor wiring plug **(see illustration)**.
6 Using an open-ended spanner, unscrew the sensor and withdraw it from position.

Refitting

Oil pressure switch

7 Examine the sealing washer for any signs of damage or deterioration, and if necessary renew.
8 Refit the switch, complete with washer, and tighten it to the specified torque where given.
9 Refit the engine undershield, and lower the vehicle to the ground.

Oil level sensor

10 Smear a little silicone sealant on the threads and refit the sensor to the cylinder block, tightening it securely.
11 Reconnect the sensor wiring plug.
12 Refit the engine undershield, and lower the vehicle to the ground.

16 Flywheel – removal, inspection and refitting

Removal

1 Remove the transmission as described in Chapter 7 Section 7, then remove the clutch assembly as described in Chapter 6 Section 6.
2 Prevent the flywheel from turning. Do not attempt to lock the flywheel in position using

the crankshaft pulley locking tool described in Section 3. Insert a 12 mm diameter rod or drill bit through the hole in the flywheel cover casting, and into a slot in the flywheel (see illustration).

3 Make alignment marks between the flywheel and crankshaft to aid refitment. Slacken and remove the flywheel retaining bolts, and remove the flywheel from the end of the crankshaft. Be careful not to drop it; it is heavy. If the flywheel locating dowel (where fitted) is a loose fit in the crankshaft end, remove it and store it with the flywheel for safe-keeping. Discard the flywheel bolts; new ones must be used on refitting.

Inspection

4 Examine the flywheel for scoring of the clutch face, and for wear or chipping of the ring gear teeth. If the clutch face is scored, the flywheel may be surface-ground, but renewal is preferable. Seek the advice of an engine reconditioning specialist to see if machining is possible. If the ring gear is worn or damaged, the flywheel must be renewed, as it is not possible to renew the ring gear separately.

5 All engines are fitted with a dual-mass flywheel. The maximum travel of the primary mass in relation to the secondary must not exceed 15 teeth (or 20 degrees). If in doubt remove the flywheel and have a suitably equipped specialist check the flywheel. Inspect the flywheel for any grease or debris from the interface between the fixed part and the movable part of the flywheel. If any doubt to the condition of the flywheel exists, despite the expense we recommend replacing it.

Refitting

6 Clean the mating surfaces of the flywheel and crankshaft. Remove any remaining locking compound from the threads of the crankshaft holes, using the correct size of tap, if available.

7 If the new flywheel retaining bolts are not supplied with their threads already pre-coated, apply a suitable thread-locking compound to the threads of each bolt.

8 Ensure that the locating dowel is in position. Offer up the flywheel, locating it on the dowel (where fitted), and fit the new retaining bolts. Where no locating dowel is fitted, align the

16.2 Lock the flywheel with a 12mm diameter rod or bolt (arrowed)

previously-made marks to ensure the flywheel is refitted in its original position.

9 Lock the flywheel using the method employed on dismantling, and tighten the retaining bolts to the specified torque (see illustration).

10 Refit the clutch as described in Chapter 6 Section 6. Remove the flywheel locking tool, and refit the transmission as described in Chapter 7 Section 7.

17 Engine/transmission mountings – inspection and renewal

General

1 The engine/transmission mountings seldom require attention, but broken or deteriorated mountings should be renewed immediately, or the added strain placed on the driveline components may cause damage or wear.

2 While separate mountings may be removed and refitted individually, if more than one is disturbed at a time – such as if the engine/transmission unit is removed from its mountings – they must be reassembled and their fasteners tightened in the position marked on removal.

3 On reassembly, the complete weight of the engine/transmission unit must not be taken by the mountings until all are correctly aligned with the marks made on removal. Tighten the engine/transmission mounting fasteners to their specified torque wrench settings.

16.9 Flywheel retaining Torx bolts

Inspection

4 During the check, the engine/transmission unit must be raised slightly, to remove its weight from the mountings.

5 Raise the front of the vehicle, and support it securely on axle stands. Remove the engine undershield. Position a jack under the sump, with a large block of wood between the jack head and the sump, then carefully raise the engine/transmission just enough to take the weight off the mountings.

⚠️ **Warning: DO NOT place any part of your body under the engine when it is supported only by a jack.**

6 Check the mountings to see if the rubber is cracked, hardened or separated from the metal components. Sometimes the rubber will split right down the centre.

7 Check for relative movement between each mounting's brackets and the engine/transmission or body (use a large screwdriver or lever to attempt to move the mountings). If movement is noted, lower the engine and check-tighten the mounting fasteners.

Renewal

Note: *The following paragraphs assume the engine is supported beneath the sump as described earlier.*

Right-hand engine mounting

8 Raise the front of the vehicle, and support it securely on axle stands, then remove the engine undershield. Position a jack under the sump, with a large block of wood between the jack head and the sump, then carefully raise the jack just enough to support the weight of the engine.

9 On models with belt driven power steering pump, undo the retaining bolt and move the PAS reservoir to one side (see illustration). Note there is no need to disconnect the pipes. On some models a vibration damper is fitted to the rear of the mounting. Where fitted unbolt and remove the damper.

10 Mark the position of the mounting on the vehicle on the right-hand inner wing panel, and then undo the bolts securing the mounting, to the inner wing panel. Then undo the 3 retaining bolts from the engine side of the mounting, and remove the complete mounting (see illustration).

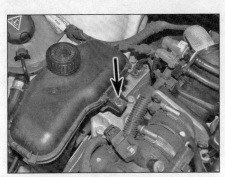

17.9 Undo the PAS reservoir retaining bolt (arrowed)

17.10 Engine mounting bolts (arrowed)

17.14 Transmission mounting

17.17 Undo the rear link-to-subframe mounting bolt (arrowed) …

17.18 … and the lower link-to-mounting bracket bolt (arrowed)

11 Re-align the marks made on removal. Tighten all fasteners to the torque wrench settings specified.

Left-hand transmission mounting

12 Remove the battery and tray, as described in Chapter 5A Section 4.

13 If not already done, undo the retaining bolts/nuts and remove the engine undershield. Place a jack beneath the transmission, with a block of wood on the jack head. Raise the jack until it is supporting the weight of the transmission.

14 With the transmission supported, note the position of the mounting then first unscrew the centre retaining nut. Remove the retaining nuts and bolts, then lift the transmission mounting from its position on the inner wing mounting bracket **(see illustration)**.

15 Refitting is a reversal of removal. Re-align the mounting in the position noted on removal, then tighten all fasteners to the specified torque wrench settings.

Lower engine rear torque link

16 Firmly apply the handbrake, and then jack up the front of the vehicle and support it securely on axle stands (see *Jacking and vehicle support*). If not already done, undo the retaining bolts/nuts and remove the engine undershield.

17 Unscrew and remove the bolt securing the rear mounting link to the subframe **(see illustration)**.

18 Remove the bolt securing the rear mounting link to the driveshaft inner bearing bracket at the rear of the cylinder block **(see illustration)**, and then remove the mounting torque reaction link.

19 To remove the intermediate bearing housing/mounting assembly it will first be necessary to remove the right-hand driveshaft as described in Chapter 8 Section 2.

20 With the driveshaft removed, undo the retaining bolts and remove the bearing

housing/ mounting from the rear of the cylinder block.

21 Check carefully for signs of wear or damage on all components, and renew them where necessary. The rubber bush fitted to the driveshaft bearing housing is available as a separate item on some models, check with your local dealer for availability of parts. If available, the rubber bush can be pressed out of the bearing housing, noting its fitted position, and then a new one pressed back into place.

22 On reassembly, fit the bearing housing assembly to the rear of the cylinder block, and tighten its retaining bolts securely. Refit the driveshaft as described in Chapter 8 Section 2.

23 Refit the rear mounting torque reaction link, and tighten both its bolts to their specified torque settings.

24 Refit the engine undershield, and then lower the vehicle to the ground.

Chapter 2 Part B
1.6 litre DOHC engine in-car repair procedures

Contents

Degrees of difficulty

| **Easy,** suitable for novice with little experience | 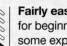 | **Fairly easy,** suitable for beginner with some experience | | **Fairly difficult,** suitable for competent DIY mechanic | | **Difficult,** suitable for experienced DIY mechanic | | **Very difficult,** suitable for expert DIY or professional | |

Specifications

General

Designation DV6ATED4, DV6AUTED4, DV6BTED4, DV6BUTED4, DV6TED4,
  DV6TED4B and DV6TED4BU

Engine codes: *
  DV6ATED4 and DV6AUTED4 . . . .   9HX
  DV6BTED4 . . . .   9HT or 9HW
  DV6BUTED4 . . . .   9HT
  DV6TED4 . . . .   9HZ
  DV6TED4B 9HV
  DV6TED4BU 9HS
Capacity . . . .   1560 cc
Bore . . . .   75.0 mm
Stroke . . . .   88.3 mm
Direction of crankshaft rotation . . . .   Clockwise (viewed from the right-hand side of vehicle)
No 1 cylinder location. . . . .   At the transmission end of block
Maximum power output:
  9HT and 9HW. . . . .   55 kW (75hp) @ 4000 rpm
  9HS, 9HV and 9HX. . . . .   66 kW (90hp) @ 4000 rpm
  9HZ . . . .   80 kW (110 hp) @ 4000 rpm
Maximum torque output:
  9HW . . . .   175 Nm @ 1750 rpm
  9HT . . . .   185 Nm @ 1750 rpm
  9HS, 9HV and 9HX . . . .   215 Nm @ 1750 rpm
  9HZ . . . .   240 Nm @ 1750 rpm
Compression ratio . . . .   18.0 : 1

The engine code is stamped on a plate attached to the front of the cylinder block.

Compression pressures (engine hot, at cranking speed)

Normal (new engine).. 20 ± 5 bar
Minimum .... 15 bar
Maximum difference between any two cylinders................. 5 bar

Cylinder head gasket

Gasket thickness:
   1 notch .... 1.35 mm
   2 notch .... 1.25 mm
   3 notch .... 1.30 mm
   4 notch .... 1.40 mm
   5 notch .... 1.45 mm
Piston protrusion (gasket required):
   0.685 to 0.734 mm .... 1 notch
   0.533 to 0.634 mm .... 2 notch
   0.635 to 0.684 mm .... 3 notch
   0.735 to 0.784 mm .... 4 notch
   0.785 to 0.886 mm .... 5 notch

Cylinder head bolts

Maximum length (measured under head)....................... 149 mm

Camshaft

Drive:
   Intake camshaft .... Toothed belt from crankshaft
   Exhaust camshaft .... Chain-drive from intake camshaft
Number of teeth 19
Length:
   Intake camshaft .... 401.0 ± 0.15 mm
   Exhaust camshaft .... 389.0 ± 0.5 mm
Endfloat 0.195 to 0.300 mm

Lubrication system

Oil pump type... Gear-type, driven directly by the right-hand end of the crankshaft, by two flats machined along the crankshaft journal

Oil pressure at 110°C:
   1000 rpm .... 1.3 bar
   4000 rpm .... 3.5 bar

Torque wrench settings

	Nm	lbf ft
Ancillary drivebelt tensioner roller	20	15
Big-end bolts: *		
Stage 1	10	7
Stage 2	Slacken 180°	
Stage 3	30	22
Stage 4	Angle-tighten a further 140°	
Camshaft bearing caps	10	7
Camshaft cover/bearing ladder:		
Studs	10	7
Bolts	10	7
Camshaft position sensor bolt	5	4
Camshaft sprocket:		
Stage 1	20	15
Stage 2	Angle-tighten a further 50°	
Coolant outlet housing bolts	7	5
Crankshaft position/speed sensor bolt	5	4
Crankshaft pulley/sprocket bolt: *		
Stage 1	35	26
Stage 2	Angle-tighten a further 190 °	
Cylinder head bolts:		
Stage 1	20	15
Stage 2	40	30
Stage 3	Angle-tighten a further 260°	
Cylinder head cover/manifold	10	7
EGR valve	10	7

Torque wrench settings (continued)

	Nm	lbf ft
Engine mountings:		
Left-hand engine/transmission mounting:		
Mounting bracket to transmission	55	41
Mounting to bracket	60	44
Rear engine/transmission mounting:		
Connecting link to mounting assembly	60	44
Connecting link-to-subframe nut/bolt	60	44
Mounting to engine	60	44
Right-hand engine mounting:		
Mounting to body	60	44
Mounting to support bracket	60	44
Support bracket to engine	55	41
Engine-to-transmission fixing bolts	54	40
Flywheel bolts: *		
Dual mass flywheel:		
Stage 1	25	18
Stage 2	Fully slacken	
Stage 3	8	6
Stage 4	30	22
Stage 5	Angle-tighten a further 90°	
Normal flywheel:		
Stage 1	25	18
Stage 2	Fully slacken	
Stage 3	8	6
Stage 4	17	13
Stage 5	Angle-tighten a further 75°	
Fuel pump sprocket	50	37
Main bearing ladder outer seam bolts:		
Stage 1	5	4
Stage 2	10	7
Main bearing ladder to cylinder block:		
Stage 1	10	7
Stage 2	Slacken 180°	
Stage 3	30	22
Stage 4	Angle-tighten a further 140°	
Piston oil jet spray tube bolt	20	15
Oil filter cover	25	18
Oil pick-up pipe	10	7
Oil pressure switch	32	24
Oil pump to cylinder block	10	7
Sump drain plug	25	18
Sump bolts/nuts	12	9
Timing belt idler pulley	35	26
Timing belt tensioner pulley	25	18
Timing chain tensioner	10	7
Vacuum pump:		
Stage 1	18	13
Stage 2	Angle-tighten a further 5°	

* Do not re-use

1 General Information

How to use this Chapter

1 This Chapter describes the repair procedures that can reasonably be carried out on the engine whilst it remains in the vehicle. If the engine has been removed from the vehicle and is being dismantled as described in Chapter 2C, any preliminary dismantling procedures can be ignored.

2 Note that, while it may be possible physically to overhaul items such as the piston/connecting rod assemblies while the engine is in the car, such tasks are not usually carried out as separate operations. Usually, several additional procedures are required (not to mention the cleaning of components and oil ways); for this reason, all such tasks are classed as major overhaul procedures, and are described in Chapter 2C.

3 Chapter 2C describes the removal of the engine/transmission from the car, and the full overhaul procedures that can then be carried out.

DV series engines

4 The 1.6 litre DV series engine is the result of development collaboration between Peugeot/Citroën and Ford. The engine in this Chapter is of double overhead camshaft (DOHC) 16-valve design. The direct injection, turbocharged, four-cylinder engine is mounted transversely, with the transmission mounted on the left-hand side.

5 A toothed timing belt drives the intake camshaft, high-pressure fuel pump and coolant pump. The intake camshaft drives the exhaust camshaft via a chain. The camshafts operate the intake and exhaust valves via rocker arms, which are supported at their pivot ends by hydraulic self-adjusting tappets. The camshafts are supported by bearings machined directly in the cylinder head and camshaft bearing housing.

6 The high-pressure fuel pump supplies fuel to the fuel rail, and subsequently to the electronically controlled injectors, which inject the fuel direct into the combustion chambers. This design differs from the previous type where an injection pump supplies the fuel at high pressure to each injector. The earlier, conventional type injection pump required fine calibration and timing, and these functions are now completed by the high-pressure pump, electronic injectors and engine management ECM (Engine Control Module).

7 The crankshaft runs in five main bearings of the usual shell type. Endfloat is controlled by thrustwashers either side of No 2 main bearing.

8 The pistons are selected to be of matching weight, and incorporate fully floating gudgeon pins retained by circlips.

Repair operations precaution

9 The engine is a complex unit with numerous accessories and ancillary components. The design of the engine compartment is such that every conceivable space has been utilised, and access to virtually all of the engine components is extremely limited. In many cases, ancillary components will have to be removed, or moved to one side, and wiring, pipes and hoses will have to be disconnected or removed from various cable clips and support brackets.

10 When working on this engine, read through the entire procedure first, look at the car and engine at the same time, and establish whether you have the necessary tools, equipment, skill and patience to proceed. Allow considerable time for any operation, and be prepared for the unexpected.

11 Because of the limited access, many of the engine photographs appearing in this Chapter were, by necessity, taken with the engine removed from the vehicle.

⚠️ **Warning: It is essential to observe strict precautions when working on the fuel system components of the engine, particularly the high-pressure side of the system. Before carrying out any engine operations that entail working on, or near, any part of the fuel system, refer to the special information given in Chapter 4A Section 1.**

Operations with engine in vehicle

a) *Compression pressure – testing.*
b) *Cylinder head cover – removal and refitting.*
c) *Crankshaft pulley – removal and refitting.*
d) *Timing belt covers – removal and refitting.*
e) *Timing belt – removal, refitting and adjustment.*
f) *Timing belt tensioner and sprockets – removal and refitting.*
g) *Camshaft oil seal – renewal.*
h) *Camshaft, rocker arms and hydraulic tappets – removal, inspection and refitting*
i) *Sump – removal and refitting.*
j) *Oil pump – removal and refitting.*
k) *Crankshaft oil seals – renewal.*
l) *Engine/transmission mountings – inspection and renewal.*
m) *Flywheel – removal, inspection and refitting.*

2 Compression and leakdown tests – description and interpretation

Compression test

Note: *A compression tester specifically designed for diesel engines must be used for this test.*

1 When engine performance is down, or if misfiring occurs which cannot be attributed to the fuel system, a compression test can provide diagnostic clues as to the engine's condition. If the test is performed regularly, it can give warning of trouble before any other symptoms become apparent.

2 A compression tester specifically intended for diesel engines must be used, because of the higher pressures involved. The tester is connected to an adapter, which screws into the glow plug or injector hole. On this engine, an adapter suitable for use in the glow plug holes will be required, so as not to disturb the fuel system components. It is unlikely to be worthwhile buying such a tester for occasional use, but it may be possible to borrow or hire one – if not, have the test performed by a garage.

3 Unless specific instructions to the contrary are supplied with the tester, observe the following points:

a) *The battery must be in a good state of charge, the air filter must be clean, and the engine should be at normal operating temperature.*
b) *All the glow plugs should be removed as described in Chapter 5B Section 2 before starting the test.*
c) *The wiring connectors on the engine management system ECM (located in the plastic fuse box next to the battery) must be disconnected.*

4 The compression pressures measured are not so important as the balance between cylinders. Values are given in the Specifications.

5 The cause of poor compression is less easy to establish on a diesel engine than on a petrol one. The effect of introducing oil into the cylinders ('wet' testing) is not conclusive, because there is a risk that the oil will sit in the swirl chamber or in the recess on the piston crown instead of passing to the rings. However, the following can be used as a rough guide to diagnosis.

6 All cylinders should produce very similar pressures; any difference greater than that specified indicates the existence of a fault. Note that the compression should build-up quickly in a healthy engine; low

compression on the first stroke, followed by gradually increasing pressure on successive strokes, indicates worn piston rings. A low compression reading on the first stroke, which does not build-up during successive strokes, indicates leaking valves or a blown head gasket (a cracked head could also be the cause). Deposits on the undersides of the valve heads can also cause low compression.

7 A low reading from two adjacent cylinders is almost certainly due to the head gasket having blown between them; the presence of coolant in the engine oil will confirm this.

8 If the compression reading is unusually high, the cylinder head surfaces, valves and pistons are probably coated with carbon deposits. If this is the case, the cylinder head should be removed and decarbonised (see Chapter 2C Section 7).

Leakdown test

9 A leakdown test measures the rate at which compressed air fed into the cylinder is lost. It is an alternative to a compression test, and in many ways it is better, since the escaping air provides easy identification of where pressure loss is occurring (piston rings, valves or head gasket).

10 The equipment needed for leakdown testing is unlikely to be available to the home mechanic. If poor compression is suspected, have the test performed by a suitably-equipped garage.

3 Engine assembly/valve timing holes – general information and usage

Note: *Do not attempt to rotate the engine whilst the crankshaft and camshaft are locked in position. If the engine is to be left in this state for a long period of time, it is a good idea to place suitable warning notices inside the vehicle, and in the engine compartment. This will reduce the possibility of the engine being accidentally cranked on the starter motor, which is likely to cause damage with the locking pins in place.*

1 Timing holes or slots are located only in the crankshaft pulley flange and camshaft sprocket hub. The holes/slots are used to position the pistons halfway up the cylinder bores. This will ensure that the valve timing is maintained during operations that require removal and refitting of the timing belt. When the holes/slots are aligned with their corresponding holes in the cylinder block and cylinder head, suitable diameter bolts/pins can be inserted to lock the crankshaft and camshaft in position, preventing rotation.

2 Note that the HDi type fuel system used on these engines does not have a conventional diesel injection pump, but instead uses a high-pressure fuel pump. Although it may be argued that timing of the fuel pump is irrelevant because it merely pressurises the fuel in the fuel rail, Peugeot/Citroën include

3.9 Insert a 5.0 mm drill bit/bolt through the round hole in the sprocket flange, into the hole in the oil pump housing (lower timing belt cover removed for clarity)

3.10a Insert an 8.0 mm drill bit/bolt through the hole in the camshaft sprocket (early model sprocket) …

3.10b … and into the corresponding hole in the cylinder head (later model sprocket)

this procedure for engines fitted with a Bosch high-pressure fuel pump, using the same timing rod/pin used for crankshaft sprocket timing. **Note:** *On the Bosch pump, the drive sprocket is keyed to the shaft. In addition, note that the hole in the fuel pump sprocket only aligns correctly with the hole in the mounting bracket every 12 revolutions of the crankshaft (or every 6 revolutions of the camshaft sprocket).*

3 To align the engine assembly/valve timing holes, proceed as follows.

4 Chock the rear wheels then jack up the front of the vehicle and support it on axle stands (see *Jacking and vehicle support*). Remove the right-hand front roadwheel.

5 To gain access to the crankshaft pulley, to enable the engine to be turned, the wheel arch plastic liner must be removed. The liner is secured by several plastic expanding rivets/nut/screws. To remove the rivets, push in the centre pins a little, and then prise the clips from place. Remove the liner from under the front wing. The crankshaft can then be turned using a suitable socket and extension bar fitted to the pulley bolt.

6 Remove the upper and lower timing belt covers as described in Section 6.

7 Temporarily refit the crankshaft pulley bolt, remove the crankshaft locking tool, then turn the crankshaft until the timing hole in the camshaft sprocket hub is aligned with the corresponding hole in the cylinder head. Note

that the crankshaft must always be turned in a clockwise direction (viewed from the right-hand side of vehicle). Use a small mirror so that the position of the sprocket hub timing slot can be observed. When the slot is aligned with the corresponding hole in the cylinder head, the camshaft is positioned correctly.

8 Remove the crankshaft drivebelt pulley as described in Section 5.

9 Insert a 5 mm diameter bolt, rod or drill through the hole in crankshaft sprocket flange and into the corresponding hole in the oil pump housing **(see illustration)**, if necessary, carefully turn the crankshaft either way until the rod enters the timing hole in the block.

10 Insert an 8 mm bolt, rod or drill through the hole in the camshaft sprocket hub and into engagement with the cylinder head. Note that a modified 3-segment camshaft sprocket is fitted to later models **(see illustrations)**.

11 If using this procedure during refitting of the timing belt, insert a 5 mm diameter bolt, rod or drill through the hole in the fuel pump sprocket and into the corresponding hole in the cylinder head **(see illustration)**. **Note:** *On some engines, a hole is provided at the 5 o'clock position for locking purposes only, however, the timing hole is at the 12 o'clock position. Note the comment in paragraph 2 – if the fuel pump sprocket holes are not aligned during removal of the timing belt, it is of no consequence, however it is important to align the holes during the refitting procedure. If*

timing alignment alone is being checked there is no need to check alignment of the pump sprocket.

12 The crankshaft and camshaft are now locked in position, preventing unnecessary rotation.

4 Cylinder head cover/intake manifold – removal and refitting

Removal

1 To make access easier, remove the scuttle panel lower grille panel as described in Chapter 11 Section 23.

2 Pull the plastic engine cover upwards at the front to release the locating pegs from the rubber mountings on top of the cylinder head cover **(see illustration)**.

3 Remove the air intake hoses, then unscrew the air filter housing upper cover bolts and remove the filter element as described in Chapter 1 Section 20. Pull the air filter lower housing from its rubber mountings.

4 Disconnect the wiring plugs from the top of each injector, undo the guide bolts, then make sure all wiring harnesses are freed from any retaining brackets on the cylinder head cover/intake manifold **(see illustration)**. Disconnect any vacuum pipes as necessary, having first noted their fitted positions.

3.11 Insert a 5.0 mm drill bit/bolt through the round hole in the fuel pump sprocket flange, into the hole in the cylinder head

4.2 Pull the plastic cover upwards to release the rubber mountings

4.4 Undo the Allen screws (arrowed) and position the wiring harness/guide to one side

4.6 Depress the release buttons and disconnect the fuel feed and return hoses

4.7a Slacken the left-hand turbocharger outlet hose bolt, undo the right-hand bolt (arrowed) …

4.7b … then slacken the hose clamps (arrowed) …

4.7c … disconnect the wiring plugs …

4.7d … and undo the securing bolts (2 bolts arrowed)

4.8 Undo the bolts and remove the oil separator (arrowed)

4.9a Prise out the clip and pull the return hose from the top of each injector

5 Remove the EGR heat exchanger as described in Chapter 4B Section 2.

6 Depress the release buttons and disconnect the fuel feed and return hoses at the right-hand end of the cylinder head, then disconnect the fuel temperature sensor wiring plug, and move the pipe/priming bulb assembly to the rear **(see illustration)**.

7 Release the clamps, undo the bolts and remove the intake ducting between the turbocharger and the intake manifold. Make a note of their fitted positions, and then disconnect the various wiring plugs, as the assembly is withdrawn **(see illustrations)**.

8 Undo the retaining bolts and remove the oil separator from the top of the cylinder head **(see illustration)**. Recover the rubber seal.

9 Prise out the retaining clips and disconnect the fuel return pipes from the injectors, then undo the unions and remove the high-pressure fuel pipes from the injectors and the common fuel rail at the rear of the cylinder head – counterhold the unions with a second spanner **(see illustrations)**. Plug the openings to prevent dirt ingress.

10 Undo the 2 bolts securing the cylinder head cover/intake manifold. Lift the assembly away **(see illustration)**. Recover the manifold rubber seals.

4.9b Use a second spanner to hold the injector port whilst slackening the fuel pipe unions

4.10 Undo the 2 remaining bolts (arrowed) and pull the cover/manifold upwards

5.2 The locking pin/bolt (arrowed) must locate in the hole in the flywheel (arrowed) to prevent rotation

5.3a Undo the retaining bolt ...

5.3b ... and remove the crankshaft pulley

Refitting

11 Refitting is a reversal of removal, bearing in mind the following points:

a) Examine the seals for signs of damage and deterioration, and renew if necessary. Smear a little clean engine oil on the manifold seals.

b) Renew the fuel injector high-pressure pipes – see Chapter 4A Section 9.

c) Refit the air intake hoses and filter element – see Chapter 1 Section 20.

d) Refit the scuttle panel – see Chapter 11 Section 23.

5 Crankshaft pulley – removal and refitting

Removal

1 Remove the auxiliary drivebelt as described in Chapter 1 Section 16.

2 To lock the crankshaft, working underneath the engine, insert Peugeot/Citroën tool No 0194-C into the hole in the right-hand face of the engine block casting over the lower section of the flywheel. Rotate the crankshaft until the tool engages in the corresponding hole in the flywheel. In the absence of the

special tool, insert a 12 mm rod or drill into the hole (see illustration). Note: The hole in the casting and the hole in the flywheel are provided purely to lock the crankshaft whilst the pulley bolt is undone, it does not position the crankshaft at TDC.

3 Using a suitable socket and extension bar, unscrew the retaining bolt, remove the washer, then slide the pulley off the end of the crankshaft (see illustrations). If the pulley is tight fit, it can be drawn off the crankshaft using a suitable puller. If a puller is being used, refit the pulley retaining bolt without the washer to avoid damaging the crankshaft as the puller is tightened.

Caution: Do not touch the outer magnetic sensor ring of the sprocket with your fingers, or allow metallic particles to come into contact with it.

Refitting

4 Refit the pulley to the end of the crankshaft, making sure the locating lug on the end of the crankshaft aligns with the slot in the rear of the pulley (see illustration).

5 Thoroughly clean the threads of the pulley retaining bolt, then apply a coat of locking compound to the bolt threads. Peugeot/Citroën recommend the use of Loctite (available from your franchised dealer); in the absence of this, any good-quality locking compound may be used.

6 Refit the crankshaft pulley retaining bolt and washer. Tighten the bolt to the specified torque, and then through the specified angle, preventing the crankshaft from turning using the method employed on removal.

7 Refit and tension the auxiliary drivebelt as described in Chapter 1 Section 16.

6 Timing belt covers – removal and refitting

⚠ Warning: Refer to the precautionary information contained in Section 1 before proceeding.

Removal

Upper cover

1 Disconnect the battery (refer to precautions in Chapter 5A Section 1).

2 Remove the scuttle panel lower grille panel as described in Chapter 11 Section 23.

3 Support the engine and remove the right-hand engine mounting as described in Section 17.

4 Release the retaining clips and unclip the fuel pipes and wiring harness from the upper cover (see illustration).

5.4 Crankshaft sprocket alignment lug (arrowed)

6.4 Unclip the fuel pipes (arrowed) and the wiring harness (arrowed)

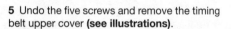

6.5a Undo the upper cover securing bolts (arrowed) …

6.5b … and remove it from over the timing belt

6.8 Timing belt lower cover retaining bolts (arrowed)

5 Undo the five screws and remove the timing belt upper cover **(see illustrations)**.

Lower cover

6 Remove the upper cover as described previously.
7 Remove the crankshaft pulley as described in Section 5.
8 Remove the auxiliary drivebelt tensioner locking tool (where applicable), then undo the five bolts and remove the lower cover **(see illustration)**.

Refitting

9 Refitting of all the covers is a reversal of the relevant removal procedure, ensuring that each cover section is correctly located, and that the cover retaining bolts are securely tightened. Ensure that all disturbed hoses are reconnected and retained by their relevant clips.

7 Timing belt – removal, inspection, refitting and tensioning

General

1 The timing belt drives the intake camshaft, high-pressure fuel pump, and coolant pump from a toothed sprocket on the end of the crankshaft. If the belt breaks or slips in service, the pistons are likely to hit the valve heads, resulting in expensive damage.
2 The timing belt should be renewed at the specified intervals, or earlier if it is

contaminated with oil, or at all noisy in operation (a 'scraping' noise due to uneven wear).
3 If the timing belt is being removed, it is a wise precaution to check the condition of the coolant pump at the same time (check for signs of coolant leakage). This may avoid the need to remove the timing belt again at a later stage should the coolant pump fail.

Removal

4 Chock the rear wheels then jack up the front of the vehicle and support it on axle stands (see *Jacking and vehicle support*). Remove the front right-hand roadwheel, wheel arch liner (to expose the crankshaft pulley), and the engine undershield. The wheel arch liner is secured by several plastic expanding rivets/plastic clips. Pull the centre pins out a little then prise the rivets from place. The engine undershield is retained by several bolts/nuts.
5 Remove the auxiliary drivebelt as described in Chapter 1 Section 16.
6 Remove the upper and lower timing belt covers, as described in Section 6.
7 Refer to Chapter 4A Section 18 and disconnect the front exhaust pipe at the flexible section.
8 Position a trolley jack under the engine, and using a block of wood on the jack head, take the weight of the engine.
9 Undo the bolts/nut and remove the right-hand engine mounting and support bracket as described in Section 17.
10 Undo the screw and remove the crankshaft position sensor adjacent to the

crankshaft sprocket flange, and move it to one side **(see illustration)**.
11 Undo the retaining screw and remove the timing belt protection bracket, again adjacent to the crankshaft sprocket flange **(see illustration)**.
12 Lock the crankshaft and camshaft in the correct position as described in Section 3. If necessary, temporarily refit the crankshaft pulley bolt to enable the crankshaft to be rotated. At this stage, it is of no consequence whether the fuel pump sprocket aligns correctly with the hole in the pump mounting bracket.
13 Insert a hexagon key into the belt tensioner pulley centre, slacken the pulley bolt, and allow the tensioner to rotate, relieving the belt tension **(see illustration)**. With the belt slack, temporarily tighten the pulley bolt.
14 Note its routing, then remove the timing belt from the sprockets.

Inspection

15 Renew the belt as a matter of course, regardless of its apparent condition. The cost of a new belt is nothing compared with the cost of repairs should the belt break in service. If signs of oil contamination are found, trace the source of the oil leak and rectify it. Wash down the engine timing belt area and all related components, to remove all traces of oil. Check that the tensioner and idler pulleys rotate freely without any sign of roughness, and also check that the coolant pump pulley rotates freely. Due to the complexity of this procedure, it is recommended that the

7.10 Undo the bolt and remove the crankshaft position sensor

7.11 Remove the timing belt protection bracket bolt (arrowed)

7.13 Slacken the bolt and allow the tensioner to rotate, relieving the tension on the belt

7.15 Tensioner and idler pulleys

7.17a Feed the timing belt around the crankshaft sprocket first ...

7.17b ... and then finally around the tensioner pulley

tensioner and idler pulleys be renewed when fitting a new timing belt **(see illustration)**.

Refitting and tensioning

16 Commence refitting by ensuring that the crankshaft and camshaft timing pins are still in position correctly. Also, where a Bosch high-pressure fuel pump is fitted, locate and lock the fuel pump sprocket in its correct position as described in Section 3.

17 Locate the timing belt on the crankshaft sprocket then, keeping it taut, locate it around the idler pulley, camshaft sprocket, high-pressure pump sprocket, coolant pump sprocket, and the tensioner pulley **(see illustrations)**. If the timing belt has directional arrows on it, make sure that they point in the direction of normal engine rotation.

18 Refit the timing belt protection bracket and tighten the retaining bolt securely.

19 Slacken the tensioner pulley bolt and, using a hexagonal key, rotate the tensioner anti-clockwise, which moves the index arm clockwise, until the index arm is aligned as shown **(see illustration)**.

20 Remove the camshaft and crankshaft and fuel pump timing pins and, using a socket on the crankshaft pulley bolt, crankshaft clockwise 6 complete revolutions. Align the camshaft and crankshaft timing holes and check that the timing pins can be inserted, then remove them. There is no requirement to check the fuel pump sprocket alignment, as it will only be aligned after 12 complete revolutions.

21 Check that the tensioner index arm is still aligned between the edges of the area shown **(see illustration 7.19)**. If it is not, remove and belt and begin the refitting process again.

22 The remainder of refitting is a reversal of removal. Tighten all fasteners to the specified torque where given.

8 Timing belt sprockets and tensioner – removal and refitting

Camshaft sprocket

Removal

1 Remove the timing belt as described in Section 7.

7.17c Timing belt routing

2 Remove the locking tool from the camshaft sprocket/hub. Slacken the sprocket hub retaining bolt. To prevent the camshaft rotating as the bolt is slackened, a sprocket holding tool will be required. In the absence of the special Peugeot/Citroën tool, an acceptable substitute can be fabricated at home (see **Tool Tip**). Do not attempt to use the engine assembly/valve timing locking tool to prevent the sprocket from rotating whilst the bolt is slackened.

3 Remove the sprocket hub retaining bolt, and slide the sprocket and hub off the end of the camshaft.

A sprocket holding tool can be made from two lengths of steel strip bolted together to form a forked end. Drill holes and insert bolts in the ends of the fork to engage with the sprocket spokes.

7.19 The index arm must align with the lug (arrowed)

4 Clean the camshaft sprocket thoroughly, and renew it if there are any signs of wear, damage or cracks.

Refitting

5 Refit the camshaft sprocket to the camshaft **(see illustration)**.

6 Refit the sprocket hub retaining bolt. Tighten the bolt to the specified torque, preventing the camshaft from turning as during removal.

7 Align the engine assembly/valve timing slot in the camshaft sprocket hub with the hole in the cylinder head and refit the timing pin to lock the camshaft in position.

8 Fit the timing belt around the pump sprocket and camshaft sprocket, and tension the timing belt as described in Section 7.

8.5 Ensure the lug on the sprocket hub engages with the slot on the end of the camshaft (arrowed)

8.11a Slide the sprocket from the crankshaft …

8.11b … and recover the Woodruff key

8.17 Insert a suitable drill bit through the sprocket into the hole in the backplate

Crankshaft sprocket

Removal

9 Remove the timing belt as described in Section 7.

10 Check that the engine assembly/valve timing holes are still aligned as described in Section 3, and the camshaft sprocket and flywheel are locked in position.

11 Slide the sprocket off the end of the crankshaft and collect the Woodruff key **(see illustrations)**.

12 Examine the crankshaft oil seal for signs of oil leakage and, if necessary, renew it as described in Section 14.

Make a sprocket releasing tool from a short strip of steel. Drill two holes in the strip to correspond with the two holes in the sprocket. Drill a third hole just large enough to accept the flats of the sprocket retaining nut.

8.25 Remove the tensioner retaining bolt

13 Clean the crankshaft sprocket thoroughly, and renew it if there are any signs of wear, damage or cracks. Recover the crankshaft locating key.

Refitting

14 Refit the key to the end of the crankshaft, then refit the crankshaft sprocket (with the flange facing the crankshaft pulley).

15 Fit the timing belt around the crankshaft sprocket, and tension the timing belt as described in Section 7.

Fuel pump sprocket

Removal

16 Remove the timing belt as described in Section 7.

17 Using a socket, undo the pump sprocket retaining nut. The sprocket can be held stationary by inserting a locking pin, drill or rod through the hole in the sprocket, and into the corresponding hole in the backplate **(see illustration)**, or by using a forked tool engaged with the holes in the sprocket (see Tool Tip in paragraph 2). **Note:** *On some engines, a hole is provided at the 5 o'clock position for locking purposes only, however, the timing position hole is at the 12 o'clock position.*

18 The pump sprocket is a taper fit on the pump shaft and it will be necessary to make up another tool to release it from the taper (see **Tool Tip**).

19 On late models where the sprocket is keyed to the shaft, unscrew the retaining nut and remove the sprocket, then recover the Woodruff key. On early models where the

8.28 Make sure the tensioner is fitted to the lug (arrowed) on the engine casing

sprocket is not keyed to the shaft, partially unscrew the sprocket retaining nut, then fit the home-made tool, and secure it to the sprocket with two suitable bolts. Prevent the sprocket from rotating as before, and unscrew the sprocket retaining nut. The nut will bear against the tool, as it is undone, forcing the sprocket off the shaft taper. Once the taper is released, remove the tool, unscrew the nut fully, and remove the sprocket from the pump shaft.

20 Clean the sprocket thoroughly, and renew it if there are any signs of wear, damage or cracks.

Refitting

21 Refit the Woodruff key (later models only) then refit the pump sprocket and retaining nut, and tighten the nut to the specified torque. Prevent the sprocket rotating as the nut is tightened using the sprocket holding tool.

22 Fit the timing belt around the pump sprocket, and tension the timing belt as described in Section 7.

Coolant pump sprocket

23 The coolant pump sprocket is integral with the pump, and cannot be removed. Coolant pump removal is described in Chapter 3 Section 8.

Tensioner pulley

Removal

24 Remove the timing belt as described in Section 7.

25 Remove the tensioner pulley retaining bolt, and remove the pulley from the cylinder block **(see illustration)**.

26 Clean the tensioner pulley, but do not use any strong solvent, which may enter the pulley bearings. Check that the pulley rotates freely, with no sign of stiffness or free play. Renew the pulley if there is any doubt about its condition, or if there are any obvious signs of wear or damage.

27 Examine the pulley locating stud for signs of damage.

Refitting

28 Refit the tensioner pulley to the cylinder block making sure it is positioned over the locating stud **(see illustration)**, and then fit the retaining bolt.

29 Refit the timing belt as described in Section 7.

Idler pulley

Removal

30 Remove the timing belt as described in Section 7.
31 Undo the retaining nut and withdraw the idler pulley from the engine (see illustration).
32 Clean the idler pulley, but do not use any strong solvent which may enter the bearings. Check that the pulley rotates freely, with no sign of stiffness or free play. Renew the idler pulley if there is any doubt about its condition, or if there are any obvious signs of wear or damage.

Refitting

33 Locate the idler pulley on the engine, and fit the retaining nut. Tighten the nut to the specified torque.
34 Refit the timing belt (see Section 7).

---

9 Camshafts, rocker arms and hydraulic tappets – removal, inspection and refitting

Removal

1 Remove the cylinder head cover/manifold as described in Section 4.
2 Remove the injectors as described in Chapter 4A Section 11.
3 Remove the camshaft sprocket as described in Section 8.
4 Refit the right-hand engine mounting, but only tighten the bolts moderately; this will keep the engine supported during the camshaft removal.
5 Undo the bolts and remove the vacuum pump. Recover the pump O-ring seals (see illustration).

6 Remove the fuel filter (see Chapter 1 Section 7), then undo the bolts and remove the fuel filter mounting bracket.
7 Release the wiring harness clips, then undo the 3 bolts and remove the timing belt inner, upper cover (see illustration).
8 Disconnect the wiring plug, unscrew the retaining bolt, and remove the camshaft position sensor from the camshaft cover/bearing ladder.
9 Undo the 5 bolts and remove the upper

rear section of the turbocharger heat shield, then working gradually and evenly, slacken and remove the bolts securing the camshaft cover/bearing ladder to the cylinder head in sequence (see illustrations). Lift the cover/ladder from position complete with the camshafts.
10 Undo the retaining bolts and remove the bearing caps. Note their fitted positions, as they must be refitted into their original positions (see illustration). Note that the bearing caps are marked A for intake, and E for exhaust, and 1 to 4 from the flywheel end of the cylinder head.
11 Undo the bolts securing the chain tensioner assembly to the camshaft cover/bearing ladder, and then lift the camshafts,

8.31 Undo the timing belt idler pulley retaining nut

9.5 Vacuum pump bolts (arrowed)

9.7 Timing belt inner, upper cover bolts (arrowed)

9.9a Undo the bolts (arrowed) and remove the rear section of the heat shield

9.9b Camshaft cover/bearing ladder bolt slackening sequence

9.10 Bearing caps are numbered 1 to 4 from the flywheel end – A for intake, and E for exhaust (arrowed)

9.11a Undo the tensioner bolts (arrowed) ...

9.11b ... then lift the camshafts, chain and tensioner from place

9.21 Refit the hydraulic tappets ...

9.22 ... and rocker arms to their original locations

chain and tensioner from place (**see illustrations**). Discard the camshaft oil seal.

12 Obtain 16 small, clean plastic containers, and number them 1 to 8 intake and 1 to 8 exhaust; alternatively, divide a larger container into 16 compartments.

13 Lift out each rocker arm. Place the rocker arms in their respective positions in the box or containers.

14 A compartmentalised container filled with engine oil is now required to retain the hydraulic tappets while they are removed from the cylinder head. Withdraw each hydraulic follower and place it in the container, keeping them each identified for correct refitting. The tappets must be totally submerged in the oil to prevent air entering them.

Inspection

15 Inspect the cam lobes and the camshaft bearing journals for scoring or other visible evidence of wear. Once the surface hardening of the cam lobes has been eroded, wear will occur at an accelerated rate. **Note:** *If these symptoms are visible on the tips of the camshaft lobes, check the corresponding rocker arm, as it will probably be worn as well.*

16 Examine the condition of the bearing surfaces in the cylinder head and camshaft bearing housing. If wear is evident, the cylinder head and bearing housing will both have to be renewed, as they are a matched assembly.

17 Inspect the rocker arms and tappets for scuffing, cracking or other damage and renew any components as necessary. Also check the condition of the tappet bores in the cylinder head. As with the camshafts, any wear in this area will necessitate cylinder head renewal.

Refitting

18 Thoroughly clean the sealant from the mating surfaces of the cylinder head and camshaft bearing housing. Use a suitable liquid gasket dissolving agent (available from Peugeot/Citroën dealers) together with a soft putty knife; do not use a metal scraper or the faces will be damaged. As there is no conventional gasket used, the cleanliness of the mating faces is of the utmost importance.

Prise out the oil injector oil seals from the camshaft bearing housing.

19 Clean off any oil, dirt or grease from both components and dry with a clean lint-free cloth. Ensure that all the oilways are completely clean.

20 Liberally lubricate the hydraulic tappet bores in the cylinder head with clean engine oil.

21 Insert the hydraulic tappets into their original bores in the cylinder head unless they have been renewed (**see illustration**).

22 Lubricate the rocker arms and place them over their respective tappets and valve stems (**see illustration**).

23 Engage the timing chain around the camshaft sprockets, aligning the black-coloured links with the marked teeth on the camshaft sprockets (**see illustration**). If the black colouring has been lost, there must be 12 chain link pins between the marks on the sprockets.

24 Fit the chain tensioner between the upper and lower runs of the chain, then lubricate the bearing surfaces with clean engine oil, and fit the camshafts into position on the underside of the camshaft cover/bearing ladder. Refit the bearing caps to their original positions and tighten the retaining bolts to the specified torque (**see illustrations**). Tighten the tensioner retaining bolts to the specified torque.

25 Apply a thin bead of sealant to the mating

9.23 Align the marks on the sprockets with the centre of the black-coloured chain links (arrowed). There must be 12 link pins between the sprocket marks

9.24a Assemble the chain tensioner between the upper and lower runs of the chain ...

9.24b ... and lower the camshafts, chain and tensioner into position

9.25 Apply sealant to the camshaft cover/bearing ladder as indicated by the heavy black lines. Ensure sealant does not enter the tensioner oil holes – marked A

9.26 Camshaft cover/bearing ladder bolt tightening sequence

surface of the camshaft cover/bearing ladder as shown. Peugeot/Citroën recommend the use of Autojoint Noir **(see illustration)**. Do not allow the sealant to obstruct the oil channels for the hydraulic chain tensioner.

26 Check that the black-coloured links on the chain are still aligned with the marks on the camshaft sprockets, then refit the camshaft cover/bearing ladder, and gradually and evenly tighten the retaining bolts until the cover/ladder is in contact with the cylinder head, then tighten the bolts to the specified torque in sequence **(see illustration)**. **Note:** *Ensure the cover/ladder is correctly located by checking the bores of the vacuum pump and camshaft oil seal at each end of the cover/ladder.*

27 Fit a new camshaft oil seal as described in Section 14.

28 Refit the camshaft sprocket, and tighten the retaining bolt finger-tight.

29 Using a spanner on the camshaft sprocket bolt, rotate the camshafts approximately 40 complete revolutions clockwise. Check the black-coloured links on the chain still align with the marks on the camshaft sprockets.

30 If the marks still align, refit the camshaft sprocket as described in Section 8.

31 Refit and adjust the camshaft position sensor as described in Chapter 4A Section 12.

32 Press the new oil seals into the bearing housing, using a tube/socket of approximately 20 mm outside diameter, ensuring the inner lip of the seal fits around the injector guide tube **(see illustrations)**. Refit the injectors as described in, Chapter 4A Section 11.

33 Refit the cylinder head cover/manifold as described in Section 4.

10 Cylinder head – removal and refitting

Removal

1 Chock the rear wheels then jack up the front of the vehicle and support it on axle stands (see *Jacking and vehicle support*). Remove the front right-hand roadwheel, the engine undershield, and the front wheel arch liner. The undershield is secured by several screws, and the wheel arch liner is secured by several plastic expanding rivets/nuts/plastic

clips. Push the centre pins in a little, then prise the rivet from place.

2 Disconnect the battery (refer to precautions in Chapter 5A Section 1).

3 Drain the cooling system as described in Chapter 1 Section 19.

4 Remove the camshafts, rocker arms and hydraulic tappets as described in Section 9.

5 Remove the turbocharger as described in Chapter 4A Section 16.

6 Remove the glow plugs as described in Chapter 5B Section 2.

7 Undo the upper mounting bolts, and pivot the alternator away from the engine, undo the oil dipstick guide tube bolt, then undo the bolts securing the alternator/power steering pump mounting bracket to the cylinder head/block.

8 Undo the coolant outlet housing (left-hand end of the cylinder head) retaining bolts, slacken the two bolts securing the housing support bracket to the top of the transmission bellhousing, and move the outlet housing away from the cylinder head a little **(see illustration)**. There is no need to disconnect the hoses.

9 Disconnect the high-pressure fuel pipe from the common rail to the pump, and disconnect

9.32a Fit the new seal around a 20 mm outside diameter socket ...

9.32b ... and push it into place

10.8 Coolant outlet housing retaining bolts (arrowed)

10.9a Remove the high-pressure pipe (arrowed) ...

10.9b ... and the bracket (arrowed)

10.9c Pump mounting bracket upper nut and lower mounting bolt (arrowed)

10.11 Free the cylinder head using angled rods

the fuel supply and return hoses. Remove the bracket at the rear of the pump, then undo the bolt/nut and remove the pump and mounting bracket as an assembly (see illustrations). Note that a new high-pressure pipe must be fitted – see Chapter 4A Section 9.

10 Working in the reverse of the sequence shown (see illustration 10.32) undo the cylinder head bolts.

11 Release the cylinder head from the cylinder block and location dowels by rocking it. The Peugeot/Citroën tool for doing this consists simply of two metal rods with 90-degree angled ends (see illustration). Do not prise between the mating faces of the cylinder head and block, as this may damage the gasket faces.

12 Lift the cylinder head from the block, and recover the gasket.

13 If necessary, remove the exhaust manifold with reference to Chapter 4A Section 14.

Preparation for refitting

14 The mating faces of the cylinder head and cylinder block must be perfectly clean before refitting the head. Peugeot/Citroën recommend the use of a scouring agent for this purpose, but acceptable results can be achieved by using a hard plastic or wood scraper to remove all traces of gasket and carbon.

15 The same method can be used to clean the piston crowns. Take particular care to avoid scoring or gouging the cylinder head/cylinder block mating surfaces during the cleaning operations, as aluminium alloy is easily damaged. Make sure that the carbon is not allowed to enter the oil and water passages – this is particularly important for the lubrication system, as carbon could block the oil supply to the engine's components. Using adhesive tape and paper, seal the water, oil and bolt holes in the cylinder block. To prevent carbon entering the gap between the pistons and bores, smear a little grease in the gap. After cleaning each piston, use a small brush to remove all traces of grease and carbon from the gap, and then wipe away the remainder with a clean rag.

16 Check the mating surfaces of the cylinder block and the cylinder head for nicks, deep scratches and other damage. If slight, they may be removed carefully with a file, but if excessive, machining may be the only alternative to renewal. If warpage of the cylinder head gasket surface is suspected, use a straight-edge to check it for distortion. Refer to Chapter 2C Section 7 if necessary.

17 Thoroughly clean the threads of the cylinder head bolt holes in the cylinder block. Ensure that the bolts run freely in their threads, and that all traces of oil and water are removed from each bolt hole. If required, pull the oil feed non-return valve from the cylinder head, and check the ball moves freely. Push a new valve into place if necessary (see illustrations).

Gasket selection

18 Remove the crankshaft timing pin, then turn the crankshaft until pistons 1 and 4 are at TDC (Top Dead Centre). Position a dial test indicator (dial gauge) on the cylinder block adjacent to the rear of No 1 piston, and zero it on the block face. Transfer the probe to the crown of No 1 piston (10.0 mm in from the rear edge), and then slowly turn the crankshaft back-and-forth past TDC, noting the highest reading on the indicator. Record this reading as protrusion A.

19 Repeat the check described in paragraph 18, this time 10.0 mm in from the front edge of the No 1 piston crown. Record this reading as protrusion B.

20 Add protrusion A to protrusion B, then divide the result by 2 to obtain an average reading for piston No 1.

21 Repeat the procedure described in paragraphs 18 to 20 on piston 4, then turn the crankshaft through 180° and carry out the procedure on the piston Nos 2 and 3 (see illustration). Check that there is a maximum difference of 0.07 mm protrusion between any two pistons.

22 If a dial test indicator is not available,

10.17a Pull the non-return valve from the cylinder head ...

10.17b ... and push a new one into place

10.21 Measure the piston protrusion using a DTI gauge

10.23 Cylinder head gasket thickness identification notches (arrowed)

10.24 Measure the length from under the bolt head to its end

10.27 Ensure the gasket locates over the dowels (arrowed)

piston protrusion may be measured using a straight-edge and feeler blades or Vernier calipers. However, this is much less accurate, and cannot therefore be recommended.

23 Note the greatest piston protrusion measurement, and use this to determine the correct cylinder head gasket from the following table. The series of notches/holes on the side of the gasket are used for thickness identification **(see illustration)**.

Piston protrusion	Gasket identification
0.685 to 0.734 mm	1 notch
0.533 to 0.634 mm	2 notch
0.635 to 0.684 mm	3 notch
0.735 to 0.784 mm	4 notch
0.785 to 0.886 mm	5 notch

Head bolt examination

24 Carefully examine the cylinder head bolts for signs of damage to the threads or head, and for any sign of corrosion. If the bolts are in a satisfactory condition, measure the length of each bolt from the underside of the head to the end of the shank. The bolts may be re-used providing that the measured length does not exceed 149.0 mm **(see illustration)**. **Note:** *Considering the stress to which the cylinder head bolts are subjected, it is highly recommended that they be all renewed, regardless of their apparent condition.*

Refitting

25 Turn the crankshaft and position Nos 1 and 4 pistons at TDC, then turn the crankshaft a quarter turn (90°) anti-clockwise.
26 Thoroughly clean the surfaces of the cylinder head and block.
27 Make sure that the locating dowels are in place, then fit the correct gasket the right way round on the cylinder block **(see illustration)**.
28 If necessary, refit the exhaust manifold to the cylinder head as described in Chapter 4A Section 14.
29 Carefully lower the cylinder head onto the gasket and block, making sure that it locates correctly onto the dowels.
30 Apply a smear of grease to the threads, and to the underside of the heads, of the cylinder head bolts. Peugeot/Citroën recommend the

use of Molykote G Rapid Plus (available from your franchised dealer); in the absence of the specified grease, any good-quality high melting-point grease may be used.
31 Carefully insert the cylinder head bolts into their holes (do not drop them in) and initially finger-tighten them.
32 Working progressively and in sequence, tighten the cylinder head bolts to their Stage 1 torque setting, using a torque wrench and suitable socket **(see illustration)**.
33 Once all the bolts have been tightened to their Stage 1 torque setting, working again in the specified sequence, tighten each bolt to the specified Stage 2 setting. Finally, angle-tighten the bolts through the specified Stage 3 angle. It is recommended that an angle-measuring gauge be used during this stage of tightening, to ensure accuracy. **Note:** *Retightening of the cylinder head bolts after running the engine is not required.*
34 Refit the hydraulic tappets, rocker arms, and camshaft housing (complete with camshafts) as described in Section 9.
35 Refit the timing belt as described in Section 7.
36 The remainder of refitting is a reversal of removal, noting the following points.
a) *Use a new seal when refitting the coolant outlet housing.*
b) *When refitting a cylinder head, it is good practice to renew the thermostat.*
c) *Refit the camshaft position sensor and set the air gap with reference to Chapter 4A Section 12.*
d) *Tighten all fasteners to the specified torque where given.*

10.32 Cylinder head bolt tightening sequence

e) *Refill the cooling system as described in Chapter 1 Section 19.*
f) *The engine may run erratically for the first few miles, until the engine management ECM relearns its stored values.*

11 Sump – removal and refitting

Removal

1 Drain the engine oil, then clean and refit the engine oil drain plug, tightening it securely. If the engine is nearing the service interval when the oil and filter are due for renewal, it is recommended that the filter is also removed, and a new one fitted. After reassembly, the engine can then be refilled with fresh oil. Refer to Chapter 1 Section 2 for further information.
2 Chock the rear wheels then jack up the front of the vehicle and support it on axle stands (see *Jacking and vehicle support*). Undo the screws and remove the engine undershield.
3 Remove the exhaust front pipe as described in Chapter 4A Section 18.
4 Where necessary, disconnect the wiring connector from the oil temperature sender unit, which is screwed into the sump.
5 Progressively slacken and remove all the sump retaining bolts/nuts. Since the sump bolts vary in length, remove each bolt in turn, and store it in its correct fitted order by pushing it through a clearly marked cardboard template. This will avoid the possibility of installing the bolts in the wrong locations on refitting.
6 Try to break the joint by striking the sump with the palm of your hand, then lower and withdraw the sump from under the car. If the sump is stuck (which is quite likely) use a putty knife or similar, carefully inserted between the sump and block. Ease the knife along the joint until the sump is released. While the sump is removed, take the opportunity to check the oil pump pick-up/strainer for signs of clogging or splitting. If necessary, remove the pump as described in Section 12, and clean or renew the strainer.

Refitting

7 Clean all traces of sealant from the mating surfaces of the cylinder block/crankcase and

11.8 Apply a bead of sealant to the sump or crankcase mating surface.
Ensure the sealant is applied on the inside of the retaining bolt holes

11.9 Refit the sump and tighten the bolts

sump, and then use a clean rag to wipe out the sump and the engine's interior.

8 On engines where the sump was fitted without a gasket, ensure that the sump mating surfaces are clean and dry, then apply a thin coating of suitable sealant to the sump or crankcase mating surface (see illustration).

9 Offer up the sump to the cylinder block/crankcase. Refit its retaining bolts/nuts, ensuring that each bolt is screwed into its original location. Tighten the bolts evenly and progressively to the specified torque setting (see illustration).

10 Where necessary, align the air conditioning compressor with its mountings on the sump, and insert the retaining bolts. Securely tighten the compressor retaining bolts, then refit the drivebelt as described in Chapter 1 Section 16.

11 Reconnect the wiring connector to the oil temperature sensor (where fitted).

12 Lower the vehicle to the ground, then refill the engine with oil as described in Chapter 1 Section 2.

12 Oil pump – removal, inspection and refitting

Removal

1 Remove the sump as described in Section 11.

2 Remove the crankshaft sprocket as described in Section 8. Recover the locating key from the crankshaft.

3 Disconnect the wiring plug, undo the bolts and remove the crankshaft position sensor, located on the right-hand end of the cylinder block.

4 Undo the three Allen screws and remove the oil pump pick-up tube from the pump/block (see illustration). Discard the oil seal; a new one must be fitted.

5 Undo the 8 bolts, and remove the oil pump (see illustration).

Inspection

6 Undo and remove the Torx bolts securing the cover to the oil pump (see illustration).

12.4 Oil pick-up tube Allen screws (arrowed)

12.5 Oil pump retaining bolts (arrowed)

12.6 Undo the Torx bolts and remove the pump cover

12.7a Remove the circlip ...

12.7b ... cap ...

12.7c ... spring ...

12.7d ... and piston

12.11 Apply a bead of sealant to the cylinder block mating surface

Examine the pump rotors and body for signs of wear and damage. If worn, the complete pump must be renewed.

7 Remove the circlip, and extract the cap, valve piston and spring, noting which way around they are fitted **(see illustrations)**. The condition of the relief valve spring can only be measured by comparing it with a new one; if there is any doubt about its condition, it should also be renewed.

8 Refit the relief valve piston and spring, and then secure them in place with the circlip.

9 Refit the cover to the oil pump, and tighten the Torx bolts securely.

Refitting

10 Remove all traces of sealant, and thoroughly clean the mating surfaces of the oil pump and cylinder block.

11 Apply a 4 mm wide bead of silicone sealant to the mating face of the cylinder block **(see illustration)**. Ensure that no sealant enters any of the holes in the block.

12 With a new oil seal fitted, refit the oil pump over the end of the crankshaft, aligning the flats in the pump drivegear with the flats machined in the crankshaft **(see illustrations)**. Note that new oil pumps are supplied with the oil seal already fitted, and a seal protector

sleeve. The sleeve fits over the end of the crankshaft to protect the seal as the pump is fitted.

13 Install the oil pump bolts and tighten them to the specified torque.

14 Refit the oil pick-up tube to the pump/cylinder block using a new O-ring seal. Ensure the oil dipstick guide tube is correctly refitted.

15 Refit the Woodruff key to the crankshaft, and slide the crankshaft sprocket into place.

16 The remainder of refitting is a reversal of removal.

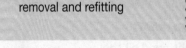

13 Oil cooler –
removal and refitting

Removal

1 Chock the rear wheels then jack up the front of the vehicle and support it on axle stands (see *Jacking and vehicle support*). Undo the retaining bolts/nuts and remove the engine undershield.

2 The oil cooler is fitted to the front of the oil filter housing. Drain the coolant as described in Chapter 1 Section 19.

3 Drain the engine oil as described in Chapter 1 Section 2, or be prepared for fluid spillage.

12.12a Fit a new seal ...

12.12b ... align the pump gear flats (arrowed) ...

12.12c ... with those of the crankshaft (arrowed)

13.4a Undo the oil cooler bolts/stud (arrowed)

13.4b Renew the O-ring seals (arrowed)

4 Undo the 5 bolts/stud and remove the oil cooler. Recover the O-ring seals (see illustrations).

Refitting

5 Fit new O-ring seals into the recesses in the oil filter housing, and refit the cooler. Tighten the bolts securely.
6 Refill or top-up the cooling system and engine oil level as described in Chapter 1 Section 19 and Chapter 1 Section 2, or *Weekly checks* (as applicable). Start the engine, and check the oil cooler for signs of leakage.

14 Oil seals – renewal

Crankshaft

Right-hand oil seal

1 Remove the crankshaft sprocket and Woodruff key as described in Section 8.
2 Measure and note the fitted depth of the oil seal.
3 Pull the oil seal from the housing using a screwdriver. Alternatively, drill a small hole in the oil seal, and use a self-tapping screw and a pair of pliers to remove it (see illustration).
4 Clean the oil seal housing and the crankshaft sealing surface.
5 The seal has a Teflon lip and must not be oiled or marked. The new seal should be

supplied with a protector sleeve, which fits over the end of the crankshaft to prevent any damage to the seal lip. With the sleeve in place, press the seal (open end first) into the pump to the previously-noted depth, using a suitable tube or socket (see illustrations).
6 Where applicable, remove the plastic sleeve from the end of the crankshaft.
7 Refit the timing belt crankshaft sprocket as described in Section 8.

Left-hand oil seal

8 Remove the flywheel, as described in Section 16.
9 Measure and note the fitted depth of the oil seal.
10 Pull the oil seal from the housing using a screwdriver (see illustration 14.3).

Alternatively, drill a small hole in the oil seal, and use a self-tapping scread a pair of pliers to remove it.
11 Clean the oil seal housing and the crankshaft sealing surface.
12 The seal has a Teflon lip and must not be oiled or marked. The new seal should be supplied with a protector sleeve, which fits over the end of the crankshaft to prevent any damage to the seal lip (see illustration). With the sleeve in place, press the seal (open end first) into the housing to the previously-noted depth, using a suitable tube or socket.
13 Where applicable, remove the plastic sleeve from the end of the crankshaft.
14 Refit the flywheel, as described in Section 16.

Camshaft

15 Remove the camshaft sprocket as described in Section 8. In principle there is no need to remove the timing belt completely, but remember that if the belt has been contaminated with oil, it must be renewed.
16 Pull the oil seal from the housing using a hooked instrument. Alternatively, drill a small hole in the oil seal and use a self-tapping screw and a pair of pliers to remove it (see illustration).
17 Clean the oil seal housing and the camshaft sealing surface.
18 The seal has a Teflon lip and must not be oiled or marked. The new seal should be supplied with a protector sleeve, which fits

14.3 Take great care not to mark the crankshaft whilst levering out the oil seal

14.5a Slide the seal and protective sleeve over the end of the crankshaft …

14.5b … and press the seal into place

14.12 Slide the seal and protective sleeve over the left-hand end of the crankshaft

14.16 Drill a hole, insert a self-tapping screw, and pull the seal from place using pliers

14.18 Fit the protective sleeve and seal over the end of the camshaft

15.3 The oil pressure switch is located on the front face of the cylinder block (arrowed)

15.5 The oil level sensor is located on the rear face of the cylinder block (arrowed)

over the end of the camshaft to prevent any damage to the seal lip **(see illustration)**. With the sleeve in place, press the seal (open end first) into the housing, using a suitable tube or socket, which bears only of the outer edge of the seal.

19 Refit the camshaft sprocket as described in Section 8.

20 Where necessary, fit a new timing belt with reference to Section 7.

15 Oil pressure switch and level sensor – removal and refitting

Removal

Oil pressure switch

1 The oil pressure switch is located at the front of the cylinder block, adjacent to the oil dipstick guide tube. Note that on some models, access to the switch may be improved if the vehicle is jacked up and supported on axle stands, then undo the bolts/nuts and remove the engine undershield so that the switch can be reached from underneath (see *Jacking and vehicle support*).

2 Remove the protective sleeve from the wiring plug (where applicable), and then disconnect the wiring from the switch.

3 Unscrew the switch from the cylinder block, and recover the sealing washer **(see illustration)**. Be prepared for oil spillage, and if the switch is to be left removed from the engine for any length of time, plug the hole in the cylinder block.

Oil level sensor

4 The oil level sensor is located at the rear of the cylinder block. Jack up the front of the vehicle and support it securely on axle stands (see *Jacking and vehicle support*). Undo the retaining bolts/nuts and remove the engine undershield.

5 Reach up between the driveshaft and the cylinder block, and disconnect the sensor wiring plug **(see illustration)**.

6 Using an open-ended spanner, unscrew the sensor and withdraw it from position.

Refitting

Oil pressure switch

7 Examine the sealing washer for any signs of damage or deterioration, and if necessary renew.

8 Refit the switch, complete with washer, and tighten it to the specified torque.

9 Refit the engine undershield, and lower the vehicle to the ground.

10 Check the engine oil level, and top-up as required (see *Weekly checks*).

11 Check for correct operation of the warning light, and for signs of oil leaks once the engine has been started and warmed-up to normal operating temperature.

Oil level sensor

12 Smear a little silicone sealant on the threads and refit the sensor to the cylinder block, tightening it securely.

13 Reconnect the sensor wiring plug.

14 Refit the engine undershield, and lower the vehicle to the ground.

15 Check the engine oil level, and top-up as required (see *Weekly checks*).

16 Check for correct operation of the warning light, and for signs of oil leaks once the engine has been started and warmed-up to normal operating temperature.

16 Flywheel – removal, inspection and refitting

Removal

1 Remove the transmission as described in Chapter 7 Section 7, then remove the clutch assembly as described in Chapter 6 Section 6.

2 Prevent the flywheel from turning by locking the ring gear teeth **(see illustration)**. Alternatively, bolt a strap between the flywheel and the cylinder block/crankcase. Do not attempt to lock the flywheel in position using the crankshaft pulley locking tool described in Section 3. Insert a 12 mm diameter rod or drill bit through the hole in the flywheel cover casting, and into a slot in the flywheel.

3 Make alignment marks between the flywheel and crankshaft to aid refitting. Slacken and remove the flywheel retaining

bolts, and remove the flywheel from the end of the crankshaft. Be careful not to drop it; it is heavy. If the flywheel locating dowel (where fitted) is a loose fit in the crankshaft end, remove it and store it with the flywheel for safekeeping. Discard the flywheel bolts; new ones must be used on refitting.

Inspection

4 Examine the flywheel for scoring of the clutch face, and for wear or chipping of the ring gear teeth. If the clutch face is scored, the flywheel may be surface-ground, but renewal is preferable. Seek the advice of an engine reconditioning specialist to see if machining is possible. If the ring gear is worn or damaged, the flywheel must be renewed, as it is not possible to renew the ring gear separately.

Refitting

5 Clean the mating surfaces of the flywheel and crankshaft. Remove any remaining locking compound from the threads of the crankshaft holes, using the correct size of tap, if available.

6 If the new flywheel retaining bolts are not supplied with their threads already pre-coated, apply a suitable thread-locking compound to the threads of each bolt.

Engines with normal flywheel

7 Ensure that the locating dowel is in position. Offer up the flywheel, locating it on the dowel (where fitted), and fit the new retaining bolts. Where no locating dowel is fitted, align the previously-made marks to ensure the flywheel

16.2 Using a tool to lock the flywheel ring gear and prevent rotation

16.8 Flywheel retaining Torx bolts

is refitted in its original position.

8 Lock the flywheel using the method employed on dismantling, and tighten the retaining bolts to the specified torque **(see illustration)**.

Engines with dual mass flywheel

9 The dual mass flywheel is designed to reduce harshness and vibration in the action of the engine, clutch and transmission. With this type of flywheel, two flywheel centralising tools are needed (available from franchised dealers). These are screwed into two opposite flywheel bolt holes in the crankshaft. As the tools are screwed down, their conical shape centralises the flywheel with regard to the crankshaft.

10 With the flywheel centralised, fit the new bolts into the remaining flywheel holes, then lock the flywheel using the same method employed on dismantling, and tighten the bolts to the specified torque.

11 Remove the two centralising tools, fit the new bolts and tighten them to the specified torque.

All models

12 Refit the clutch as described in Chapter 6 Section 6. Remove the flywheel locking tool, and refit the transmission as described in Chapter 7 Section 7.

17 Engine/transmission mountings – inspection and renewal

General

1 The engine/transmission mountings seldom require attention, but broken or deteriorated mountings should be renewed immediately, or the added strain placed on the driveline components may cause damage or wear.

2 While separate mountings may be removed and refitted individually, if more than one is disturbed at a time – such as if the engine/transmission unit is removed from its mountings – they must be reassembled and their fasteners tightened in the position marked on removal.

3 On reassembly, the complete weight of the engine/transmission unit must not be taken by the mountings until all are correctly aligned with the marks made on removal. Tighten the engine/transmission mounting fasteners to their specified torque wrench settings.

Inspection

4 During the check, the engine/transmission unit must be raised slightly, to remove its weight from the mountings.

5 Raise the front of the vehicle, and support it securely on axle stands. Remove the engine undershield. Position a jack under the sump, with a large block of wood between the jack head and the sump, then carefully raise the engine/transmission just enough to take the weight off the mountings.

 Warning: DO NOT place any part of your body under the engine when it is supported only by a jack.

6 Check the mountings to see if the rubber is cracked, hardened or separated from the metal components. Sometimes the rubber will split right down the centre.

7 Check for relative movement between each mounting's brackets and the engine/transmission or body (use a large screwdriver or lever to attempt to move the mountings). If movement is noted, lower the engine and check-tighten the mounting fasteners.

Renewal

Note: *The following paragraphs assume the engine is supported beneath the sump as described earlier.*

Right-hand engine mounting

8 Raise the front of the vehicle, and support it securely on axle stands, then remove the engine undershield. Position a jack under the sump, with a large block of wood between the jack head and the sump, then carefully raise the jack just enough to support the weight of the engine.

9 On models with belt driven power steering pump, undo the retaining bolt and move the PAS reservoir to one side **(see illustration)**. Note there is no need to disconnect the pipes. On some models a vibration damper is fitted to the rear of the mounting. Where fitted unbolt and remove the damper.

10 Mark the position of the mounting on the vehicle on the right-hand inner wing panel, and then undo the bolts securing the mounting, to the inner wing panel. Then undo the 3 retaining bolts from the engine side of the mounting, and remove the complete mounting **(see illustration)**.

11 Re-align the marks made on removal. Tighten all fasteners to the torque wrench settings specified.

Left-hand transmission mounting

12 Remove the battery and tray, as described in Chapter 5A Section 4.

13 If not already done, undo the retaining bolts/nuts and remove the engine undershield. Place a jack beneath the transmission, with a block of wood on the jack head. Raise the jack until it is supporting the weight of the transmission.

14 With the transmission supported, note the

17.9 Undo the PAS reservoir retaining bolt (arrowed)

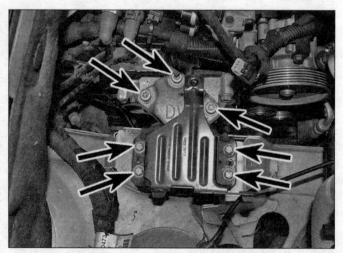

17.10 Engine mounting bolts (arrowed)

17.14 Transmission mounting

17.17 Undo the rear link-to-subframe mounting bolt (arrowed) ...

position of the mounting then first unscrew the centre retaining nut. Remove the retaining nuts and bolts, then lift the transmission mounting from its position on the inner wing mounting bracket **(see illustration)**.

15 Refitting is a reversal of removal. Re-align the mounting in the position noted on removal, then tighten all fasteners to the specified torque wrench settings.

Lower engine rear torque link

16 Firmly apply the handbrake, and then jack up the front of the vehicle and support it securely on axle stands (see *Jacking and vehicle support*). If not already done, undo the retaining bolts/nuts and remove the engine undershield.

17 Unscrew and remove the bolt securing the rear mounting link to the subframe **(see illustration)**.

18 Remove the bolt securing the rear mounting link to the driveshaft inner bearing bracket at the rear of the cylinder block **(see**

illustration), and then remove the mounting torque reaction link.

19 To remove the intermediate bearing housing/mounting assembly it will first be necessary to remove the right-hand driveshaft as described in Chapter 8 Section 2.

20 With the driveshaft removed, undo the retaining bolts and remove the bearing housing/ mounting from the rear of the cylinder block.

21 Check carefully for signs of wear or damage on all components, and renew them where necessary. The rubber bush fitted to the driveshaft bearing housing is available as a separate item on some models, check with your local dealer for availability of parts. If available, the rubber bush can be pressed out of the bearing housing, noting its fitted position, and then a new one pressed back into place.

22 On reassembly, fit the bearing housing assembly to the rear of the cylinder block, and

17.18 ... and the lower link-to-mounting bracket bolt (arrowed)

tighten its retaining bolts securely. Refit the driveshaft as described in Chapter 8 Section 2.

23 Refit the rear mounting torque reaction link, and tighten both its bolts to their specified torque settings.

24 Refit the engine undershield, and then lower the vehicle to the ground.

Chapter 2 Part C
Engine removal and overhaul procedures

Contents

Degrees of difficulty

| Easy, suitable for novice with little experience | Fairly easy, suitable for beginner with some experience | Fairly difficult, suitable for competent DIY mechanic | Difficult, suitable for experienced DIY mechanic | Very difficult, suitable for expert DIY or professional |

Specifications

Cylinder block

Cylinder bore diameter . . . . 75.00 mm (nominal)

Cylinder head

SOHC engine:
  Maximum gasket face distortion . . . . 0.03 mm
  Maximum permitted re-grind . . . . NO re-grind permitted
DOHC engines:
  New cylinder head height . . . . 124.0 ± 0.05 mm
  Maximum gasket face distortion . . . . 0.05 mm
  Maximum permitted re-grind . . . . 0.4 mm

Valves and springs	**Intake**	**Exhaust**
Valve head diameter:		
SOHC engines	30.15 ± 0.1 mm	27.51 ± 0.1 mm
DOHC engines	25.6 ± 0.1 mm	23.4 ± 0.1 mm
Valve stem diameter:		
All engines	5.485 +0.0 -0.015 mm	5.475 +0.0 -0.015 mm
Valve spring free height:		
SOHC	50 mm	50 mm
DOHC	No measurement given	No measurement given

Pistons

Piston diameter:
   All engines:
      Nominal dimension . . . .   74.945 mm ± 0.075 mm
      Repair dimension . . . .   75.345 mm ± 0.075 mm

Piston ring end gaps

All engines:
   Top compression ring . . . .   0.15 to 0.25 mm
   Second compression (sealing) ring . . . .   0.30 to 0.50 mm
   Oil control (scraper) ring . . . .   0.35 to 0.55 mm

Crankshaft

Endfloat:
   All engines . . . .   0.10 to 0.30 mm (thrustwasher thickness 2.40 ± 0.05 mm)

Torque wrench settings

1.6 litre SOHC engines

Refer to Chapter 2A, Specifications

1.6 litre DOHC engines

Refer to Chapter 2B, Specifications

1 General Information

1 Included in this Chapter are details of removing the engine/transmission from the car and general overhaul procedures for the cylinder head, cylinder block/crankcase and all other engine internal components.

2 The information given ranges from advice concerning preparation for an overhaul and the purchase of parts, to detailed step-by-step procedures covering removal, inspection, renovation and refitting of engine internal components.

3 After Section 5, all instructions are based on the assumption that the engine has been removed from the car. For information concerning in-car engine repair, as well as the removal and refitting of those external components necessary for full overhaul, refer to Chapter 2A or Chapter 2B, as applicable and to Section 5. Ignore any preliminary dismantling operations that are no longer relevant once the engine has been removed from the car.

4 Apart from torque wrench settings, which are given at the beginning of Chapter 2A or Chapter 2B, all specifications relating to engine overhaul are at the beginning of this Chapter.

2 Engine overhaul – general information

1 It is not always easy to determine when, or if, an engine should be completely overhauled, as a number of factors must be considered.

2 High mileage is not necessarily an indication that an overhaul is needed, while low mileage does not preclude the need for an overhaul. Frequency of servicing is probably the most important consideration. An engine, which has had regular and frequent oil and filter changes, as well as other required maintenance, should give many thousands of miles of reliable service. Conversely, a neglected engine may require an overhaul very early in its life.

3 Excessive oil consumption is an indication that piston rings, valve seals and/or valve guides are in need of attention. Make sure that oil leaks are not responsible before deciding that the rings and/or guides are worn. Perform a compression test, as described in Chapter 2A or Chapter 2B (as applicable), to determine the likely cause of the problem.

4 Check the oil pressure with a gauge fitted in place of the oil pressure switch, and compare it with that specified. If it is extremely low, the main and big-end bearings, and/or the oil pump, are probably worn out.

5 Loss of power, rough running, knocking or metallic engine noises, excessive valve gear noise, and high fuel consumption may also point to the need for an overhaul, especially if they are all present at the same time. If a complete service does not remedy the situation, major mechanical work is the only solution.

6 A full engine overhaul involves restoring all internal parts to the specification of a new engine. During a complete overhaul, the pistons and the piston rings are renewed. New main and big-end bearings are generally fitted; if necessary, the crankshaft may be reground, to compensate for wear in the journals. The valves are also serviced as well, since they are usually in less-than-perfect condition at this point. While the engine is being overhauled, other components, such as the starter and alternator, can be overhauled as well. Always pay careful attention to the condition of the oil pump when overhauling the engine, and renew it if there is any doubt as to its serviceability. The end result should be an as-new engine that will give many trouble-free miles.

7 Critical cooling system components such as the hoses, thermostat and water pump should be renewed when an engine is overhauled. The radiator should be checked carefully, to ensure that it is not clogged or leaking. Also, it is a good idea to renew the oil pump whenever the engine is overhauled.

8 Before beginning the engine overhaul, read through the entire procedure, to familiarise yourself with the scope and requirements of the job. Overhauling an engine is not difficult if you follow carefully all of the instructions, have the necessary tools and equipment, and pay close attention to all specifications. It can, however, be time-consuming. Plan on the car being off the road for a minimum of two weeks, especially if parts must be taken to an engineering works for repair or reconditioning. Check on the availability of parts and make sure that any necessary special tools and equipment are obtained in advance. Most work can be done with typical hand tools, although a number of precision measuring tools are required for inspecting parts to determine if they must be renewed. Often the engineering works will handle the inspection of parts and offer advice concerning reconditioning and renewal.

9 Always wait until the engine has been completely dismantled, and until all components (especially the cylinder block/ crankcase and the crankshaft) have been inspected, before deciding what service and repair operations must be performed by an engineering works. The condition of these components will be the major factor to consider when determining whether to overhaul the original engine, or to buy a reconditioned unit. Do not, therefore,

purchase parts or have overhaul work done on other components until they have been thoroughly inspected. As a general rule, time is the primary cost of an overhaul, so it does not pay to fit worn or sub-standard parts.

10 As a final note, to ensure maximum life and minimum trouble from a reconditioned engine, everything must be assembled with care, in a spotlessly clean environment.

3 Engine removal –
methods and precautions

1 If you have decided that the engine must be removed for overhaul or major repair work, several preliminary steps should be taken.

2 Locating a suitable place to work is extremely important. Adequate workspace, along with storage space for the car, will be needed. Engine/transmission removal is extremely complicated and involved on these vehicles. It must be stated, that unless the vehicle can be positioned on a ramp, or raised and supported on axle stands over an inspection pit, it will be more difficult to carry out the work involved.

3 Cleaning the engine compartment and engine/transmission before beginning the removal procedure will help keep tools clean and organised.

4 An engine hoist or A-frame will also be necessary. Make sure the equipment is rated in excess of the weight of the engine. Safety is of primary importance, considering the potential hazards involved in lifting the engine/transmission out of the car.

5 The help of an assistant is essential. Apart from the safety aspects involved, there are many instances when one person cannot simultaneously perform all of the operations required during engine/transmission removal.

6 Plan the operation ahead of time. Before starting work, arrange for the hire of or obtain all of the tools and equipment you will need. Some of the equipment necessary to perform engine/transmission removal and installation safely and with relative ease (in addition to an engine hoist) is as follows: a heavy duty trolley jack, complete sets of spanners and sockets (see Tools and working facilities), wooden

blocks, and plenty of rags and cleaning solvent for mopping-up spilled oil, coolant and fuel. If the hoist must be hired, make sure that you arrange for it in advance, and perform all of the operations possible without it beforehand. This will save you money and time.

7 Plan for the car to be out of use for quite a while. An engineering machine shop or engine reconditioning specialist will be required to perform some of the work, which cannot be accomplished without special equipment. These places often have a busy schedule, so it would be a good idea to consult them before removing the engine, in order to accurately estimate the amount of time required to rebuild or repair components that may need work.

8 During the engine/transmission removal procedure, it is advisable to make notes of the locations of all brackets, cable-ties, earthing points, etc, as well as how the wiring harnesses, hoses and electrical connections are attached and routed around the engine and engine compartment. An effective way of doing this is to take a series of photographs of the various components before they are disconnected or removed; the resulting photographs will prove invaluable when the engine/transmission is refitted.

9 The engine can be removed complete with the transmission as an assembly. Remove the front bumper, crossmember and radiator panel, and then the assembly is removed from the front of the vehicle.

10 Always be extremely careful when removing and refitting the engine/transmission. Serious injury can result from careless actions. Plan ahead and take your time, and a job of this nature, although major, can be accomplished successfully.

4 Engine – removal and refitting

Note: *Such is the complexity of the power unit arrangement on these vehicles, and the variations that may be encountered according to model and optional equipment fitted, the following should be regarded as a guide to the work involved, rather than a* *step-by-step procedure. Where differences are encountered, or additional component disconnection or removal is necessary, make notes of the work involved as an aid to refitting.*

Removal

1 Remove the battery and battery support tray (see Chapter 5A, Section 4). Wait five minutes, and then disconnect the engine wiring harness plugs at the fusebox or ECM (Electroninc Control Module) depending on model **(see illustration)**. Release the wiring harness from the retaining clips on the timing cover at the right-hand end of the engine (where applicable).

2 Apply the handbrake, then jack up the front of the vehicle and support it on axle stands (see *Jacking and vehicle support*). Remove both front roadwheels. Undo the retaining bolts/nuts and remove the engine undershield, also release the securing clips and remove the front wheel arch liners.

3 Remove the upper trim covers from the top of the engine, these simply pull upwards to release from the locating pegs.

4 Drain the cooling system with reference to Chapter 1 Section 19.

5 Drain the transmission oil/fluid as described in Chapter 7 Section 2. Refit the drain and filler plugs, and tighten them to their specified torque settings.

6 If the engine is to be dismantled, drain the engine oil and remove the oil filter as described in Chapter 1 Section 2. Clean and refit the drain plug, tightening it securely.

7 Refer to Chapter 8 Section 2 and remove both front driveshafts.

8 Remove the front bumper and bumper bar as described in Chapter 11 Section 6. Also, remove the headlamps (see Chapter 12 Section 7).

9 Refer to Chapter 1 Section 16 and remove the auxiliary drivebelt.

10 Remove the radiator/cooling fan and front panel assembly as described in Chapter 3 Section 6. On air conditioned models, tie the condenser to one side. Do not disconnect the refrigerant pipes.

11 Undo the securing bolts and remove the front panel lower crossmember and side rails **(see illustrations)**.

4.1 Disconnect the ECU wiring plugs

4.11a Remove the front panel lower crossmember ...

4.11b ... and the side rails

4.30 The stud must be removed to access the front transmission-to-engine bolt

12 On turbo diesel engines, remove the air hoses leading from the intercooler to the turbocharger located on the right-hand side of the radiator, and to the intake manifold.

13 Remove the air cleaner housing and ducting, then remove the exhaust system with reference to Chapter 4A Section 4 and Chapter 4A Section 18.

14 Note their fitted positions and harness routing, then disconnect all wiring plugs from the transmission. If necessary label the connectors as they are unplugged. Undo the nut and remove the heater control box (still connected) from the front left-hand corner of the engine compartment.

15 Disconnect the hose from the vacuum pump on the left-hand end of the cylinder head – see Chapter 9 Section 20

16 Disconnect the fuel feed and return hoses. Plug the end of the hoses to prevent dirt ingress.

17 Disconnect the selector cable(s) from the transmission as described in Chapter 7 Section 3.

18 On manual transmission models, unbolt the clutch slave cylinder, then tie it to one side, without disconnecting the fluid pipe (see Chapter 6 Section 4). Use an elastic band around the cylinder to prevent the piston from coming out.

19 From underneath the vehicle, slacken and remove the nuts and bolts securing the rear engine mounting connecting link to the mounting assembly and subframe, and remove the connecting link. Refer to Chapter 2A Section 17 or Chapter 2B Section 17.

20 On models with air conditioning, refer to Chapter 3 Section 12 and unbolt the compressor from the engine. Do not disconnect the refrigerant lines. Support or tie the compressor to one side.

21 Using a hoist attached to the lifting eyes on the cylinder head, take the weight of the engine and transmission.

22 Remove the right-hand and left-hand engine mountings and support brackets as described in Chapter 2A or 2B.

23 Completely pull out the wire retaining clips and disconnect the heater hoses at the engine compartment bulkhead.

24 Make a final check to ensure all wiring; hoses and brackets that would prevent the removal of the assembly have been disconnected.

25 Move the engine/transmission forwards and out from the front of the vehicle. Enlist the help of an assistant during this procedure, as it may be necessary to tilt and twist the assembly slightly to clear the body panels and adjacent components. Move the unit clear of the car and lower it to the ground.

Separation

26 With the engine/transmission assembly removed, support the assembly on suitable blocks of wood on a workbench (or failing that, on a clean area of the workshop floor).

27 Undo the retaining bolts, and remove the flywheel lower cover plate (where fitted) from the transmission.

28 Slacken and remove the retaining bolts, and remove the starter motor from the transmission.

29 Disconnect any remaining wiring connectors at the transmission, then move the main engine wiring harness to one side.

30 Ensure that both engine and transmission are adequately supported, then slacken and remove the remaining bolts securing the transmission housing to the engine. Note the correct fitted positions of each bolt (and the relevant brackets) as they are removed, to use as a reference on refitting. On some models, the left-hand catalytic converter mounting stud must be removed to access the front transmission-to-engine bolt **(see illustration)**.

31 Carefully withdraw the transmission from the engine, ensuring that the weight of the transmission is not allowed to hang on the input shaft while it is engaged with the clutch friction disc.

32 If they are loose, remove the locating dowels from the engine or transmission, and keep them in a safe place.

Refitting

33 If the engine and transmission have not been separated, perform the operations described below from paragraph 40 onwards.

34 Apply a smear of high melting-point grease (Peugeot/Citroën recommend the use of Molykote BR2 plus – available from your franchised dealer) to the splines of the transmission input shaft. Do not apply too much; otherwise there is a possibility of the grease contaminating the clutch friction disc. **Note:** *On late models, Peugeot/Citroën recommend no grease be applied.*

35 Ensure that the locating dowels are correctly positioned in the engine or transmission, and then carefully offer the transmission to the engine until the locating dowels are engaged. On manual transmission models, ensure that the weight of the transmission is not allowed to hang on the input shaft as it is engaged with the clutch friction disc.

36 Refit the transmission housing-to-engine bolts, ensuring that all the necessary brackets are correctly positioned, and tighten them securely.

37 Refit the starter motor, and securely tighten its retaining bolts.

38 Refit the lower flywheel cover plate (where fitted) to the transmission, and securely tighten the bolts.

39 Reconnect the hoist and lifting tackle to the engine lifting brackets. With the aid of an assistant, lift the assembly into the engine compartment, taking care not to damage surrounding components.

40 Refit the right-hand engine mounting and support bracket, but leave the bolts finger-tight at this stage.

41 Working on the left-hand mounting, refit the mounting to the transmission and finger-tighten.

42 Remove the hoist.

43 From underneath the vehicle, refit the rear mounting connecting link and finger-tighten the bolts.

44 Rock the engine to settle it on its mountings, then go around and tighten all the mounting nuts and bolts to their specified torque settings.

45 The remainder of the refitting procedure is a direct reversal of the removal sequence, with reference to the relevant chapters and noting the following points:

a) *Ensure that the wiring loom is correctly routed and retained by all the relevant retaining clips; all connectors should be correctly and securely reconnected.*

b) *Prior to refitting the driveshafts to the transmission, renew the driveshaft oil seals as described in Chapter 7 Section 4 and Chapter 8 Section 2.*

c) *Ensure that all coolant hoses are correctly reconnected, and securely retained by their retaining clips.*

d) *Refill the engine and transmission with the correct quantity and type of lubricant.*

e) *Refill the cooling system as described in Chapter 1 Section 19.*

f) *Initialise the engine management ECM as follows. Start the engine and run to normal temperature. Carry out a road test during which the following procedure should be made. Engage third gear and stabilise the engine at 1000 rpm. Now accelerate fully to 3500 rpm.*

5 Engine overhaul – dismantling sequence

1 It is much easier to dismantle and work on the engine if it is mounted on a portable engine stand. These stands can often be hired from a tool hire shop. Before the engine is mounted on a stand, the flywheel/driveplate should be removed, so that the stand bolts can be tightened into the end of the cylinder block/crankcase.

2 If a stand is not available, it is possible to dismantle the engine with it blocked up on a sturdy workbench, or on the floor. Be extra careful not to tip or drop the engine when working without a stand.

3 If you are going to obtain a reconditioned engine, all the external components must be removed first, to be transferred to the new engine (just as they will if you are doing a complete engine overhaul yourself). These components include the following:
a) *Ancillary unit mounting brackets (oil filter, starter, alternator, power steering pump, etc)*
b) *Thermostat and housing (Chapter 3 Section 5).*
c) *Dipstick tube/sensor.*
d) *All electrical switches and sensors.*
e) *Intake and exhaust manifolds – where applicable.*
f) *Flywheel/driveplate (Chapter 2A Section 16 or Chapter 2B Section 16).*

Note: *When removing the external components from the engine, pay close attention to details that may be helpful or important during refitting. Note the fitted position of gaskets, seals, spacers, pins, washers, bolts, and other small items.*

4 If you are obtaining a 'short' engine (which consists of the engine cylinder block/crankcase, crankshaft, pistons and connecting rods all assembled), then the cylinder head, sump, oil pump, and timing chain/belt will have to be removed also.

5 If you are planning a complete overhaul, the engine can be dismantled, and the internal components removed, in the order given below, referring to Chapter 2A or Chapter 2B unless otherwise stated.
a) *Intake and exhaust manifolds – where applicable (Chapter 4A).*
b) *Timing chains/belts, sprockets and tensioner(s).*
c) *Cylinder head.*
d) *Flywheel/driveplate.*
e) *Sump.*
f) *Oil pump.*
g) *Piston/connecting rod assemblies (Section 9).*
h) *Crankshaft (Section 10).*

6 Before beginning the dismantling and overhaul procedures, make sure that you have all of the correct tools necessary. Refer to *Tools and working facilities* for further information.

6 Cylinder head – dismantling

Note: *New and reconditioned cylinder heads are available from the manufacturer, and from engine overhaul specialists. Be aware that some specialist tools are required for the dismantling and inspection procedures, and new components may not be readily available. It may therefore be more practical and economical for the home mechanic to purchase a reconditioned head, rather than dismantle, inspect and recondition the original head.*

1 Remove the cylinder head as described in Chapter 2A Section 10 or Chapter 2B Section 10 (as applicable).
2 If not already done, remove the intake and the exhaust manifolds with reference to Chapter 4A. Remove any remaining brackets or housings as required.
3 Remove the camshafts, hydraulic followers and rockers (as applicable) as described in Chapter 2A or Chapter 2B.
4 If not already done, remove the glow plugs as described in Chapter 5B Section 2.
5 On all models, using a valve spring compressor, compress each valve spring in turn until the split collets can be removed. Release the compressor, and lift off the spring retainer, spring and, where fitted, the spring seat. Using a pair of pliers, carefully extract the valve stem oil seal from the top of the guide. On 16-valve engines, the valve stem oil seal also forms the spring seat and is deeply recessed in the cylinder head. It is also a tight fit on the valve guide making it difficult to remove with pliers or a conventional valve stem oil seal removal tool. It can be easily removed, however, using a self-locking nut of suitable diameter screwed onto the end of a bolt and locked with a second nut. Push the nut down onto the top of the seal; the locking portion of the nut will grip the seal allowing it to be withdrawn from the top of the valve guide. Access to the valves is limited, and it may be necessary to make up an adapter out of metal tube – cut out a 'window' so that the valve collets can be removed **(see illustrations)**.
6 If, when the valve spring compressor is screwed down, the spring retainer refuses to free and expose the split collets, gently tap the top of the tool, directly over the retainer, with a light hammer. This will free the retainer.

6.5a Compress the valve spring using a spring compressor …

6.5b … then extract the collets and release the spring compressor

6.5c Remove the spring retainer …

6.5d … followed by the valve spring …

6.5e … and the spring seat (not all models)

6.5f Use a pair of pliers to remove the valve stem oil seal. On some models the spring seat is integral with the seal

7 Withdraw the valve from the combustion chamber. Remove the valve stem oil seal from the top of the guide, then lift out the spring seat where fitted.

8 It is essential that each valve is stored together with its collets, retainer, spring, and spring seat. The valves should also be kept in their correct sequence, unless they are so badly worn that they are to be renewed. If they are going to be kept and used again, place each valve assembly in a labelled polythene bag or similar small container **(see illustration)**. Note that No 1 valve is nearest to the transmission (flywheel/driveplate) end of the engine.

7 Cylinder head and valves – cleaning and inspection

1 Thorough cleaning of the cylinder head and valve components, followed by a detailed inspection, will enable you to decide how much valve service work must be carried out during the engine overhaul. **Note:** *If the engine has been severely overheated, it is best to assume that the cylinder head is warped – check carefully for signs of this.*

Cleaning

2 Scrape away all traces of old gasket material from the cylinder head.

3 Scrape away the carbon from the combustion chambers and ports, then wash the cylinder head thoroughly with paraffin or a suitable solvent.

4 Scrape off any heavy carbon deposits that may have formed on the valves, then use a power-operated wire brush to remove deposits from the valve heads and stems.

Inspection

Note: *Be sure to perform all the following inspection procedures before concluding that the services of a machine shop or engine overhaul specialist are required. Make a list of all items that require attention.*

Cylinder head

5 Inspect the head very carefully for cracks, evidence of coolant leakage, and other

6.8 Place each valve and its associated components in a labelled bag

damage. If cracks are found, a new cylinder head should be obtained. Use a straight-edge and feeler blade to check that the cylinder head gasket surface is not distorted **(see illustration)**. If it is, it may be possible to have it machined, provided that the cylinder head height is not significantly reduced.

6 Examine the valve seats in each of the combustion chambers. If they are severely pitted, cracked, or burned, they will need to be renewed or recut by an engine overhaul specialist. If they are only slightly pitted, this can be removed by grinding-in the valve heads and seats with fine valve grinding compound, as described below. If in any doubt, have the cylinder head inspected by an engine overhaul specialist.

7 Check the valve guides for wear by inserting the relevant valve, and checking for side-to-side motion of the valve. A very small amount of movement is acceptable. If the movement seems excessive, remove the valve. Measure the valve stem diameter (see below), and renew the valve if it is worn. If the valve stem is not worn, the wear must be in the valve guide, and the guide must be renewed. The renewal of valve guides is best carried out by a Citroën/Peugeot dealer or engine overhaul specialist, who will have the necessary tools available. Where no valve stem diameter is specified, seek the advice of a Citroën/Peugeot dealer on the best course of action.

8 If renewing the valve guides, the valve seats should be recut or reground only after the guides have been fitted.

7.5 Check the cylinder head gasket surface for distortion

9 Where applicable, examine the camshaft oil supply non-return valve in the oil feed bore at the timing belt/chain end of the cylinder head. Check that the valve is not loose in the cylinder head and that the ball is free to move within the valve body. If the valve is a loose fit in its bore, or if there is any doubt about its condition, it should be renewed. The non-return valve can be removed (assuming it is not loose), using compressed air, such as that generated by a tyre foot pump. Place the pump nozzle over the oil feed bore of the camshaft bearing journal and seal the corresponding oil feed bore with a rag. Apply the compressed air and the valve will be forced out of its location in the underside of the cylinder head **(see illustrations)**. Fit the new non-return valve to its bore on the underside of the head ensuring it is fitted the correct way. Oil should be able to pass upwards through the valve to the camshafts, but the ball in the valve should prevent the oil from returning back to the cylinder block. Use a thin socket or similar to push the valve fully into position.

Valves

10 Examine the head of each valve for pitting, burning, cracks, and general wear. Check the valve stem for scoring and wear ridges. Rotate the valve, and check for any obvious indication that it is bent. Look for pits or excessive wear on the tip of each valve stem. Renew any valve that shows any such signs of wear or damage.

11 If the valve appears satisfactory at this stage, measure the valve stem diameter at several points using a micrometer **(see illustration)**. Any

7.9a Apply compressed air to the oil feed bore of the intake camshaft, seal the bore in the exhaust camshaft bore with a rag ...

7.9b ... and the camshaft oil supply non-return valve will be ejected from the underside of the cylinder head

7.11 Measure the valve stem diameter with a micrometer

7.14 Grinding-in a valve

8.1a Locate the valve stem oil seal on the valve guide …

8.1b … and press the seal firmly onto the guide using a suitable socket

8.1c On some models, the valve stem oil seal is integral with the spring seat

8.2 Lubricate the stem of the valve and insert it into the guide

significant difference in the readings obtained indicates wear of the valve stem. Should any of these conditions be apparent, the valve must be renewed.

12 If the valves are in satisfactory condition, they should be ground (lapped) into their respective seats, to ensure a smooth, gas-tight seal. If the seat is only lightly pitted, or if it has been recut, fine grinding compound only should be used to produce the required finish. Coarse valve-grinding compound should not be used, unless a seat is badly burned or deeply pitted. If this is the case, the cylinder head and valves should be inspected by an expert, to decide whether seat recutting, or even the renewal of the valve or seat insert (where possible) is required.

13 Valve grinding is carried out as follows. Place the cylinder head upside-down on a bench.

14 Smear a trace of (the appropriate grade of) valve-grinding compound on the seat face, and press a suction grinding tool onto the valve head (see illustration). With a semi-rotary action, grind the valve head to its seat, lifting the valve occasionally to redistribute the grinding compound. A light spring placed under the valve head will greatly ease this operation.

15 If coarse grinding compound is being used, work only until a dull, matt even surface is produced on both the valve seat and the valve, then wipe off the used compound, and repeat the process with fine compound. When a smooth unbroken ring of light grey matt finish is produced on both the valve and seat, the grinding operation is complete. Do not grind-in the valves any further than absolutely necessary, or the seat will be prematurely sunk into the cylinder head.

16 When all the valves have been ground-in, carefully wash off all traces of grinding compound using paraffin or a suitable solvent, before reassembling the cylinder head.

Valve components

17 Examine the valve springs for signs of damage and discoloration. No minimum free length is specified by Peugeot/Citroën, so the

only way of judging valve spring wear is by comparison with a new component.

18 Stand each spring on a flat surface, and check it for squareness. If any of the springs are damaged, distorted or have lost their tension, obtain a complete new set of springs. It is normal to renew the valve springs as a matter of course if a major overhaul is being carried out.

19 Renew the valve stem oil seals regardless of their apparent condition.

8 Cylinder head – reassembly

1 Working on the first valve assembly, refit the spring seat then dip the new valve stem oil seal in fresh engine oil. Locate the seal on the valve guide and press the seal firmly onto the guide using a suitable socket (see illustrations). Note that the seal is integral with the lower spring seat.

2 Lubricate the stem of the first valve, and insert it in the guide (see illustration).

3 Locate the valve spring on top of its seat, and then refit the spring retainer.

4 Compress the valve spring, and locate the split collets in the recess in the valve stem. Release the compressor, then repeat the procedure on the remaining valves. Ensure that each valve is inserted into its original location. If new valves are being fitted, insert

them into the locations to which they have been ground.

5 With all the valves installed, support the cylinder head and, using a hammer and interposed block of wood, tap the end of each valve stem to settle the components.

6 Refit the camshafts, hydraulic followers and rocker arms (as applicable) as described in Chapter 2A or Chapter 2B.

7 Refit any remaining components using the reverse of the removal sequence and with new seals or gaskets as necessary.

8 The cylinder head can then be refitted as described in Chapter 2A Section 10 or Chapter 2B Section 10.

9 Piston/connecting rod assembly – removal

Note: The main bearing ladder must be removed before the piston/connecting rods, can be withdrawn.

1 Remove the cylinder head, sump and oil pump as described in Chapter 2A or Chapter 2B.

2 If there is a pronounced wear ridge at the top of any bore, it may be necessary to remove it with a scraper or ridge reamer, to avoid piston damage during removal. Such a ridge indicates excessive wear of the cylinder bore.

3 Using quick-drying paint, mark each connecting rod and big-end bearing cap

9.3 Connecting rod and big-end bearing cap identification marks (No 3 shown)

9.5 Remove the big-end bearing shell and cap

9.6 To protect the crankshaft journals, tape over the connecting rod stud threads

with its respective cylinder number on the flat machined surface provided; if the engine has been dismantled before, note carefully any identifying marks made previously **(see illustration)**. Note that No 1 cylinder is at the transmission (flywheel) end of the engine.

4 Turn the crankshaft to bring pistons 1 and 4 to BDC (Bottom Dead Centre). Remove the main bearing ladder, as described in Section 10.

5 Unscrew the nuts or bolts, as applicable, from No 1 piston big-end bearing cap. Take off the cap, and recover the bottom half bearing shell **(see illustration)**. If the bearing shells are to be re-used, tape the cap and the shell together.

6 Where applicable, to prevent the possibility of damage to the crankshaft bearing journals, tape over the connecting rod stud threads **(see illustration)**.

7 Using a hammer handle, push the piston up through the bore, and remove it from the top of the cylinder block. Recover the bearing shell, and tape it to the connecting rod for safekeeping.

8 Loosely refit the big-end cap to the connecting rod, and secure with the nuts/ bolts – this will help to keep the components in their correct order.

9 Remove number 4 piston assembly in the same way.

10 Turn the crankshaft through 180° to bring pistons 2 and 3 to BDC (Bottom Dead Centre), and remove them in the same way.

10 Crankshaft – removal

1 Remove the crankshaft sprocket and the oil pump as described in Chapter 2A or Chapter 2B (as applicable).

2 Remove the pistons and connecting rods, as described in Section 9. If no work is to be done on the pistons and connecting rods, there is no need to remove the cylinder head, or to push the pistons out of the cylinder bores. The pistons should just be pushed far enough up the bores so that they are positioned clear of the crankshaft journals. **Note:** *The main bearing ladder must be removed before the piston/connecting rods, can be withdrawn.*

3 Check the crankshaft endfloat as described in Section 13, then proceed as follows.

4 Work around the outside of the cylinder block, and unscrew all the small bolts securing the main bearing ladder to the base of the cylinder block. Note the correct fitted depth of the left-hand crankshaft oil seal in the cylinder block/main bearing ladder.

5 Working in a diagonal sequence, evenly and progressively slacken the large main bearing ladder retaining bolts by a turn at a time. Once all the bolts are loose, remove them from the ladder. **Note:** *Prise up the two caps at the flywheel end of the ladder to expose the two end main bearing bolts (see illustration).*

6 With all the retaining bolts removed, carefully lift the main bearing ladder casting

away from the base of the cylinder block. Recover the lower main bearing shells, and tape them to their respective locations in the casting. If the two locating dowels are a loose fit, remove them and store them with the casting for safekeeping.

7 Undo the big-end bolts and remove the pistons/connecting rods as described in Section 9. Lift out the crankshaft, and discard both the oil seals.

8 Recover the upper main bearing shells, and store them along with the relevant lower bearing shell. Also recover the two thrustwashers (one fitted either side of No 2 main bearing) from the cylinder block.

11 Cylinder block/crankcase – cleaning and inspection

Cleaning

1 Remove all external components and electrical switches/sensors from the block. For complete cleaning, the core plugs should ideally be removed **(see illustration)**. Drill a small hole in the plugs, and then insert a self-tapping screw into the hole. Pull out the plugs by pulling on the screw with a pair of grips, or by using a slide hammer.

2 Where applicable, undo the retaining bolts and remove the piston oil jet spray tubes (there is one for each piston) from inside the cylinder block **(see illustration)**.

10.5 Prise up the two caps to expose the main bearing bolts at the flywheel end

11.1 Cylinder block core plugs (arrowed)

11.2 Piston oil jet spray tube (arrowed) in the cylinder block

11.8 Use a suitable tap to clean the cylinder block threaded holes

11.17a On aluminium block engines, remove each liner ...

11.17b ... and recover the bottom O-ring seal (arrowed)

3 Scrape all traces of gasket from the cylinder block/crankcase, and from the main bearing ladder/caps (as applicable), taking care not to damage the gasket/sealing surfaces.

4 Remove all oil gallery plugs (where fitted). The plugs are usually very tight – they may have to be drilled out, and the holes retapped. Use new plugs when the engine is reassembled.

5 If any of the castings are extremely dirty, all should be steam-cleaned.

6 After the castings are returned, clean all oil holes and oil galleries one more time. Flush all internal passages with warm water until the water runs clear. Dry thoroughly, and apply a light film of oil to all mating surfaces, to prevent rusting. If you have access to compressed air, use it to speed up the drying process, and to blow out all the oil holes and galleries.

 Warning: Wear eye protection when using compressed air.

7 If the castings are not very dirty, you can do an adequate cleaning job with hot (as hot as you can stand), soapy water and a stiff brush. Take plenty of time, and do a thorough job. Regardless of the cleaning method used, be sure to clean all oil holes and galleries very thoroughly, and to dry all components well. On cast-iron block engines, protect the cylinder bores as described above, to prevent rusting.

8 All threaded holes must be clean, to ensure accurate torque readings during reassembly. To clean the threads, run the correct-size tap into each of the holes to remove rust, corrosion, thread sealant or sludge, and to restore damaged threads **(see illustration)**. If possible, use compressed air to clear the holes of debris produced by this operation.

9 Apply suitable sealant to the new oil gallery plugs, and insert them into the holes in the block. Tighten them securely. Also apply suitable sealant to new core plugs, and drive them into the block using a tube or socket.

10 Where applicable, clean the threads of the piston oil jet retaining bolts, and apply a drop of thread-locking compound (Peugeot/Citroën recommend Loctite Frenetanch) to each bolt threads. Refit the piston oil jet spray tubes to the cylinder block, and tighten the retaining bolts to the specified torque setting.

11 If the engine is not going to be reassembled right away, cover it with a large plastic bag to keep it clean; protect all mating surfaces and the cylinder bores as described above, to prevent rusting.

Inspection

Cast-iron cylinder block

12 Visually check the castings for cracks and corrosion. Look for stripped threads in the threaded holes. If there has been any history of internal water leakage, it may be worthwhile having an engine overhaul specialist check the cylinder block/crankcase with special equipment. If defects are found, have them repaired if possible, or renew the assembly.

13 Check each cylinder bore for scuffing and scoring. Check for signs of a wear ridge at the top of the cylinder, indicating that the bore is excessively worn.

14 If the necessary measuring equipment is available, measure the bore diameter of each cylinder at the top (just under the wear ridge), centre, and bottom of the cylinder bore, parallel to the crankshaft axis.

15 Next, measure the bore diameter at the same three locations, at right angles to the crankshaft axis. Compare the results with the figures given in the Specifications. If there is any doubt about the condition of the cylinder bores, seek the advice of a Citroën/Peugeot dealer or suitable engine reconditioning specialist.

16 At the time of writing, it was not clear whether oversize pistons were available for all models. Consult your Peugeot/Citroën dealer or engine specialist for the latest information on piston availability. If oversize pistons are available, then it may be possible to have the cylinder bores rebored and fit the oversize pistons. If oversize pistons are not available, and the bores are worn, renewal of the block seems to be the only option.

Aluminium cylinder block

17 Remove the liner clamps (where used), and then use a hardwood drift to tap out each liner from the inside of the cylinder block. When all the liners are released, tip the cylinder block/crankcase on its side and remove each liner from the top of the block. As each liner is removed, stick masking tape on its left-hand (transmission side) face, and write the cylinder

number on the tape. No 1 cylinder is at the transmission (flywheel/driveplate) end of the engine. Remove the sealing ring from the base of each liner, and discard **(see illustrations)**.

18 Check each cylinder liner for scuffing and scoring. Check for signs of a wear ridge at the top of the liner, indicating that the bore is excessively worn.

19 Take the liners to a Peugeot/Citroën dealer or engine reconditioning specialist and have their bores measured to determine if renewal is necessary. If it is, the dealer or specialist will be able to advise you regarding piston/liner availability.

20 Prior to installing the liners, check the liner protrusion as follows. Thoroughly clean the mating surfaces of the liner and cylinder block. Insert the liners into the block, without a sealing ring, ensuring each one is correctly seated; if the original liners are being refitted, ensure the liners are fitted in their original locations. With all four liners correctly installed, use a dial gauge (or a straight-edge and feeler blade) to check that the protrusion of each liner above the upper surface of the cylinder block is within the limits given in the Specifications. The maximum difference between any two liners must not be exceeded. **Note:** *If new liners are being fitted, it is permissible to interchange them to bring the difference in protrusion within limits. Remember to keep each piston with its respective liner. If liner protrusion is not within the specified limits, seek the advice of a Citroën/Peugeot dealer or engine reconditioning specialist before proceeding with the engine rebuild.*

21 Once the protrusions have been checked, remove the liners from the block and fit a new sealing ring carefully to the base of each liner. Lubricate the base of each liner with a smear of oil to aid installation.

22 Insert each liner into the cylinder block, taking care not to damage the O-ring, and press it home as far as possible by hand. Using a hammer and a block of wood, tap each liner lightly but fully onto its locating shoulder. If the original liners are being refitted, use the marks made on removal to ensure that each is refitted the correct way round, and is inserted into its original bore.

23 Wipe clean, then lightly oil all exposed liner surfaces, to prevent rusting. Where necessary, clamp the liners back in position.

12.2 Remove the piston rings with the aid of a feeler gauge

12.14a Prise out the circlip …

12.14b … and withdraw the gudgeon pin

12 Piston/connecting rod assembly – inspection

1 Before the inspection process can begin, the piston/connecting rod assemblies must be cleaned, and the original piston rings removed from the pistons.

2 Carefully expand the old rings over the top of the pistons. The use of two or three old feeler blades will be helpful in preventing the rings dropping into empty grooves **(see illustration)**. Be careful not to scratch the piston with the ends of the ring. The rings are brittle, and will snap if they are spread too far. They are also very sharp – protect your hands and fingers. Note that the third ring incorporates an expander. Always remove the rings from the top of the piston. Keep each set of rings with its piston if the old rings are to be re-used.

3 Scrape away all traces of carbon from the top of the piston. A hand-held wire brush (or a piece of fine emery cloth) can be used, once the majority of the deposits have been scraped away.

4 Remove the carbon from the ring grooves in the piston, using an old ring. Break the ring in half to do this (be careful not to cut your fingers – piston rings are sharp). Be careful to remove only the carbon deposits – do not remove any metal, and do not nick or scratch the sides of the ring grooves.

5 Once the deposits have been removed, clean the piston/connecting rod assembly with paraffin or a suitable solvent, and dry thoroughly. Make sure that the oil return holes in the ring grooves are clear.

6 If the pistons and cylinder bores are not damaged or worn excessively, and if the cylinder block does not need to be re-bored (where possible), the original pistons can be refitted. Normal piston wear shows up as even vertical wear on the piston thrust surfaces, and slight looseness of the top ring in its groove. New piston rings should always be used when the engine is reassembled.

7 Carefully inspect each piston for cracks around the skirt, around the gudgeon pin holes, and at the piston ring 'lands' (between the ring grooves).

8 Look for scoring and scuffing on the piston skirt, holes in the piston crown, and burned areas at the edge of the crown. If the skirt is scored or scuffed, the engine may have been suffering from overheating, and/or abnormal combustion, which caused excessively high operating temperatures. The cooling and lubrication systems should be checked thoroughly. Scorch marks on the sides of the pistons show that blow-by has occurred. A hole in the piston crown, or burned areas at the edge of the piston crown, indicates that abnormal combustion (pre-ignition, knocking, or detonation) has been occurring. If any of the above problems exist, the causes must be investigated and corrected, or the damage will occur again. The causes may include incorrect ignition/injection pump timing, or a faulty injector (as applicable).

9 Corrosion of the piston, in the form of pitting, indicates that coolant has been leaking into the combustion chamber and/or the crankcase. Again, the cause must be corrected, or the problem may persist in the rebuilt engine.

10 On engines with wet liners, it is not possible to renew the pistons separately; pistons are only supplied with piston rings and a liner, as a part of a matched assembly (see Section 11). On iron-block engines, pistons can be purchased from a Peugeot/Citroën dealer or engine reconditioning specialist.

11 Examine each connecting rod carefully for signs of damage, such as cracks around the big-end and small-end bearings. Check that the rod is not bent or distorted. Damage is highly unlikely, unless the engine has been seized or badly overheated. Detailed checking of the connecting rod assembly can only be carried out by a Citroën/Peugeot dealer or engine specialist with the necessary equipment.

12 The connecting rod big-end cap bolts/ nuts must be renewed whenever they are disturbed. Although Citroën/Peugeot do not specify that the bolts must also renewed, it is recommended that the nuts and bolts are renewed as a complete set.

13 The gudgeon pins are of the floating type, secured in position by two circlips. On these engines, the pistons and connecting rods can be separated as described in the following paragraphs.

14 Using a small flat-bladed screwdriver, prise out the circlips, and push out the gudgeon pin **(see illustrations)**. Hand pressure should be sufficient to remove the pin. Identify the piston and rod to ensure correct reassembly. Discard the circlips – new ones must be used on refitting.

15 Examine the gudgeon pin and connecting rod small-end bearing for signs of wear or damage. Wear can be cured by renewing both the pin and bush (where possible) or connecting rod. Bush renewal, however, is a specialist job – press facilities are required, and the new bush must be reamed accurately.

16 The connecting rods themselves should not be in need of renewal, unless seizure or some other major mechanical failure has occurred. Check the alignment of the connecting rods visually, and if the rods are not straight, take them to an engine overhaul specialist for a more detailed check.

17 Examine all components, and obtain any new parts from your Peugeot/Citroën dealer. If new pistons are purchased, they will be supplied complete with gudgeon pins and circlips. These circlips can also be purchased individually.

18 Position the piston as shown **(see illustration)**.

12.18 Piston and connecting rod assembly

1 Connecting rod
2 Big-end shells
3 Big-end bolt
4 Piston rings
5 Gudgeon pin
6 Circlips

13.2 The crankshaft endfloat can be checked with a dial gauge ...

13.3 ... or with feeler gauges

14.2 Typical bearing failures

19 Ensure the piston and connecting rod are correctly positioned then apply a smear of clean engine oil to the gudgeon pin. Slide it into the piston and through the connecting rod small-end. Check that the piston pivots freely on the rod, then secure the gudgeon pin in position with two new circlips. Ensure that each circlip is correctly located in its groove in the piston.

13 Crankshaft – inspection

Checking endfloat

1 If the crankshaft endfloat is to be checked, this must be done when the crankshaft is still installed in the cylinder block/crankcase, but is free to move (see Section 10).
2 Check the endfloat using a dial gauge in contact with the end of the crankshaft. Push the crankshaft fully one way, and then zero the gauge. Push the crankshaft fully the other way, and check the endfloat. The result can be compared with the specified amount, and will give an indication as to whether new thrustwashers are required **(see illustration)**.
3 If a dial gauge is not available, feeler blades can be used. First push the crankshaft fully towards the flywheel end of the engine, and then use feeler blades to measure the gap between the web of No 2 crankpin and the thrustwasher **(see illustration)**.

Inspection

4 Clean the crankshaft using paraffin or a suitable solvent, and dry it, preferably with compressed air if available. Be sure to clean the oil holes with a pipe cleaner or similar probe, to ensure that they are not obstructed.

 Warning: Wear eye protection when using compressed air.

5 Check the main and big-end bearing journals for uneven wear, scoring, pitting and cracking.
6 Big-end bearing wear is accompanied by distinct metallic knocking when the engine is running (particularly noticeable when the engine is pulling from low speed) and some loss of oil pressure.

7 Main bearing wear is accompanied by severe engine vibration and rumble – getting progressively worse as engine speed increases – and again by loss of oil pressure.
8 Check the bearing journal for roughness by running a finger lightly over the bearing surface. Any roughness (which will be accompanied by obvious bearing wear) indicates that the crankshaft requires regrinding (where possible) or renewal.
9 Check the oil seal contact surfaces at each end of the crankshaft for wear and damage. If the seal has worn a deep groove in the surface of the crankshaft, consult an engine overhaul specialist; repair may be possible, but otherwise a new crankshaft will be required.
10 Take the crankshaft to a Peugeot/Citroën dealer or engine reconditioning specialist to have it measured for journal wear. If excessive wear is evident, they will be able to advise you with regard to regrinding the crankshaft and supplying new bearing shells.
11 If the crankshaft has been reground, check for burrs around the crankshaft oil holes (the holes are usually chamfered, so burrs should not be a problem unless regrinding has been carried out carelessly). Remove any burrs with a fine file or scraper, and thoroughly clean the oil holes as described previously.
12 At the time of writing, it was not clear whether Peugeot/Citroën produce undersize bearing shells for all of these engines. On some engines, if the crankshaft journals have not already been reground, it may be possible to have the crankshaft reconditioned, and to fit undersize shells. If no undersize shells are available and the crankshaft has worn beyond the specified limits, it will have to be renewed. Consult your Peugeot/Citroën dealer or engine specialist for further information on parts availability.

14 Main and big-end bearings – inspection

1 Even though the main and big-end bearings should be renewed during the engine overhaul, the old bearings should be retained for close examination, as they may reveal

valuable information about the condition of the engine. The bearing shells are graded by thickness, the grade of each shell being indicated by the colour code marked on it.
2 Bearing failure can occur due to lack of lubrication, the presence of dirt or other foreign particles, overloading the engine, or corrosion **(see illustration)**. Regardless of the cause of bearing failure, the cause must be corrected (where applicable) before the engine is reassembled, to prevent it from happening again.
3 When examining the bearing shells, remove them from the cylinder block/crankcase, the main bearing ladder/caps (as appropriate), the connecting rods and the connecting rod big-end bearing caps. Lay them out on a clean surface in the same general position as their location in the engine. This will enable you to match any bearing problems with the corresponding crankshaft journal. Do not touch any shell's bearing surface with your fingers while checking it, or the delicate surface may be scratched.
4 Dirt and other foreign matter gets into the engine in a variety of ways. It may be left in the engine during assembly, or it may pass through filters or the crankcase ventilation system. It may get into the oil, and from there into the bearings. Metal chips from machining operations and normal engine wear are often present. Abrasives are sometimes left in engine components after reconditioning, especially when parts are not thoroughly cleaned using the proper cleaning methods. Whatever the source, these foreign objects often end up embedded in the soft bearing material, and are easily recognised. Large particles will not embed in the bearing, and will score or gouge the bearing and journal. The best prevention for this cause of bearing failure is to clean all parts thoroughly, and

keep everything spotlessly clean during engine assembly. Frequent and regular engine oil and filter changes are also recommended.

5 Lack of lubrication (or lubrication breakdown) has a number of interrelated causes. Excessive heat (which thins the oil), overloading (which squeezes the oil from the bearing face) and oil leakage (from excessive bearing clearances, worn oil pump or high engine speeds) all contribute to lubrication breakdown. Blocked oil passages, which usually are the result of misaligned oil holes in a bearing shell, will also oil-starve a bearing, and destroy it. When lack of lubrication is the cause of bearing failure, the bearing material is wiped or extruded from the steel backing of the bearing. Temperatures may increase to the point where the steel backing turns blue from overheating.

6 Driving habits can have a definite effect on bearing life. Full-throttle, low-speed operation (labouring the engine) puts very high loads on bearings, tending to squeeze out the oil film. These loads cause the bearings to flex, which produces fine cracks in the bearing face (fatigue failure). Eventually, the bearing material will loosen in pieces, and tear away from the steel backing.

7 Short-distance driving leads to corrosion of bearings, because insufficient engine heat is produced to drive off the condensed water and corrosive gases. These products collect in the engine oil, forming acid and sludge. As the oil is carried to the engine bearings, the acid attacks and corrodes the bearing material.

8 Incorrect bearing installation during engine assembly will lead to bearing failure as well. Tight-fitting bearings leave insufficient bearing running clearance, and will result in oil starvation. Dirt or foreign particles trapped behind a bearing shell result in high spots on the bearing, which lead to failure.

9 Do not touch any shell's bearing surface with your fingers during reassembly; there is a risk of scratching the delicate surface, or of depositing particles of dirt on it.

10 As mentioned at the beginning of this Section, the bearing shells should be renewed as a matter of course during engine overhaul; to do otherwise is false economy.

15 Engine overhaul – reassembly sequence

1 Before reassembly begins, ensure that all new parts have been obtained, and that all necessary tools are available. Read through the entire procedure to familiarise yourself with the work involved, and to ensure that all items necessary for reassembly of the engine are at hand. In addition to all normal tools and materials, thread-locking compound will be needed. A tube of suitable liquid sealant will also be required for the joint faces that are fitted without gaskets. It is recommended that the manufacturers own product(s) be used, which are specially formulated for this purpose; the relevant product names are quoted in the text of each Section where they are required.

2 In order to save time and avoid problems, engine reassembly can be carried out in the following order, referring to Chapter 2A or Chapter 2B unless otherwise stated:
a) *Crankshaft (see Section 17).*
b) *Piston/connecting rod assemblies (See Section 18).*
c) *Oil pump.*
d) *Sump.*
e) *Flywheel/driveplate.*
f) *Cylinder head.*
g) *Injection pump and mounting bracket (Chapter 4A Section 9).*
h) *Timing chain/belt tensioner pulley(s) and sprockets, and timing chain/belt.*
i) *Engine external components.*

3 At this stage, all engine components should be absolutely clean and dry, with all faults repaired. The components should be laid out (or in individual containers) on a completely clean work surface.

16 Piston rings – refitting

1 Before fitting new piston rings, the ring end gaps must be checked as follows.

2 Lay out the piston/connecting rod assemblies and the new piston ring sets, so that the ring sets will be matched with the same piston and cylinder during the end gap measurement and subsequent engine reassembly.

3 Insert the top ring into the first cylinder, and push it down the bore using the top of the piston. This will ensure that the ring remains square with the cylinder walls. Position the ring near the bottom of the cylinder bore, at the lower limit of ring travel. Note that the top and second compression rings are different. The second ring can be identified by its taper and the top ring has a chamfer on its upper/outer edge.

4 Measure the end gap using feeler blades.

5 Repeat the procedure with the ring at the top of the cylinder bore, at the upper limit of its travel **(see illustration)**, and compare the measurements with the figures given in the Specifications. If the end gaps are incorrect, check that you have the correct rings for your engine and for the cylinder bore size.

6 Repeat the checking procedure for each ring in the first cylinder, and then for the rings in the remaining cylinders. Remember to keep rings, pistons and cylinders matched up.

7 Once the ring end gaps have been checked and if necessary corrected, the rings can be fitted to the pistons.

8 Fit the oil control ring expander (where fitted) then install the ring. The ring gap should be positioned 180° from the expander gap.

9 The second and top rings are different and can be identified from their cross-sections; the top ring is symmetrical whilst the second ring is tapered. Fit the second ring, ensuring its identification (TOP) marking is facing upwards, and then install the top ring **(see illustrations)**. Arrange the second and top ring end gap so they are equally spaced 120° apart. **Note:** *Always follow any instructions supplied with the new piston ring sets – different manufacturers may specify different procedures. Do not mix up the top and second compression rings, as they have different cross-sections.*

16.5 Measure the piston rings end gaps with a feeler gauge

16.9a Piston ring fitting diagram (typical)

1 Oil control ring
2 Second compression ring
3 Top compression ring

16.9b Piston rings

1 Top compression ring
2 Second compression ring
3 Oil control ring

17 Crankshaft – refitting

Selection of bearing shells

1 Have the crankshaft inspected and measured by an engine reconditioning specialist. They will be able to carry out any regrinding/repairs, and supply suitable main and big-end bearing shells.

Crankshaft refitting

Note: *New main bearing cap/lower crankcase bolts must be used when refitting the crankshaft.*

2 Where applicable, ensure that the oil spray jets are fitted to the bearing locations in the cylinder block.

3 Place the bearing shells in their locations. If new shells are being fitted, ensure that all traces of protective grease are cleaned off using paraffin. Wipe dry the shells with a lint-free cloth. The upper bearing shells all have a grooved surface, whereas the lower shells have a plain surface. On these engines, it's essential that the lower bearing shells are centrally located in the bearing cap housing/ladder. To ensure this use Peugeot/Citroën tool No 0194-QZ positioned over the housing/ladder, and insert the bearing shells through the slots in the tool **(see illustration)**.

4 Liberally lubricate each bearing shell in the cylinder block with clean engine oil then lower the crankshaft into position.

5 Insert the thrustwashers to either side of No 2 main bearing upper location and push them around the bearing journal until their edges are horizontal **(see illustration)**. Ensure that the oilway grooves on each thrustwasher face outwards (away from the bearing journal).

6 Thoroughly degrease the mating surfaces of the cylinder block and the crankshaft

17.3 Main bearing shell refitment

1 *Bearing shell*   3 *Citroën tool*
2 *Main bearing ladder*   4 *Aligning pins*

bearing cap housing. Apply a thin bead of RTV sealant to the bearing cap housing mating surface **(see illustration)**. Peugeot/Citroën recommend the use of Loctite Autojoint Noir for this purpose.

7 Lubricate the lower bearing shells with clean engine oil, then refit the bearing cap housing, ensuring that the shells are not displaced, and that the locating dowels engage correctly.

8 Install the ten large diameter and sixteen smaller diameter crankshaft bearing cap housing retaining bolts, and screw them in until they are just making contact with the housing.

9 Working in sequence, tighten the bolts to the torque settings given in Chapter 2A or Chapter 2B **(see illustration)**.

10 With the bearing cap housing in place, check that the crankshaft rotates freely.

11 Refit the piston/connecting rod assemblies to the crankshaft as described in Section 18.

12 Refit the oil pump and sump, as described in Chapter 2A and Chapter 2B.

13 Fit a new crankshaft left-hand oil seal, then refit the flywheel, as described in Chapter 2A and Chapter 2B.

17.5 Place the thrustwashers each side of the No 2 bearing upper location

14 Refit the cylinder head (where removed) and also refit the crankshaft sprocket and timing belt.

18 Piston/connecting rod assembly – refitting

Note: *New big-end cap nuts/bolts must be used on refitting.*

1 Clean the backs of the bearing shells, and the bearing locations in both the connecting rod and bearing cap.

2 Lubricate the cylinder bores, the pistons and piston rings, then lay out each piston/connecting rod assembly in its respective position.

3 Start with assembly No 1. Make sure that the piston rings are still spaced as described in Section 16, and then clamp them in position with a piston ring compressor.

4 Insert the piston/connecting rod assembly into the top of cylinder number 1; ensuring the DIST mark or arrow on the piston crown is towards the timing belt end of the engine.

5 Once the piston is correctly positioned, using a block of wood or hammer handle against the piston crown, tap the assembly

17.6 Apply a thin bead of RTV sealant to the bearing cap housing mating surface

17.9 Main bearing ladder bolts tightening sequence

18.5 Tap the piston into the bore using a hammer handle

H44712

18.7 Big-end bearing shell positioning

1 Tool No 0194-P   2 Bearing shell

into the cylinder until the piston crown is flush with the top of the cylinder **(see illustration)**.

6 The connecting rod is made in one piece, and the big-end bearing cap is 'cracked' off. This ensures that the cap fits onto the connecting rod only in one position, and with maximum rigidity. Consequently, there are no locating notches for the bearing shells to fit into.

7 To ensure that the big-end bearing shells are centrally located in the connecting rod and cap, two special tools are available from Peugeot/Citroën. These half-moon shaped tools are pressed in from either side of the rod/cap and locate the shell exactly in the centre **(see illustration)**. Fit the shells into the connecting rods and big-end caps and lubricate them with plenty of clean engine oil.

8 Pull the connecting rods and pistons down the bores and onto the crankshaft journals. Fit the big-end caps – they will only fit properly one way round (see paragraph 10), and insert the new bolts.

9 Tighten the bolts to the Stage 1 torque setting, then slacken them 180° (Stage 2). Tighten the bolts to the Stage 3 setting, followed by the Stage 4 angle-tightening setting.

10 Once the bearing cap retaining nuts have been correctly tightened, rotate the crankshaft. Check that it turns freely; some stiffness is to be expected if new components have been fitted, but there should be no signs of binding or tight spots.

11 Refit the cylinder head and oil pump as described in Chapter 2A or Chapter 2B (as applicable).

19 Engine – initial start-up after overhaul

1 With the engine refitted in the vehicle, double-check the engine oil and coolant levels. Make a final check that everything has

been reconnected, and that there are no tools or rags left in the engine compartment.

2 On the models covered in this Manual, the oil pressure warning light is linked to the STOP warning light, and is not illuminated when the ignition is initially switched on. Therefore it is not possible to check the oil pressure warning light when turning the engine on the starter motor.

3 Prime the fuel system (refer to Chapter 4A Section 3).

4 Fully depress the accelerator pedal, turn the ignition key to position M, and wait for the preheating warning light to go out.

5 Start the engine, noting that this may take a little longer than usual, due to the fuel system components having been disturbed.

6 While the engine is idling, check for fuel, water and oil leaks. Don't be alarmed if there are some odd smells and smoke from parts getting hot and burning off oil deposits.

7 Assuming all is well; keep the engine idling until hot water is felt circulating through the top hose, then switch off the engine.

8 After a few minutes, recheck the oil and coolant levels as described in *Weekly checks*, and top-up as necessary.

9 Note that there is no need to retighten the cylinder head bolts once the engine has first run after reassembly.

10 If new pistons, rings or crankshaft bearings have been fitted, the engine must be treated as new, and run-in for the first 500 miles. Do not operate the engine at full-throttle, or allow it to labour at low engine speeds in any gear. It is recommended that the oil and filter be changed at the end of this period.

Chapter 3
Cooling, heating and ventilation systems

Contents

Degrees of difficulty

| Easy, suitable for novice with little experience | | Fairly easy, suitable for beginner with some experience | Fairly difficult, suitable for competent DIY mechanic | Difficult, suitable for experienced DIY mechanic | Very difficult, suitable for expert DIY or professional | |

Specifications

General

Maximum system pressure	1.4 bars
Engine coolant temperature sensor resistance (approx):	
60°C	1266 ohms
80°C	642 ohms

Thermostat

Start of opening temperature.	83°C

Air conditioning compressor oil

Quantity	135 cc
Type	Sanden SP10

Note: *DENSO ND8 oil is compatible with SANDEN SP10 oil*

Compressor

All engines	SD 7C 16

Refrigerant

Quantity	450 ± 25 g
Type	R134a

Torque wrench settings

	Nm	lbf ft
Air conditioning compressor mounting bolts	25	18
Coolant outlet housing:		
Stage 1	3	
Stage 2	8	
Coolant pump:		
Stage1	5	
Stage 2	9	

1 General information and precautions

1 The cooling system is of pressurised type, comprising a coolant pump driven by the timing belt, an aluminium radiator, an expansion tank, an electric cooling fan, a thermostat, a heater matrix, and all associated hoses and switches.
2 The system functions as follows. Cold coolant in the bottom of the radiator passes through the bottom hose to the coolant pump, where it is pumped around the cylinder block and head passages. After cooling the cylinder bores, combustion surfaces and valve seats, the coolant reaches the underside of the thermostat, which is initially closed. The coolant passes through the heater, and is returned via the cylinder block to the coolant pump.
3 When the engine is cold, the coolant circulates only through the cylinder block, cylinder head, and heater. When the coolant reaches a predetermined temperature, the thermostat opens, and the coolant passes through the top hose to the radiator. As the coolant passes down through the radiator, it is cooled by the inrush of air when the car is in forward motion. The airflow is supplemented by the action of the electric cooling fan when necessary. Upon reaching the bottom of the radiator, the coolant has now cooled, and the cycle is repeated.
4 On models with automatic transmission, a proportion of the coolant is recirculated through the transmission fluid cooler mounted on the transmission. On models fitted with an engine oil cooler, the coolant is also passed through the oil cooler.
5 The operation of the electric cooling fan(s) is controlled by the engine management control unit.

⚠ *Warning: Do not attempt to remove the expansion tank filler cap, or to disturb any part of the cooling system, while the engine is hot, as there is a high risk of scalding. If the expansion tank filler cap must be removed before the engine and radiator*

have fully cooled (even though this is not recommended), the pressure in the cooling system must first be relieved. Cover the cap with a thick layer of cloth to avoid scalding, and slowly unscrew the filler cap until a hissing sound is heard. When the hissing has stopped, indicating that the pressure has reduced, slowly unscrew the filler cap until it can be removed; if more hissing sounds are heard, wait until they have stopped before unscrewing the cap. At all times keep well away from the filler cap opening, and protect your hands.

⚠ *Warning: Do not allow antifreeze to come into contact with your skin, or with the painted surfaces of the vehicle. Rinse off spills immediately, with plenty of water. Never leave antifreeze lying around in an open container, or in a puddle in the driveway or on the garage floor. Children and pets are attracted by its sweet smell, but antifreeze can be fatal if ingested.*

⚠ *Warning: If the engine is hot, the electric cooling fan(s) may start rotating even if the engine is not running. Be careful to keep your hands, hair, and any loose clothing well clear when working in the engine compartment.*

⚠ *Warning: Refer to Section 11 for precautions to be observed when working on models equipped with air conditioning.*

2 Cooling system hoses – disconnection and renewal 🔧

Note: *Refer to the warnings given in Section 1 of this Chapter before proceeding. Hoses should only be disconnected once the engine has cooled sufficiently to avoid scalding.*
1 If the checks described in the hose and fluid leak check in Chapter 1 Section 3 reveal a faulty hose, it must be renewed as follows.
2 First drain the cooling system (see Chapter 1 Section 19). If the coolant is not due for renewal, it may be re-used, providing it is collected in a clean container.

3 To disconnect a hose, proceed as follows, according to the type of hose connection.

Conventional connections

4 On conventional connections, the clips used to secure the hoses in position may be either standard worm-drive clips, spring clips or disposable crimped types. The crimped type of clip is not designed to be re-used and should be updated with a worm-drive type on reassembly. The clips mainly used by Peugeot/Citroen are of the spring clip type **(see illustration)**.
5 To disconnect a hose, release the retaining clips and move them along the hose, clear of the relevant inlet/outlet. Carefully work the hose free. The hoses can be removed with relative ease when new – on an older car they may have stuck **(see illustration)**.
6 If a hose proves to be difficult to remove, try to release it by rotating its ends before attempting to free it. Gently prise the end of the hose with a blunt instrument (such as a flat-bladed screwdriver), but do not apply too much force, and take care not to damage the pipe stubs or hoses. Note in particular that the radiator inlet stub is fragile; do not use excessive force when attempting to remove the hose. If all else fails, cut the hose with a sharp knife, then slit it so that it can be peeled off in two pieces. Although this may prove expensive if the hose is otherwise undamaged, it is preferable to buying a new radiator. Check first, however, that a new hose is readily available.
7 When fitting a hose, first slide the clips onto the hose, and then work the hose into position. If crimped-type clips were originally fitted, use standard worm-drive clips when refitting the hose.
8 Work the hose into position, checking that it is correctly routed, and the alignment markings **(see illustration)** on the hoses, are in line with the markings on the coolant pipe stubs. Once in position, slide each clip back along the hose until it passes over the flared end of the relevant inlet/outlet, before tightening the clip securely.
9 Refill the cooling system (see Chapter 1 Section 19).

2.4 Spring clip type upper hose retaining clip

2.5 Release the retaining clip and move it along the hose

2.8 Hose alignment markings (arrowed)

2.12 Where click-fit connectors are used, prise out the circlip then disconnect the hose

2.13 Ensure the sealing ring and circlip (arrowed) are correctly fitted to the hose union before reconnecting a connector

3.2 Squeeze the clips to disconnect the coolant pipe

10 Check thoroughly for leaks as soon as possible after disturbing any part of the cooling system.

Click-fit connections

Note: New sealing ring should be used when reconnecting the hose.
11 On certain models, some cooling system hoses are secured in position with click-fit connectors where the hose is retained by a large circlip.
12 To disconnect this type of hose fitting, carefully prise the wire clip out of position then disconnect the hose connection **(see illustration)**. Once the hose has been disconnected, refit the wire clip to the hose union. Inspect the hose unit sealing ring for signs of damage or deterioration and renew if necessary.
13 On refitting, ensure that the sealing ring is in position and the wire clip is correctly located in the groove in the union **(see illustration)**. Lubricate the sealing ring with a smear of soapy water, to ease installation, and then push the hose into its union until it is heard to click into position.
14 Ensure the hose is securely retained by the wire clip then refill the cooling system as described in Chapter 1 Section 19.
15 Check thoroughly for leaks as soon as possible after disturbing any part of the cooling system.

3.3 Disconnect the sensor wiring connector

3 Coolant expansion tank – removal and refitting

Removal

1 Referring to Chapter 1 Section 19, drain the cooling system sufficiently to empty the contents of the expansion tank. Do not drain any more coolant than is necessary.
2 Squeeze together the collar, and then pull the plastic hose from the top of the expansion tank **(see illustration)**.
3 Disconnect the level sensor wiring plug – where fitted **(see illustration)**.
4 Unscrew the mounting bolt and free

3.4 Coolant reservoir mounting bolt (arrowed)

the tank from its mount **(see illustration)**. Withdraw the expansion tank forwards from the mounting rubbers in the mounting bracket. Lift the expansion tank upwards to access the lower coolant hose.
5 Release the securing clip and disconnect the remaining hose from the bottom of the expansion tank, as it is removed.

Refitting

6 Refitting is the reverse of removal, ensuring the hoses are securely reconnected. On completion, top-up the coolant level as described in *Weekly checks*.

4 Radiator – removal, inspection and refitting

Note: If leakage is the reason for removing the radiator, bear in mind that minor leaks can often be cured using a radiator sealant with the radiator still in position.

Removal

1 Drain the cooling system (see Chapter 1 Section 19).
2 Remove the front bumper as described in Chapter 11 Section 6.
3 Release the retaining clips and disconnect the upper and lower coolant hoses from the radiator **(see illustrations)**. The lower hose may have already been removed to drain the cooling system, see paragraph 1.

4.3a Disconnect the upper hose retaining clip (arrowed) …

4.3b … and the lower radiator hose retaining clip (arrowed)

4.4 Squeeze the clips to disconnect the coolant pipe (arrowed)

4.5a Undo the radiator upper mounting screws (arrowed)…

4.5b …and remove the upper mounting brackets

4 Squeeze together the collar, then pull the plastic hose to disconnect it from the top of the radiator **(see illustration)**.

5 Slacken and remove the retaining screws securing the radiator upper mounting brackets to the front panel. Move the radiator away from the front panel and unclip both brackets from the top of the radiator **(see illustrations)**.

6 On models with air-conditioning, unclip the condenser from the front of the radiator, then carefully lift the radiator out of position, taking care not to damage the radiator fins.

Inspection

7 If the radiator has been removed due to suspected blockage, reverse-flush it as described in Chapter 1 Section 19. Clean dirt and debris from the radiator fins, using an airline (in which case, wear eye protection) or a soft brush. Be careful, as the fins are sharp, and easily damaged.

8 If necessary, a radiator specialist can perform a 'flow test' on the radiator, to establish whether an internal blockage exists.

9 A leaking radiator must be referred to a specialist for permanent repair. Do not attempt to weld or solder a leaking radiator, as damage to the plastic components may result.

10 Inspect the condition of the radiator mounting rubbers, and renew them if necessary. Check that the two radiator

lower mounting rubbers are in position **(see illustration)**, before refitting.

Refitting

11 Refitting is a reversal of removal, bearing in mind the following points:
a) *Ensure that the lower lugs on the radiator are correctly engaged with the mounting rubbers in the body panel*
b) *Reconnect the hoses with reference to Section 2, using new sealing rings where applicable.*
c) *On completion, refill the cooling system as described in Chapter 1 Section 19.*

5 Thermostat – removal, testing and refitting

Removal

1 The thermostat is located in the coolant outlet housing on the left-hand end of the cylinder head. On all later models the thermostat is integral with the housing, requiring removal of the complete housing.

2 Drain the cooling system (see Chapter 1 Section 19).

3 To make access easier remove the air cleaner ducting as described in Chapter 4A Section 4 and also the battery as described in Chapter 5A Section 4.

4 Unclip the plastic wiring loom support from the top of the housing by releasing the lower securing clip **(see illustration)**. As the loom is moved to one side, disconnect the wiring connector(s) from the sensor(s) at the rear of the coolant housing.

5 Note the fitted position of the hoses on the coolant housing, and then release the securing clips to disconnect them.

6 Unscrew the four retaining bolts, and then remove the housing from the left-hand end of the cylinder head. Recover the gasket/seal a new one will be required for refitting.

Testing

7 A rough test of the thermostat may be made by suspending it with a piece of string in a container full of water. Heat the water to bring it to the boil – the thermostat must open by the time the water boils. If not, renew it.

8 If a thermometer is available, the precise opening temperature of the thermostat may be determined; compare with the figures given in the Specifications. The opening temperature may also be marked on the thermostat.

9 A thermostat which fails to close as the water cools must also be renewed.

Refitting

10 Refitting is a reversal of removal, bearing in mind the following points.
a) *Renew the coolant housing gasket/seal.*

4.10 Radiator lower rubber mounting (one side arrowed)

5.4 Release the wiring support securing clip (arrowed)

6.2 Release the securing clip (arrowed)

6.3 Unclip the louvered vent panel

6.4a Undo the four cooling fan bolts (arrowed) ...

b) *Make sure all wiring connectors are fitted securely.*
c) *On completion, refill the cooling system as described in Chapter 1 Section 19.*

8 Disconnect the two wiring connectors from the fan control resistor, note the locking clip has to be released on the lower connector before it can be disconnected **(see illustration)**.

9 Undo the retaining screw, and then remove the resistor from the front panel **(see illustrations)**.

Refitting

10 Refitting is a reversal of removal.

6 Electric cooling fan and resistor – removal and refitting

Removal

1 Remove the front bumper as described in Chapter 11 Section 6.

Cooling fan

2 Release the locking clip, then disconnect the fan wiring plug connector and release it from the securing clip on the radiator front panel **(see illustration)**.
3 Unclip the louvered vent panel from the radiator front panel to allow for the wiring to be withdrawn **(see illustration)**.
4 Slacken and remove the four bolts and washers securing the cooling fan to the radiator front panel. Recover the collar from the rear of each mounting rubber **(see illustrations)**.
5 Remove the cooling fan from the front panel, and withdraw the fan and wiring out from the front panel **(see illustrations)**.

Cooling fan resistor

6 The cooling fan resistor is fitted to the radiator front panel and is located next to the cooling fan.
7 Unclip the plastic cover from the front panel **(see illustration)**.

6.4b ... noting the collars fitted to the bolts for refitting

6.5a Remove the fan from the front panel

6.5b ... and withdraw the wiring connector from the front panel

6.7 Unclip the plastic cover from the resistor

6.8 Securing clip (arrowed) on lower connector

6.9a Undo the retaining screw ...

6.9b ... and remove the cooling fan resistor

7 Cooling system electrical sensors – general information, removal and refitting

General information

1 The coolant temperature sensor is fitted to the coolant housing on the left-hand end of the cylinder head (see Section 5). The coolant temperature gauge and the cooling fan are all operated by the engine management ECM (Electronic Control Module), using the signal supplied by this sensor.

2 To make access easier remove the air cleaner ducting as described in Chapter 4A Section 4 and also the battery as described in Chapter 5A Section 4.

Removal

Note: *Ensure the engine is cold before removing a temperature sensor.*

3 Partially drain the cooling system to just below the level of the sensor (as described in Chapter 1 Section 19). Alternatively, have ready a suitable bung to plug the sensor aperture whilst the sensor is removed. If this method is used, take great care not to damage the switch aperture or use anything that will allow foreign matter to enter the cooling system.

4 Disconnect the wiring connector from the sensor **(see illustration)**. **Note:** *Depending on model, the sensor may be on the front or rear of the coolant housing.*

5 The sensor is clipped in place; prise out the sensor retaining circlip, and then remove the sensor and sealing ring from the housing. If the system has not been drained, plug the sensor aperture to prevent further coolant loss.

Refitting

6 Fit a new sealing ring to the sensor, and then apply some lubricant (coolant) to the seal to aid refitting. Push the sensor firmly into the housing and secure it in position with the circlip, ensuring it is correctly located in the housing groove.

7 Reconnect the wiring connector then refit any components removed from access. Refit the air cleaner and if removed, refit the battery.

8 Top-up the cooling system as described in *Weekly checks*.

8 Coolant pump – removal and refitting

1 Drain the cooling system (see Chapter 1 Section 19).

2 Remove the timing belt as described in Chapter 2A Section 7 or Chapter 2B Section 7

3 Slacken and remove the retaining bolts from the coolant pump in the reverse order of the tightening sequence shown **(see illustration 8.5)**, then withdraw it from the cylinder block. Recover the pump sealing ring/gasket (as applicable) and discard it; a new one must be used on refitting. **Note:** *The sealing ring may not be available separately from the pump – check with your Peugeot/Citroën dealer.*

4 Ensure that the pump and cylinder block/housing mating surfaces are clean and dry.

5 Fit the new sealing ring/gasket (as applicable) to the pump, and then refit the pump assembly, tightening its retaining bolts in the correct sequence **(see illustration)** to the specified torque setting.

6 Refit the timing belt as described in Chapter 2A Section 7 or Chapter 2B Section 7.

7 Refill the cooling system as described in Chapter 1 Section 19 (as applicable).

9 Heating and ventilation system – general information

Note: *Refer to Section 11 for information on the air conditioning side of the system.*

Manually-controlled system

1 The heating/ventilation system consists of a four-speed blower motor (housed behind the right-hand side of the fascia), face level vents in the centre and at each end of the fascia, and air ducts to the front footwells.

2 The control unit is located in the fascia, and the controls operate flap valves to deflect and mix the air flowing through the various parts of the heating/ventilation system. The flap valves are contained in the air distribution housing, which acts as a central distribution unit, passing air to the various ducts and vents.

3 Cold air enters the system through the grille in the scuttle. If required, the airflow is boosted by the blower, and then flows through the various ducts, according to the settings of the controls. Stale air is expelled through ducts at the rear of the vehicle. If warm air is required, the cold air is passed over the heater matrix, which is heated by the engine coolant.

4 A recirculation button enables the outside air supply to be closed off, while the air inside the vehicle is recirculated. This can be useful to prevent unpleasant odours entering from outside the vehicle, but should only be used briefly, as the recirculated air inside the vehicle will soon become stale.

5 On some models an electric heater is fitted into the heater housing. When the coolant temperature is cold, the heater warms the air before it enters the heater matrix. This quickly increases the temperature of the heater matrix on cold starts, resulting in warm air being available to heat the vehicle interior soon after start-up.

Automatic climate control

6 A fully automatic electronic climate control system was offered as an option on some models. The main components of the system are exactly the same as those described for the manual system, the only major difference being that the temperature and distribution flaps in the heating/ventilation housing are operated by electric motors rather than cables.

7 The operation of the system is controlled

7.4 Temperature sensor (arrowed) – shown on front of housing

8.5 Coolant pump tightening sequence

9.9 Vehicle diagnostic plug connector (arrowed)

10.1 Unclip the trim cover and remove the screws (arrowed)

10.2 Remove the control panel

by the electronic control module (which is incorporated in the blower motor assembly) along with the following sensors.

a) *The passenger compartment sensor – informs the control module of the temperature of the air inside the passenger compartment.*

b) *Evaporator temperature sensor – informs the control module of the evaporator temperature.*

c) *Heater matrix temperature sensor – informs the control module of the heater matrix temperature.*

8 Using the information from the above sensors, the control module determines the appropriate settings for the heating/ventilation system housing flaps to maintain the passenger compartment at the desired setting on the control panel.

9 If the system develops a fault, the vehicle should be taken to a Peugeot/Citroën dealer. A complete test of the system can then be carried out, using a special electronic diagnostic test unit, which is simply plugged into the system's diagnostic connector. This is located inside the glovebox compartment **(see illustration)**.

---

10 Heater/ventilation components – removal and refitting

Control panel

1 Carefully unclip the trim panel from below

the heater control panel, and then undo the two retaining screws **(see illustration)**.

2 Push the control panel inside the facia and manoeuvre it out through the aperture **(see illustration)** complete with wiring and control cables (on manually-operated system). if required, to make access easier, remove the switch panel from below the heater control panel as described in Chapter 11 Section 28

3 Disconnect the wiring connectors from the rear of the control panel **(see illustration)**.

4 On manually-operated systems, note the position of the control cables, then release the securing clips from the outer cables and unhook the inner cable from the operating levers on the control panel **(see illustration)**.

5 Refitting is the reverse of removal. On manually-operated systems, ensure the control cables are correctly reconnected and securely held by the retaining clips; check the operation of the control knobs before refitting the trim panels and switch panel (where removed).

Control cables – manually operated system

6 Remove the control panel as described previously in this Section.

7 Before disconnecting the cables from the rear of the control panel note their fitted position. The cable with the black outer cable connects to the black operating lever (temperature control), and the cable with the white outer cable connects to the white operating lever (air flow direction control).

8 Release the retaining clip and then detach the relevant cable from the lever on the rear of the control panel **(see illustrations)**.

9 To access the lower end of the cable on the passenger side, remove the glovebox as described in Chapter 11 Section 28

10 Unclip the heater ducting from the side of the heater housing **(see illustration)**.

11 Unclip the outer cable from the retaining clip and then detach the inner cable from the

10.3 Disconnect the wiring connectors

10.4 Release the securing clips (arrowed)

10.8a Release the securing clip...

10.8b ... and disconnect the inner cable from the operating lever

10.10 Removing the heater ducting

10.11 Heater control cable on side of heater housing

10.14 Using hose clamps to prevent the loss of fluid

10.15 Press in the locking clips (arrowed) to release the heater hoses

10.16a Remove the heater pipe retaining plate ...

lever on the heater housing **(see illustration)**. The cable can then be withdrawn out from the facia panel.

12 Refitting is the reverse of removal, ensuring the cable is routed correctly and secured in place by its retaining clips. Check the operation of the control panel and cables.

Heater matrix

13 To improve access to the matrix unions on the bulkhead, remove the battery as described in Chapter 5A Section 4. Where necessary also remove the air cleaner housing intake duct (see Chapter 4A Section 4).

14 Drain the cooling system (see Chapter 1 Section 19). Alternatively, clamp the heater matrix coolant hoses to minimise coolant loss **(see illustration)**.

15 Release the retaining clips and disconnect

10.16b ... and bulkhead rubber seal

the coolant hoses from the heater matrix pipe unions on the engine compartment bulkhead **(see illustration)**. Press on the locking clips to release the heater hoses. **Note:** *To help evacuate the heater matrix of coolant, an air gun can be used at the inlet pipe, to blow the coolant through the matrix. At the outlet pipe, catch the coolant in a container, to prevent it going over the engine compartment.*

16 Slacken and remove the screw securing the heater matrix pipe unions on the engine compartment bulkhead **(see illustrations)**.

17 Remove the glovebox assembly, as described in, Chapter 11 Section 28.

18 Unclip the heater ducting from the side of the heater housing **(see illustration 10.10)**.

19 Position a container or some rags inside the passenger footwell, beneath the heater matrix pipe union to catch any spilt coolant.

20 Undo the retaining bolt, and remove the

wiring loom mounting bracket from around the two heater pipes, at the side of the heater housing **(see illustration)**. Move the wiring loom and bracket to one side.

21 Undo the retaining bolt, and remove the mounting bracket from around the two heater pipes, at the rear of the heater housing **(see illustration)**.

22 Release the retaining clamps from around the two heater pipe connections to the heater matrix **(see illustration)**.

23 Carefully free the heater pipes from the matrix, catching any spilt coolant as the pipes are disconnected. Recover any sealing rings (where applicable) fitted to the pipe unions and discard them; new ones should be used on refitting. If required, the coolant pipes can be withdrawn from the bulkhead.

24 Release the retaining clips and slide the matrix out from the heater housing. Keep the matrix unions uppermost as the matrix is removed to prevent any coolant spillage.

25 On refitting, ease the matrix into the housing, until it is fitted securely in the heater housing.

26 Fit a new sealing ring (where applicable) to each of the pipe unions, and then manoeuvre the pipes into position and secure them to the matrix with the retaining clamps.

27 Make sure the heater pipes are located correctly at the bulkhead, and then refit the mounting bracket to the rear of the heater housing and tighten the securing bolt. Also refit the wiring loom mounting bracket around the heater pipes, and tighten the securing bolt.

10.20 Undo the retaining bolt (arrowed)

10.21 Undo the retaining bolt (arrowed)

10.22 Release the two retaining clamps (arrowed)

10.33 Remove the trim panel

10.34a Remove the screws (arrowed) – upper bolt behind facia

10.34b Removing the blower motor – front panel removed for clarity

28 Working inside the engine compartment, refit the seal and retaining plate to the top end of the matrix pipes at the bulkhead.

29 Reconnect the heater coolant hoses, securing them in position with the retaining clips. Where fitted, remove the clamps from the heater hoses and refill the cooling system (see Chapter 1 Section 19).

30 Refit the battery (see Chapter 5A Section 4).

31 Working back inside the passenger side front footwell, refit the heater ducting to the side of the heater housing and refit the glovebox assembly, as described in Chapter 11 Section 28

Heater blower motor

32 The blower motor is fitted to part of the heating/ventilation housing, located on the right-hand side, above the accelerator pedal.

33 Working inside the drivers side footwell, release the securing clips and remove the trim panel from under the facia above the pedal assembly **(see illustration)**.

34 Disconnect the wiring connector from the blower motor, undo the four retaining screws and lower the heater blower motor out from under the facia **(see illustrations)**.

35 Refitting is the reverse of removal.

Heater blower motor resistor

36 The resistor is located at the side of the heater blower motor, in the heater housing **(see illustration)**.

37 Working inside the drivers side footwell, release the securing clips and remove the trim panel from under the facia above the pedal assembly **(see illustration 10.33)**.

38 Reach under the facia and disconnect the wiring connector from the resistor.

39 Undo the retaining bolt and withdraw the resistor from the heater housing **(see illustration)**.

40 To refit manoeuvre the resistor into position in the heater housing and tighten the securing screw. Connect the wiring connector and refit any components removed for access.

Housing assembly

Models without air conditioning

41 To improve access to the matrix unions on the bulkhead, remove the battery as described in Chapter 5A Section 4. Where necessary also remove the air cleaner housing intake duct (see Chapter 4A Section 4).

42 Drain the cooling system (see Chapter 1 Section 19). Alternatively, working in the engine compartment, clamp the heater matrix coolant hoses to minimise coolant loss.

43 Release the retaining clips and disconnect the coolant hoses from the heater matrix pipe unions on the engine compartment bulkhead **(see illustration 10.15)**.

44 Slacken and remove the screw securing the heater matrix pipes to the bulkhead and remove the retaining plate and seal **(see illustrations 10.16a and 10.16b)**.

45 Slacken and remove the bolt securing the heating/ventilation housing to the bulkhead **(see illustration)**.

46 Remove the facia assembly as described in, Chapter 11 Section 28.

47 Disconnect the wiring connectors from the heating/ventilation housing components then remove the housing assembly from the vehicle. Keep the heater matrix pipe unions uppermost as the assembly is removed to prevent coolant spillage.

48 Recover the seal and retaining plate from the heater matrix pipes, and the seal from the housing mounting. Renew the seals if they show signs of damage or deterioration.

49 Refitting is the reverse of removal ensuring the seals are in position on the pipes and housing mounting. On completion, refill the cooling system (see Chapter 1 Section 19).

Models with air conditioning

⚠ *Warning: Refer to Section 11 for precautions to be observed when working on models equipped with air conditioning. Do not attempt the following procedure unless the system has been professionally discharged.*

50 Have the air conditioning system discharged by an air conditioning specialist and obtain some plugs to seal the air conditioning pipe unions whilst the system is disconnected.

51 Carry out the operations described in paragraphs 41 to 44.

10.36 Location of blower motor resistor (arrowed)

10.39 Withdraw the resistor

10.45 Heater/ventilation housing retaining bolt (arrowed)

10.52 Undo the two nuts (arrowed) securing the air conditioning pipes

10.63 Location of additional heater (arrowed) – where fitted

52 Unscrew the two nuts securing the air conditioning pipe union to the bulkhead **(see illustration)**. Separate the pipes from the evaporator and quickly seal the pipe and evaporator unions to prevent the entry of moisture into the refrigerant circuit. Discard the sealing rings, new ones must be used on refitting.

⚠ *Warning: Failure to seal the refrigerant pipe unions will result in the dehydrator reservoir become saturated, necessitating its renewal.*

53 Remove the heating/ventilation housing assembly as described in paragraphs 45 to 48 and recover the seal from the evaporator.
54 Ensure the bulkhead seals are correctly fitted to the evaporator, matrix pipes and housing mounting. Manoeuvre the housing assembly into position, locating the housing drain hose correctly in its hole in the floor.
55 Loosely refit the housing mounting bolt then refit the retaining plate to the heater matrix pipe and loosely install the retaining screw.
56 Lubricate the new evaporator union sealing rings with compressor oil. Remove the plugs and install the sealing rings then quickly fit the refrigerant pipe union to the evaporator. Ensure the refrigerant pipes and evaporator

are correctly joined then refit the retaining nuts and tighten them securely.
57 Tighten the matrix pipe retaining screw securely and securely tighten the housing mounting bolt.
58 The remainder of refitting is the reverse of removal. On completion, refill the cooling system (see Chapter 1 Section 19).

Interior air temperature sensor

59 Depending on model, there may be two air temperature sensors fitted, to the rear left- and right-hand sides of the heater housing.
60 Remove centre console as described in Chapter 11, Section 27, and then remove the trims from under the facia in each of the footwells. Also to make access easier on the left-hand side of the ehater housing, remove the glovebox as described in Chapter 11 Section 28
61 Disconnect the wiring plug connector and then turn the sensor a quarter of a turn anti-clockwise to remove it from the heater housing.
62 Refitting is a reversal of removal.

Additional heater

63 Depending on model, there may be an additional heater fitted, to the left-hand side of the heater housing, next to the heater matrix **(see illustration)**.

64 On right-hand drive models, remove the glovebox as described in Chapter 11 Section 28
65 On left-hand drive models, remove the trim panel above the pedals, undo the two fasteners and remove the trim panel at the front of the centre console, adjacent to the pedals.
66 Unclip the heater ducting from the side of the heater housing**(see illustration 10.10)**.
67 Slide the locking clip downwards to release the wiring plug connector, and then disconnect it from the heater element **(see illustration)**.
68 Undo the retaining bolt/screw, and slide the heater element out from the housing **(see illustrations)**.
69 Refitting is the reverse of removal.

Air control motors

70 On models with an automatic (climate control) heater control system, there may be a number of control motors fitted to the heater housing assembly. On manually-operated heater systems, control cables operate the heater flaps.
71 Remove the glovebox and passenger's side central kick panel to access the control motors on the left-hand side of the heater housing.
72 Remove the steering column lower trim

10.67 Pull down on the locking clip (arrowed) to release wiring

10.68a Remove the bolt/screw...

10.68b ...and withdraw the heater element

10.73a Disconnect the wiring connector ...

10.73b ... and undo the retaining screws (arrowed)

10.74 Air flap control motor (arrowed)

panels and driver's side central kick panel to gain access to the control motors on the right-hand side of the heater housing.

73 Disconnect the wiring plug from the control motor, then undo the retaining bolts, and remove it from the side of the heater housing (**see illustrations**).

74 All models have an air flap control motor fitted to the heater housing above the air blower motor (**see illustration**).

75 Refitting is a reversal of removal.

Ambient temperature sensor

76 The ambient temperature sensor is located on the underside of the driver's side exterior door mirror. To remove the sensor, remove the mirror upper and lower rear covers as described in Chapter 11, Section 19.

77 Twist the sensor and unclip it from the mirror housing (**see illustrations**). To renew or remove the sensor completely, the two wires going to the sensor will need to be cut, as they go into the door wiring harness. The wires must be cut about 30 mm away from the sensor.

78 When refitting the new sensor, make sure the connections are made correctly, and insulated using a heat-shrink sleeve.

Rain/Sunlight Bi-sensor

79 Twist the mirror clockwise approx. 60 degrees, to remove it from the mirror base on the screen. Then unclip the plastic trim from around the rain sensor.

10.77a Unclip the sensor (arrowed)

10.77b ... and cut the wires to the sensor

80 Disconnect the wiring plug connector and then release the two securing clips one at each side of the sensor to remove it from the mounting base on the windscreen (**see illustrations**). If the sensor is going to be refitted, keep the sensor outer surface (which fits against the screen) protected to prevent any damage.

81 Refitting is a reversal of removal, noting the following points:

a) *Make sure the surface of the screen is clean before fitting sensor*

b) *If fitting a new sensor, remove the protective cover before fitting*

c) *Do not touch the surface of the sensor that fits against the screen*

10.80a ... disconnect the wiring connector ...

10.80b ... and unclip the sensor from the mounting bracket

11 Air conditioning system – general information and precautions

1 An air conditioning system is available on all models. It enables the temperature of incoming air to be lowered, and also dehumidifies the air, which makes for rapid demisting and increased comfort.

2 The cooling side of the system works in the same way as a domestic refrigerator. Refrigerant gas is drawn into a belt-driven compressor, and passes into a condenser mounted on the front of the radiator, where it loses heat and becomes liquid. The liquid passes through an expansion valve to an evaporator, where it changes from liquid under high pressure to gas under low pressure. This change is accompanied by a drop in temperature, which cools the evaporator. The refrigerant returns to the compressor, and the cycle begins again.

3 Air blown through the evaporator passes to the heating/ventilation housing, where it is mixed with hot air blown through the heater matrix to achieve the desired temperature in the passenger compartment.

4 The heating side of the system works in the same way as on models without air conditioning (see Section 9).

5 The operation of the system is controlled electronically by the ECM integral with the

11.5 Air conditioning high- and low-pressure circuits service ports (arrowed)

12.3a Disconnect the wiring connector

12.3b On some models there are two connectors

control panel. Any problems with the system should be referred to a Peugeot/Citroën dealer, or suitably-equipped specialist **(see illustration)**.

Precautions

6 When an air conditioning system is fitted, it is necessary to observe special precautions whenever dealing with any part of the system, or its associated components. The refrigerant is potentially dangerous, and should only be handled by qualified persons. Uncontrolled discharging of the refrigerant is dangerous and damaging to the environment for the following reasons.

• If it is splashed onto the skin, it can cause frostbite.
• The refrigerant is heavier then air and so displaces oxygen. In a confined space, which is not adequately ventilated, this could lead to a risk of suffocation. The gas is odourless and colourless so there is no warning of its presence in the atmosphere.
• Although not poisonous, in the presence of a naked flame (including a cigarette) it forms a noxious gas that causes headaches, nausea, etc.

⚠️ *Warning: Never attempt to open any air conditioning system refrigerant pipe/hose union without first having the system fully discharged by an air conditioning specialist. On completion of work, have the system recharged with the correct type and amount of fresh refrigerant.*

⚠️ *Warning: Always seal disconnected refrigerant pipe/hose unions as soon as they are disconnected. Failure to form an airtight seal on any union will result in the dehydrator reservoir become saturated, necessitating its renewal. Also renew all sealing rings disturbed.*
Caution: Do not operate the air conditioning system if it is known to be short of refrigerant as this could damage the compressor.

12 Air conditioning system components – removal and refitting 🔧

⚠️ *Warning: Refer to the precautions given in Section 11 and have the system discharged by an air conditioning specialist before carrying out any work on the air conditioning system.*

Compressor

1 Have the air conditioning system fully discharged and evacuated by an air conditioning specialist.
2 Remove the auxiliary drivebelt as described in Chapter 1, Section 16.
3 Disconnect the compressor wiring connector(s), and unclip the wiring harness from the retaining clips **(see illustrations)**.
4 Unscrew the nuts securing the refrigerant

pipes retaining plates to the compressor **(see illustration)**. Separate the pipes from the compressor and quickly seal the pipe and compressor unions to prevent the entry of moisture into the refrigerant circuit. Discard the sealing rings, new ones must be used on refitting.

⚠️ *Warning: Failure to seal the refrigerant pipe unions will result in the dehydrator reservoir become saturated, necessitating its renewal.*

5 Unscrew the compressor mounting bolts and nuts then free the compressor from its mounting bracket and remove it from the engine **(see illustration)**. Take care not to lose the spacers from the compressor rear mountings (where fitted).
6 If the compressor is to be renewed, drain the refrigerant oil from the old compressor. The specialist who recharges the refrigerant system will need to add this amount of oil to the system. Check for the amount of oil to be added, depending on specific model.
7 Ensure the spacers are correctly fitted to the rear mountings then manoeuvre the compressor into position and fit the mounting bolts and nuts.
8 Tighten the compressor front (drivebelt pulley) end mounting bolts to the specified torque first then tighten the rear bolts.
9 Lubricate the new refrigerant pipe sealing rings with compressor oil. Remove the plugs and install the sealing rings then quickly fit the refrigerant pipes to the compressor. Ensure the refrigerant pipes are correctly joined then refit the retaining bolt, tighten it securely.
10 Reconnect the wiring connector then refit the auxiliary drivebelt (see Chapter 1 Section 16).
11 Have the air conditioning system recharged with the correct type and amount of refrigerant by a specialist before using the system. Remember to inform the specialist which components have been renewed, so they can add the correct amount of oil.

Condenser

12 Have the air conditioning system fully discharged by an air conditioning specialist.
13 Remove the radiator as described in Section 4.

12.4 Undo the nuts (arrowed) securing the refrigerant pipes to the compressor

12.5 Remove the compressor mounting bolts (arrowed)

12.14 Undo the nuts (arrowed) securing the refrigerant pipes to the condenser

12.16a Make sure the rubber mountings are fitted securely ...

12.16b ... and the lower pegs locate in the rubber mountings (arrowed)

14 Undo the retaining nuts and disconnect the refrigerant pipes from the right-hand side of the condenser. Recover the O-ring seals **(see illustration)**.

⚠ *Warning: Failure to seal the refrigerant pipe unions will result in the dehydrator reservoir become saturated, necessitating its renewal.*

15 Move the top of the condenser to the rear and withdraw it upwards and out from the engine compartment.

16 Refitting is a reversal of removal. Noting the following points:
a) *Ensure the upper and lower mounting rubbers are correctly fitted then seat the condenser in position in the front panel (see illustrations)*
b) *Lubricate the sealing rings with compressor oil. Remove the plugs and install the sealing rings then quickly fit the refrigerant pipes to the condenser. Securely tighten the dehydrator pipe union nut and ensure the compressor pipe is correctly joined.*
c) *Have the air conditioning system recharged with the correct type and amount of refrigerant by a specialist before using the system.*

Receiver/drier

17 The receiver/drier is located on the left-hand side of the condenser **(see illustration)**. See paragraphs 12 to 15 to remove the condenser. The receiver/drier is not available separately; see your local dealer for further information.

Pressure switch

18 The switch is located in the high-pressure pipe on the right-hand side of the engine compartment **(see illustration)**.
19 Have the air conditioning system fully discharged by an air conditioning specialist.
20 Disconnect the wiring connector, and then unscrew the switch from the high-pressure pipe. Quickly seal the condenser union

to prevent the entry of moisture into the refrigerant circuit.

⚠ *Warning: Failure to seal the refrigerant pipe unions will result in the dehydrator reservoir become saturated, necessitating its renewal.*

21 Refitting is a reversal of removal noting the following points:
a) *Lubricate the switch seal with compressor oil.*
b) *Have the air conditioning system recharged with the correct type and amount of refrigerant by a specialist prior to using the system.*

Evaporator

22 Have the air conditioning system fully discharged and evacuated by an air conditioning specialist.
23 Remove the heating/ventilation housing as described in Section 10.
24 Note their fitted positions, and then disconnect the wiring plugs and harness from the housing.
25 Release the retaining clips, undo the screws and separate the two halves of the heater housing.
26 With the two halves of the housing separated, undo the screws, remove the pipe cover, and then slide the evaporator from the housing.

12.17 Receiver/drier (arrowed) fitted to the side of the condenser

27 Refitting is a reversal of removal but have the air conditioning system recharged with the correct type and amount of refrigerant by a specialist prior to using the system.

Expansion valve

28 Have the air conditioning system fully discharged and evacuated by an air conditioning specialist.
29 Remove the sound insulation material/heat shield from the engine compartment bulkhead (where fitted).
30 Undo the nuts securing the refrigerant pipes to the connection at the engine compartment bulkhead. Plug/cover the openings to prevent contamination/saturation. Recover and discard the O-ring seals – new ones must be fitted.

⚠ *Warning: Failure to seal the refrigerant pipe unions will result in the receiver/drier becoming saturated, necessitating its renewal.*

31 Pull the seal from around the pipes connection at the bulkhead, and then undo the 2 studs using a Torx socket, and remove the expansion valve. Recover and discard the O-ring seals – new ones must be fitted.
32 Refitting is a reversal of removal but have the air conditioning system recharged with the correct type and amount of refrigerant by a specialist prior to using the system.

12.18 Pressure switch location (arrowed)

Chapter 4 Part A
Fuel and exhaust systems

Contents

Degrees of difficulty

Easy, suitable for novice with little experience	**Fairly easy,** suitable for beginner with some experience	**Fairly difficult,** suitable for competent DIY mechanic	**Difficult,** suitable for experienced DIY mechanic	**Very difficult,** suitable for expert DIY or professional

Specifications

General

System type	HDi (high-pressure diesel injection) with full electronic control, direct injection and turbocharger
Designation	Bosch EDC 16C 34, Bosch EDC 17C 10 or Siemens SID 807
Firing order	1-3-4-2 (No 1 at flywheel end)
Fuel system operating pressure..............................	200 to 1800 bars (according to engine speed)

Injectors

Type	Electromagnetic or Piezo

Turbocharger

Type	MHI TD025S2 or Garret GT1544V
Boost pressure:	
@2500 rpm..	0.2 ± 0.1 bar
@4000 rpm..	0.7 ± 0.1 bar
Movement of wastegate valve rod:	
MHI	
200 mbars...	3.7 ± 1.5 mm
500 mbars...	12.2 ± 0.6 mm
Garret	
800 mbars...	6 ± 2 mm

Torque wrench settings

	Nm	lbf ft
Camshaft position sensor bolt	6	4
Common rail mounting bolts	23	17
Engine knock sensor	20	15
Exhaust manifold nuts	20	15
Exhaust system fasteners:		
Catalytic converter-to-manifold nuts	40	30
Clamping ring nuts	20	15
Fuel filter water sensor	25	18
Fuel injector clamp bolts/nuts:		
Stage 1	4	3
Stage 2	Angle-tighten a further 65°	
Fuel pipe unions	25	18
Fuel pressure regulator:		
Screw-in type	28	20
With retaining screws:		
Stage 1	3	2
Stage 2	Slacken 180°	
Stage 3	2	1
Stage 4	3	2
Stage 5	6	4
High-pressure fuel pump mounting bolts	25	18
High-pressure fuel pump rear mounting bolts/nut (8 mm)	17	13
High-pressure fuel pump sprocket nut	50	37
Intake manifold bolts	10	7
Turbocharger mounting bolts/nuts	25	18
Turbocharger oil feed pipe banjo bolts	30	20
Turbocharger oil return pipe bolts	30	20

1 General information and system operation

1 The fuel system consists of a rear-mounted fuel tank with an immersed level sensor, a fuel pump, a fuel filter with integral water separator, a fuel cooler mounted under the car (depending on model), and an electronically-controlled high-pressure diesel injection (HDi) system, together with a single turbocharger.

2 The exhaust system is conventional, but to meet the latest emission levels an unregulated catalytic converter and an exhaust gas recirculation system are fitted to all models. On some models, an exhaust emission particulate filter may be fitted – refer to Section 18, for further details.

3 The HDi system (generally known as a 'common rail' system) derives its name from the fact that a common rail, or fuel reservoir, is used to supply fuel to all the fuel injectors. Instead of an in-line or distributor type injection pump, which distributes the fuel directly to each injector, a high-pressure pump is used, which generates a very high fuel pressure (up to 1800 bar at high engine speed) in the common rail. The common rail stores fuel, and maintains a constant fuel pressure with the aid of a pressure control valve. Each injector is supplied with high-pressure fuel from the common rail, and the injectors are individually controlled via signals from the system Electronic Control Module (ECM). The injectors are electronically operated.

4 In addition to the various sensors used on models with a conventional fuel injection pump; common rail systems also have a fuel pressure sensor. The fuel pressure sensor allows the ECM to maintain the required fuel pressure, via the pressure control valve.

System operation

5 For the purposes of describing the operation of a common rail injection system, the components can be divided into three sub-systems; the low-pressure fuel system, the high-pressure fuel system and the electronic control system.

Low-pressure fuel system

6 The low-pressure fuel system consists of the following components:
a) Fuel tank.
b) Fuel pump.
c) Fuel cooler.
d) Fuel heater (not all models).
e) Fuel filter/water trap.
f) Low-pressure fuel lines.

7 The low-pressure system (fuel supply system) is responsible for supplying clean fuel to the high-pressure fuel system.

High-pressure fuel system

8 The high-pressure fuel system consists of the following components:
a) High-pressure fuel pump with pressure control valve.
b) High-pressure fuel common rail.
c) Fuel injectors.
d) High-pressure fuel lines.

9 After passing through the fuel filter, the fuel reaches the high-pressure pump, which forces it into the common rail. As diesel fuel has certain elasticity, the pressure in the common rail remains constant, even though fuel leaves the rail each time one of the injectors operates. Additionally, a pressure control valve mounted on the high-pressure pump ensures that the fuel pressure is maintained within preset limits.

10 The pressure control valve is operated by the ECM. When the valve is opened, fuel is returned from the high-pressure pump to the tank, via the fuel return lines, and the pressure in the common rail falls. To enable the ECM to trigger the pressure control valve correctly, the pressure in the common rail is measured by a fuel pressure sensor.

11 The electronically controlled fuel injectors are operated individually, via signals from the ECM, and each injector injects fuel directly into the relevant combustion chamber. The fact that high fuel pressure is always available allows very precise and highly flexible injection in comparison to a conventional injection pump: for example combustion during the main injection process can be improved considerably by the pre-injection of a very small quantity of fuel.

Electronic control system

12 The electronic control system consists of the following components:
a) Electronic control module (ECM).
b) Crankshaft speed/position sensor.
c) Camshaft position sensor.
d) Accelerator pedal position sensor.
e) Coolant temperature sensor.
f) Fuel temperature sensor.

g) *Airflow meter.*
h) *Fuel pressure sensor.*
i) *Fuel injectors.*
j) *Fuel pressure control valve.*
k) *Preheating control module.*
l) *EGR solenoid valve.*
m) *Air temperature sensor.*
n) *Atmospheric pressure sensor – integral with the ECM.*
o) *Intake manifold pressure sensor.*

13 The information from the various sensors is passed to the ECM, which evaluates the signals. The ECM contains electronic 'maps' which enable it to calculate the optimum quantity of fuel to inject, the appropriate start of injection, and even pre- and post-injection fuel quantities, for each individual engine cylinder under any given condition of engine operation.

14 Additionally, the ECM carries out monitoring and self-diagnostic functions. Any faults in the system are stored in the ECM memory, which enables quick and accurate fault diagnosis using appropriate diagnostic equipment (such as a suitable fault code reader).

2 High-pressure diesel injection system – special information

Warnings and precautions

⚠️ *It is essential to observe strict precautions when working on the fuel system components, particularly the high-pressure side of the system. Before carrying out any operations on the fuel system, refer to the precautions given in* Safety first! *at the beginning of this manual, and to the following additional information.*

• *Do not carry out any repair work on the high-pressure fuel system unless you are competent to do so, have all the necessary tools and equipment required, and are aware of the safety implications involved.*

• *Before starting any repair work on the fuel system, wait at least 30 seconds after switching off the engine to allow the fuel circuit pressure to reduce.*

• *Never work on the high-pressure fuel system with the engine running.*

• *Keep well clear of any possible source of fuel leakage, particularly when starting the engine after carrying out repair work. A leak in the system could cause an extremely high-pressure jet of fuel to escape, which could result in severe personal injury.*

• *Never place your hands or any part of your body near to a leak in the high-pressure fuel system.*

• *Do not use steam cleaning equipment or compressed air to clean the engine or any of the fuel system components.*

2.3 Typical plastic plug and cap set for sealing disconnected fuel pipes and components

Procedures and information

1 Strict cleanliness must be observed at all times when working on any part of the fuel system. This applies to the working area in general, the person doing the work, and the components being worked on.

2 Before working on the fuel system components, they must be thoroughly cleaned with a suitable degreasing fluid. Specific cleaning products may be obtained from Citroën dealers. Alternatively, a suitable brake cleaning fluid may be used. Cleanliness is particularly important when working on the fuel system connections at the following components:

a) *Fuel filter.*
b) *High-pressure fuel pump.*
c) *Common rail.*
d) *Fuel injectors.*
e) *High-pressure fuel pipes.*

3 After disconnecting any fuel pipes or components, the open union or orifice must be immediately sealed to prevent the entry of dirt or foreign material. Plastic plugs and caps in various sizes are available in packs from motor factors and accessory outlets, and are particularly suitable for this application **(see illustration)**. Fingers cut from disposable rubber gloves should be used to protect components such as fuel pipes, fuel injectors and wiring connectors, and can be secured in place using elastic bands. Suitable gloves of this type are available at no cost from most petrol station forecourts.

3.1a Hand-priming pump – DOHC engines

2.6 Two crow-foot adapters will be necessary for tightening the fuel pipe unions

4 Whenever any of the high-pressure fuel pipes are disconnected or removed, new pipes must be obtained for refitting.

5 On the completion of any repair on the high-pressure fuel system, Peugeot/Citroën recommend the use of a leak-detecting compound. This is a powder which is applied to the fuel pipe unions and connections, and turns white when dry. Any leak in the system will cause the product to darken indicating the source of the leak.

6 The torque wrench settings given in the Specifications must be strictly observed when tightening component mountings and connections. This is particularly important when tightening the high-pressure fuel pipe unions. To enable a torque wrench to be used on the fuel pipe unions, two Peugeot/Citroën crow-foot adapters are required. Suitable alternatives are available from motor factors and accessory outlets **(see illustration)**.

3 Fuel system – priming and bleeding

1 Should the fuel supply system be disconnected between the fuel tank and high-pressure pump, it is necessary to prime the fuel system. This is achieved by operating the hand-priming pump until resistance is felt **(see illustrations)**.

2 If vehicle will still not run, it may be necessary to connect a hose (special Peugeot/

3.1b Hand-priming pump (arrowed) – SOHC engines

4.3a Disconnect the air intake pipe...

4.3b ...and remove it from the engine compartment

4.4 Disconnect wiring connector

4.5 Remove the locating bolts (arrowed)

4.6a Disconnect the air intake hose...

4.6b ...and remove the lower housing

Citroën hose No 444-T may be available) from the fuel filter outlet pipe to the fuel return pipe and forcing fuel through the filter into the return system. If the special manufacturer hose is not available, it will suffice to connect a length of hose to the filter outlet, with the other end of the hose into a container.

4 Air cleaner assembly – removal and refitting

Removal

1 If required, to make access easier, undo the two screws securing the brake/clutch master cylinder upper reservoir and move it to one side.

2 Remove the air cleaner upper housing and air filter element, as described in Chapter 1, Section 20.

SOHC engines

3 Disconnect the air intake pipe from the mounting bracket at the rear of the near-side headlight unit. Then unclip the other end of the air intake pipe from the air cleaner lower housing, and remove it from the engine compartment **(see illustrations)**.

4 Disconnect the wiring connector from the air flow meter **(see illustration)**.

5 Undo the two cover locating bolts from the top of the cylinder head cover **(see illustration)**.

6 Disconnect the air intake hose from the air flow meter, then lift the air cleaner lower housing out from the rear of the engine compartment **(see illustrations)**.

DOHC engines

7 Pull the air filter lower housing upwards from the rubber mounting grommets **(see illustrations)**.

Refitting

8 Refitting is a reverse of the removal procedure. Examine the condition of the seals and retaining clips, and renew if necessary.

5 Accelerator pedal – removal and refitting

Removal

1 Release the fasteners along the edge of the trim panel and remove it from above the pedal assembly **(see illustration)**.

4.7a Withdraw the lower part of the housing ...

4.7b ... noting the rubber mountings (arrowed) are still in place

5.1 Remove the lower trim panel (arrowed)

5.2 Disconnect the wiring connector

5.3 Undo the three retaining nuts (arrowed)

6.1 Location of fuel pump/gauge sender unit

2 Disconnect the accelerator pedal position sensor wiring plug from the top of the pedal **(see illustration)**.
3 Undo the three nuts and remove the pedal assembly **(see illustration)**.

Refitting

4 Refitting is a reversal of the removal procedure.

---

6 Fuel lift pump –
removal and refitting

Note: *The fuel pump/gauge sender unit is only available as a complete assembly – no components are available separately.*

Removal

1 The fuel pump/gauge sender unit is located in the top of the fuel tank **(see illustration)**. Therefore the fuel tank will need to be lowered from under the floor panel, to allow for enough space to lift the pump/gauge sender unit out the fuel tank.
Caution: It is recommended that the fuel level in the tank, should be as low as possible for this operation.
2 Before carrying out any of the following procedures, disconnect the battery (refer to precautions in Chapter 5A, Section 1). Reconnect the battery on completion of refitting.
3 Chock the front wheels then jack up the rear of the vehicle and support it safely on axle stands (see *Jacking and vehicle support*).
4 To make access to the rear of the fuel tank easier, remove the spare wheel, then unhook

the spare wheel carrier from brackets on the rear body panel **(see illustration)**, and remove it from under the vehicle.
5 Working under the vehicle, release the securing clips and remove the heat shield(s) from under the fuel tank and around the exhaust pipe **(see illustrations)**.
6 Where applicable, remove the particulate filter additive reservoir from the right-hand side of the fuel tank, as described in Chapter 4B, Section 2.
7 Slacken the retaining nuts securing the fuel tank straps, one at the front, two at the rear and one at the left-hand side of the fuel tank **(see illustrations)**. Unscrew the retaining nuts until they are at the ends of the threaded studs, do not remove the nuts completely.
8 There is also a retaining nut to the right-hand side of the fuel tank, which will require slackening on models without

6.4 Unhook the spare wheel carrier

6.5a Remove the securing clips...

6.5b ...and remove the heatshield

6.7a Undo the retaining nut at the front (arrowed)...

6.7b ...two at the rear...

6.7c ...and one at the left-hand side

6.10 Disconnect the pump wiring plug connector

6.11 Place a plastic bag around the pipes to prevent dirt ingress

6.12a Fuel sender alignment marks – using a mirror

6.12b Using a special tool to slacken the locking ring

6.12c Remove the locking ring

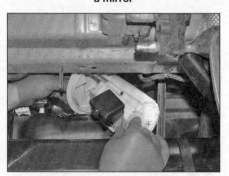

6.13 Lift the fuel pump assembly, taking care not to damage the float arm

particulate filter additive tank. On models with particulate filter additive tank fitted, this would have been removed as it secures the additive tank in position.

9 With the fuel tank lowered this amount, it should give sufficient room to remove the fuel pump/gauge sender unit out from the top of the fuel tank. Take care when lowering the fuel tank as to not damage the filler neck, which goes up the left-hand side of the vehicle and under the wheel arch liner.

10 Disconnect the wiring connector from the fuel pump **(see illustration)**.

11 Depress the retaining clips and detach the fuel pipe(s) from the top of the pump, bearing in mind the information given in Section 2 on warnings and precautions to be taken with the fuel system before disconnecting. Plug the pipe end(s) to minimise fuel loss and prevent the entry of dirt **(see illustration)**. **Note:** *Depending on model, the amount of pipes to*

the top of the pump will vary note their fitted position, before removal.

12 Using a mirror, note the alignment marks on the tank **(see illustrations)**, pump cover and the locking ring, unscrew the ring and remove it from the tank. This is best accomplished by using a special tool, which fits over the locking ring and allows it to be released using a spanner or a ratchet and socket. Alternatively, it may be possible to undo the locking ring using a screwdriver on the raised ribs of the locking ring. Carefully tap the screwdriver to turn the ring anti-clockwise until it can be unscrewed by hand.

13 Carefully lift the fuel pump assembly out of the fuel tank, taking great care not to damage the fuel gauge sender unit float arm **(see illustration)**. The pump/gauge sender will hold fuel, so be aware of spillage. Recover the rubber sealing ring and discard it – a new one must be used on refitting.

14 If the fuel pump is going to be left out of the fuel tank for a while, screw the ring back to the top of the fuel tank to prevent it from going out of shape. Cover the access hole in the tank to prevent dirt ingress.

Refitting

15 Fit the new sealing ring to the top of the fuel tank **(see illustration)**.

16 Carefully manoeuvre the pump assembly into the fuel tank, taking care not to damage the float arm.

17 Align the notch in the top of the fuel tank with the arrows on the fuel pump cover to locate the pump assembly into position **(see illustration)**.

18 Press down on the pump and refit the locking ring, tighten it securely until its alignment mark aligns with the alignment marks on the fuel tank, as noted on removal **(see illustration)**.

6.15 Fit a new sealing ring to the top of the tank

6.17 Align the pump with the cut-out in the fuel tank

6.18 Hold the pump in position, whilst fitting the locking ring

19 Securely reconnect the fuel pipe(s) to the pump/gauge sender unit, then reconnect the pump wiring connector.

20 Tighten the fuel tank securing strap retaining nuts, then refit the particulate filter additive tank (where applicable) and heatshields once the fuel tank is back in position.

21 Prime the fuel system (see Section 3). Start the engine and check the fuel pump feed and return hoses unions for signs of leakage.

7 Fuel gauge sender unit – removal and refitting

1 The fuel gauge sender unit is an integral part of the fuel lift pump assembly and is not available separately. Refer to Section 6 for removal and refitting details.

8 Fuel tank and cooler – removal and refitting

Fuel tank

Note: *Refer to the warnings and precautions in Section 2 before proceeding.*

1 Before removing the fuel tank, all fuel must be drained from the tank. Since a fuel tank drain plug is not provided, it is therefore preferable to carry out the removal operation when the tank is nearly empty. Before proceeding, disconnect the battery (refer to precautions in Chapter 5A Section 1), and then siphon or hand-pump the remaining fuel from the tank.

2 Disconnect the wiring connectors and fuel pipes from the top of the fuel sender/pump assembly, with reference to Section 6 of this Chapter. Plug the pipe end(s) to minimise fuel loss and prevent the entry of dirt. Note the fitted position of the fuel pipes for refitting.

3 Chock the front wheels then jack up the rear of the vehicle and support it on axle stands (see *Jacking and vehicle support*). **Note:** *As the filler neck of the fuel tank is part of the fuel tank assembly and cannot be removed separately, there will need to be sufficient height to remove the complete assembly.*

4 Remove the left-hand rear roadwheel and inner wheel arch liner. Inside the wheel arch, undo the upper retaining bolt from the fuel filler neck **(see illustration)**, and then unclip it from the fuel flap housing.

5 Working under the vehicle, release the securing clips and remove the heat shield(s) from under the fuel tank and around the exhaust pipe **(see illustrations 6.5a and 6.5b)**.

6 Where applicable, remove the particulate filter additive reservoir from the right-hand side of the fuel tank, as described in Chapter 4B, Section 2

7 Remove the rear part of the exhaust system as described in Section 18.

8 Place a trolley jack with a flat/long piece of

8.4 Filler neck retaining bolt (arrowed)

wood beneath the tank, to spread the weight. Then raise the jack until it is supporting the weight of the tank.

9 Slacken and remove the nuts securing the fuel tank to the body **(see illustrations 6.7a, 6.7b and 6.7c)**. Release the filler neck from the body at the filler cap aperture.

10 There is also a retaining nut to the right-hand side of the fuel tank **(see illustration)**. On models with particulate filter additive tank fitted, this also secures the additive tank in position, so this will have already been removed.

11 Reaching up at the rear of the fuel tank, disconnect the wiring connector **(see illustration)**.

12 Start to lower the fuel tank, once it is lowered enough, reach up and disconnect the fuel pipes and wiring connector(s) from the top of the fuel pump/gauge sender unit. Depress the retaining clips and detach the fuel pipe(s), bearing in mind the information given in, Section 2 on warnings and precautions to be taken with the fuel system before disconnecting. Plug the pipe end(s) to minimise fuel loss and prevent the entry of dirt **(see illustration 6.11)**. Depending on model, the amount of pipes to the top of the pump will vary note their fitted position, before removal.

13 With the wiring and fuel pipes disconnected slowly lower the fuel tank; ensuring the filler neck assembly is guided out of position without placing any stress on it. As the fuel tank is lowered, remove the long spacers from above the tank and remove them from under the vehicle. Check all pipes and wiring are disconnected from the fuel tank as it is lowered.

14 If the tank is contaminated with sediment

8.11 Disconnect the wiring connector

8.10 Fuel/additive tank retaining nut (arrowed)

or water, remove the fuel pump (Section 6), and swill the tank out with clean fuel. The tank is injection-moulded from a synthetic material – if seriously damaged, it should be renewed. However, in certain cases, it may be possible to have small leaks or minor damage repaired. Seek the advice of a specialist before attempting to repair the fuel tank.

15 It is not possible to separate the filler neck from the tank. If damaged, the complete assembly must be renewed.

16 Refitting is the reverse of the removal procedure, noting the following points:

a) *Ensure the wiring connectors and fuel pipes are securely reconnected and retained by all the relevant clips. When lifting the tank back into position, take care to ensure that the pipes/wiring do not become trapped between the tank and vehicle body.*

b) *Make sure the spacer(s) are fitted correctly between the fuel tank and the floor panel.*

c) *Refit the particulate filter additive tank as described in Chapter 4B, Section 2.*

d) *Refit the exhaust as described in Section 18.*

e) *On completion, refill the tank with a small amount of fuel and prime the fuel system as described in Section 3. Check for signs of leakage prior to taking the vehicle out on the road.*

Fuel cooler

Note: *The fuel cooler is not fitted to all models.*
17 The fuel cooler is located under the right-hand side of the vehicle **(see illustration)**. Jack up the rear of the vehicle, and support it on axle stands (see *Jacking and vehicle support*).

8.17 Fuel cooler fitted under floor panel

8.19 Undo the nuts (arrowed) securing the fuel cooler

9.4a On DOHC engines, remove the air filter support bracket (arrowed) …

9.4b … and the brackets around the fuel pump (arrowed)

18 Where fitted, undo the fasteners and remove the plastic undershield from the right-hand underside of the vehicle.

19 Working underneath the vehicle, undo the two retaining nuts, and release the cooler bracket from the locating holes in the floor panel **(see illustration)**.

20 Release the locking clips and disconnect the fuel feed and return hoses from the end of the cooler. Be prepared for fuel spillage, and plug the hose and cooler openings to prevent dirt ingress.

21 Refitting is a reversal of removal.

---

9 High-pressure fuel pump –
removal and refitting

⚠️ *Warning: Refer to the information contained in Section 2 before proceeding.*

Note: *A new fuel pump-to-common rail high-pressure fuel pipe will be required for refitting.*

Removal

1 Disconnect the battery (refer to precautions in Chapter 5A Section 1) and remove the timing belt as described in Chapter 2A Section 7 or Chapter 2B Section 7. After removal of the timing belt, temporarily refit the right-hand engine mounting but do not fully-tighten the bolts.

2 Remove the air cleaner assembly as described in Section 4.

3 Remove the EGR heat exchanger/cooler as described in Chapter 4B Section 2.

4 Undo the bolts/nuts and remove the support brackets above the fuel common rail and the high-pressure pump **(see illustrations)**.

5 Undo the union nuts and remove the high-pressure fuel pipe between the fuel common rail and the high-pressure pump. Plug the openings to prevent contamination.

6 Disconnect the wiring plug from the high-pressure fuel pump.

7 Depress the release buttons and disconnect the fuel supply and return hoses from the pump. Note that the hoses may have a release button on each side of the fitting. Plug the openings to prevent contamination.

8 Hold the pump sprocket stationary, and loosen the centre nut securing it to the pump shaft (see **Tool Tip 1**).

9 The fuel pump sprocket is a taper fit on the pump shaft and it will be necessary to make up a tool to release it from the taper (see **Tool Tip 2**). Partially unscrew the sprocket retaining nut, fit the home-made tool, and secure it to the sprocket with two 7.0 mm bolts and nuts. Prevent the sprocket from rotating as before, and screw down the nuts, forcing the sprocket off the shaft taper. Once the taper is released, remove the tool, unscrew the nut fully, and remove the sprocket from the pump shaft.

10 Undo the three bolts, and remove the pump from the mounting bracket.

Caution: The high-pressure fuel pump is manufactured to extremely close tolerances and must not be dismantled in any way. Do not unscrew the fuel pipe male union on the rear of the pump, or attempt to remove the sensor, piston de-activator switch, or the seal on the pump shaft. No parts for the pump are available separately and if the unit is in any way suspect, it must be renewed.

11 Undo the bolts securing the bracket to the rear of the pump (where fitted), then undo the bolts and pull the pump from the inner timing cover.

Refitting

12 Refitting is a reversal of removal, noting the following points:

a) *Always renew the pump-to-common rail high-pressure pipe.*

b) *Renew the fuel pump drive seal.*

c) *With everything reassembled and reconnected, and observing the precautions listed in Section 2, start the engine and allow it to idle. Check for leaks at the high-pressure fuel pipe unions with the engine idling. If satisfactory, increase the engine speed to 3000 rpm and check again for leaks.*

d) *Take the car for a short road test and check for leaks once again on return. If any leaks are detected, obtain and fit another new high-pressure fuel pipe. Do not attempt to cure even the slightest leak by further tightening of the pipe unions.*

---

10 Common rail –
removal and refitting

⚠️ *Warning: Refer to the information contained in Section 2 before proceeding.*

Note: *A complete new set of high-pressure fuel pipes will be required for refitting.*

TOOL TiP 1

A sprocket holding tool can be made from two lengths of steel strip bolted together to form a forked end. Bend the ends of the strip through 90° to form the fork 'prongs'.

TOOL TiP 2

Make a sprocket releasing tool from a short strip of steel. Drill two holes in the strip to correspond with the two holes in the sprocket. Drill a third hole just large enough to accept the flats of the sprocket retaining nut.

10.6 Undo the bolts (arrowed) and move the coolant pump outlet assembly aside

10.8 The pressure sensor is located at the end of the accumulator rail (arrowed)

10.9 Accumulator rail mounting bolt/stud (arrowed)

Removal

1 Disconnect the battery (refer to precautions in Chapter 5A, Section 1).
2 Remove the trim cover from the top of the engine.
3 Drain the coolant as described in Chapter 1, Section 19.

DOHC engines

4 Remove the cylinder head cover/intake manifold as described in Chapter 2B.
5 Remove the EGR heat exchanger/cooler as described in Chapter 4B Section 2.
6 Undo the 2 mounting bolts, slacken the clamps, and move the coolant pump outlet assembly aside **(see illustration)**.
7 Clean around the pipe, then undo the unions and remove the high-pressure pipe from the common rail to the high-pressure pump. Plug the openings to prevent contamination.
8 Disconnect the pressure sensor wiring plug from the common rail **(see illustration)**.
9 Unscrew the two rail mounting bolts and manoeuvre it from place **(see illustration)**.
Note: *Peugeot/Citroën insist that the fuel pressure sensor on the common rail must not be removed.*
Caution: Do not attempt to remove the four high-pressure fuel pipe male unions from the common rail. These parts are not available separately and if disturbed are likely to result in fuel leakage on reassembly.

SOHC engines

10 Slacken the hose clamp and remove the hose from the throttle body. Disconnect the wiring plug from the throttle body.
11 Remove the bolts, slacken the hose clamp and remove the throttle body and inlet hose as a single part.
12 Remove the protection bracket from the fuel filter and then remove the fuel hoses. Seal the fuel lines.
13 Unbolt the fuel filter and move it to one side.
14 At the rear of the engine disconnect the vacuum lines from the EGR vacuum control.
15 Remove the rear coolant hoses and then unbolt the EGR pipe from the inlet manifold.
16 Remove the 3 bolts at the cylinder head

and the 3 bolts at the support bracket and then remove the inlet manifold.
17 Slacken the unions on the high pressure fuel lines – use another spanner to counter hold the union at the injector of the pipe **(see illustration)**.
18 Slacken the unions on the high pressure pipe on the fuel pump and then at the fuel rail. Remove all the high pressure fuel lines and dispose of them – they must be replaced.
19 Disconnect the wiring plug from the fuel pressure sensor and then unbolt and remove the fuel rail **(see illustrations 10.8 and 10.9)**.

Refitting

20 Locate the common rail in position, refit and finger-tighten the mounting bolts/nuts.
21 Reconnect the common rail wiring plug(s).
22 Fit the new pump-to-rail high-pressure pipe, and only finger-tighten the unions at first, then tighten the unions to the specified torque setting. Use a second spanner to counterhold the union screwed into the pump body.
23 Fit the new set of rail-to-injector high pressure pipes, and finger-tighten the unions. If it's not possible to fit the new pipes to the injector unions, remove and refit the injectors as described in Section 11, and then try again.
24 Tighten the common rail mounting bolts/nuts to the specified torque.
25 Tighten the rail-to-injector pipe unions to the specified torque setting. Use a second spanner to counterhold the injector unions.

10.17 Counter hold the injector with a second spanner whilst slackening the union

26 The remainder of refitting is a reversal of removal, noting the following points:
a) *Ensure all wiring connectors and harnesses are correctly refitting and secured.*
b) *Reconnect the battery, referring to precautions in Chapter 5A Section 1.*
c) *Observing the precautions listed in Section 2, start the engine and allow it to idle. Check for leaks at the high-pressure fuel pipe unions with the engine idling. If satisfactory, increase the engine speed to 3000 rpm and check again for leaks. Take the car for a short road test and check for leaks once again on return.*
d) *If any leaks are detected, obtain and fit additional new high-pressure fuel pipes as required. Do not attempt to cure even the slightest leak by further tightening of the pipe unions.*

11 Fuel injectors – removal and refitting

⚠ *Warning: Refer to the information contained in Section 2 before proceeding.*

Removal

1 Disconnect the battery (refer to precautions in Chapter 5A, Section 1).
2 Remove the trim cover from the top of the engine, pull it upwards to release it from its mountings.
Note: *The following procedure describes the removal and refitting of the injectors as a complete set, however each injector may be removed individually if required. New copper washers, upper seals, and a high-pressure fuel pipe will be required for each disturbed injector when refitting.*

DOHC engines

3 Remove the EGR heat exchanger/cooler as described in Chapter 4B Section 2.
4 Undo the bolts, slacken the clamps and remove the air intake ducting assembly from between the turbocharger and the intake manifold. Note their fitted positions, and

11.4a Intake ducting securing clamps (arrowed) ...

11.4b ... and retaining bolts (arrowed)

11.6 Wiring harness support bracket bolts (arrowed)

disconnect the various wiring plugs as the assembly is withdrawn **(see illustrations)**.

5 Disconnect the injector wiring plugs.

6 Undo the bolts and move aside the wiring harness support bracket **(see illustration)**.

7 Release the manual fuel priming pump and its support.

8 Extract the retaining circlip and disconnect the leak-off pipe from each fuel injector **(see illustration)**.

9 Clean the area around the high-pressure fuel pipes between the injectors and the common rail, then unscrew the pipe unions. Use a second spanner to counterhold the union screwed into the injector body **(see illustration)**. The injectors' screwed-in unions must not be allowed to move. Remove the bracket above the common rail unions, and then remove the pipes. Plug the openings in the common rail and injectors to prevent dirt ingress.

10 Unscrew the injector retaining nuts, and carefully pull or lever the injector from place. If necessary, use an open-ended spanner and twist the injector to free it from position **(see illustrations)**. Do not lever against or pull on the solenoid housing at the top of the injector. If improved access is required, undo the bolts and remove the oil separator housing from the front of the cylinder head cover.

11 Note down the 8-digit injector classification number – this may be needed during the refitting procedure if the ECM has been renewed **(see illustration)**.

SOHC engines

12 Slacken the hose clips and remove the air intake hose from the air inlet metering unit **(see illustration)**.

13 Remove the air cleaner assembly as described in, Section 4

14 Remove the sound insulation from the top of the injectors **(see illustration)**.

15 Disconnect the fuel injector return pipe and plug the end to prevent dirt ingress **(see illustration)**.

11.8 Prise out the clip and pull the return pipe from each injector

11.9 Use a second spanner to counterhold the high-pressure pipe union nuts

11.10a Injector retaining nuts (arrowed)

11.10b Use a spanner to twist the injector and free it from position

11.11 Bosch injector classification number

11.12 undo the securing clips (arrowed)

11.14 Remove the insulation

11.15 Disconnect fuel return pipe (arrowed)

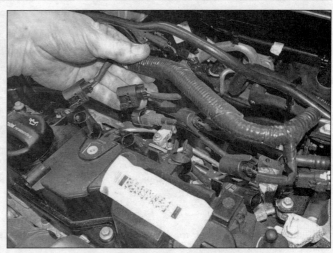

11.16 Disconnect the wiring plugs

16 Disconnect the wiring plugs from the fuel injectors **(see illustration)**.

17 Compress the wings of the locking collars and remove the bleed off hoses from the 4 fuel injectors **(see illustrations)**. Disconnect the hose assembly at the junction with the fuel return pipe and remove it from the vehicle. Seal the now exposed bleed off ports on the injectors

18 Clean the area around the high-pressure fuel pipes between the injectors and the common rail, then unscrew the pipe unions. Use a second spanner to counter-hold the union screwed into the injector body **(see illustration)**. The injectors screwed-in unions must not be allowed to move. Plug the openings in the common rail and injectors to prevent dirt ingress. Dispose of the high pressure pipes, they must be replaced.

19 Unscrew the injector retaining bolt **(see illustration)** and carefully pull or lever the injector from place. If necessary, use an open-ended spanner and twist the injector to free it from position. Do not lever against or pull on the solenoid housing at the top of the injector. Note that special tools (consisting of a slide hammer and collar that locks onto the injector) are available to help with the removal of the injectors. In extreme cases a hydraulic

puller tool may be required. A specialist or well equipped garage should have these tools.

All engines

20 Note down the injector's position – if the injectors are to be refitted, they must be refitted to their original locations. Where possible keep the injectors vertical at all times and store them in a suitable place **(see illustration)**.

21 Remove the copper washer and the upper seal from each injector, or from the cylinder head if they remained in place during injector removal. New copper washers and upper seals will be required for refitting. Cover the

injector hole in the cylinder head to prevent dirt ingress.

22 Examine each injector visually for any signs of obvious damage or deterioration. If any defects are apparent, renew the injector(s).

Caution: The injectors are manufactured to extremely close tolerances and must not be dismantled in any way. Do not unscrew the fuel pipe union on the side of the injector, or separate any parts of the injector body. Do not attempt to clean carbon deposits from the injector nozzle or carry out any form of ultrasonic or pressure testing.

11.17a Compress the locking collar and...

11.17b ...remove the bleed off hoses

11.18 Use a second spanner to counter hold the high-pressure pipe union nuts

11.19 Remove the injector retaining bolts (arrowed)

11.20 Store the injectors upright at all times

11.24a Unscrew the old injector retaining studs ...

11.24b ... and fit new studs

Refitting

23 Clean out the injector recess in the cylinder head and make sure it is free from any dirt.

DOHC engines

24 Unscrew the injector retaining studs from the cylinder head and renew **(see illustrations)**.

11.25a Fit a new upper seal ...

11.25b ... and use a length of wire to guide the new sealing washer into place

25 Locate a new upper seal in the cylinder head, and place a new copper washer down the injector recess in the cylinder head **(see illustrations)**.

26 Where fitted, refit the injector clamp locating dowels to the cylinder head.

27 Ensure the injector clamps are in place over their respective circlips on the injector bodies, and then fit the injectors into place in the cylinder head. If the original injectors are being refitted, ensure they are fitted into their original positions **(see illustrations)**.

28 Fit the injector retaining bolts/nuts, but only finger-tighten them at this stage **(see illustration)**. When tightening the nuts/bolts, ensure the clamps stay horizontal.

29 Working on one fuel injector at a time, remove the blanking plugs from the fuel pipe unions on the common rail and the relevant injector. Locate a new high-pressure fuel pipe over the unions and screw on the union nuts **(see illustration)**. Take care not to cross-thread the nuts or strain the fuel pipes as they are fitted. Once the union nut threads have started, finger-tighten the nuts to the ends of the threads.

30 When all the fuel pipes are in place, tighten the injector clamp retaining nuts/bolts to the specified torque and angle **(see illustration)**.

31 Using an open-ended spanner, hold each fuel pipe union in turn and tighten the union nut to the specified torque using a torque wrench and crow-foot adapter **(see illustration)**. Tighten all the disturbed union nuts in the same way.

11.27a Ensure the circlip (arrowed) is in place (where applicable) ...

11.27b ... then fit the injectors into their original positions

11.28 Fit new injector securing nuts

11.29 Screw the high-pressure fuel pipes to the fuel rail

11.30 Using an angle gauge to tighten the injector securing nuts

11.31 Using a crow-foot adapter to tighten the injector pipes

11.33 Upper seal (A) and copper washer (B)

11.37 Tighten the high-pressure pipe unions nuts using a crows foot wrench

32 If new injectors have been fitted, their classification numbers must be programmed into the engine management ECM using dedicated diagnostic equipment/scanner. If this equipment is not available, entrust this task to a Peugeot/Citroën dealer or suitably-equipped repairer. Note that it should be possible to drive the vehicle, albeit with reduced performance/increased emissions, to a repairer for the numbers to be programmed.

SOHC engines

33 Fit new seals to the injectors (see illustration). For future reference (or where new injectors have been fitted) note down the classification numbers from each injector. Refit the refurbished injectors to the cylinder head.

34 Align the locking collars and tighten the injectors to the specified torque.

35 Working on one fuel injector at a time, remove the blanking plugs from the fuel pipe unions on the common rail and the relevant injector. Locate a new high-pressure fuel pipe over the unions and screw on the union nuts. Take care not to cross-thread the nuts or strain the fuel pipes as they are fitted. Once the union nut threads have started, finger-tighten the nuts only at this stage, to the ends of the threads.

36 When all the fuel pipes are in place, tighten the injector clamp retaining nuts/bolts to the specified torque and angle.

37 Using an open-ended spanner, hold each fuel pipe union in turn and tighten the union nut to the specified torque using a torque wrench and crow's-foot adapter (see illustration). Tighten all the disturbed union nuts in the same way.

38 If new injectors have been fitted, their classification numbers must be programmed into the engine management ECM using dedicated diagnostic equipment. If this equipment is not available, entrust this task to a Peugeot/Citroen dealer or suitably-equipped repairer. Note that it should be possible to drive the vehicle, albeit with reduced performance/increased emissions, to a repairer for the numbers to be programmed.

All engines

39 The remainder of refitting is a reversal of removal, noting the following points:
a) Ensure all wiring connectors and harnesses are correctly refitting and secured.
b) Reconnect the battery as described in Chapter 5A Section 4.
c) Observing the precautions listed in Section 2, start the engine and allow it to idle. Check for leaks at the high-pressure fuel pipe unions with the engine idling. If satisfactory, increase the engine speed to 3000 rpm and check again for leaks. Take the car for a short road test and check for leaks once again on return. If any leaks are detected, obtain and fit additional new high-pressure fuel pipes as required.
d) Do not attempt to cure even the slightest leak by further tightening of the pipe unions.

12 Electronic control system components – testing, removal and refitting

Testing

1 If a fault is suspected in the electronic control side of the system, first ensure that all the wiring connectors are securely connected and free of corrosion. Ensure that the suspected problem is not of a mechanical nature, or due to poor maintenance; ie, check that the air filter element is clean, the engine breather hoses are clear and undamaged, and that the cylinder compression pressures are correct.

2 If these checks fail to reveal the cause of the problem, the vehicle should be taken to a Peugeot/Citroën dealer or suitably-equipped garage for testing. A diagnostic socket is located inside the glovebox to the right-hand side (see illustration) to which a fault code reader or other suitable test equipment can be connected. By using the code reader or test equipment, the engine management ECM – Engine Control Module (and the various other vehicle system ECMs) can be interrogated, and any stored fault codes can be retrieved. This will allow the fault to be quickly and simply traced, alleviating the need to test all the system components individually, which is a time-consuming operation that carries a risk of damaging the ECM.

Removal and refitting

3 Before carrying out any of the following procedures, disconnect the battery (refer to precautions in Chapter 5A Section 1). Reconnect the battery on completion of refitting.

Electronic control Module (ECM)

Note: If a new ECM is being fitted, the vehicle will not start until the immobiliser ECM has been matched to the engine management ECM. This can only be performed using dedicated test equipment. Consequently, entrust the procedure to a Peugeot/Citroën dealer or suitably-equipped specialist.

4 Disconnect the battery (refer to precautions in Chapter 5A Section 1).

5 The ECM is located on the left-hand side of the engine compartment, inside the engine compartment fusebox.

6 Remove the plastic cover from the top of the fusebox (see illustration).

7 Where fitted, the security plate will need to be removed from over the wiring connectors on the ECM. This is held in position with shear bolts (bolts that fitted to a specific torque, the head of the bolt snaps off).

8 Use a centre punch to mark the centre of the security plate retaining bolts (shear bolts),

12.2 Vehicle diagnostic socket (arrowed)

12.6 Remove the fusebox cover

12.8 Security plate retaining bolts (arrowed)

12.9 Release the locking clips and disconnect the ECU wiring plugs

12.14 Disconnect the crankshaft position sensor wiring plug (arrowed)

12.20 Remove the air intake pipes (SOHC shown)

12.21a Camshaft sensor retaining bolt (arrowed) – DOHC engine

12.21b Camshaft sensor retaining bolt (arrowed) – SOHC engine

then using a drill and an extractor, remove the bolts **(see illustration)**. New bolts will be required for refitting. Once the bolts have been removed the security plate can be removed from over the wiring connectors.

9 Release the locking clips and disconnect the wiring connectors from the top of the ECM **(see illustration)**.

10 Lift the ECM upwards and withdraw it out from the engine compartment fusebox.

11 Refitting is a reverse of the removal procedure ensuring the wiring connectors are securely reconnected. Fit new shear bolts to the security cover.

Crankshaft speed/position sensor

12 The crankshaft position sensor is located adjacent to the crankshaft pulley on the right-hand end of the engine. Slacken the

right-hand front roadwheel bolts, and then jack the front of the vehicle up and support it on axle stands (see *Jacking and vehicle support*). Remove the right-hand front roadwheel.

13 Push in the centre pins a little, then prise out the rivets and remove the wheel arch liner.

14 Disconnect the sensor wiring plug **(see illustration)**.

15 Undo the bolt and remove the sensor.

16 Refitting is a reversal of removal, tightening the sensor retaining bolt securely.

Camshaft position sensor

17 The camshaft position sensor is mounted on the right-hand end of the cylinder head cover, directly behind the camshaft sprocket.

18 On DOHC engines, remove the upper timing belt cover, as described in Chapter 2B Section 6.

19 Unplug the sensor wiring connector.

20 To access the sensor, undo the retaining bolts and hose clips and remove the air intake pipes from the top of the engine **(see illustration)**.

21 Undo the bolt and pull the sensor from position **(see illustrations)**.

22 On DOHC engines, upon refitting, position the sensor so that the air gap between the sensor end and the webs of the signal wheel is 1.2 mm, measured with feeler gauges **(see illustrations)**. If a new sensor is being fitted, position it so the nipple of the sensor is just in contact with the camshaft signal wheel. Tighten the sensor retaining bolt to the specified torque.

23 The remainder of refitting is a reversal of removal.

Accelerator pedal position sensor

24 The pedal sensor is integral with the accelerator pedal assembly. Refer to Section 5 of this Chapter for the pedal removal procedure.

Coolant temperature sensor

25 Refer to Chapter 3 Section 7.

Fuel temperature sensor

 Warning: Refer to the information contained in Section 2 before proceeding.

26 The sensor (where fitted) is clipped in to the plastic fuel manifold at the right-hand rear end of the cylinder head. To remove the sensor, disconnect the wiring plug, and

12.22a The gap between the end of the used sensor and signal wheel (arrowed) ...

12.22b ... must be 1.2 mm measured with a feeler gauge

12.26 Fuel temperature sensor (arrowed)

12.29 Disconnect airflow meter wiring plug – SOHC engine shown

12.30 Disconnect air intake hose

then unclip the sensor from the manifold. Be prepared for fuel spillage **(see illustration)**.

27 Refitting is a reversal of removal. Observing the precautions listed in Section 2, start the engine and allow it to idle. Check for leaks at the fuel temperature sensor with the engine idling. If satisfactory, increase the engine speed to 4000 rpm and check again for leaks. Take the car for a short road test and check for leaks once again on return. If any leaks are detected, obtain and fit a new sensor.

Airflow meter

28 The airflow meter is located in the intake ducting from the air cleaner housing.

29 Disconnect the meter wiring plug **(see illustration)**.

30 Slacken the retaining clips (where fitted) and disconnect the air intake ducting from the airflow meter **(see illustration)**. Suitably plug or cover the turbocharger intake duct, using clean rag to prevent any dirt or foreign material from entering.

31 Undo the retaining screws and disconnect the airflow meter from the air cleaner housing.

32 Refitting is reverse of the removal procedure.

Fuel pressure sensor

33 The fuel pressure sensor is integral with the common rail, and is not available separately. Peugeot/Citroën insist that the sensor is not removed from the rail.

Fuel pressure regulator

34 The fuel pressure regulator is located in

the high-pressure fuel pump. Depending on fuel system, the regulator may be screwed into the fuel pump or it may have two retaining screws securing it to the fuel pump.

35 Disconnect the wiring connector from the fuel pressure regulator.

36 Thoroughly clean the area around the sensor and its location.

37 Suitably protect the components below the sensor and have plenty of clean rags handy. Be prepared for considerable fuel spillage.

38 Depending on type fitted, either unscrew the regulator and remove it from the fuel pump or undo the two retaining screws and remove the regulator from the pump.

39 Refitting is a reversal of removal, tightening the sensor to the specified torque.

40 Observing the precautions listed in Section 2, start the engine and allow it to idle. Check for leaks at the fuel temperature sensor with the engine idling. If satisfactory, increase the engine speed to 4000 rpm and check again for leaks. Take the car for a short road test and check for leaks once again on return. If any leaks are detected, obtain and fit a new sensor.

EGR solenoid valve

41 Refer to Chapter 4B Section 2.

Vehicle speed sensor

42 The engine management ECM receives the vehicle speed signal from the wheel speed sensors via the ABS ECM. Refer to Chapter 9 Section 19 for wheel speed sensor removal.

13 Intake manifold – removal and refitting

1 The intake manifold is integral with the cylinder head cover. For the removal and refitting procedure, refer to Chapter 2A, Section 10, or Chapter 2B, Section 10

14 Exhaust manifold – removal and refitting

Removal

1 Remove the turbocharger as described in Section 16.

2 Undo the retaining nuts, recover the spacers (where fitted), and remove the manifold. Recover the gasket **(see illustrations)**.

Refitting

3 Refitting is a reverse of the removal procedure, bearing in mind the following points:

a) Ensure that the manifold and cylinder head mating faces are clean, with all traces of old gasket removed.

b) Use new gaskets when refitting the manifold to the cylinder head.

c) Tighten the exhaust manifold retaining nuts to the specified torque, starting with the ones at the centre and then working your way to the outer ones.

15 Turbocharger – description and precautions

1 A turbocharger is fitted to increase engine efficiency by raising the pressure in the intake manifold above atmospheric pressure. Instead of the air simply being sucked into the cylinders, it is forced in.

2 Energy for the operation of the turbocharger comes from the exhaust gas. The gas flows through a specially shaped housing (the turbine housing) and, in so doing, spins the turbine wheel. The turbine wheel is attached to a shaft, at the end of which is another vaned wheel known

14.2a Undo the exhaust manifold nuts, recover the spacers, and remove the manifold

14.2b Recover the manifold gasket

16.5 Disconnect the vacuum pipe from the wastegate control assembly (arrowed)

16.6 Undo the bolts and remove the turbocharger heat shield (arrowed)

as the compressor wheel. The compressor wheel spins in its own housing, and compresses the intake air on the way to the intake manifold.

3 Boost pressure (the pressure in the intake manifold) is limited by a wastegate, which diverts the exhaust gas away from the turbine wheel in response to a pressure-sensitive actuator. The turbocharger incorporates a variable intake nozzle to improve boost pressure at low engine speeds.

4 The turbo shaft is pressure-lubricated by an oil feed pipe from the main oil gallery. The shaft 'floats' on a cushion of oil. A drain pipe returns the oil to the sump.

Precautions

The turbocharger operates at extremely high speeds and temperatures. Certain precautions must be observed, to avoid premature failure of the turbo, or injury to the operator.

• *Do not operate the turbo with any of its parts exposed, or with any of its hoses removed. Foreign objects falling onto the rotating vanes could cause excessive damage, and (if ejected) personal injury.*

• *Do not race the engine immediately after start-up, especially if it is cold. Give the oil a few seconds to circulate.*

• *Always allow the engine to return to idle speed before switching it off – do not blip the throttle and switch off, as this will leave the turbo spinning without lubrication.*

• *Allow the engine to idle for several minutes before switching off after a high-speed run.*

• *Observe the recommended intervals for oil and filter changing, and use a reputable oil of the specified quality. Neglect of oil changing, or use of inferior oil, can cause carbon formation on the turbo shaft, leading to subsequent failure.*

16 Turbocharger – removal, inspection and refitting

Removal

1 Chock the rear wheels then jack up the front of the vehicle and support it on axle stands (see *Jacking and vehicle support*). Undo the screws and remove the engine undershield.

2 Disconnect the battery, (refer to precautions in Chapter 5A Section 1).

3 Place a sheet of thick cardboard over the rear of the radiator to protect it from accidental damage.

4 Slacken the clamps, undo the bolts, and remove the air ducts to and from the turbocharger and intake manifold **(see illustration 12.20)**. Note their fitted positions and disconnect the various wiring plugs, as the assembly is withdrawn.

5 Disconnect the vacuum hose from the turbocharger wastegate control assembly **(see illustration)**.

6 Undo the mounting bolts **(see illustration)**, and remove the heat shield from above turbocharger.

7 Remove the catalytic converter/particulate filter (where applicable) as described in Section 18.

8 Undo the oil supply pipe banjo bolts and recover the sealing washers **(see illustration)**.

9 Slacken the retaining clip and disconnect the oil return pipe from the turbocharger and cylinder block.

10 Unscrew the four nuts, and the nut securing the support bracket, then remove the turbocharger from the exhaust manifold **(see illustration)**.

Inspection

11 With the turbocharger removed, inspect the housing for cracks or other visible damage.

12 Spin the turbine or the compressor wheel to verify that the shaft is intact and to feel for excessive shake or roughness. Some play is normal, since in use the shaft is 'floating' on a film of oil. Check that the wheel vanes are undamaged.

13 If oil contamination of the exhaust or induction passages is apparent, it is likely that turbo shaft oil seals have failed.

14 No DIY repair of the turbo is possible and none of the internal or external parts are available separately. If the turbocharger is suspect in any way a complete new unit must be obtained. Do not attempt to dismantle the turbocharger control assemblies.

16.8 Turbocharger oil supply and return pipes (arrowed)

16.10 Undo the 3 nuts (arrowed – one hidden) and remove the support bracket bolt (arrowed)

Refitting

15 Refitting is a reverse of the removal procedure, bearing in mind the following points:

a) *Renew the turbocharger retaining nuts and gaskets.*

b) *When fitting the new clamp to the pre-catalyst, align the clamp on the flange (see illustrations).*

c) *If a new turbocharger is being fitted, change the engine oil and filter. Also renew the filter in the oil feed pipe.*

d) *Prime the turbocharger by injecting clean engine oil through the oil feed pipe union before reconnecting the union.*

17 Intercooler – removal and refitting

Removal

1 Remove the front bumper as described in Chapter 11 Section 6.

2 The intercooler is located at the front of the engine compartment, on the right-hand side of the radiator.

3 Slacken the retaining clips and disconnect the air intake and outlet hoses from the top of the intercooler **(see illustration)**.

4 Unclip the coolant reservoir overflow pipe to the radiator from the cross panel and move it to one side **(see illustration)**.

5 Undo the upper retaining bolts, and then lift the intercooler, releasing it from its lower mountings in the radiator front panel **(see illustrations)**.

16.15a Unclip the old inner sealing washer from the old clamp

6 If required, undo the retaining bolts, and remove the panel from across the top of the intercooler **(see illustration)**.

Refitting

7 Refitting is a reversal of removal.

18 Exhaust system – general information and component renewal

General information

1 According to model, the exhaust system consists of either three or four sections. Three-section systems consist of a catalytic converter, an intermediate pipe, and a rear silencer. Four-section systems consist of a pre-catalyst after the turbocharger, followed by a catalytic converter, particulate filter

16.15b Fit the alignment mark on the new clamp (arrowed) with the upper flange of the pre-cat

(not all models), intermediate pipe, and rear silencer.

2 The exhaust joints are of either the spring-loaded ball type (to allow for movement in the exhaust system) or clamp-ring type.

3 The system is suspended throughout its entire length by rubber mountings.

Removal

4 Each exhaust section can be removed individually, or alternatively, the complete system can be removed as a unit.

5 To remove the system or part of the system, first jack up the front or rear of the car, and support it on axle stands (see *Jacking and vehicle support*). Alternatively, position the car over an inspection pit, or on car ramps.

Catalytic converter/particulate filter

6 Undo the retaining bolts/nuts and remove the engine undershield.

17.3 Remove the upper hose clamps (arrowed) from the intercooler

17.4 Unclip the coolant overflow pipe from the retaining clip

17.5a Undo the mounting bolts (arrowed) ...

17.5b ... and withdraw the intercooler from the engine compartment

17.5c Make sure the lower mounting rubbers are still in place

17.6 Remove the upper cross panel

18.7a Unscrew the pressure take-off union from the side of the catalyst/filter …

18.7b … and the one at the base

18.10 Exhaust flexible pipe-to-catalyst/ filter clamp (arrowed)

7 Unscrew the pressure take-off unions from the side and base of the assembly **(see illustrations)**.

8 Disconnect the sensor wiring plug on the side of the catalytic converter.

9 Undo the bolts and remove the heat shield from the catalytic converter/particulate filter.

10 Slacken the retaining clamps joining the catalytic converter to the turbocharger and exhaust pipe. Take care not to damage the

flexible section of the front exhaust pipe **(see illustration)**.

11 Slacken the clamp securing the catalytic converter to the turbocharger.

12 Undo the 2 nuts securing the catalytic converter to the cylinder block and manoeuvre it down and out of the engine compartment **(see illustration)**.

13 If required, note its fitted position, then slacken the clamp and detach the particulate

filter from the base of the catalytic converter **(see illustration)**.

Intermediate pipe

14 Slacken the clamping ring bolts, and disengage both clamps from the flange joints at each end of the pipe.

15 Release the pipe from its mounting rubbers and remove it from underneath the vehicle **(see illustration)**. Alternatively, undo the nuts securing the mounting bracket to the vehicle body.

Rear silencer

16 Slacken the rear silencer clamping ring bolts, and disengage the clamp from the flange joint.

17 Unhook the rear silencer from its mounting rubbers, and remove it from the vehicle **(see illustrations)**. Alternatively, undo the nuts/bolts securing the mounting bracket to the vehicle body.

Heat shield(s)

18 The heat shields are secured to the underside of the body by various fasteners. Each shield can be removed once the relevant exhaust section has been removed **(see illustration)**. If a shield is being removed to gain access to a component located behind it, it may prove sufficient in some cases to remove the fasteners and simply lower the shield, without disturbing the exhaust system.

18.12 Catalytic converter/particulate filter retaining nuts (arrowed)

18.13 Undo the clamp (arrowed) and slide the particulate filter from the catalytic converter

18.15 Exhaust system front mounting bracket (arrowed)

18.17a Exhaust rear silencer side rubber mounting (arrowed) …

Refitting

19 Each section is refitted by reversing the removal sequence, noting the following points:

a) *Ensure that all traces of corrosion have been removed from the flanges, and renew all necessary gaskets.*

b) *Inspect the rubber mountings for signs of damage or deterioration, and renew as necessary.*

c) *On joints secured together by a clamping ring, apply a smear of exhaust system jointing paste to the flange joint, to ensure a gas-tight seal. Tighten the clamping ring nuts evenly and progressively, so that the clearance between the clamp halves remains equal on either side.*

d) *Prior to tightening the exhaust system fasteners, ensure that all rubber mountings are correctly located, and that there is adequate clearance between the exhaust system and vehicle underbody.*

18.17b … and front rubber mounting (arrowed)

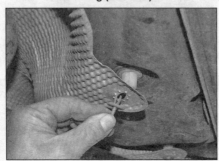

18.18 Heat shield fasteners

Chapter 4 Part B
Emission control systems

Contents

Degrees of difficulty

| Easy, suitable for novice with little experience | | Fairly easy, suitable for beginner with some experience | | Fairly difficult, suitable for competent DIY mechanic | | Difficult, suitable for experienced DIY mechanic | | Very difficult, suitable for expert DIY or professional | |

1 General Information

1 All diesel engines are designed to meet strict emission requirements and are equipped with a crankcase emission control system and a catalytic converter. To further reduce exhaust emissions, all diesel engines are also fitted with an exhaust gas recirculation (EGR) system. Additionally, some diesel models may be equipped with a particulate emission filter, which uses porous silicon carbide substrate to trap particulates of carbon as the exhaust gases pass through.

Crankcase emission control

2 To reduce the emission of unburned hydrocarbons from the crankcase into the atmosphere, the engine is sealed and the blow-by gases and oil vapour are drawn from inside the crankcase, through a wire mesh oil separator, into the intake tract to be burned by the engine during normal combustion.

3 Under all conditions the gases are forced out of the crankcase by the (relatively) higher crankcase pressure; if the engine is worn, the raised crankcase pressure (due to increased blow-by) will cause some of the flow to return under all manifold conditions.

Exhaust emission control

4 To minimise the level of exhaust pollutants released into the atmosphere, a catalytic converter is fitted in the exhaust system of all models.

5 The catalytic converter consists of a canister containing a fine mesh impregnated with a catalyst material, over which the hot exhaust gases pass. The catalyst speeds up the oxidation of harmful carbon monoxide, un-burnt hydrocarbons and soot, effectively reducing the quantity of harmful products released into the atmosphere via the exhaust gases.

Exhaust gas recirculation system

6 This system is designed to recirculate small quantities of exhaust gas into the intake tract, and therefore into the combustion process. This process reduces the level of oxides of nitrogen present in the final exhaust gas, which is released into the atmosphere.

7 The volume of exhaust gas recirculated is controlled by the system electronic control unit.

8 A vacuum-operated valve is fitted to the exhaust manifold, to regulate the quantity of exhaust gas recirculated. The valve is operated by the vacuum supplied by the solenoid valve.

Particulate filter system

9 The particulate filter is combined with the catalytic converter in the exhaust system on some models, and its purpose it to trap particles of carbon (soot) as the exhaust gases pass through, in order to comply with latest emission regulations.

10 The filter can be automatically regenerated (cleaned) by the system's ECM on-board the vehicle. The engine's high-pressure injection system is utilised to inject fuel into the exhaust gases during the post-injection period; this causes the filter temperature to increase sufficiently to oxidise the particulates, leaving an ash residue. The regeneration period is automatically controlled by the on-board ECM. Subsequently, at the correct service interval the filter must be removed from the exhaust system, and renewed.

11 To assist the combustion of the trapped carbon (soot) during the regeneration process, a fuel additive (cerium-based Eolys) is automatically mixed with the diesel fuel in the fuel tank. The additive is stored in a container attached to the left-hand side of the fuel tank, and the ECM regulates the amount of additive to send to the fuel tank by means of an additive injector located on the top of the fuel tank.

2 Emission control systems – testing and component renewal

Crankcase emission control

1 The components of this system require no attention other than to check that the hose(s) are clear and undamaged at regular intervals.

Exhaust emission control

2 The performance of the catalytic converter can be checked only by measuring the exhaust gases, using a good quality, carefully calibrated exhaust gas analyser.

3 If the catalytic converter is thought to be faulty, before assuming the catalytic converter is faulty, it is worth checking the problem is not due to a faulty injector. Refer to your Citroën dealer for further information.

Catalytic converter renewal

4 Refer to Chapter 4A Section 18.

Exhaust gas recirculation system

5 Testing of the system should ideally be entrusted to a Peugeot/Citroën dealer since

2.9 EGR heat exchanger-to-valve clamp (arrowed)

a vacuum pump and vacuum gauge are required.

EGR valve renewal

6 To make access easier, remove the battery and tray, as described in Chapter 5A, Section 4. Before disconnecting the battery, refer to precautions in Chapter 5A, Section 1

7 The EGR valve is located at the rear of the cylinder head, bolted to the left-hand end of the heat exchanger. The EGR valve can be removed separately from the heat exchanger.

8 Remove the air cleaner housing and air ducting, as described in Chapter 4A Section 4, and then, where fitted, remove the heat shield from over the EGR valve.

DOHC engine

9 Slacken and remove the securing clamp from between the heat exchanger and EGR valve (see illustration). It may be necessary to undo the heat exchanger mounting bracket nuts and move it to one side.

10 Disconnect the wiring connector from the top of the EGR valve.

11 There are two bolts securing the EGR valve, undo the bolts and remove the valve (see illustration). Discard the metal gasket from the valve, and the O-ring seal from the pipe – new ones must be fitted.

12 Refitting is a reversal of removal.

SOHC engine

13 Disconnect the wiring connector from the top of the EGR valve.

14 There are two bolts securing the EGR valve, undo the bolts and carefully lever the

2.11 EGR valve mounting bolts (arrowed – one hidden)

valve upwards to release it from the housing (see illustration). Discard the gasket/seal from the valve, as a new one must be fitted.

15 Refitting is a reversal of removal.

EGR heat exchanger renewal

16 To make access easier, remove the battery and tray, as described in Chapter 5A, Section 4. Before disconnecting the battery, refer to precautions in Chapter 5A, Section 1.

17 Drain the cooling system (see Chapter 1 Section 19). Alternatively, fit hose clamps to the hoses connected to the EGR heat exchanger.

18 Remove the air cleaner housing and air ducting, as described in Chapter 4A Section 4, and then remove the heat shield (where fitted) from over the EGR valve.

DOHC engines

19 Slacken and remove the securing clamp from between the heat exchanger and EGR valve (see illustration 2.9). It may be necessary to undo the heat exchanger mounting bracket nuts and move it to one side.

20 Slacken and remove the securing clamp from between the heat exchanger and EGR pipe (see illustration).

21 Loosen the clips and disconnect the coolant hoses from the EGR heat exchanger (see illustration).

22 If not already done, undo the heat exchanger mounting bracket nuts and remove the heat exchanger from the rear of the engine.

23 Refitting is a reversal of removal.

2.14 EGR valve location (arrowed)

2.20 EGR cooler-to-pipe clamp (arrowed)

2.21 Release the coolant hose retaining clamps (arrowed)

SOHC engines

24 Anticipating some fuel spillage, remove the fuel lines from the fuel filter and from the rear of the cylinder head.

25 Disconnect the wiring plugs from the fuel injectors, the fuel pressure sensor, the EGR control valve and the fuel filter. Release the wiring loom from the various cable clips and then move the loom to the side.

26 Unplug the vacuum lines from the control valve at the rear of the cylinder head.

27 Disconnect the coolant hoses from the EGR cooler. Anticipate some coolant spillage.

28 Unbolt the EGR pipe from inlet pipe and then remove the remove the 4 mounting bolts and single nut. Withdraw the cooler from the engine and recover the gaskets.

29 Refitting is a reversal of removal, but remember to replace the gasket and tighten the bolts to the specified torque where given.

Particulate filter

Fuel additive system

30 It is possible to check the fuel additive pump delivery pressure, but this should be made by a Peugeot/Citroën dealer or specialist.

Fuel additive reservoir renewal

Note: *Ideally, the additive reservoir should be empty before removing it, otherwise take precautions against spillage.*

 Warning: Wear protective gloves and eye protection when handling the reservoir.

31 To remove the fuel additive reservoir, chock the front wheels then jack up the rear of the vehicle and support on axle stands (see *Jacking and vehicle support*). The reservoir is attached to the right-hand side of the fuel tank.

32 Undo the retaining nuts and remove the plastic shield from over the fuel pipes **(see illustration)**.

33 Remove the heatshield(s) from beneath the fuel tank/additive reservoir **(see illustration)**.

34 Slacken and remove the retaining nut at the front of the additive reservoir tank **(see illustration)**.

2.32 Plastic shield over fuel pipes

2.34 Undo the retaining nut (arrowed)

35 Slide the additive tank away from the exhaust pipe to release it from the locating lugs on the base of the fuel tank **(see illustration)**.

36 As the additive tank is removed, disconnect the wiring connector from the additive pump unit **(see illustration)**.

37 Depress the release button and disconnect the pipe from the additive pump unit **(see illustration)**. Keep the tank with the pump facing upwards to prevent spillage of any additive still left in the tank. Plug the openings to prevent dirt ingress.

38 The reservoir can now be carefully removed from under the vehicle.

39 Refitting is a reversal of removal.

40 Have the reservoir refilled by a Peugeot/Citroën dealer or specialist.

2.33 Remove the heatshield

2.35 Release the additive tank from the locating lugs

Particulate filter

41 Renewal of the particulate filter is described in Chapter 4A Section 18.

Exhaust gas pressure sensor

42 This sensor measures the pressure at the entrance and exit of the particulate filter, and is located in the engine compartment **(see illustration)**. It is fitted to the right-hand front of the engine unit, on a mounting bracket above the alternator. **Note:** *Depending on model and year of the vehicle this location may change.*

43 Note the fitted position of the hoses, and then disconnect the hoses and wiring connectors from the pressure sensor.

44 Undo the mounting nuts and remove the sensor from the mounting bracket.

45 Refitting is a reversal of removal.

2.36 Disconnect the wiring connector

2.37 Disconnect the pipe(s)

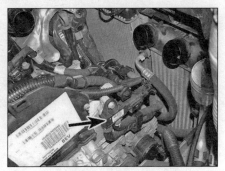

2.42 Pressure sensor (arrowed) – SOHC engine shown

3 Catalytic converter – general information and precautions

1 The catalytic converter is a reliable and simple device which needs no maintenance in itself, but there are some facts of which an owner should be aware if the converter is to function properly for its full service life.

a) *DO NOT use fuel or engine oil additives – these may contain substances harmful to the catalytic converter.*

b) *DO NOT continue to use the car if the engine burns oil to the extent of leaving a visible trail of blue smoke.*

c) *Remember that the catalytic converter operates at very high temperatures. DO NOT, therefore, park the car in dry undergrowth, over long grass or piles of dead leaves after a long run.*

d) *Remember that the catalytic converter is FRAGILE – do not strike it with tools.*

e) *If the converter is no longer effective it must be renewed.*

Chapter 5 Part A
Starting and charging systems

Contents

Degrees of difficulty

Easy, suitable for novice with little experience	**Fairly easy,** suitable for beginner with some experience	**Fairly difficult,** suitable for competent DIY mechanic	**Difficult,** suitable for experienced DIY mechanic	**Very difficult,** suitable for expert DIY or professional

Specifications

System type . . . . 12 volt, negative earth

Battery
Type . . . . Low maintenance or 'maintenance-free' sealed for life
Capacity . . . . 60, 70 or 80 Ah (depending on model)

Alternator
Type . . . . Valeo, Denso, Bosch, Magneti Marelli or Mitsubishi (depending on model)
Rating . . . . 120 or 150 amp

Starter motor
Type . . . . Valeo, Bosch, Ducellier, Mitsubishi or Iskra (depending on model)

Torque wrench settings	Nm	lbf ft
Alternator mounting bolts:		
Front upper bolt	40	30
Rear bolts	49	36
Auxiliary belt idler roller-to-mounting bracket	45	33
Auxiliary belt tensioner-to-cylinder block bolt	20	15
Oil level sensor	27	20
Oil pressure switch	20	15
Starter motor	20	15

1 General information and precautions

General information

1 The engine electrical system consists mainly of the charging and starting systems. Because of their engine-related functions, these components are covered separately from the body electrical devices such as the lights, instruments, etc (which are covered in Chapter 12). Refer to Chapter 5B Section 1 for information on the preheating system.

2 The electrical system is of the 12 volt negative earth type.

3 The battery is of the low maintenance or 'maintenance-free' (sealed for life) type and is charged by the alternator, which is belt-driven from the crankshaft pulley.

4 The starter motor is of the pre-engaged type incorporating an integral solenoid. On starting, the solenoid moves the drive pinion into engagement with the flywheel ring gear before the starter motor is energised. Once the engine has started, a one-way clutch prevents the motor armature being driven by the engine until the pinion disengages from the flywheel.

Precautions

5 Further details of the various systems are given in the relevant Sections of this Chapter. While some repair procedures are given, the usual course of action is to renew the component concerned.

6 It is necessary to take extra care when working on the electrical system to avoid damage to semi-conductor devices (diodes and transistors), and to avoid the risk of personal injury. In addition to the precautions given in *Safety first!* at the beginning of this manual, observe the following when working on the system:

• *Always remove rings, watches, etc, before working on the electrical system. Even with the battery disconnected, capacitive discharge could occur if a component's live terminal is earthed through a metal object. This could cause a shock or nasty burn.*

• *Do not reverse the battery connections. Components such as the alternator, electronic control units, or any other components having semi-conductor circuitry could be irreparably damaged.*

• *If the engine is being started using jump leads and a slave battery, connect the batteries positive-to-positive and negative-to-negative (see Jump starting). This also applies when connecting a battery charger.*

• *Never disconnect the battery terminals, the alternator, any electrical wiring or any test instruments when the engine is running.*

• *Do not allow the engine to turn the alternator when the alternator is not connected.*

• *Never 'test' for alternator output by 'flashing' the output lead to earth.*

• *Never use an ohmmeter of the type incorporating a hand-cranked generator for circuit or continuity testing.*

• *Always ensure that the battery negative lead is disconnected when working on the electrical system.*

• *Before using electric-arc welding equipment on the car, disconnect the battery, alternator and components such as the fuel injection/ignition electronic control unit to protect them from the risk of damage.*

2 Electrical fault finding – general information

1 Refer to Chapter 12 Section 2.

3 Battery – testing and charging

Testing

1 A 'sealed for life' maintenance-free battery is fitted to these models, topping-up and testing of the electrolyte in each cell is not possible. The condition of the battery can therefore only be tested using a battery condition indicator or a voltmeter.

2 Certain models may be fitted with a built-in charge condition indicator. The indicator is located in the top of the battery casing, and indicates the condition of the battery from its colour **(see illustration)**. If the indicator shows green, then the battery is in a good state of charge. If the indicator shows black, then the battery requires charging, as described later in this Section. If the indicator shows blue, then the electrolyte level in the battery is too low to allow further use, and the battery should be renewed.

Caution: *Do not attempt to charge, load or jump start a battery when the indicator shows clear/yellow.*

3 If testing the battery using a voltmeter, connect the voltmeter across the battery and check for a reading of approx. 12.7 volts.

3.2 Battery charge condition indicator (arrowed)

The test is only accurate if the battery has not been subjected to any kind of charge for the previous six hours. If this is not the case, switch on the headlights for 30 seconds, then wait four to five minutes before testing the battery after switching off the headlights. All other electrical circuits must be switched off, so check that the doors and tailgate are fully shut when making the test.

4 If the voltage reading is less than 12.2 volts, then the battery is discharged, whilst a reading of 12.2 to 12.4 volts indicates a partially discharged condition.

5 If the battery is to be charged, remove it from the vehicle (Section 4) and charge it as described later in this Section.

Charging

Note: *The following is intended as a guide only. Always refer to the manufacturer's recommendations (often printed on a label attached to the battery) before charging a battery.*

6 A maintenance-free battery takes considerably longer to fully recharge than the standard type, the time taken being dependent on the extent of discharge, but it can take anything up to three days.

7 A constant voltage type charger is required to be set, when connected, to 13.9 to 14.9 volts with a charger current below 25 amps. Using this method, the battery should be usable within three hours, giving a voltage reading of 12.5 volts, but this is for a partially discharged battery and, as mentioned, full charging can take considerably longer.

8 If the battery is to be charged from a fully discharged state (condition reading less than 12.2 volts), have it recharged by your Peugeot/Citroën dealer or local automotive electrician, as the charge rate is higher and constant supervision during charging is necessary.

4 Battery and tray – removal and refitting

Note: *The audio unit fitted as standard equipment by Peugeot/Citroën is equipped with an anti-theft system, to deter thieves. If the power source is disconnected, the unit will automatically recode itself as long as it is still fitted to the correct vehicle. If the unit is removed it will not operate in another vehicle.*

Note: *Prior to disconnecting the battery, wait 5 minutes after switching off the ignition to allow the vehicle's ECMs to store all learned values in their memories, and also the power consuming equipment can switch to standby.*

Removal

Battery

1 Prior to disconnecting the battery, close all windows and the sunroof (where fitted), and ensure that the vehicle alarm system is deactivated (see Owner's Handbook).

4.4 Lift up the quick-release lever and disconnect the positive lead

4.5a Unclip the red cover from the top of the battery …

4.5b … release the securing clip (arrowed) …

2 The battery is located on the left-hand side of the engine compartment.

3 To make access easier and depending on model, release the fasteners and remove the air intake ducting from the front left-hand side of the engine compartment.

4 Unclip the battery positive terminal cover, then lift up the quick-release lever and disconnect the positive lead from the battery **(see illustration)**.

5 Unclip the red plastic cover from the additional fuses on top of the battery cover. Release the securing clips and slide the additional fuse link assembly upwards and away from the battery cover **(see illustrations)**. Unclip the cables from the securing clip on the battery cover and move the assembly to one side.

6 Withdraw the battery cover upwards, releasing it from the lower plastic inner tray and remove it from the battery **(see illustrations)**.

7 Undo the securing nut and disconnect the negative terminal connector from the rear of the battery **(see illustration)**.

8 Unscrew the securing bolt and remove the battery retaining clamp **(see illustration)**.

9 The battery can now be lifted out of the engine compartment **(see illustration)**.

Battery tray

10 Undo the two securing nuts and withdraw the plastic battery inner tray from the engine

4.5c … and the lower securing clip …

4.5d … then slide the fused link assembly upwards

4.6a Remove the cover from the battery …

4.6b … releasing it from the locating peg (arrowed)

4.7 Undo the negative lead securing nut (arrowed)

4.8 Release the securing clamp bolt (arrowed) …

4.9 … and then lift out the battery

4.10a Undo the two retaining nuts (arrowed) …

4.10b … and lift out the battery plastic inner tray

4.13a Undo the battery tray fasteners (arrowed) …

4.13b … including the bolt (arrowed) under the wheel arch

4.14a Release the wiring clips at the rear (arrowed) …

4.14b … and at the front of the battery tray

compartment **(see illustrations)**. Where applicable, note the fitted position of any wiring loom securing clips, and disconnect them from the plastic battery tray as it is removed.

11 Slacken the left-hand front roadwheel bolts, then jack up the front of the vehicle and support it securely on axle stands (see *Jacking and vehicle support*).

12 Remove the left-hand front road wheel, then release the various fasteners and remove the wheel arch liner from under the front wing.

13 Working inside the engine compartment, undo the fasteners securing the metal battery tray to the inner wing panel, including the one on the outside from under the wheel arch **(see illustrations)**.

14 Note the fitted position of the wiring loom

4.15 … and then lift the battery tray out from the engine compartment

securing clips, and disconnect them from the metal battery tray **(see illustrations)**.

15 Carefully move aside all cables and hoses, and then lift the metal battery tray out of the engine compartment **(see illustration)**.

Refitting

16 Refitting is a reversal of removal, but smear petroleum jelly on the terminals after reconnecting the leads. Due to the design of the cover over the battery, reconnect the negative lead first, before the cover is fitted and the positive lead last, after the cover is fitted.

17 With the battery reconnected, switch on the ignition and wait at least 1 minute before starting the engine. This will allow the vehicle electronic systems and control units to stabilise. Check that there are no error messages on the instrument panel, if required use a diagnostic tool to clear any faults. Also refer to Chapter 12 Section 20; on models with the anti-theft alarm system.

18 On models with a sunroof, after reconnecting the battery, re-initialise the sunroof mechanism as follows:

a) *Turn the switch to the maximum partial-opening position (3rd position to the right).*

b) *Keep the control switch pressed in. The sunroof will reach the maximum partially-open position, then close slightly.*

c) *Release the switch within 6 seconds.*

d) *Press the switch within 6 seconds. The sunroof starts to close after 4 seconds from the switch being pressed, then opens completely, then closes completely*

5 Charging system – testing

Note: *Refer to the warnings given in* Safety first! *and in Section 1 of this Chapter before starting work.*

1 If the ignition warning light fails to illuminate when the ignition is switched on, first check the alternator wiring connections for security. If satisfactory, check that the warning light bulb has not blown, and that the bulbholder is secure in its location in the instrument panel. If the light still fails to illuminate, check the continuity of the warning light feed wire from the alternator to the bulbholder. If all is satisfactory, the alternator is at fault and should be renewed or taken to an auto-electrician for testing and repair.

2 If the ignition warning light illuminates when the engine is running, stop the engine and check that the drivebelt is correctly fitted and tensioned (see Chapter 1 Section 16) and that the alternator connections are secure. If all is so far satisfactory, have the alternator checked by an auto-electrician for testing and repair.

3 If the alternator output is suspect even though the warning light functions correctly, the regulated voltage may be checked as follows.

4 Connect a voltmeter across the battery terminals and start the engine.

7.3 Remove the air intake hoses from the intercooler

7.6a Remove the rubber cover and undo the securing nut (arrowed) ...

7.6b ... then disconnect the alternator wiring and plug ...

5 Increase the engine speed until the voltmeter reading remains steady; the reading should be approximately 12 to 13 volts, and no more than 14 volts.

6 Switch on as many electrical accessories as possible (eg, the headlights, heated rear window and heater blower), and check that the alternator maintains the regulated voltage of around 13 to 14 volts.

7 If the regulated voltage is not as stated, the fault may be due to worn brushes, weak brush springs, a faulty voltage regulator, a faulty diode, a severed phase winding or worn or damaged slip-rings. The alternator should be renewed or taken to an auto-electrician for testing and repair.

7.6c ... release the wiring loom (arrowed) from the rear of the alternator

7.7 Undo the auxiliary drivebelt tensioner bolts (arrowed)

6 Alternator drivebelt
– removal, refitting and tensioning

1 Refer to the procedure given for the auxiliary drivebelt in Chapter 1, Section 16.

7 Alternator –
removal and refitting

Removal

1 Disconnect the battery (see Section 4).
2 Remove the auxiliary drivebelt as described

in Chapter 1, Section 16. On some models, it may be necessary to undo the bolts and remove the auxiliary drivebelt idler pulley bracket bolts, which obscures the lower alternator mounting bolt.

3 Slacken the retaining clips and remove the intercooler air intake hoses, to gain better access to the alternator **(see illustration)**.

4 Undo the retaining bolts and remove the wiring connector mounting bracket (where applicable) from above the alternator.

5 On models with belt driven power steering pump, remove the pump and move it to one side with reference to Chapter 10, Section 22. Note the pipes/hoses do not have to be completely removed from the pump for this operation. Undo the pump retaining bolts and move it to one side.

6 Remove the rubber cover from the

alternator terminal, then unscrew the retaining nut and disconnect the wiring from the rear of the alternator **(see illustrations)**. Prise out the retaining clip to release the wiring harness routed around the end of the alternator.

7 Where an auxiliary drivebelt tensioner is fitted, undo the three bolts and remove it from the alternator mounting bracket **(see illustration)**.

8 Where an elasticated auxiliary drivebelt is fitted, undo the idler roller retaining bolt and remove it from the alternator mounting bracket **(see illustration)**. **Note:** *The idler roller retaining bolt is also the alternator lower bolt.*

9 Unscrew the alternator mounting bolts **(see illustrations)**. Manoeuvre the alternator away from its mounting brackets and out from the engine compartment.

7.8 Undo the auxiliary drivebelt pulley bolt (arrowed)

7.9a Alternator outer mounting bolts (arrowed) ...

7.9b ... and inner mounting bolts (arrowed)

7.10 On some models, the upper bolt acts as a centraliser

8.2 Undo the screw/nuts (arrowed) and remove the cover from the alternator

Refitting

10 Refitting is a reversal of removal, tensioning the auxiliary drivebelt as described in Chapter 1, Section 16, and ensuring that the alternator mountings are securely tightened. Note that on diesel models, one of the bolts acts as a centraliser and should be tightened first **(see illustration)**.

8 Alternator brushes, regulator and drive pulley – inspection and renewal

Note: *If the alternator is thought to be suspect, check on the cost of repairs before proceeding, as it may prove more economical to obtain a new or exchange alternator. The alternator fitted may vary slightly, depending on model*

and age; the model shown in the following sequence is for a Valeo type alternator.

Brushes and regulator

1 Remove the alternator as described in Section 7.
2 Unscrew the nuts/screws securing the cover to the rear of the alternator **(see illustration)**.
3 Using a screwdriver, lever off the cover, and remove it from the rear of the alternator.
4 Unscrew and remove the three retaining screws, and remove the regulator/brush holder from the rear of the alternator **(see illustration)**.
5 Check the brushes for excessive wear and damage. No specifications for brush length are given by Citroën. If the brushes are suspect, renew them along with the regulator as a complete assembly.

6 If the brushes are in good condition, clean them and check that they move freely in their holders.
7 Wipe clean the alternator slip-rings, and check them for signs of scoring or burning **(see illustration)**. It may be possible to have the slip-rings renovated by an electrical specialist.
8 Use a paper clip to restrain the brushes, then refit the regulator/brush holder assembly and securely tighten the retaining screws **(see illustration)**.
9 Refit the cover, then insert and tighten the retaining screws/nuts.
10 Refit the alternator with reference to Section 7.

Drive pulley

11 The alternator drive pulley is fitted with a one-way clutch to reduced wear and stress on the auxiliary drivebelt. In order to remove the pulley, a special tool will be required to hold the alternator shaft whilst unscrewing the pulley. This tool should be available from auto electrical specialists/automotive tool specialists.
12 Prise the plastic cap from the pulley.
13 Insert the special tool into the splines of the pulley, engaging the central Torx bit with the alternator shaft **(see illustrations)**. Unscrew the pulley anti-clockwise whilst holding the shaft with the Torx bit, and remove the pulley.
14 Fit the pulley to the alternator shaft, and tighten it securely using the special tool.

8.4 Undo the bolts (arrowed) and remove the regulator/brush pack

8.7 Check the condition of the slip-rings

8.8 Use a screwdriver to push back the brushes against the springs, then insert a thin rod (arrowed) to hold them in place

8.13a A special tool is required to remove the alternator pulley

8.13b Insert the central Torx bit into the end of the alternator shaft, unscrew the pulley …

8.13c … and remove the pulley from the shaft

9 Starting system – testing

Note: *Refer to the precautions given in* Safety first! *and in Section 1 of this Chapter before starting work.*

1 If the starter motor fails to operate when the ignition key is turned to the appropriate position, the following possible causes may be to blame.
a) *The engine immobiliser is faulty.*
b) *The battery is faulty.*
c) *The electrical connections between the switch, solenoid, battery and starter motor are somewhere failing to pass the necessary current from the battery through the starter to earth.*
d) *The solenoid is faulty.*
e) *The starter motor is mechanically or electrically defective.*

2 To check the battery, switch on the headlights. If they dim after a few seconds, this indicates that the battery is discharged – recharge (see Section 3) or renew the battery. If the headlights glow brightly, operate the ignition switch and observe the lights. If they dim, then this indicates that current is reaching the starter motor, therefore the fault must lie in the starter motor. If the lights continue to glow brightly (and no clicking sound can be heard from the starter motor solenoid), this indicates that there is a fault in the circuit or solenoid – see following paragraphs. If the starter motor turns slowly when operated, but the battery is in good condition, then this indicates that either the starter motor is faulty, or there is considerable resistance somewhere in the circuit.

3 If a fault in the circuit is suspected, disconnect the battery leads (including the earth connection to the body), the starter/solenoid wiring and the engine/transmission earth strap – located on the top of the transmission housing **(see illustration)**. Thoroughly clean the connections and reconnect the leads and wiring, then use a voltmeter or test lamp to check that full battery voltage is available at the battery positive

9.3 Engine/transmission earth strap connection (arrowed)

lead connection to the solenoid, and that the earth is sound. Smear petroleum jelly around the battery terminals to prevent corrosion – corroded connections are amongst the most frequent causes of electrical system faults.

4 If the battery and all connections are in good condition, check the circuit by disconnecting the wire from the solenoid blade terminal. Connect a voltmeter or test lamp between the wire end and a good earth (such as the battery negative terminal), and check that the wire is live when the ignition switch is turned to the 'start' position. If it is, then the circuit is sound – if not the circuit wiring can be checked as described in Chapter 12 Section 2.

5 The solenoid contacts can be checked by connecting a voltmeter or test lamp between the battery positive feed connection on the starter side of the solenoid, and earth. When the ignition switch is turned to the 'start' position, there should be a reading or lighted bulb, as applicable. If there is no reading or lighted bulb, the solenoid is faulty and should be renewed.

6 If the circuit and solenoid are proved sound, the fault must lie in the starter motor. In this event, it may be possible to have the starter motor overhauled by a specialist, but check on the cost of spares before proceeding, as it may prove more economical to obtain a new or exchange motor.

10.5 Vacuum reservoir retaining bolt (arrowed)

10 Starter motor –
removal and refitting

Removal

1 Disconnect the battery (see Section 4).
2 So that access to the motor can be gained both from above and below, apply the handbrake then jack up the front of the vehicle and support it on axle stands (see *Jacking and vehicle support*). Undo the retaining bolts/nuts and remove the engine undershield.
3 Remove the battery and the battery tray as described in Section 4.
4 Remove the air cleaner housing and air ducting as described in Chapter 4A Section 4.
5 Depending on model, undo the retaining bolt and remove the vacuum reservoir from below the starter motor, on the rear of the engine **(see illustration)**.
6 Disconnect the wiring connectors from the starter motor solenoid, and where fitted, recover the washers under the nuts **(see illustrations)**.
7 Release the wiring loom from the retaining clips, and then if required, undo the bolt securing the wiring loom support plate above the starter motor **(see illustration)**.
8 Undo the three mounting bolts (two at the rear of the motor, and one which comes through from the top of the transmission

10.6a Undo the two nuts (arrowed) and disconnect the starter motor wiring – early models

10.6b Undo the nut and wiring connector (arrowed) from the starter motor – later models

10.7 Undo the bolt (arrowed) securing the wiring loom support plate

housing), supporting the starter motor as the bolts are withdrawn. Recover the washers from under the bolt heads and note the locations of any wiring or hose brackets secured by the bolts **(see illustration)**.

9 Manoeuvre the starter motor out from underneath the engine; recover the locating dowel(s) from the motor/transmission so that they do not get lost **(see illustration)**.

Refitting

10 Refitting is a reversal of removal, ensuring that the locating dowel(s) are correctly positioned. Also make sure that any wiring or hose brackets are in place under the bolt heads as noted prior to removal.

11 Starter motor –
testing and overhaul

1 If the starter motor is thought to be suspect, it should be removed from the vehicle and taken to an auto-electrician for testing. Most auto-electricians will be able to supply and fit brushes at a reasonable cost. However, check on the cost of repairs before proceeding, as it may prove more economical to obtain a new or exchange motor.

12 Ignition switch –
removal and refitting

1 The ignition switch is integral with the steering column lock, and can be removed as described in Chapter 10, Section 18.

13 Oil pressure warning light
switch – removal and refitting

Removal

1 The switch is fitted at the front of the cylinder block, adjacent to the oil dipstick

10.8 Starter motor mounting bolts (arrowed)

guide tube on the front of the cylinder block.

2 Note that on some models access to the switch may be improved if the vehicle is jacked up and supported on axle stands, and the engine undershield removed, so that the switch can be reached from underneath (see *Jacking and vehicle support*).

3 Remove the protective sleeve from the wiring plug (where applicable), and then release the securing clip and disconnect the wiring from the switch **(see illustration)**.

4 Unscrew the switch from the cylinder block, and recover the sealing washer **(see illustration)**. Be prepared for oil spillage, and if the switch is to be left removed from the engine for any length of time, plug the hole in the cylinder block.

Refitting

5 Examine the sealing washer for signs of damage or deterioration and if necessary renew.

6 Refit the switch, complete with washer, and tighten it securely. Reconnect the wiring connector.

7 Lower the vehicle to the ground and then check the oil level. If necessary, top-up the engine oil as described in *Weekly checks*.

10.9 Remove the starter motor

14 Oil level sensor –
removal and refitting

1 The sensor, is located in the rear lower part of the cylinder block, at the centre **(see illustration)**.

2 So that access to the sensor can be gained from below, apply the handbrake then jack up the front of the vehicle and support it on axle stands (see *Jacking and vehicle support*). Undo the retaining bolts/nuts and remove the engine undershield.

3 Release the securing clip and disconnect the wiring from the switch.

4 Unscrew the switch from the cylinder block, and recover the sealing washer (where fitted). Be prepared for oil spillage, and if the switch is to be left removed from the engine for any length of time, plug the hole in the cylinder block.

5 Examine the sealing washer (where fitted) for signs of damage or deterioration and if necessary renew.

6 Refit the switch, complete with washer, and tighten it securely. Reconnect the wiring connector.

7 Lower the vehicle to the ground and then check the oil level. If necessary, top-up the engine oil as described in *Weekly checks*

13.3 Disconnect the wiring connector from the oil pressure switch

13.4 Unscrew the switch from the cylinder block

14.1 Disconnect the wiring connector from the oil level sensor

Chapter 5 Part B
Pre/post-heating system

Contents

Degrees of difficulty

Easy, suitable for novice with little experience	Fairly easy, suitable for beginner with some experience	Fairly difficult, suitable for competent DIY mechanic	Difficult, suitable for experienced DIY mechanic	Very difficult, suitable for expert DIY or professional

Specifications

Preheating system
Preheating period at ambient temperatures of (approximate values):

-30°C	15 seconds
-25°C	10 seconds
-10°C	5 seconds
0°C	0.5 seconds
20°C	0 seconds

Post-heating system
Post-heating period at ambient temperatures of (approximate values):

-30°C	3 minutes
-20°C	3 minutes
-10°C	3 minutes
0°C	3 minutes
20°C	0.5 seconds
80°C	0 seconds

Torque wrench settings	Nm	lbf ft
Glow plugs	9	7

1 Pre/post-heating system – description and testing

Description

1 To assist cold starting, diesel engines are fitted with a preheating system, which consists of four glow plugs (one per cylinder), a glow plug relay unit, a facia-mounted warning lamp, the engine management ECM, and the associated electrical wiring.
2 The glow plugs are miniature electric heating elements, encapsulated in a metal case with a probe at one end and electrical connection at the other. Each combustion chamber has one glow plug threaded into it, with the tip of the glow plug probe positioned directly in line with incoming spray of fuel from the injectors. When the glow plug is energised, it heats up rapidly, causing the fuel passing over the glow plug probe to be heated to its optimum temperature, ready for combustion. In addition, some of the fuel passing over the glow plugs is ignited and this helps to trigger the combustion process.
3 The preheating system begins to operate as soon as the ignition key is switched to the second position, but only if the engine coolant temperature is below 20° C and the engine is turned at more than 70 rpm for 0.2 seconds. A facia-mounted warning lamp informs the driver that preheating is taking place. The lamp extinguishes when sufficient preheating has taken place to allow the engine to be started, but power will still be supplied to the glow plugs for a further period until the engine is started. If no attempt is made to start the engine, the power supply to the glow plugs is switched off after 10 seconds, to prevent battery drain and glow plug burn-out.

1.12 Pull the connector from the glow plug

2.2a Using a pair of long-nose pliers to disconnect connector

2.2b Undo the nuts securing the glow plug connections (arrowed)

4 With the electronically controlled diesel injection systems fitted to models in this manual, the glow plug relay unit is controlled by the engine management system ECM, which determines the necessary preheating time based on inputs from the various system sensors. The system monitors the temperature of the intake air, and then alters the preheating time (the length for which the glow plugs are supplied with current) to suit the conditions.

5 Post-heating takes place after the ignition key has been released from the 'start' position, but only if the engine coolant temperature is below 20°C, the injected fuel flow is less than a certain rate, and the engine speed is less than 2000 rpm. The glow plugs continue to operate for a maximum of 180 seconds, helping to improve fuel combustion whilst the engine is warming-up, resulting in quieter, smoother running and reduced exhaust emissions.

Testing

6 If the system malfunctions, testing is ultimately by substitution of known good units, but some preliminary checks may be made as follows.

7 Connect a voltmeter or 12 volt test lamp between the glow plug supply cable and earth (engine or vehicle metal). Make sure that the live connection is kept clear of the engine and bodywork.

8 Have an assistant switch on the ignition, and check that voltage is applied to the glow plugs. Note the time for which the warning light is lit, and the total time for which voltage

is applied before the system cuts out. Switch off the ignition.

9 Compare the results with the information given in the Specifications. Warning light time will increase with lower temperatures and decrease with higher temperatures.

10 If there is no supply at all, the control module or associated wiring is at fault.

11 To gain access to the glow plugs for further testing, remove the following components, according to model:
a) *1.6 litre DOHC engine: Remove the cylinder head cover/manifold assembly as described in Chapter 2B, Section 4.*
b) *1.6 litre SOHC engine: Working as described in Chapter 4A, Section 4, remove the air cleaner assembly.*

12 Disconnect the main supply cable and the interconnecting wire or strap from the top of the glow plugs. Pull the wiring connector upwards to release it from the top of the glow plug **(see illustration)**. On engines with securing nuts holding the wiring to the top of the glow plug, undo the retaining nut, taking care not to drop the nuts and washers.

13 Use a continuity tester or a 12 volt test lamp connected to the battery positive terminal to check for continuity between each glow plug terminal and earth. The resistance of a glow plug in good condition is very low (less than 1 ohm), so if the test lamp does not light or the continuity tester shows a high resistance, the glow plug is certainly defective.

14 If an ammeter is available, the current draw of each glow plug can be checked.

After an initial surge of 15 to 20 amps, each plug should draw 12 amps. Any plug that draws much more or less than this is probably defective.

15 As a final check, the glow plugs can be removed and inspected as described in the following Section. On completion, refit any components removed for access.

2 Glow plugs – removal, inspection and refitting

Caution: If the preheating system has just been energised, or if the engine has been running, the glow plugs will be very hot.

Removal

1 Ensure the ignition is turned off. To gain access to the glow plugs, remove the components described in Section 1, paragraph 11, according to engine.

2 Either pull the connector upwards to disconnect the wiring connector from the top of the glow plug or unscrew the nuts from the glow plug terminals, and recover the washers **(see illustrations)**.

3 Where applicable, carefully move any obstructing pipes or wires to one side to enable access to the relevant glow plug(s).

4 Unscrew the glow plug(s) and remove from the cylinder head **(see illustrations)**.

Inspection

5 Inspect each glow plug for physical damage. Burnt or eroded glow plug tips can be caused by a bad injector spray pattern. Have the injectors checked if this sort of damage is found.

6 If the glow plugs are in good physical condition, check them electrically using a 12 volt test lamp or continuity tester as described in the previous Section.

7 The glow plugs can be energised by applying 12 volts to them to verify that they heat up evenly and in the required time. Observe the following precautions.
a) *Support the glow plug by clamping it carefully in a vice or self-locking pliers. Remember it will become red-hot.*
b) *Make sure that the power supply or test*

2.4a Unscrew the glow plugs – SOHC engine ...

2.4b ... and remove them from the cylinder head – DOHC engine

3.1 Location of the pre/post-heating relay (arrowed)

3.3 Release the wiring connector (arrowed) and undo the mounting nut

lead incorporates a fuse or overload trip to protect against damage from a short circuit.

c) *After testing, allow the glow plug to cool for several minutes before attempting to handle it.*

8 A glow plug in good condition will start to glow red at the tip after drawing current for 5 seconds or so. Any plug that takes much longer to start glowing, or which starts glowing in the middle instead of at the tip is defective.

Refitting

9 Refit by reversing the removal operations. Apply a smear of copper-based anti-seize

compound to the plug threads and tighten the glow plugs to the specified torque. Do not overtighten, as this can damage the glow plug element.

10 Refit any components removed for access.

3 Pre/post-heating system relay unit – removal and refitting

Removal

1 The unit is located on the left-hand front side of the engine compartment where it is

mounted just in front of the fuse/relay box **(see illustration)**.

2 Disconnect the battery (see precautions in Chapter 5A Section 1).

3 Slide out the wiring connector locking clip and disconnect the wiring connector from the relay unit, then undo the securing nut and remove the relay unit from the front of the engine compartment fusebox **(see illustration)**.

Refitting

4 Refitting is a reversal of removal, ensuring that the wiring connector is correctly connected.

Chapter 6
Clutch

Contents

Degrees of difficulty

Easy, suitable for novice with little experience	Fairly easy, suitable for beginner with some experience	Fairly difficult, suitable for competent DIY mechanic	Difficult, suitable for experienced DIY mechanic	Very difficult, suitable for expert DIY or professional

Specifications

Type
All models . . . . Single dry disc with diaphragm spring, hydraulic operation

Friction disc diameter
All engines . . . . 235 mm

Torque wrench settings

	Nm	lbf ft
Clutch slave cylinder bolts (5-speed)	19	14
Clutch slave cylinder/release bearing bolts (6-speed)	10	7
Pressure plate retaining bolts	20	15

1 General Information

1 The clutch consists of a friction disc, a pressure plate assembly, and a release bearing; all of these components are contained in the large cast-aluminium alloy bellhousing, sandwiched between the engine and the transmission. The release mechanism is hydraulic, operated by a master cylinder and a slave cylinder, which on some models is part of the thrust bearing inside the bellhousing. The hydraulic master cylinder is located in the bulkhead, directly behind the brake pedal, and the clutch fluid reservoir is shared with the brake fluid reservoir on top of the brake master cylinder.

2 The friction disc is fitted between the engine flywheel and the clutch pressure plate, and is allowed to slide on the transmission input shaft splines.

3 The pressure plate assembly is bolted to the engine flywheel. When the engine is running, drive is transmitted from the crankshaft, via the flywheel, to the friction disc (these components being clamped securely together by the pressure plate assembly) and from the friction disc to the transmission input shaft.

4 To interrupt the drive, the spring pressure must be relaxed by the hydraulically operated release mechanism. Depressing the clutch pedal operates the master cylinder, which in turn, through the hydraulic system, presses the release bearing against the pressure plate spring fingers. This causes the springs to deform and releases the clamping force on the pressure plate. When the pedal is released the diaphragm spring forces the pressure plate into contact with the friction linings on the friction plate. The friction disc is now firmly sandwiched between the pressure plate and the flywheel, thus transmitting engine power to the transmission.

5 The clutch pedal is connected to the clutch master cylinder by a short pushrod. The master cylinder is mounted on the engine side of the bulkhead in front of the driver and receives its hydraulic fluid supply from the brake master cylinder reservoir. Depressing the clutch pedal moves the piston in the master cylinder forwards, so forcing hydraulic fluid through the clutch hydraulic pipe to the slave cylinder.

6 On models with external slave cylinder, the piston in the slave cylinder moves forward on the entry of the fluid and actuates the clutch release fork by means of a short pushrod. The release fork pivots on its mounting stud, and the other end of the fork then presses the release bearing against the pressure plate spring fingers. This causes the springs to deform and releases the clamping force on the pressure plate.

7 On models where the slave cylinder is part of the release bearing, the fluid is pushed through the system and the release bearing moves forward against the pressure plate spring fingers. This causes the springs to deform and releases the clamping force on the pressure plate.

8 On all models the clutch operating mechanism is self-adjusting, and no manual adjustment is required.

2 Clutch hydraulic system – bleeding

⚠️ *Warning: Hydraulic fluid is poisonous; wash off immediately and thoroughly in the case of skin contact, and seek immediate medical advice if any fluid is swallowed or gets into the eyes. Certain types of hydraulic fluid are inflammable, and may ignite when allowed into contact with hot components; when servicing any hydraulic system, it is safest to assume that the fluid IS inflammable, and to take precautions against the risk of fire as though it is petrol that is being handled. Hydraulic fluid is also an effective paint stripper, and will attack plastics. If any is spilt, it should be washed off immediately, using copious quantities of clean water. When topping-up or renewing the fluid, always use the recommended type, and ensure that it comes from a freshly opened sealed container.*

1 Obtain a clean container, a suitable length of rubber or clear plastic tubing that is a tight fit over the bleed screw on the clutch slave cylinder, and a tin of the specified hydraulic fluid. The help of an assistant will also be required. If a one-man do-it-yourself bleeding kit for bleeding the brake hydraulic system is available, this can be used quite satisfactorily for the clutch also. Full information on the use of these kits may be found in Chapter 9 Section 2.

2 Remove the air cleaner intake ducting from the front left-hand side of the engine compartment (see Chapter 4A Section 4), to access the clutch bleed screw.

3 Remove the filler cap from the brake master cylinder reservoir, and if necessary top-up the fluid. Keep the reservoir topped-up during subsequent operations.

4 On models with external slave cylinder, remove the dust cap from the slave cylinder bleed screw, located on the lower front facing side of the transmission (see illustration).

5 On models where the slave cylinder is part of the release bearing, remove the dust cap from the bleed screw at the hydraulic connection, located on the lower front facing side of the transmission (see illustration).

6 Connect one end of the bleed tube to the bleed screw, and insert the other end of the tube in the jar containing sufficient clean hydraulic fluid to keep the end of the tube submerged (see illustration).

7 Open the bleed screw half a turn and have your assistant depress the clutch pedal and then slowly release it. Continue this procedure until clean hydraulic fluid, free from air bubbles, emerges from the tube. Now tighten the bleed screw at the end of a downstroke. Make sure that the brake master cylinder reservoir is checked frequently to ensure that the level does not drop too far, allowing air into the system.

8 Check the operation of the clutch pedal. After a few strokes it should feel normal. Any sponginess would indicate air still present in the system.

9 On completion remove the bleed tube and refit the dust cover. Top-up the master cylinder reservoir if necessary and refit the cap. Fluid expelled from the hydraulic system should now be discarded, as it will be contaminated with moisture, air and dirt, making it unsuitable for further use.

2.4 Remove the dust cap from the bleed screw – external slave cylinder

2.5 Dust cap (arrowed) – slave cylinder part of the release bearing

2.6 Air bleed bottle connected to bleed screw

3.1 Unclip the trim panel (arrowed) from under the facia

3.2 Release the end of the pushrod (arrowed) from the pedal

3.5 Release the clips (arrowed), and disconnect the pipes from the master cylinder

3 Clutch master cylinder – removal and refitting

Note: *Before starting work, refer to the note at the beginning of Section 2 concerning the dangers of hydraulic fluid.*

Removal

1 Working inside the driver's footwell, prise up the centre pins, lever out the complete expanding plastic rivets, and remove the trim panel above the pedals **(see illustration)**. Disconnect the interior light from the trim as it is removed.

2 Release the securing clips, and then using a flat ended screwdriver, carefully prise the master cylinder pushrod end from the pedal pin **(see illustration)**.

Caution: There are different types of pushrod fitted, depending on year and model. Check the type of fitment before using any force to remove the pushrod. Some are a ball and socket that just unclip, but some have retaining clips, which need to be released before removal.

3 To minimise hydraulic fluid loss, remove the brake master cylinder reservoir filler cap then tighten it down onto a piece of polythene to obtain an airtight seal.

4 Working inside the engine compartment, down the back of the engine, place absorbent rags under the clutch master cylinder pipe connections in the engine compartment and be prepared for hydraulic fluid loss.

5 Release the master cylinder hydraulic pressure pipe and supply pipe from there retaining clips on the engine compartment bulkhead, then prise out the retaining wire clips and disconnect the pipes from the master cylinder **(see illustration)**. Suitably plug or cap the pipe end to prevent further fluid loss and dirt entry.

6 Rotate the master cylinder 45 degrees clockwise, and remove it from the bulkhead **(see illustration)**.

Refitting

7 Refitting the master cylinder is the reverse sequence to removal, bearing in mind the following points.

a) Ensure all retaining clips are correctly refitted.
b) Remove the piece of polythene from the top of the reservoir.
c) Bleed the clutch hydraulic system as described in Section 2.

4 Clutch slave cylinder – removal and refitting

Note: *Before starting work, refer to the note at the beginning of Section 2 concerning the dangers of hydraulic fluid.*

Removal

External slave cylinder

1 To minimise hydraulic fluid loss, remove the brake master cylinder reservoir filler cap then tighten it down onto a piece of polythene to obtain an airtight seal.

2 Remove the air cleaner intake ducting from the front left-hand side of the engine compartment (see Chapter 4A Section 4), to access the clutch slave cylinder.

3 Place absorbent rags under the clutch slave cylinder located on the lower front facing side of the transmission. Be prepared for hydraulic fluid loss.

4 Where necessary for access, release the wiring harness from the retaining clips and move the harness clear of the slave cylinder.

5 Lever out the retaining clip a little, and then disconnect the hydraulic pipe from the side of the slave cylinder **(see illustration)**. Suitably plug or cap the pipe end to prevent further fluid loss and dirt entry.

6 Undo the two retaining bolts and remove the cylinder from the transmission housing **(see illustration)**.

Slave cylinder part of release bearing

7 On some models, the clutch slave cylinder is part of the release bearing assembly. Refer to Section 7 for the removal and refitting procedure.

3.6 Turn the master cylinder 45° clockwise, and remove it from the bulkhead

4.5 Lever out the hydraulic pipe retaining clip

4.6 Undo the two bolts (arrowed) and remove the clutch slave cylinder

5.4 Clutch return spring assembly (arrowed)

5.5 Pedal pivot bolt retaining nut (arrowed)

Refitting

8 Refitting the slave cylinder is the reverse sequence to removal, bearing in mind the following points.

a) *Apply a little Molykote BR2 Plus grease to the end of the slave cylinder pushrod.*

b) *Remove the piece of polythene from the top of the reservoir.*

c) *Bleed the clutch hydraulic system as described in Section 2.*

5 Clutch pedal – removal and refitting

Removal

1 Release the securing clips and remove the trim panel from above the driver's pedals **(see illustration 3.1)**.

2 Release the securing clips, and then using a flat-bladed screwdriver, prise the master cylinder pushrod end from the pedal pin **(see illustration 3.2)**.

3 To prevent the clutch return spring assembly coming apart when removed a cable tie can be used. Pass the cable tie through the upper mounting point, and then through the lower mounting point to secure it together.

4 Move the clutch pedal upwards and remove the clutch return spring from the lower mounting point and the locating peg on the pedal **(see illustration)**.

5 Undo the nut from the clutch pedal pivot bolt and withdraw the bolt **(see illustration)**.

6.2 Mark the position of the pressure plate on the flywheel

Do not withdraw the bolt completely, as it is also the brake pedal pivot bolt.

6 Remove the clutch pedal from the pedal bracket and recover the bush (where applicable) from the pedal pivot.

7 Check the condition of the pedal, pivot bush and return spring assembly and renew any components as necessary.

Refitting

8 Lubricate the pedal pivot bolt with multipurpose grease, then locate the pedal in the bracket and insert the pivot bolt. Refit the pivot bolt nut and tighten it securely.

9 Reconnect the return spring to the pedal and pedal bracket; making sure it locates correctly. Cut the cable-tie from around the spring once it is in its fitted position.

10 Reconnect the clutch master cylinder pushrod to the clutch pedal.

11 Depress the pedal two or three times and check the operation of the clutch release mechanism.

12 Refit the facia lower trim panel and secure with the plastic clips.

6 Clutch assembly – removal, inspection and refitting

⚠️ **Warning: Dust created by clutch wear and deposited on the clutch components may be a health hazard. DO NOT blow it out with compressed air, nor inhale any of it. DO NOT use petrol or petroleum-based**

6.3 Undo the pressure plate bolts (arrowed)

solvents to clean off the dust. Brake system cleaner or methylated spirit should be used to flush the dust into a suitable receptacle. After the clutch components are wiped clean with rags, dispose of the contaminated rags and cleaner in a sealed, marked container.

Note: *Although most friction materials no longer contain asbestos, it is safest to assume that some still do, and to take precautions accordingly.*

Removal

1 Unless the complete engine/transmission unit is to be removed from the car and separated for major overhaul (see Chapter 2C Section 3), the clutch can be reached by removing the transmission as described in Chapter 7 Section 7.

2 Before disturbing the clutch, use chalk or a marker pen to mark the relationship of the pressure plate assembly to the flywheel **(see illustration)**.

3 Working in a diagonal sequence, slacken the pressure plate bolts by half a turn at a time, until spring pressure is released and the bolts can be unscrewed by hand **(see illustration)**.

4 Prise the pressure plate assembly off its locating dowels, and collect the friction disc, noting which way round the disc is fitted.

Inspection

Note: *Due to the amount of work necessary to remove and refit clutch components, it is considered good practice to renew the clutch friction disc, pressure plate assembly and release bearing as a matched set, even if only one of these is worn enough to require renewal. It is worth considering the renewal of the clutch components on a preventative basis if the engine and/or transmission have been removed for some other reason.*

5 When cleaning clutch components, read the warning at the beginning of this Section first; remove dust using a clean, dry cloth, and working in a well-ventilated atmosphere.

6 Check the friction disc facings for signs of wear, damage or oil contamination. If the friction material is cracked, burnt, scored or damaged, or if it is contaminated with oil or grease (shown by shiny black patches), the friction disc must be renewed.

7 If the friction material is still serviceable, check that the centre boss splines are unworn, that the torsion springs are in good condition and securely fastened, and that all the rivets are tight. If any wear or damage is found, the friction disc must be renewed.

8 If the friction material is fouled with oil, this must be due to an oil leak from the crankshaft left-hand oil seal, from the sump-to-cylinder block joint, or from the transmission input shaft. Renew the seal or repair the joint, as appropriate, as described in Chapter 2A or Chapter 2B, or Chapter 7 Section 4, before installing the new friction disc.

9 Check the pressure plate assembly for

obvious signs of wear or damage; shake it to check for loose rivets or worn or damaged fulcrum rings, and check that the drive straps securing the pressure plate to the cover do not show signs (such as a deep yellow or blue discoloration) of overheating. If the diaphragm spring is worn or damaged, or if its pressure is in any way suspect, the pressure plate assembly should be renewed.

10 Examine the machined bearing surfaces of the pressure plate and of the flywheel; they should be clean, completely flat, and free from scratches or scoring. If either is discoloured from excessive heat, or shows signs of cracks, it should be renewed – although minor damage of this nature can sometimes be polished away using emery paper.

11 Check that the release bearing contact surface rotates smoothly and easily, with no sign of noise or roughness. Also check that the surface itself is smooth and unworn, with no signs of cracks, pitting or scoring. If there is any doubt about its condition, the bearing must be renewed.

Refitting

12 On reassembly, ensure that the bearing surfaces of the flywheel and pressure plate are completely clean, smooth, and free from oil or grease. Use solvent to remove any protective grease from new components.

13 Fit the friction disc so that its spring hub assembly faces away from the flywheel; there may be a marking showing which way round the disc is to be refitted **(see illustrations)**.

Models with self-adjusting clutch

14 On these models, the clutch pressure plate has a pre-adjustment mechanism to compensate for wear in the friction disc (this is termed by Peugeot/Citroën as a self-adjusting clutch (SAC), which is slightly ambiguous as all clutches fitted to these models are essentially self-adjusting). However, this mechanism must be reset before refitting the pressure plate. A new plate may be supplied preset, in which case this procedure can be ignored.

15 A large diameter bolt (M14 at least) long enough to pass through the pressure plate, a matching nut, and several large diameter

6.13a Fit the disc so the spring hub assembly faces away from the flywheel

6.13b ... or the protruding hub away from the flywheel

washers, will be needed for this procedure. Mount the bolt head in the jaws of a sturdy bench vice, with one large washer fitted.

16 Offer the plate over the bolt, friction disc surface facing down, and locate it centrally over the bolt and washer – the washer should bear on the centre hub **(see illustration)**.

17 Fit several further large washers over the bolt, so that they bear on the ends of the spring fingers, then add the nut and tighten by hand to locate the washers.

18 The purpose of the procedure is to turn the plate's internal adjuster disc so that the three small coil springs visible on the plate's outer surface are fully compressed. Tighten the nut just fitted until the adjuster disc is free to turn. Using a pair of thin-nosed, or circlip, pliers in one of the two windows in the top surface, open the jaws of the pliers to turn the adjuster disc anti-clockwise, so that the springs are fully compressed **(see illustration)**.

19 Hold the pliers in this position, and then unscrew the centre nut. Once the nut is released, the adjuster disc will be gripped in position, and the pliers can be removed. Take the pressure plate from the vice, and it is ready to fit.

All models

20 Refit the pressure plate assembly, aligning the marks made on dismantling (if the original pressure plate is re-used), and locating the pressure plate on its three locating dowels. Fit the pressure plate bolts, but tighten them only finger-tight, so that the friction disc can still be moved.

21 The friction disc must now be centralised, so that when the transmission is refitted, its input shaft will pass through the splines at the centre of the friction disc.

22 Centralisation can be achieved by passing a screwdriver or other long bar through the friction disc and into the hole in the crankshaft; the friction disc can then be moved around until it is centred on the crankshaft hole. Alternatively, a clutch-aligning tool can be used to eliminate the guesswork; these can be obtained from most accessory shops **(see illustration)**.

23 When the friction disc is centralised, tighten the pressure plate bolts evenly and in a diagonal sequence to the specified torque setting.

24 Apply a thin smear of molybdenum disulphide grease (Peugeot/Citroën recommend the use of Molykote BR2 Plus) to the splines of the friction disc and the transmission input shaft, and also to the release bearing bore and release fork shaft.

25 Refit the transmission as described in Chapter 7 Section 7.

7 Clutch release mechanism – removal, inspection and refitting

Note: *Refer to the warning concerning the dangers of asbestos dust at the beginning of Section 2.*

6.16 Using some threaded rod, washers and nuts, compress the spring and the pressure plate together ...

6.18 ... then move the adjusting ring (arrowed) anti-clockwise to the stop

6.22 Centralise the friction plate on the flywheel using a clutch aligning tool

7.2 Squeeze the tabs of the retaining clip together and remove the release fork …

7.3 … disengage the release bearing as the fork is removed

7.4a Recover the shim …

Removal

1 Unless the complete engine/transmission unit is to be removed from the car and separated for major overhaul (see Chapter 2C Section 4), the clutch release mechanism can be reached by removing the transmission only, as described in Chapter 7 Section 7.

Transmission with external slave cylinder

2 With the transmission removed, squeeze together the tabs of the retaining clip and pull the release fork off the pivot ball-stud **(see illustration)**.

3 Slide the release bearing off the guide tube and disengage the arms off the release fork **(see illustration)**.

4 If required, recover the shim where fitted and unscrew the mounting stud from the transmission housing **(see illustrations)**.

Transmissions with the slave cylinder part of the release bearing

5 With the transmission removed, undo the three mounting bolts from inside the bellhousing **(see illustration)**.

6 Withdraw the slave cylinder/release bearing by sliding it over the transmission input shaft.

Inspection

7 Check that the release bearing contact surface rotates smoothly and easily, with no sign of noise or roughness, and that the surface itself is smooth and unworn, with no signs of cracks, pitting or scoring. If there is any doubt about its condition, the bearing must be renewed.

8 On external slave cylinder transmissions, check the bearing surfaces and points of contact on the release fork and pivot ball-stud, renewing any component, which is worn or damaged.

7.4b … then unscrew the pivot ball-stud (arrowed)

Refitting

9 Apply a smear of molybdenum disulphide grease to the pivot ball-stud.

10 On external slave cylinder transmissions, insert the outer end of the release fork through the rubber boot in the side of the transmission bellhousing. Engage the arms of the release fork with the release bearing collar, then slide the release bearing onto the guide tube. Position the shim over the tabs of the pivot

7.10a Refit the release fork into the rubber gaiter and release bearing

7.5 Undo the slave cylinder/release bearing retaining bolts

ball-stud clip, then push the fork over the stud, ensuring the tabs of the retaining clip engage correctly with the fork **(see illustrations)**.

11 On transmissions where the slave cylinder is part of the release bearing, slide the slave cylinder/release bearing over the transmission input shaft and tighten the retaining bolts to the specified torque setting.

12 Refit the transmission as described in Chapter 7, Section 7.

7.10b Ensure the retaining tabs (arrowed) engage correctly with the release fork

Chapter 7
Manual transmission

Contents

Degrees of difficulty

Easy, suitable for novice with little experience	Fairly easy, suitable for beginner with some experience	Fairly difficult, suitable for competent DIY mechanic	Difficult, suitable for experienced DIY mechanic	Very difficult, suitable for expert DIY or professional

Specifications

General
Type . . . . Manual, five forward speeds and reverse. Synchromesh on all forward speeds
Designation BE4/5

Lubrication
Capacity . . . . Refer to Chapter 1
Recommended oil type . . . . See *Lubricants and fluids*

Torque wrench settings

	Nm	lbf ft
Clutch release bearing guide sleeve bolts	15	11
Engine-to-transmission fixing bolts	Refer to Chapter 2A or 2B	
Gearchange lever mounting nuts	8	6
Left-hand engine/transmission mounting	Refer to Chapter 2A or 2B	
Neutral sensor bolt	10	7
Oil drain plug	35	26
Oil filler/level plug	22	16
Reversing light switch	25	18
Roadwheel bolts	100	74
Speedometer drive housing bolts	15	11

1 General Information

1 The transmission is contained in a cast-aluminium alloy casing bolted to the engine's left-hand end, and consists of the gearbox and final drive differential – often called a transaxle.

2 Drive is transmitted from the crankshaft via the clutch to the input shaft that has a splined extension to accept the clutch friction disc, and rotates in sealed ball-bearings. From the input shaft, drive is transmitted to the output shaft, which rotates in a roller bearing at its right-hand end, and a sealed ball-bearing at its left-hand end. From the output shaft, the drive is transmitted to the differential crownwheel, which rotates with the differential case and planetary gears, thus driving the sun gears and driveshafts. The rotation of the planetary gears on their shaft allows the inner roadwheel to rotate at a slower speed than the outer roadwheel when the car is cornering.

3 The input and output shafts are arranged side-by-side, parallel to the crankshaft and driveshafts, so that their gear pinion teeth are in constant mesh. In the neutral position, the output shaft gear pinions rotate freely, so that drive cannot be transmitted to the crownwheel.

4 On some transmissions, the oil level cannot be checked, as there is no filler/level plug fitted. These transmissions do not require regular maintenance and are filled for life. If the transmission develops a leak or is removed for other work, the oil needs to be completely drained and refilled with the correct amount of oil. The transmission will then be refilled through the vent on the top of the transmission.

5 Gear selection is via a facia-mounted lever and two cables, which pass through the floor panel to the top of the transmission housing. The selector/gearchange cables cause the appropriate selector fork to move its respective synchro-sleeve along the shaft, to lock the gear pinion to the synchro-hub. Since the synchro-hubs are splined to the output shaft, this locks the pinion to the shaft, so that drive can be transmitted. To ensure that gearchanging can be made quickly and quietly, a synchromesh system is fitted to all forward gears, consisting of baulk rings and spring-loaded fingers, as well as the gear pinions and synchro-hubs. The synchromesh cones are formed on the mating faces of the baulk rings and gear pinions.

2 Manual transmission – draining and refilling

Note: *A suitable square section wrench may be required to undo the transmission filler/level and drain plugs on some models. These wrenches can be obtained from most motor factors or your Peugeot/Citroën dealer.*

2.3 Oil drain plug (arrowed)

1 This operation is much quicker and more efficient if the car is first taken on a journey of sufficient length to warm the engine/transmission up to normal operating temperature.

2 Park the car on level ground, switch off the ignition and apply the handbrake firmly. For improved access, jack up the front of the car and support it securely on axle stands (see *Jacking and vehicle support*). Note that on models with filler/level plug fitted, the car must be level to ensure accuracy when refilling and checking the oil level. Undo the screws and remove the engine undershield.

3 Position a suitable container under the drain plug (situated on the final drive casing at the rear of the transmission) and unscrew the plug **(see illustration)**.

4 Allow the oil to drain completely into the container. If the oil is hot, take precautions against scalding. Clean the drain plug, being especially careful to wipe any metallic particles off the magnetic inserts. Discard the original sealing washer, as it should be renewed whenever it is disturbed.

Models with filler/level plug

5 To improve access to the filler/level plug, remove the left-hand front wheel and wheel arch liner.

6 Wipe clean the area around the filler/level plug; it is situated on the left-hand end of the transmission, next to the end cover. The filler/level plug is the largest bolt among those securing the end cover to the transmission.

2.13a Vent on top of transmission housing (arrowed)

2.6 Oil filler/level plug (arrowed)

Remove the filler/level plug from the transmission and recover the sealing washer **(see illustration)**.

7 When the oil has finished draining, clean the drain plug threads and those of the transmission casing, fit a new sealing washer and refit the drain plug, tightening it to the specified torque wrench setting. Refit the undercover (where fitted), and then check that the vehicle is level before refilling.

8 Refilling the transmission is an extremely awkward operation. Above all, allow plenty of time for the oil level to settle properly before checking it. Note that the car must be parked on flat level ground when checking the oil level.

9 Refill the transmission with the exact amount of the specified type of oil, and then check the oil level as described in Chapter 1, Section 21 if the correct amount was poured into the transmission and a large amount flows out on checking the level, refit the filler/level plug and roadwheel, then take the car on a short journey so that the new oil is distributed fully around the transmission components, then check the level again on your return.

10 Once the oil level is correct securely refit the inner cover/wheel arch liner and roadwheel; tighten to the specified torque.

Models without filler/level plugs

Note: *The oil level cannot be checked, as there is no level plug fitted. These transmissions do not require regular maintenance and are filled for life. If the transmission develops a leak or is removed for other work, the oil needs to be*

2.13b Unclip the breather/vent cap and add the exact amount of fluid specified using a funnel

3.3a Undo the retaining screw…

3.3b …and unclip the outer cable

3.4 Release the locking clip to disconnect cable

completely drained and refilled with the correct amount of oil. The transmission will then be refilled through the vent/breather on the top of the transmission (see illustration 2.13a).

11 Remove the battery and battery tray as described in Chapter 5A Section 4.

12 When the oil has finished draining, clean the drain plug threads and those of the transmission casing, fit a new sealing washer and refit the drain plug, tightening it to the specified torque wrench setting. Refit the undercover (where fitted) then lower the vehicle to the ground.

13 Carefully prise off the breather cap from the top of the transmission casing, and then using a funnel, add the exact amount of transmission oil specified **(see illustrations)**.

14 Clean up any spilt oil, and then refit the breather cap.

15 Refit the battery tray and battery with reference to Chapter 5A Section 4 if required.

3.7 Prise the gearchange cables (arrowed) from their balljoints

3.9 Gearchange cable rubber grommet (arrowed) fitted in floor panel

outer cable from the gear lever housing **(see illustrations)**.

4 Push the securing clip on the end of the inner cable connection, and then disconnect the cable from the ball joint on the gear lever assembly **(see illustration)**. Carry out the same procedure on the second gearchange cable.

5 Undo the bolts securing the gearchange lever housing to the facia mounting bracket and remove the housing assembly from the vehicle. The gearchange lever is integral with the housing, and is not available separately.

6 Working inside the engine compartment, remove the battery and battery tray, as described in Chapter 5A, Section 4.

7 Note their fitted locations, then carefully prise the two gearchange cable balljoints from the selector levers on the transmission **(see illustration)**.

8 Rotate the collars on the outer cables,

then pull the outer cables upwards to release them from the support bracket on top of the transmission housing. Note the cables fitted position for refitting.

9 Release the cable sealing grommet from the floor, and manoeuvre the cables from the vehicle **(see illustration)**. Note on some models it may be necessary to remove the exhaust heat shield from under the vehicle to access the cable grommet.

Refitting

10 Refitting is a reversal of the removal procedure.

Adjustment

Note: *Peugeot/Citroen have a special tool (0317-AV), that fits around the gear lever to hold it in the neutral position. If this is not available, then make sure that the gear lever inside the vehicle, and the levers on the top of the transmission are in the neutral position.*

11 If not already done, remove the lower facia panel from around the gear lever assembly, as described in Chapter 11 Section 28

12 Use a small screwdriver to lever back the yellow locking clips on the ends of the gearchange cables **(see illustration)**. The gear selection cables are then in the adjustment position.

13 Make sure the gear lever and transmission are in the neutral position, then push the yellow locking clips back into position to secure the cables **(see illustration)**.

14 Check the operation of the gearchange lever. If all is satisfactory, refit the lower facia trim panel.

3 Gearchange lever and cables – removal, refitting and adjustment

Removal

1 Firmly apply the handbrake, and then jack up the front of the vehicle and support it on axle stands (see *Jacking and vehicle support*).

2 Remove the lower facia panel from around the gear lever assembly, as described in Chapter 11 Section 28.

3 Undo the retaining screw and release the

3.12 Lever the locking clips out from the inner cable

3.13 Press the locking clip inwards to reset the gearchange cable

4.2 Use a large flat-bladed screwdriver to prise out the driveshaft oil seals

4.3a Fit the new seal to the transmission, noting the plastic seal protector ...

4.3b ... and tap it into position using a tubular drift/socket

4 Oil seals – renewal

Driveshaft oil seals

1 Remove the appropriate driveshaft as described in Chapter 8, Section 2.

2 Carefully prise the oil seal out of the transmission, using a large flat-bladed screwdriver (see illustration).

3 Remove all traces of dirt from the area around the oil seal aperture, then apply a smear of grease to the outer lip of the new oil seal. Fit the new seal into its aperture, and drive it squarely into position using a suitable tubular drift (such as a socket) which bears only on the hard outer edge of the seal until it abuts its locating shoulder. If the seal was

supplied with a plastic protector sleeve, leave this in position until the driveshaft has been refitted (see illustrations).

4 Apply a thin film of grease to the oil seal lip.

5 Refit the driveshaft as described in Chapter 8 Section 2.

Input shaft oil seal

Note: *On some transmission, the oil seal appears to be integral with the guide sleeve. Check with your Peugeot/Citroën parts specialist before removal.*

6 Remove the transmission as described in Section 7, and the clutch release mechanism as described in, Section 7.

7 Undo the three bolts (two bolts on some models) securing the clutch release bearing guide sleeve in position, and slide the guide off the input shaft, along with its sealing ring or gasket (as applicable) (see illustrations).

Recover any shims or thrustwashers, which have stuck to the rear of the guide sleeve, and refit them to the input shaft.

8 Where applicable, carefully lever the oil seal out of the guide using a suitable flat-bladed screwdriver (see illustration).

9 Before fitting a new seal, check the input shaft's seal rubbing surface for signs of burrs, scratches or other damage, which may have caused the seal to fail in the first place. It may be possible to polish away minor faults of this sort using fine abrasive paper; however, more serious defects will require the renewal of the input shaft. Ensure that the input shaft is clean and greased, to protect the seal lips on refitting.

10 Where applicable, dip the new seal in clean oil, and fit it to the guide sleeve.

11 On transmissions where the seals are integral with the guide sleeve, lubricate the lips of the seal before refitting.

12 Fit a new sealing ring or gasket (as applicable) to the rear of the guide sleeve, then carefully slide the sleeve into position over the input shaft. Refit the retaining bolts and tighten them to the specified torque setting (see illustration).

13 Take the opportunity to inspect the clutch components if not already done (Chapter 6, Section 6). Finally, refit the transmission as described in Section 7.

Selector shaft oil seal

14 Park the car on level ground, apply the handbrake, slacken the left-hand front roadwheel bolts, then jack up the front of the vehicle and support it on axle stands (see *Jacking and vehicle support*). Remove the left-hand front roadwheel.

15 Using a large flat-bladed screwdriver, lever the link rod balljoint off the transmission selector shaft, and disconnect the link rod.

16 Using a large flat-bladed screwdriver, carefully prise the selector shaft seal out of the housing, and slide it off the end of the shaft.

17 Before fitting a new seal, check the selector shaft's seal rubbing surface for signs of burrs, scratches or other damage, which may have caused the seal to fail in the first place. It may be possible to polish away minor faults of this sort using fine abrasive paper;

4.7a Undo the three bolts (arrowed) and remove the guide sleeve ...

4.7b ... and any shims, where fitted

4.8 Remove the input shaft seal from the guide sleeve

4.12 Fit a new O-ring/gasket (as applicable) to the guide sleeve

5.1 Location of reversing light switch

7.5 Remove the intercooler hoses – turbo models

7.7 Front lower crossmember retaining bolts (arrowed)

however, more serious defects will require the renewal of the selector shaft.

18 Apply a smear of grease to the new seal's outer edge and sealing lip, then carefully slide the seal along the selector rod. Press the seal fully into position in the transmission housing.

19 Refit the link rod to the selector shaft, ensuring that its balljoint is pressed firmly onto the shaft. Lower the car to the ground.

5 Reversing light switch – testing, removal and refitting

Testing

1 The reversing light circuit is controlled by a plunger-type switch, which is screwed into the front of the transmission housing **(see illustration)**. If a fault develops, first ensure that the circuit fuse has not blown.

2 To test the switch, disconnect the wiring connector, and use a multimeter (set to the resistance function) or a battery-and-bulb test circuit to check that there is continuity between the switch terminals only when reverse gear is selected. If this is not the case, and there are no obvious breaks or other damage to the wires, the switch is faulty, and must be renewed.

Removal

3 Where necessary, to improve access to

7.8 Remove the front strengthener bar (arrowed)

the switch, remove the battery and tray (see Chapter 5A, Section 4).

4 Disconnect the wiring connector, and then unscrew the switch from the transmission casing along with its sealing washer.

Refitting

5 Fit a new sealing washer to the switch, then screw it back into position in the top of the transmission housing and tighten it to the specified torque setting. Refit the wiring plug, and test the operation of the circuit. Refit any components removed for access.

6 Speedometer drive – general information

1 The speedometer receives vehicle speed data from the engine management ECM, which is supplied by the wheel speed sensors and the ABS ECM.

7 Manual transmission – removal and refitting

Removal

1 Chock the rear wheels, then firmly apply the handbrake. Slacken both front roadwheel

7.12 Release the retaining clip (arrowed), to disconnect the fluid supply pipe

bolts. Jack up the front of the vehicle, and securely support it on axle stands (see *Jacking and vehicle support*). Remove both front roadwheels, and the plastic engine undershields.

2 Drain the transmission oil as described in Section 2, and then refit the drain and filler plugs (where applicable).

3 Remove both driveshafts as described in Chapter 8, Section 2.

4 In order to prevent any damage, remove the exhaust front flexible pipe as described in Chapter 4A, Section 18.

5 On turbocharged diesel engines, remove the air intake hoses from the top of the intercooler to prevent any damage as the engine is tilted to allow the transmission to be removed **(see illustration)**.

6 Remove the front bumper as described in Chapter 11, Section 6.

7 Undo the retaining bolts and remove the lower crossbeam from the front of the vehicle **(see illustration)**.

8 Undo the retaining bolts and remove the strengthener bar (where fitted) from across the front of the main subframe and the subframe side-member **(see illustration)**.

9 Remove the battery and battery tray as described in Chapter 5A, Section 4.

10 Remove the starter motor (Chapter 5A, Section 10).

11 On transmissions with external slave cylinders, detach the clutch slave cylinder from the front of the transmission as described in Chapter 6, Section 4. Note the slave cylinder can be moved to one side; there is no need to disconnect the fluid pipe from the cylinder.

12 On transmissions with integral release bearing/slave cylinder, disconnect the fluid supply pipe to the front of the transmission **(see illustration)**, as described in Chapter 6, Section 4. Plug the ends of the fluid pipes, to prevent dirt ingress.

13 Disconnect the wiring connector from the reversing light switch on the upper front part of the transmission housing.

14 Disconnect the gearchange cables from the transmission and support bracket as described in Section 3.

15 Undo the retaining bolt and disconnect the

7.15 Disconnect the earth cable (arrowed) from the top of the transmission

7.16 Remove the impact absorber (arrowed) from the transmission

7.20 Remove the transmission mounting

earth cable from the top of the transmission housing **(see illustration)**.

16 Where fitted, undo the retaining bolts and remove the impact absorber from the rear of the differential casing **(see illustration)**.

17 Depending on model, there may be a lower cover plate fitted to the transmission. Where fitted, undo the retaining bolts, and remove the cover plate from the transmission.

18 Place a jack with a block of wood beneath the engine, to take the weight of the engine. Alternatively, attach a couple of lifting eyes to the engine, and fit a hoist or support bar to take the engine weight.

19 Place a jack and block of wood beneath the transmission, and raise the jack to take the weight of the transmission.

20 Slacken and remove the mounting bolts/nuts from the left-hand transmission mounting and remove it from the top of the transmission **(see illustration)**. Refer to Chapter 2A, Section 17 or Chapter 2B Section 17, for further information on engine/transmission mountings.

21 Undo the retaining bolts and remove the mounting stud bracket from the top of the transmission housing.

22 Note their fitted positions, and then disconnect all wiring plugs/retaining clips from around the transmission. Note the harness routing and move the harness to one side.

23 With the jack positioned beneath the transmission taking the weight, slacken and remove the remaining bolts securing the transmission housing to the engine. Note the correct fitted positions of each bolt and the necessary brackets as they are removed, to use as a reference on refitting. With the nuts removed, slacken the studs from the top and front edge of the transmission, to allow for the removal of the transmission.

24 Make a final check that all components have been disconnected, and are positioned clear of the transmission so that they will not hinder the removal procedure.

Caution: As the engine is lowered, make sure no wiring, hoses or cables are being stretched or damaged in any way.

25 With the bolts/nuts removed, move the trolley jack and transmission to the left, to free it from its locating dowels. Lower the engine slightly to enable the transmission to be freed. *Caution: Take great care not to damage the radiator if the engine is moved – place a sheet of thick cardboard over the rear face of the radiator. On models equipped with air conditioning, care must also be taken to ensure the auxiliary drivebelt pulleys do not damage the air conditioning pipes on the right-hand side of the engine compartment.*

26 Once the transmission is free, lower the jack and manoeuvre the unit out from under the car. Remove the locating dowels from the transmission or engine if they are loose, and keep them in a safe place.

Refitting

27 The transmission is refitted by a reversal of the removal procedure, bearing in mind the following points:

a) Prior to refitting, check the clutch assembly and release mechanism components (see Chapter 6, Section 6). Lubricate the release-bearing guide with a little high melting-point grease (Peugeot/Citroën recommend the use of Molykote BR2 Plus). Do not apply too much grease, otherwise there is a possibility of the grease contaminating the clutch friction disc, and ensure no grease is applied to the input shaft/friction disc splines.

b) Ensure that the locating dowels are correctly positioned prior to installation.

c) Tighten all nuts and bolts to the specified torque (where given).

d) Renew the driveshaft oil seals (Section 4), then refit the driveshafts (see Chapter 8, Section 2).

e) Refit the slave cylinder (see Chapter 6, Section 4).

f) On completion, refill the transmission with the specified type and quantity of lubricant, as described in Section 2.

8 Manual transmission overhaul – general information

1 Overhauling a manual transmission is a difficult and involved job for the DIY home mechanic. In addition to dismantling and reassembling many small parts, clearances must be precisely measured and, if necessary, changed by selecting shims and spacers. Internal transmission components are also often difficult to obtain, and in many instances, extremely expensive. Because of this, if the transmission develops a fault or becomes noisy, the best course of action is to have the unit overhauled by a specialist repairer, or to obtain an exchange reconditioned unit.

2 Nevertheless, it is not impossible for the more experienced mechanic to overhaul the transmission, provided the special tools are available, and the job is done in a deliberate step-by-step manner, so that nothing is overlooked.

3 The tools necessary for an overhaul include internal and external circlip pliers, bearing pullers, slide hammer, set of pin punches, dial test indicator, and possibly a hydraulic press. In addition, a large, sturdy workbench and a vice will be required.

4 During dismantling of the transmission, make careful notes of how each component is fitted, to make reassembly easier and more accurate.

5 Before dismantling the transmission, it will help if you have some idea what area is malfunctioning. Certain problems can be closely related to specific areas in the transmission, which can make component examination and renewal easier. Refer to Fault finding for more information.

Chapter 8
Driveshafts

Contents

Degrees of difficulty

Easy, suitable for novice with little experience	Fairly easy, suitable for beginner with some experience	Fairly difficult, suitable for competent DIY mechanic	Difficult, suitable for experienced DIY mechanic	Very difficult, suitable for expert DIY or professional

Specifications

Lubrication (overhaul only – see text)

Lubricant type/specification .... Use only special grease supplied in sachets with gaiter kits – joints are otherwise pre-packed with grease and sealed

Torque wrench settings

	Nm	lbf ft
Driveshaft retaining nut	312	232
Right-hand driveshaft intermediate bearing retaining bolt	10	7
Roadwheel bolts	100	74
Suspension strut-to-hub carrier bolts	90	66

1 General Information

1 Drive is transmitted from the differential to the front wheels by means of two solid-steel driveshafts of unequal length.

2 Both driveshafts are splined at their outer ends, to accept the wheel hubs, and are threaded so that each hub can be fastened by a large nut. The inner end of each driveshaft is splined, to accept the differential sun gear.

3 Constant velocity (CV) joints are fitted to each end of the driveshafts, to ensure that the smooth and efficient transmission of power at all suspension and steering angles. The outer constant velocity joints are of the ball-and-cage type, and the inner constant velocity joints are of the tripod type.

4 On the right-hand side, due to the length of the driveshaft, the inner constant velocity joint is situated approximately halfway along the shaft's length, and an intermediate support bearing is mounted in the engine/transmission rear mounting bracket. The inner end of the driveshaft passes through the bearing (which prevents any lateral movement of the driveshaft inner end) and the inner constant velocity joint outer member. On automatic transmission models, the inboard end of the right-hand driveshaft fits over a splined shaft from the transmission differential.

2 Driveshafts – removal and refitting

Removal

1 Remove the wheel trim/hub cap (as applicable) then withdraw the R-clip and remove the locking cap from the driveshaft retaining nut. Slacken the driveshaft nut with the vehicle resting on its wheels. Also slacken the wheel bolts.

2 Chock the rear wheels of the car, firmly apply the handbrake, and then jack up the

2.5a Use a screwdriver to prise out the R-clip

front of the car and support it on axle stands (see *Jacking and vehicle support*). Remove the appropriate front roadwheel.

3 Drain the transmission oil as described in Chapter 7, Section 2 .

4 Unclip the wiring for the ABS wheel speed sensor, to make sure that it does not get damaged as the hub assembly is moved.

5 Slacken and remove the driveshaft retaining nut. If the nut was not slackened with the wheels on the ground (see paragraph 1), withdraw the R-clip and remove the locking cap **(see illustration)**. Refit at least two roadwheel bolts to the front hub, tightening them securely, then have an assistant firmly depress the brake pedal to prevent the front hub from rotating, whilst you slacken and remove the driveshaft retaining nut. Alternatively, a tool can be fabricated from two lengths of steel strip (one long, one short) and a nut and bolt; the nut and bolt forming the pivot of a forked tool **(see illustration)**.

6 Undo the brake caliper guide pin or guide pin bolts and slide the caliper from the disc (refer to Chapter 9, Section 8, if required). Suspend the caliper from the suspension coil spring using a cable-tie to prevent straining the brake hose. Discard the guide pin bolts, new ones must be fitted.

7 Undo the retaining nut and disconnect the track rod end from the stub axle **(see illustration)**.

2.5b Using a fabricated tool to hold the front hub stationary whilst the driveshaft nut is slackened

Left-hand driveshaft

8 Slacken and remove the two bolts securing the steering hub carrier to the base of the suspension strut **(see illustration)**.

9 Pull the hub carrier outwards to free it from the strut. **Note:** *After releasing the hub carrier, rotate the base of the strut 90° towards the rear of the vehicle to minimise the chances of damaging the rubber driveshaft gaiter* **(see illustration)**.

10 Turn the steering to full left-hand lock, carefully pull the swivel hub assembly outwards, and withdraw the driveshaft outer constant velocity joint from the hub assembly. If necessary, the shaft can be tapped out of the hub using a soft-faced mallet.

11 Support the driveshaft, and then withdraw the inner constant velocity joint from the transmission, taking care not to damage the driveshaft oil seal. Remove the driveshaft from the vehicle. **Note:** *Do not allow the vehicle to rest on its wheels with one or both driveshafts removed, as damage to the wheel bearing(s) may result. If moving the vehicle is unavoidable, temporarily insert the outer end of the driveshaft(s) in the hub(s) and tighten the driveshaft nut(s). Support the inner end(s) of the driveshaft(s) to avoid damage.*

Right-hand driveshaft

12 Loosen the two intermediate bearing retaining bolt, then rotate the retaining plate

2.7 Disconnect the track rod end

2.8 Note the fitted position of the two bolts (arrowed)

2.9 Rotate the base of the strut 90° towards the rear to minimise any chance of damaging the driveshaft gaiter

2.12 Slacken the two intermediate bearing retaining bolts (arrowed)

2.24a Tighten the driveshaft nut to the specified torque, then refit the locking cap ...

2.24b ... and secure it in position with the R-clip

anti-clockwise, so that it is clear of the bearing outer race (see illustration).

13 Slacken and remove the two bolts securing the steering hub carrier to the base of the suspension strut. Pull the hub carrier outwards to free it from the strut. Note: After releasing the hub carrier, rotate the *base of the strut 90° towards the rear of the vehicle to minimise the chances of damaging the rubber driveshaft gaiter* (see illustrations 2.8 and 2.9).

14 Carefully pull the swivel hub assembly outwards, and withdraw the driveshaft outer constant velocity joint from the hub assembly. If necessary, the shaft can be tapped out of the hub using a soft-faced mallet.

15 Support the outer end of the driveshaft, then pull on the inner end of the shaft to free the intermediate bearing from its mounting bracket.

16 Once the driveshaft end is free from the transmission, slide the dust seal (where fitted) off the inner end of the shaft, noting which way around it is fitted, and remove the driveshaft from the vehicle. Check the condition of the splined shaft O-ring. Note: *Do not allow the vehicle to rest on its wheels with one or both driveshafts removed, as damage to the wheel bearing(s) may result. If moving the vehicle is unavoidable, temporarily insert the outer end of the driveshaft(s) in the hub(s) and tighten the driveshaft nut(s). Support the inner end(s) of the driveshaft(s) to avoid damage.*

Refitting

17 Before installing the driveshaft, examine the driveshaft oil seal in the transmission for signs of damage or deterioration and, if necessary, renew it as described in Chapter 7, Section 4. It is highly recommended that the seal be renewed, regardless of its apparent condition.

18 Thoroughly clean the driveshaft splines, and the apertures in the transmission and hub assembly. Apply a thin film of grease to the oil seal lips, and to the driveshaft splines and shoulders. Check that all gaiter clips are securely fastened.

Left-hand driveshaft

19 Offer up the driveshaft, and locate the joint splines with those of the differential sun gear, taking great care not to damage the oil seal. Push the joint fully into position.

20 Locate the outer constant velocity joint splines with those of the swivel hub, and slide the joint back into position in the hub.

21 Rotate the base of the strut 90° and align the hub carrier with the brackets on the strut. Insert the bolts and tighten them to the specified torque.

22 Refit the track rod end to the stub axle and tighten the retaining nut.

23 Refit the ABS wheel speed sensor wiring back into its retaining clips and refit the brake caliper as described in Chapter 9, Section 8 .

24 Lubricate the inner face and threads of the driveshaft nut with clean engine oil, and refit it to the end of the driveshaft. Use the method employed on removal to prevent the hub from rotating (see paragraph 5), and tighten the driveshaft retaining nut to the specified torque. Check that the hub rotates freely then engage the locking cap with the driveshaft nut, so that one of its cut-outs is aligned with the driveshaft hole, and secure the cap in position with the R-clip (see illustrations). Alternatively, depending on type of wheel fitted, lightly tighten the nut at this stage, and tighten it to the specified torque once the car is resting on its wheels again.

25 Refit the roadwheel, then lower the vehicle to the ground and tighten the roadwheel bolts to the specified torque. If not already done, tighten the driveshaft retaining nut to the specified torque then refit the locking cap, aligning its cut-outs with the driveshaft hole, and secure it in position with the R-clip.

26 Refill the transmission with the specified type and amount of oil, and check the level using the information given in Chapter 7, Section 2 .

Right-hand driveshaft

27 Check that the intermediate bearing rotates smoothly, without any sign of roughness or undue free play between its inner and outer races. If necessary, renew the bearing as described in Section 5 .

Examine the dust seal for signs of damage or deterioration, and renew if necessary. Check the condition of the differential splined shaft O-ring seal and renew if necessary.

28 Apply a smear of grease to the outer race of the intermediate bearing, and to the inner lip of the dust seal (where fitted).

29 Pass the inner end of the shaft through the bearing mounting bracket then, where necessary, carefully slide the dust seal into position on the driveshaft, ensuring that its flat surface is facing the transmission (see illustration).

30 Carefully locate the inner driveshaft splines with those of the differential sun gear, taking care not to damage the oil seal.

31 Align the intermediate bearing with its mounting bracket, and push the driveshaft fully into position. If necessary, use a soft-faced mallet to tap the outer race of the bearing into position in the mounting bracket.

32 Locate the outer constant velocity joint splines with those of the swivel hub, and slide the joint back into position in the hub.

33 Ensure that the intermediate bearing is correctly seated, and then rotate its retaining plate back into position against the bearing outer race. Tighten the retaining bolts to the specified torque. Where necessary, ensure that the dust seal is tight against the driveshaft oil seal.

34 Carry out the operations described above in paragraphs 19 to 26.

2.29 Locate the dust seal (where fitted) on the inner end of the right-hand driveshaft

3.0 Make of driveshaft (PSA) written on label (arrowed)

3.3a Pull back the gaiter ...

3.3b ... and clean out the old grease

3 Driveshaft rubber gaiters – renewal

Note: *There are three makes of driveshaft fitted to these models: GKN, PSA and NTN (see illustration).*

Note: *The outer joint on GKN type driveshaft cannot be removed from the driveshaft; to renew the outer gaiter on this type, the inner joint will need to be removed and the gaiter fitted from that end.*

Note: *The inner tripod joint on PSA type driveshaft cannot be removed from the driveshaft; to renew the inner gaiter on this type, the outer joint will need to be removed and the gaiter fitted from that end.*

Outer joint (PSA and NTN type)

1 Remove the driveshaft from the vehicle as described in Section 2 .

2 Secure the driveshaft in a vice equipped with soft jaws, and release the two outer gaiter retaining clips. If necessary, the gaiter retaining clips can be cut to release them.

3 Slide the rubber gaiter down the shaft, to expose the outer constant velocity joint. Scoop out the excess grease (**see illustrations**).

4 Using a hammer and suitable soft metal drift, sharply strike the inner member of the outer joint to drive it off the end of the shaft (**see illustration**). The joint is retained on the driveshaft by a circlip, and striking the joint in this manner forces the circlip into its groove, so allowing the joint to slide off.

5 Once the joint assembly has been removed, remove the circlip from the groove in the driveshaft splines, and discard it. A new circlip must be fitted on reassembly.

6 Withdraw the rubber gaiter from the driveshaft. Where applicable, slide the gaiter inner end plastic bush off the driveshaft (**see illustration**).

7 With the constant velocity joint removed from the driveshaft, thoroughly clean the joint using paraffin, or a suitable solvent, and dry it thoroughly. Carry out a visual inspection of the joint.

8 Move the inner splined driving member from side-to-side, to expose each ball in turn at the top of its track. Examine the balls for cracks, flat spots, or signs of surface pitting.

9 Inspect the ball tracks on the inner and outer members. If the tracks have widened, the balls will no longer be a tight fit. At the same time, check the ball cage windows for wear or cracking between the windows.

10 If, on inspection, any of the constant velocity joint components are found to be worn or damaged, it will be necessary to renew the complete joint assembly (where available), or even the complete driveshaft (where no joint components are available separately). Refer to your Peugeot/Citroën dealer for further information on parts availability. If the joint is in satisfactory condition, obtain a repair kit consisting of a new gaiter, circlip, retaining clips, and the correct type and quantity of grease.

11 To install the new gaiter, perform the operations shown (**see illustrations**). Be sure to stay in order, and follow the captions carefully. Note that the hard plastic rings and plastic bushes are not fitted to all gaiters, and the gaiter retaining clips supplied with the repair kit may be different to those shown in the sequence.

12 To secure the other type of clip in position, lock the ends of the clip together, and then remove any slack in the clip by carefully compressing the raised section of the clip using a pair of special pliers or side-cutters (**see illustration**).

13 Check that the constant velocity joint

3.4 Using a soft metal drift to release the outer joint

3.6 Where applicable, remove the plastic bush

3.11a Where applicable, fit the hard plastic rings to the outer gaiter …

3.11b … then slide on the new plastic bush (arrowed – where fitted), and seat it in its recess in the shaft. Slide the gaiter onto the shaft …

3.11c … and seat the gaiter inner end on top of the plastic bush (as applicable)

3.11d Fit the new circlip to its groove in the driveshaft splines …

3.11e … then locate the joint outer member on the splines, and slide it into position over the circlip. Ensure that the joint is securely retained by the circlip

3.11f Pack the joint with grease, working it into the ball tracks while twisting the joint, then locate the gaiter outer lip in its groove on the outer member

3.11g Fit the outer gaiter retaining clip and, using a hook fabricated out of welding rod and a pair of pliers, pull the clip tight to remove all the slack

3.11h Bend the clip end back over the buckle, then cut off the excess

3.11i Fold the clip end underneath the buckle …

3.11j … then fold the buckle firmly down onto the clip to secure the clip in position

3.11k Carefully lift the gaiter inner end to equalise the air pressure in the gaiter, then secure the inner gaiter retaining clip in position using the same method

3.12 Using a pair of special pliers to secure the retaining clip

3.15a Cut the retaining clip ...

3.15b ... and remove the clip and gaiter

3.18a Slide the joint apart ...

3.18b ... and retrieve the spring (where applicable)

3.19a Release the circlip ...

3.19b ... and mark the position (arrowed) of the joint on the shaft

moves freely in all directions, and then refit the driveshaft to the vehicle as described in Section 2 .

Inner joint (GKN and NTN type)

14 Remove the driveshaft from the vehicle as described in Section 2.
15 Secure the driveshaft in a vice equipped with soft jaws, and release the two outer gaiter retaining clips. If necessary, the gaiter retaining clips can be cut to release them **(see illustrations)**. Take care not to damage the driveshaft when cutting the retaining clip.
16 Slide the rubber gaiter down the shaft to expose the outer constant velocity joint. Scoop out the excess grease.
17 If the gaiter is to be renewed, it can be cut off and removed from the driveshaft.
18 Slide the outer member off the tripod joint and remove the spring and/or cup from

inside the outer member of the joint **(see illustrations)**.
19 Using circlip pliers, extract the circlip securing the tripod joint to the driveshaft **(see illustrations)**. Mark the position of the tripod in relation to the driveshaft, using a dab of paint or a punch.
20 The tripod joint can now be removed **(see illustration)**. If it is tight, draw the joint off the driveshaft end using a puller. Ensure that the legs of the puller are located behind the joint inner member and do not contact the joint rollers. Alternatively, support the inner member of the tripod joint, and press the shaft out using a hydraulic press, again ensuring that no load is applied to the joint rollers.
21 With the tripod joint removed, if not removed already, slide the gaiter off the end of the driveshaft.
22 Wipe clean the joint components, taking

care not to remove the alignment marks made on dismantling. Do not use paraffin or other solvents to clean this type of joint.
23 Examine the tripod joint, rollers and outer member for any signs of scoring or wear. Check that the rollers move smoothly on the tripod stems. If wear is evident, check with your local dealer to see if the tripod joint and roller assembly can be renewed. Obtain a new gaiter, retaining clips and a quantity of the special lubricating grease.
24 Tape over the splines on the end of the driveshaft, then carefully slide the inner retaining clip and gaiter onto the shaft **(see illustration)**.
25 Remove the tape, then, aligning the marks made on dismantling, engage the tripod joint with the driveshaft splines **(see illustration)**. Use a hammer and soft metal drift to tap the joint onto the shaft, taking great care not to damage the driveshaft splines or joint rollers.

3.20 Slide the joint from the end of the shaft

3.24 Make sure the inner retaining clip is put on the shaft

3.25 Align the marks up for refitting

3.26 Refit the circlip to secure the tripod joint

3.27a Pack the outer joint with grease ...

3.27b ... and insert the spring (where fitted)

Alternatively, support the driveshaft, and press the joint into position using a hydraulic press and suitable tubular spacer, which bears only on the joint inner member.

26 Secure the tripod joint in position with the circlip, ensuring that it is correctly located in the driveshaft groove **(see illustration)**.

27 Evenly distribute the grease contained in the repair kit inside the outer member, and then refit the spring and cup (where fitted) in the outer member **(see illustrations)**.

28 Pack the gaiter with the remainder of the grease and slide the two halves of the joint together **(see illustration)**.

29 Slide the gaiter up the driveshaft. Locate the gaiter in the grooves on the driveshaft and outer member.

30 Fit the inner retaining clip into place over the inner end of the gaiter.

31 Using a blunt rod, carefully lift the outer lip of the gaiter to equalise the air pressure.

32 Slip the new retaining clip into place to secure the outer lip of the gaiter to the outer member. Remove any slack in the gaiter retaining clip by carefully compressing the raised section of the clip (depending on type of clip supplied). In the absence of the special tool, a pair of pincers may be used **(see illustration)**. Secure the small retaining clip using the same procedure.

3.28 Refit the tripod joint into the outer joint

33 Check that the constant velocity joint moves freely in all directions, then refit the driveshaft as described in Section 2.

Inner gaiter (PSA type)

34 Remove the outer constant velocity joint as described above in paragraphs 1 to 5.

35 Tape over the splines on the driveshaft, and carefully remove the outer constant velocity joint rubber gaiter, and (where fitted) the gaiter inner end plastic bush. It is recommended that the outer joint gaiter be also renewed, regardless of its apparent condition.

3.32 Secure the gaiter in position with the securing clips

36 Release the retaining clips, then slide the inner gaiter off the shaft and (where fitted) remove its plastic bush **(see illustration 3.6)**.

37 As the gaiter is released, the joint outer member will also be freed from the end of the shaft **(see illustrations)**.

38 Thoroughly clean the joint using paraffin, or a suitable solvent, and dry it thoroughly. Check the tripod joint bearings and joint outer member for signs of wear, pitting or scuffing on their bearing surfaces. Check that the bearing rollers rotate smoothly and easily around the tripod joint, with no traces of roughness.

3.37a Release the inner gaiter retaining clips and remove the joint outer member

3.37b Slide the gaiter off the end of the driveshaft

3.41 Locate the new gaiter in the groove on the driveshaft

3.42 Fit the new clips and crimp them into place

5.3 Using a long-reach bearing puller to remove the intermediate bearing from the right-hand driveshaft

39 If, on inspection, the tripod joint or outer member reveal signs of wear or damage, it will be necessary to renew the complete driveshaft assembly, since the joint is not available separately. If the joint is in a satisfactory condition, obtain a repair kit consisting of a new gaiter, retaining clips, and the correct type and quantity of grease.

40 On reassembly, pack the inner joint with the grease supplied in the gaiter kit. Work the grease well into the bearing tracks and rollers, while twisting the joint.

41 Clean the shaft, using emery cloth to remove any rust or sharp edges which may damage the gaiter, then slide the plastic bush (where fitted) and inner joint gaiter along the driveshaft. Locate the plastic bush in its recess on the shaft, and seat the inner end of the gaiter on top of the bush; where no bush is fitted, seat the inner end of the driveshaft in the recess on the shaft **(see illustration)**.

42 Fit the outer member over the end of the shaft, and locate the gaiter in the groove on the joint outer member. Push the outer member onto the joint, so that it's spring-loaded plunger is compressed, then lift the outer edge of the gaiter to equalise air pressure in the gaiter. Fit both the inner and outer retaining clips, securing them in position using the information given in paragraph 11. Ensure that the gaiter retaining clips are securely tightened, and then check that the joint moves freely in all directions **(see illustration)**.

43 Refit the outer constant velocity joint components using the information given in paragraphs 11 to 13.

4 Driveshaft overhaul – general information

1 If any of the checks described in Chapter 1, Section 5, reveal wear in any driveshaft joint, first remove the roadwheel trim or centre cap (as appropriate).

2 If the R-clip is still in position, the driveshaft nut should be correctly tightened; if in doubt, remove the R-clip and locking cap, and use a torque wrench to check that the nut is securely fastened. Once tightened, refit the locking cap and R-clip, and then refit the centre cap or trim. Repeat this check on the remaining driveshaft nut.

3 Road test the vehicle, and listen for a metallic clicking from the front as the vehicle is driven slowly in a circle on full-lock. If a clicking noise is heard, this indicates wear in the outer constant velocity joint. This means that the joint must be renewed; reconditioning is not possible.

4 If vibration, consistent with roadspeed, is felt through the car when accelerating, there is a possibility of wear in the inner joints.

5 To check the joints for wear, remove the driveshafts, and then dismantle them as described in Section 3 ; if any wear or free play is found, the affected joint must be renewed. In the case of the inner joints (and on some models, the outer joints), this means that the complete driveshaft assembly must be renewed, as the joints are not available

separately. Refer to your Peugeot/Citroën dealer for latest information on the availability of driveshaft components.

5 Right-hand driveshaft intermediate bearing – renewal

Note: *A suitable bearing puller will be required, to draw the bearing and collar off the driveshaft end.*

1 Remove the right-hand driveshaft as described in Section 2 of this Chapter.

2 Check that the bearing outer race rotates smoothly and easily, without any signs of roughness or undue free play between the inner and outer races. If necessary, renew the bearing as follows.

3 Using a long-reach universal bearing puller, carefully draw the collar and intermediate bearing off the driveshaft inner end **(see illustration)**. Apply a smear of grease to the inner race of the new bearing, and then fit the bearing over the end of the driveshaft. Using a hammer and suitable piece of tubing which presses only against the bearing inner race, tap the new bearing into position on the driveshaft, until it abuts the constant velocity joint outer member. Once the bearing is correctly positioned, tap the bearing collar onto the shaft until it contacts the bearing inner race.

4 Check that the bearing rotates freely, then refit the driveshaft as described in Section 2.

Chapter 9
Braking system

Contents

Degrees of difficulty

| Easy, suitable for novice with little experience | Fairly easy, suitable for beginner with some experience | Fairly difficult, suitable for competent DIY mechanic | Difficult, suitable for experienced DIY mechanic | Very difficult, suitable for expert DIY or professional |

Specifications

Front brakes
Type . . . . Vented disc, with single-piston sliding caliper
Caliper make . . . . Teves (FN3 – 60/26)
Piston diameter . . . . 60 mm
Disc diameter: . . . . 283 mm
Disc thickness:
    New . . . . 26 mm
    Minimum. . . . . 24 mm
Maximum disc run-out. . . . . 0.05 mm
Brake pad friction material thickness:
    New . . . . 12.0 mm
    Minimum. . . . . 2.0 mm

Rear disc brakes
Type . . . . Solid disc (non-vented), with single-piston sliding caliper
Caliper make . . . . TRW (type: C1 38HR – PE)
Piston diameter . . . . 38 mm
Disc diameter . . . . 268 mm
Disc thickness:
    New . . . . 12.0 mm
    Minimum thickness. . . . . 10.0 mm
Maximum disc run-out. . . . . 0.05 mm
Brake pad friction material thickness:
    New . . . . 11.0 mm
    Minimum. . . . . 3.0 mm

Vacuum pump pressure (engine at idle)

Engine temperature at 80°C:

4.5 seconds	500 mbars
18 seconds	800 mbars

Master cylinder

Make	TRW
Diameter of cylinder	23.8 mm

Servo unit

Make	TRW
Diameter of servo	255mm

ABS hydraulic valve block

Make	Bosch
Type	ABS 8.1 (8.1 ESP)

Torque wrench settings

	Nm	lbf ft
ABS system components:		
Hydraulic hose/pipe union nuts:		
Without ESP	15	11
With ESP	18	13
Hydraulic/modulator unit mounting nuts	8	6
Hydraulic/modulator unit mounting bracket bolts	15	11
Wheel sensor retaining bolts	8	6
Gyrometer/accelerometer sensor nuts	8	6
Caliper bleed screws	10	7
Crossover linkage housing nuts and bolts (right-hand drive models)	25	18
Disc retaining screws	10	7
Front brake caliper:		
Hydraulic hose to caliper	15	11
Guide pins	30	22
Mounting bracket bolts: *		
With washers:		
Stage 1	33	24
Stage 2	Angle-tighten a further 45°	
Without washers:		
Stage 1	90	66
Stage 2	Angle-tighten a further 45°	
Handbrake lever nuts	15	11
Master cylinder:		
Retaining nuts	20	15
Hydraulic hose/pipe union nuts:		
Without ESP	15	11
With ESP	18	13
Rear brake caliper:		
Hydraulic hose to caliper	18	13
Guide pin bolts*	30	22
Mounting bracket bolts: *		
Stage 1	30	22
Stage 2	Angle-tighten a further 35°	
Rear hub nut	300	221
Roadwheel bolts	100	74
Vacuum pump:		
Stage 1	5	4
Stage 2	18	13
Vacuum servo unit mounting nuts	22	16

* Do not re-use.

1 General Information

1 The braking system is of the servo-assisted, dual-circuit hydraulic type. The arrangement of the hydraulic system is such that each circuit operates one front and one rear brake from a tandem master cylinder. Under normal circumstances, both circuits operate in unison. However, in the event of hydraulic failure in one circuit, full braking force will still be available at two wheels.

2 All models are equipped with disc brakes on all wheels. ABS is fitted as standard (refer to Section 18 for further information on ABS operation).

3 The disc brakes are actuated by single-piston sliding type calipers, which ensure that equal pressure is applied to each disc pad.

4 On all models, the handbrake provides an independent mechanical means of rear brake application. All models are fitted with rear brake calipers with an integral handbrake function. The handbrake cable operates a lever on the caliper that forces the piston to press the pad against the disc surface. A self-adjust mechanism is incorporated to automatically compensate for brake pad wear.

5 There is a vacuum pump fitted to provide sufficient vacuum to operate the servo unit, this is mounted on the left-hand end of the cylinder head, and is driven directly off the end of the camshaft.

Note: *When servicing any of the system, work carefully and methodically; also observe scrupulous cleanliness when overhauling any of the hydraulic system. Always renew components (in axle sets, where applicable) if in doubt about their condition, and use only genuine Peugeot/Citroën parts, or at least those of known good quality. Note the warnings given in* Safety first! *and at relevant points in this Chapter concerning the dangers of asbestos dust and hydraulic fluid.*

2 Hydraulic system – bleeding

⚠️ **Warning: Hydraulic fluid is poisonous; wash off immediately and thoroughly in the case of skin contact, and seek immediate medical advice if any fluid is swallowed or gets into the eyes. Certain types of hydraulic fluid are inflammable, and may ignite when allowed into contact with hot components; when servicing any hydraulic system, it is safest to assume that the fluid is inflammable, and to take precautions against the risk of fire as though it is petrol that is being handled. Hydraulic fluid is also an effective paint stripper, and will attack plastics; if any is spilt, it should be washed**

off immediately, using copious quantities of fresh water. Finally, it is hygroscopic (it absorbs moisture from the air) – old fluid may be contaminated and unfit for further use. When topping-up or renewing the fluid, always use the recommended type, and ensure that it comes from a freshly opened sealed container.

Caution: Ensure the ignition is switched off before starting the bleeding procedure, to avoid any possibility of voltage being applied to the hydraulic modulator before the bleeding procedure is complete. Ideally, the battery should be disconnected. If voltage is applied to the modulator before the bleeding procedure is complete, this will effectively drain the hydraulic fluid in the modulator, rendering the unit unserviceable. Do not, therefore, attempt to 'run' the modulator in order to bleed the brakes.

Note: *If difficulty is experienced in bleeding the braking circuit, this maybe due to air being trapped in the ABS modulator unit. If this is the case then the vehicle should be taken to a Peugeot/Citroën dealer or suitably-equipped specialist so that the system can be bled using special electronic test equipment.*

Note: *A hydraulic clutch shares its fluid reservoir with the braking system, and may also need to be bled (see Chapter 6 Section 2).*

General

1 The correct operation of any hydraulic system is only possible after removing all air from the components and circuit; this is achieved by bleeding the system.

2 During the bleeding procedure, add only clean, unused hydraulic fluid of the recommended type; never re-use fluid that has already been bled from the system. Ensure that sufficient fluid is available before starting work.

3 If there is any possibility of incorrect fluid being already in the system, the brake components and circuit must be flushed completely with uncontaminated, correct fluid, and new seals should be fitted to the various components.

4 If hydraulic fluid has been lost from the system, or air has entered because of a leak, ensure that the fault is cured before proceeding further.

5 Park the vehicle on level ground, switch off the engine and select first or reverse gear, then chock the wheels and release the handbrake.

6 Check that all pipes and hoses are secure, unions tight and bleed screws closed. Clean any dirt from around the bleed screws.

7 Unscrew the master cylinder reservoir cap, and top the master cylinder reservoir up to the MAX level line **(see illustration)**; refit the cap loosely, and remember to maintain the fluid level at least above the MIN/DANGER level line throughout the procedure, or there is a risk of further air entering the system.

8 There is a number of one-man, do-it-yourself brake bleeding kits currently available from motor accessory shops. It is recommended that one of these kits is used whenever possible, as they greatly simplify the bleeding operation, and also reduce the risk of expelled air and fluid being drawn back into the system. If such a kit is not available, the basic (two-man) method must be used, which is described in detail below.

9 If a kit is to be used, prepare the vehicle as described previously, and follow the kit manufacturer's instructions, as the procedure may vary slightly according to the type being used; generally, they are as outlined below in the relevant sub-section.

10 Whichever method is used, the same sequence must be followed (paragraphs 11 and 12) to ensure that the removal of all air from the system.

Bleeding

Sequence

11 If the system has been only partially disconnected, and suitable precautions were taken to minimise fluid loss, it should be necessary only to bleed that of the system (ie, the primary or secondary circuit).

12 If the complete system is to be bled, then it should be done working in the following sequence:
a) *Left-hand front brake.*
b) *Right-hand front brake.*
c) *Left-hand rear brake.*
d) *Right-hand rear brake.*

Basic (two-man) method

13 Collect a clean glass jar, a suitable length of plastic or rubber tubing which is a tight fit over the bleed screw, and a ring spanner to fit the screw. The help of an assistant will also be required.

14 Remove the dust cap from the first screw in the sequence. Fit the spanner and tube to the screw, place the other end of the tube in the jar, and pour in sufficient fluid to cover the end of the tube.

15 Ensure that the master cylinder reservoir fluid level is maintained at least above the MIN/DANGER level line throughout the procedure.

2.7 Fluid MAX level line

16 Have the assistant fully depress the brake pedal several times to build up pressure, and then maintain it on the final downstroke.

17 While pedal pressure is maintained, unscrew the bleed screw (approximately one turn) and allow the compressed fluid and air to flow into the jar. The assistant should maintain pedal pressure, following it down to the floor if necessary, and should not release it until instructed to do so. When the flow stops, tighten the bleed screw again, have the assistant release the pedal slowly, and recheck the reservoir fluid level.

18 Repeat the steps given in paragraphs 16 and 17 until the fluid emerging from the bleed screw is free from air bubbles. If the master cylinder has been drained and refilled, and air is being bled from the first screw in the sequence, allow approximately five seconds between cycles for the master cylinder passages to refill.

19 When no more air bubbles appear, tighten the bleed screw securely, remove the tube and spanner, and refit the dust cap. Do not overtighten the bleed screw.

20 Repeat the procedure on the remaining screws in the sequence, until all air is removed from the system and the brake pedal feels firm again.

Using a one-way valve kit

21 As their name implies, these kits consist of a length of tubing with a one-way valve fitted, to prevent expelled air and fluid being drawn back into the system; some kits include a translucent container, which can be positioned so that the air bubbles can be more easily seen flowing from the end of the tube.

22 The kit is connected to the bleed screw, which is then opened **(see illustration)**. The user returns to the driver's seat, depresses the brake pedal with a smooth, steady stroke, and slowly releases it; this is repeated until the expelled fluid is clear of air bubbles.

23 Note that these kits simplify work so much that it is easy to forget the master cylinder reservoir fluid level; ensure that this is maintained at least above the MIN/DANGER level line at all times.

Using a pressure-bleeding kit

24 These kits are usually operated by the

reservoir of pressurised air contained in the spare tyre. However, note that it will probably be necessary to reduce the pressure to a lower level than normal; refer to the instructions supplied with the kit.

25 By connecting a pressurised, fluid-filled container to the master cylinder reservoir, bleeding can be carried out simply by opening each screw in turn (in the specified sequence), and allowing the fluid to flow out until no more air bubbles can be seen in the expelled fluid.

26 This method has the advantage that the large reservoir of fluid provides an additional safeguard against air being drawn into the system during bleeding.

27 Pressure-bleeding is particularly effective when bleeding 'difficult' systems, or when bleeding the complete system at the time of routine fluid renewal.

All methods

28 When bleeding is complete, and firm pedal feel is restored, wash off any spilt fluid, tighten the bleed screws securely, and refit their dust caps.

29 Check the hydraulic fluid level in the master cylinder reservoir, and top-up if necessary (see *Weekly checks*).

30 Discard any hydraulic fluid that has been bled from the system; it will not be fit for re-use.

31 Check the feel of the brake pedal. If it feels at all spongy, air must still be present in the system, and further bleeding is required. Failure to bleed satisfactorily after a reasonable repetition of the bleeding procedure may be due to worn master cylinder seals.

3 Hydraulic pipes and hoses – renewal

Caution: Ensure the ignition is switched off before disconnecting any braking system hydraulic union and do not switch it on until after the hydraulic system has been bled. Failure to do this could lead to air entering the modulator unit requiring the unit to be bled using special test equipment (see Section 2).

Note: Before starting work, refer to the note at the beginning of Section 2 concerning the dangers of hydraulic fluid.

1 If any pipe or hose is to be renewed, minimise fluid loss by first removing the master cylinder reservoir cap, then tightening it down onto a piece of polythene to obtain an airtight seal. Alternatively, flexible hoses can be sealed, if required, using a proprietary brake hose clamp; metal brake pipe unions can be plugged (if care is taken not to allow dirt into the system) or capped immediately they are disconnected. Place a wad of rag under any union that is to be disconnected, to catch any spilt fluid.

2 If a flexible hose is to be disconnected, unscrew the brake pipe union nut before removing the spring clip that secures the hose to its mounting bracket **(see illustration)**.

3 To unscrew the union nuts, it is preferable to obtain a brake pipe spanner of the correct size; these are available from most large motor accessory shops. Failing this, a close-fitting open-ended spanner will be required, though if the nuts are tight or corroded, their flats may be rounded-off if the spanner slips. In such a case, a self-locking wrench is often the only way to unscrew a stubborn union, but it follows that the pipe and the damaged nuts must be renewed on reassembly. Always clean a union and surrounding area before disconnecting it. If disconnecting a component with more than one union, make a careful note of the connections before disturbing any of them.

4 If a brake pipe is to be renewed, it can be obtained cut to length and with the union nuts and end flares in place, from Peugeot/Citroën dealers. All that is then necessary is to bend it to shape, following the line of the original, before fitting it to the car. Alternatively, most motor accessory shops can make up brake pipes from kits, but this requires very careful measurement of the original, to ensure that the new one is of the correct length. The safest answer is usually to take the original to the shop as a pattern.

5 On refitting, do not overtighten the union nuts. It is not necessary to exercise brute force to obtain a sound joint.

6 Ensure that the pipes and hoses are correctly routed, with no kinks, and that they are secured in the clips or brackets provided. After fitting, remove the polythene from the reservoir, and bleed the hydraulic system as described in Section 2. Wash off any spilt fluid, and then check the brake system carefully for fluid leaks.

4 Front brake pads – renewal

⚠️ *Warning: Disc brake pads must be renewed on both front wheels at the same time – never renew the pads on only one wheel, as*

2.22 Connect the bleed kit to the bleed screw

3.2 Slacken the union nut (arrowed) and then remove the spring clip

4.2a Release the spring clips …

4.2b … from the caliper and mounting bracket

4.4 Unclip the two plastic caps (arrowed)

4.5 Unscrew the guide pins

4.6a Remove the caliper …

4.6b … then tie it to the suspension strut

uneven braking may result. Also, the dust created by wear of the pads may contain asbestos, which is a health hazard. Never blow it out with compressed air and don't inhale any of it. An approved filtering mask should be worn when working on the brakes. DO NOT use petroleum based solvents to clean brake parts. Use brake cleaner or methylated spirit only.

1 Apply the handbrake, slacken the front roadwheel bolts, then jack up the front of the vehicle and support it on axle stands. Remove the front roadwheels.

2 Use a thin screwdriver to unclip and release the spring clip from the caliper mounting bracket **(see illustrations)**. Note the spring clips fitted position for refitting.

3 Unclip the brake hose from the mounting bracket on the lower part of the strut.

4 Unclip the two plastic plugs from the end of the guide pins **(see illustration)**.

5 Unscrew the two caliper guide pins from the rear of the caliper **(see illustration)**.

6 With the guide pins removed, lift the caliper away from the brake disc and move it to one side. The inner brake pad has a clip attached to it that locates in the caliper piston, so the pad will come away with the caliper **(see illustrations)**. Do not let the brake caliper hang on the brake hose; fasten it up using a piece of wire.

7 Withdraw the two brake pads, one from

the carrier bracket and one from the caliper. If required, the thickness of the pads can be checked at this stage using a steel rule **(see illustration)**.

8 Before refitting the pads, check that the guide pins are free to slide in the caliper and check that the rubber dust excluders around the guide pins are undamaged. Brush the dust and dirt from the caliper and piston but do not inhale it, as it is injurious to health. Inspect the dust excluder around the piston for damage and inspect the piston for evidence of fluid leaks, corrosion or damage. If attention to any of these components is necessary, refer to Section 8.

9 Make sure that the caliper piston is fully retracted in its bore. If not, fit a bleed bottle and tube to the bleed screw, open the bleed

screw and carefully push the piston in, preferably using a G-clamp or, alternatively, using a flat bar or screwdriver as a lever **(see illustration)**. As the piston is retracted, the fluid will be pushed out of the bleed screw and into the bleed bottle. Tighten the bleed screw, when the piston is fully retracted. **Note:** *The ABS unit contains hydraulic components that are very sensitive to impurities in the brake fluid. Even the smallest particles can cause the system to fail through blockage. The pad retraction method described here prevents any debris in the brake fluid expelled from the caliper from being passed back to the ABS unit, as well as preventing any chance of damage to the master cylinder seals.*

10 To refit the brake pads, place them in

4.7 Measure the thickness of the pad's friction material

4.9 Open the bleed screw and push the piston back (piston retraction tool shown)

4.10a Fit the new brake pads …

4.10b … locating the inner one in the caliper piston

4.13 Make sure the spring clip is secure

position on the carrier bracket and in the caliper piston (see illustrations).

11 Position the caliper in place over the brake disc, then fit the guide pins starting with the lowest one first. Tighten the pins to the specified torque. Refit the two plastic plugs to the ends of the guide pins.

12 Reconnect the brake hose to the mounting bracket on the lower part of the strut. Note: Make sure the brake hose and ABS sensor wiring are secure and will not foul any other components.

13 Refit the spring clip to the caliper mounting bracket, making sure it is fitted correctly as noted on removal (see illustration).

14 Refit the roadwheel, then repeat the renewal procedure on the remaining rear brake.

15 Depress the brake pedal repeatedly, until the pads are pressed into firm contact with the brake disc, and normal (non-assisted) pedal pressure is restored.

16 If not already done, refit the roadwheels, and then lower the vehicle to the ground and tighten the roadwheel bolts to the specified torque.

17 On completion, check the fluid level in the reservoir, check the hydraulic fluid level as described in Weekly checks.

Caution: New pads will not give full braking efficiency until they have bedded-in. Be prepared for this, and avoid hard braking as far as possible for the first hundred miles or so after pad renewal.

5 Rear brake pads – renewal

Warning: Renew both sets of rear brake pads at the same time – never renew the pads on only one wheel, as uneven braking may result. Note that the dust created by wear of the pads may contain asbestos, which is a health hazard. Never blow it out with compressed air, and don't inhale any of it. An approved filtering mask should be worn when working on the brakes. DO NOT use petrol or petroleum-based solvents to clean brake parts; use brake cleaner or methylated spirit only.

Note: New guide pin bolts must be fitted on reassembly.

1 Chock the front wheels, slacken the rear roadwheel bolts, and then jack up the rear of the vehicle and support it on axle stands (see Jacking and vehicle support). Remove the rear roadwheels.

2 Using a socket and spanner, slacken and remove the caliper upper and lower guide pin bolts. Withdraw the caliper from the brake pads and disc, then move the caliper to one side, and secure it in place (see illustrations).

5.2a Using a socket and spanner...

5.2b ...remove the guide pin bolts...

5.2c ...then withdraw the caliper...

5.2d and move to one side – using length of wire to secure

5.3a Withdraw the outer …

5.3b … and inner pads

5.3c Remove the shims – noting their fitted position

5.4 Measure the thickness of the friction material

5.6a Check the guide sleeves move freely

5.6b Grease the guide pins if required

3 Withdraw the outer and inner brake pads from the caliper mounting bracket, and note the location of any shims fitted between the pads and caliper **(see illustrations)**.

4 First measure the thickness of the friction material of each brake pad **(see illustration)**. If either pad is worn at any point to the specified minimum thickness or less, all four pads must be renewed. Also, the pads should be renewed if any are fouled with oil or grease; there is no satisfactory way of degreasing friction material, once contaminated. If any of the brake pads are worn unevenly, or fouled with oil or grease, trace and rectify the cause before reassembly. Examine the retaining pins for signs of wear and renew if necessary. New brake pads and retaining pin kits are available from Peugeot/Citroën dealers.

5 If the brake pads are still serviceable, carefully clean them using a clean, fine wire brush or similar, paying particular attention to the sides and back of the metal backing. Clean out the grooves in the friction material, and pick out any large embedded particles of dirt or debris. Carefully clean the pad locations in the caliper body/mounting bracket.

6 Prior to fitting the pads, check that the guide sleeves are free to slide easily in the caliper body, and check that the rubber guide sleeve gaiters are undamaged **(see illustrations)**. Brush the dust and dirt from the caliper and piston, but do not inhale it, as it is a health hazard. Inspect the dust seal around the piston for damage, and the piston for evidence of fluid leaks, corrosion or damage.

If attention to any of these components is necessary, refer to Section 9.

7 If new brake pads are to be fitted, the caliper piston must be pushed back into the cylinder to make room for them. In order to retract the piston, the piston must be turned clockwise as it is pushed into the caliper. Peugeot/Citroën tool No DF61 is available to retract the pistons, as are several available from good accessory/parts retailers **(see illustration)**. Clamp off the flexible brake hose leading to the caliper then connect a brake bleeding kit to the caliper bleed nipple. Open the bleed nipple as the piston is retracted, the surplus brake fluid will then be collected in the bleed kit vessel. Close the bleed nipple just before the caliper piston is pushed fully into the caliper. This should ensure no air enters the hydraulic system. **Note:** *The ABS unit*

contains hydraulic components that are very sensitive to impurities in the brake fluid. Even the smallest particles can cause the system to fail through blockage. The pad retraction method described here prevents any debris in the brake fluid expelled from the caliper from being passed back to the ABS unit, as well as preventing any chance of damage to the master cylinder seals.

8 Some inner brake pads have a lug on the rear metal face of the brake pad, for this type of pad the slots in the caliper piston will need to be in a vertical position **(see illustration)**. If the piston is not in correct position the pad will bind against the disc and cause uneven wear.

9 Slide the brake pads into position in the caliper; ensuring each pad's friction material is facing the brake disc. If the shims where

5.7 Use a retraction tool to rotate the piston whilst pushing at the same time

5.8 Position of slots (arrowed) to locate lug on inner pad

5.9 Ensure the shims are fitted correctly –
as noted on removal

6.3 Use a micrometer to measure the disc
thickness

6.4 Check the disc run-out using a dial
gauge

removed from the caliper mounting bracket, either fit new shims or clean and refit the old shims **(see illustration)**.

10 Release the caliper from the securing wire and lower it back into position over the brake pads. Insert the new caliper guide pin bolts, and tighten it to the specified torque.

11 Depress the brake pedal repeatedly until the pads are pressed into firm contact with the brake disc, and normal (non-assisted) pedal pressure is restored.

12 Repeat the above procedure on the remaining rear brake caliper.

13 Check the operation of the handbrake, and if necessary, carry out the adjustment procedure as described in Section 14.

14 Refit the roadwheels, then lower the vehicle to the ground and tighten the roadwheel bolts to the specified torque setting.

15 Check the hydraulic fluid level as described in *Weekly checks*.

Caution: New pads will not give full braking efficiency until they have bedded-in. Be prepared for this, and avoid hard braking as far as possible for the first hundred miles or so after pad renewal.

6 Front brake disc – inspection, removal and refitting

Note: *Before starting work, refer to the note at the beginning of Section 4 concerning the dangers of asbestos dust.*

Inspection

Note: *If either disc requires renewal, BOTH should be renewed at the same time, to ensure even and consistent braking. New brake pads should also be fitted.*

1 Apply the handbrake, slacken the front roadwheel bolts, then jack up the front of the car and support it on axle stands (see *Jacking and vehicle support*). Remove the appropriate front roadwheel.

2 Slowly rotate the brake disc so that the full area of both sides can be checked; remove the brake pads if better access is required to the inboard surface. Light scoring is normal in the area swept by the brake pads, but if heavy scoring or cracks are found, the disc must be renewed.

3 It is normal to find a lip of rust and brake dust around the disc's perimeter; this can be scraped off if required. If, however, a lip has formed due to excessive wear of the brake pad swept area, then the disc's thickness must be measured using a micrometer. Take measurements at several places around the disc, at the inside and outside of the pad swept area; if the disc has worn at any point to the specified minimum thickness or less, the disc must be renewed **(see illustration)**.

4 If the disc is thought to be warped, it can be checked for run-out. Either use a dial gauge mounted on any convenient fixed point, while the disc is slowly rotated, or use feeler blades to measure (at several points all around the disc) the clearance between the disc and a fixed point, such as the caliper

mounting bracket **(see illustration)**. If the measurements obtained are at the specified maximum or beyond, the disc is excessively warped, and must be renewed; however, it is worth checking first that the hub bearing is in good condition (Chapter 1, Section 4. Also try the effect of removing the disc and turning it through 180°, to reposition it on the hub; if the run-out is still excessive, the disc must be renewed.

5 Check the disc for cracks, especially around the wheel bolt holes, and any other wear or damage, and renew if necessary.

Removal

6 Slacken and remove the two bolts securing the brake caliper mounting bracket to the hub carrier **(see illustrations)**, discard the bolts, as new ones will be required for refitting. Slide the assembly off the disc and tie it to the coil spring, using a piece of wire or string, to avoid placing any strain on the hydraulic brake hose.

7 Use chalk or paint to mark the relationship of the disc to the hub, then remove the screws securing the brake disc to the hub, and remove the disc **(see illustration)**. If it is tight, lightly tap its rear face with a hide or plastic mallet.

Refitting

8 Refitting is the reverse of the removal procedure, noting the following points:
a) Ensure that the mating surfaces of the disc and hub are clean and flat.
b) Align (if applicable) the marks made on

6.6a Undo the mounting bolts (arrowed) …

6.6b … and withdraw the caliper and bracket from over the disc

6.7 Undo the two Torx screws, and remove the disc

7.4 Slacken the two caliper mounting bracket Torx screws (arrowed)

7.5 Remove the cap from the disc/hub …

7.6 … and remove the rear hub nut

removal, and tighten the disc retaining screws to the specified torque setting.

c) *If a new disc has been fitted, use a suitable solvent to wipe any preservative coating from the disc, before refitting the caliper.*

d) *Fit new bolts to the caliper mounting bracket and tighten to the specified torque setting.*

e) *Refit the roadwheels, and then lower the vehicle to the ground and tighten the wheel bolts to the specified torque.*

f) *Apply the footbrake several times to force the pads back into contact with the disc before driving the vehicle.*

7 Rear brake disc – inspection, removal and refitting

Note: *Before starting work, refer to the warning at the beginning of Section 5 concerning the dangers of harmful brake dust.*

Inspection

Note: *If either disc requires renewal, BOTH should be renewed at the same time, to ensure even and consistent braking. New brake pads should also be fitted.*

1 Chock the front wheels, engage reverse gear (or P on models with automatic transmission) and release the handbrake. Jack up the rear of the vehicle and support it securely on axle stands (see *Jacking and vehicle support*). Remove the relevant roadwheel.

7.9 Clean around the ABS magnetic ring before refitting

2 Inspect the rear brake discs, as described for the front brake discs in Section 6.

Removal

Note: *New hub/disc retaining nut must be fitted on reassembly.*

3 Remove the brake pads as described in Section 5.

4 Unscrew the two screws securing the brake caliper mounting bracket to the hub carrier, and move it clear of the disc **(see illustration)**.

5 Using a hammer and suitable chisel (or large flat-bladed screwdriver), carefully tap and prise the cap from the centre of the brake disc **(see illustration)**.

6 Using a socket and long bar, slacken and remove the rear hub nut – this will be very tight, so ensure that the car is well supported, and that only good quality, close-fitting tools are used **(see illustration)**. Discard the hub nut; a new one must be used on refitting

7 It should now be possible to withdraw the brake disc and hub bearing assembly from the stub axle by hand.

Refitting

8 If a new disc is being fitted, use a suitable solvent to wipe any preservative coating from the disc before refitting. Note that new discs may be supplied with new wheel bearings already fitted; see Chapter 10, Section 11, for further information on rear wheel bearings.

9 Before refitting the disc, carefully clean the ABS magnetic ring on the back of the hub bearing **(see illustration)**.

10 Slide the disc back into position on the

8.2 To minimise fluid loss, fit a brake hose clamp to the flexible hose

stub axle and fit the new rear hub nut; tighten it to the specified torque. Tap the cap back into place, in the centre of the disc (if the cap is in poor condition a new one should be fitted).

11 Apply a few drops of locking fluid onto the threads of the caliper mounting bracket bolts. Offer up the bracket and refit the bolts, tightening them to the specified torque.

12 Refit the brake pads as described in Section 5.

13 Refit the roadwheel, then lower the vehicle to the ground and tighten the roadwheel bolts to the specified torque.

14 On completion, depress the brake pedal several times to bring the brake pads into contact with the disc.

8 Front brake caliper – removal, overhaul and refitting

Caution: *Ensure the ignition is switched off before disconnecting any braking system hydraulic union and do not switch it on until after the hydraulic system has been bled. Failure to do this could lead to air entering the modulator unit requiring the unit to be bled using special Peugeot/ Citroën test equipment (see Section 2).*

Note: *Before starting work, refer to the note at the beginning of Section 2 concerning the dangers of hydraulic fluid, and to the warning at the beginning of Section 4 concerning the dangers of harmful dust.*

Note: *New caliper mounting bracket bolts will be required on reassembly.*

Removal

1 Apply the handbrake, slacken the relevant front roadwheel bolts, then jack up the front of the vehicle and support it on axle stands (see *Jacking and vehicle support*). Remove the appropriate roadwheel.

2 Minimise fluid loss by first removing the master cylinder reservoir cap, and then tightening it down onto a piece of polythene, to obtain an airtight seal. Alternatively, use a brake hose clamp, a G-clamp or a similar tool to clamp the flexible hose **(see illustration)**.

3 Clean the area around the caliper hose

8.3 Slacken the brake hose nut (arrowed)

union and place a wad of rag under the union, to catch any spilt fluid. It is only possible to slacken the brake hose fitting on the caliper at this point, as the hose will twist (see illustration).

4 Slacken and remove the upper and lower caliper guide pin bolts or pins, refer to Section 4. Lift the caliper away from the brake disc, and then unscrew the caliper from the end of the brake hose. Note that the brake pads need not be disturbed, and can be left in position in the caliper mounting bracket.

5 If required, the caliper mounting bracket can be unbolted from the hub carrier. Discard the bolts, as new ones must be fitted.

Overhaul

Note: Check the availability of repair kits for the caliper before dismantling.

6 With the caliper on the bench, wipe away all traces of dust and dirt, but avoid inhaling the dust, as it is a health hazard.

7 Withdraw the partially ejected piston from the caliper body, and remove the dust seal.

8 Using a small screwdriver, extract the piston hydraulic seal, taking great care not to damage the caliper bore.

9 Thoroughly clean all components, using only methylated spirit, isopropyl alcohol or clean hydraulic fluid as a cleaning medium. Never use mineral-based solvents such as petrol or paraffin, as they will attack the hydraulic system's rubber components. Dry the components immediately, using compressed air or a clean, lint-free cloth. Use compressed air to blow clear the fluid passages.

10 Check all components, and renew any that are worn or damaged. Check particularly the cylinder bore and piston; these should be renewed (note that this means the renewal of the complete body assembly) if they are scratched, worn or corroded in any way. Similarly check the condition of the guide pins and their gaiters; both pins should be undamaged and (when cleaned) a reasonably tight sliding fit in the caliper bracket. If there is any doubt about the condition of any component, renew it.

11 If the assembly is fit for further use, then obtain the appropriate repair kit; the components should be available

from Peugeot/Citroën dealers in various combinations. All rubber seals should be renewed as a matter of course; these should never be re-used.

12 On reassembly, ensure that all components are clean and dry.

13 Soak the piston and the new piston (fluid) seal in clean brake fluid. Smear clean fluid on the cylinder bore surface.

14 Fit the new piston (fluid) seal, using only your fingers (no tools) to manipulate it into the cylinder bore groove.

15 Fit the new dust seal to the rear of the piston and seat the outer lip of the seal in the caliper body groove. Carefully ease the piston squarely into the cylinder bore using a twisting motion. Press the piston fully into position, and seat the inner lip of the dust seal in the piston groove.

16 If the guide pins are being renewed, lubricate the pin shafts with the special grease supplied in the repair kit, and fit the gaiters to the pin grooves. Insert the pins into the caliper bracket and seat the gaiters correctly in bracket grooves.

Refitting

17 If previously removed, refit the caliper mounting bracket to the hub carrier, and tighten the new bolts to the specified torque.

18 Screw the caliper body fully onto the flexible hose union.

19 Ensure that the brake pads are correctly fitted in the caliper mounting bracket and refit the caliper (see Section 4).

20 If the threads of the new guide pin bolts are not already pre-coated with locking compound, apply a suitable locking compound to them (Peugeot/Citroën recommend Loctite Frenetanch). Fit the new lower guide pin bolt, then press the caliper into position and fit the new upper guide pin bolt. Tighten both guide pin bolts to the specified torque.

21 Tighten the brake hose union nut to the specified torque, then remove the brake hose clamp or polythene (where fitted).

22 Bleed the hydraulic system as described in Section 2. Note that, providing the precautions described were taken to minimise brake fluid loss, it should only be necessary to bleed the relevant front brake.

9.3 Unscrew the brake pipe union nut (arrowed)

23 Depress the brake pedal repeatedly, until the pads are pressed into firm contact with the brake disc, and normal (non-assisted) pedal pressure is restored.

24 Refit the roadwheel, then lower the vehicle to the ground and tighten the roadwheel bolts to the specified torque.

9 Rear brake caliper – removal, overhaul and refitting

Caution: Ensure the ignition is switched off before disconnecting any braking system hydraulic union and do not switch it back on until after the hydraulic system has been bled. Failure to do this could lead to air entering the modulator unit requiring the unit to be bled using special Peugeot/ Citroën test equipment (see Section 2).

Note: Before starting work, refer to the note at the beginning of Section 2 concerning the dangers of hydraulic fluid, and to the warning at the beginning of Section 5 concerning the dangers of asbestos dust.

Note: New caliper mounting bracket bolts and guide pin bolts when be required on reassembly.

Removal

1 Chock the front wheels, slacken the relevant rear roadwheel bolts, then jack up the rear of the vehicle and support on axle stands (see Jacking and vehicle support). Remove the relevant rear wheel.

2 Minimise fluid loss by first removing the master cylinder reservoir cap, and then tightening it down onto a piece of polythene to obtain an airtight seal. Alternatively, use a brake hose clamp, a G-clamp or a similar tool to clamp the flexible hose at the nearest convenient point to the brake caliper (see illustration 8.2).

3 Wipe away all traces of dirt around the brake pipe union on the caliper (see illustration). Unscrew the union nut and disconnect the brake pipe from the caliper. Plug the pipe and caliper unions to minimise fluid loss and prevent dirt entry.

4 Remove the brake pads (see Section 5).

5 Slacken and remove the upper guide pin bolt, to remove the caliper from the vehicle. If required, the caliper mounting bracket can be unbolted from the hub carrier. Discard the bolts, as new ones must be fitted.

Overhaul

6 At the time of writing, no parts were available to recondition the rear caliper assembly, with the excepting of the guide pin bolts, guide pins and guide pin gaiters. Check the condition of the guide pins and their gaiters; both pins should be undamaged and (when cleaned) a reasonably tight sliding fit in the caliper bracket. If there is any doubt about the condition of any component, renew it (see illustrations 5.6a and 5.6b).

Refitting

7 If previously removed, refit the caliper mounting bracket to the hub carrier, and tighten the new bolts to the specified torque.

8 Refit the brake pads as described in Section 5.

9 Refit the caliper and insert the new guide pin bolts, tightening them to the specified torque settings.

10 Reconnect the brake pipe to the caliper, and tighten the brake hose union nut to the specified torque. Remove the brake hose clamp or polythene (where fitted).

11 Bleed the hydraulic system as described in Section 2. Note that, providing the precautions described were taken to minimise brake fluid loss, it should only be necessary to bleed the relevant rear brake.

12 Depress the brake pedal repeatedly, until the pads are pressed into firm contact with the brake disc, and normal (non-assisted) pedal pressure is restored.

13 Refit the roadwheel, then lower the vehicle to the ground and tighten the roadwheel bolts to the specified torque.

10 Master cylinder –
removal, overhaul and refitting

Caution: Ensure the ignition is switched off before disconnecting any braking system hydraulic union and do not switch it back on until after the hydraulic system has been bled. Failure to do this could lead to air entering the modulator unit requiring the unit to be bled using special Peugeot/Citroën test equipment (see Section 2).

Note: *Before starting work, refer to the warning at the beginning of Section 2 concerning the dangers of hydraulic fluid.*

Removal

1 Remove the battery and battery tray, as described in Chapter 5A, Section 4.

2 Remove the master cylinder reservoir cap and filter, and siphon the hydraulic fluid from the reservoir. **Note:** *Do not siphon the fluid by mouth, as it is poisonous; use a syringe or an old antifreeze tester. Alternatively, open any convenient bleed screw in the system, and*

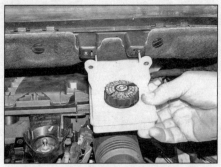

10.3 Undo the two screws securing the upper reservoir

gently pump the brake pedal to expel the fluid through a plastic tube connected to the screw until the reservoir is emptied (see Section 2).

3 Undo the two retaining screws and remove the upper reservoir from the rear panel. Depress the release button and disconnect the plastic pipe from the upper reservoir and remove it from the engine compartment **(see illustration)**. Be prepared for some fluid spillage.

4 Disconnect the wiring connector from the brake fluid level sender unit fitted to top of the reservoir.

5 Empty the lower reservoir by disconnecting the clutch master cylinder fluid supply pipe and draining the fluid into a container **(see illustration)**. Plug the pipe opening to prevent dirt ingress.

6 Wipe clean the area around the brake pipe unions on the side of the master cylinder, and place absorbent rags beneath the pipe unions to catch any surplus fluid. Make a note of the correct fitted positions of the unions, then unscrew the union nuts and carefully withdraw the pipes **(see illustration)**. Plug or tape over the pipe ends and master cylinder orifices, to minimise the loss of brake fluid, and to prevent the entry of dirt into the system. Wash off any spilt fluid immediately with cold water.

7 Slacken and remove the two nuts securing the master cylinder to the vacuum servo unit **(see illustration)**. Release the plastic servo pipe clip from the mounting stud, and then withdraw the master cylinder from the engine compartment. If the sealing ring fitted to the rear of the master cylinder shows signs of

10.5 Clutch fluid supply pipe (arrowed)

damage or deterioration, it must be renewed.

8 If required, undo the retaining screw and separate the reservoir from the master cylinder **(see illustration)**.

Overhaul

9 The master cylinder may be overhauled after obtaining the relevant repair kit from a Peugeot/Citroën dealer. Ensure that the correct repair kit is obtained for the master cylinder being worked on. Note the locations of all components to ensure correct refitting, and lubricate the new seals using clean brake fluid. Follow the assembly instructions supplied with the repair kit.

Refitting

10 Remove all traces of dirt from the master cylinder and servo unit mating surfaces and ensure that the sealing ring is correctly fitted to the rear of the master cylinder.

11 If removed, press the mounting seals fully into the master cylinder ports then carefully ease the fluid reservoir into position. Secure it in position, making sure the retaining clips are correctly located.

12 Fit the master cylinder to the servo unit. Refit the master cylinder mounting nuts, and tighten them to the specified torque.

13 Wipe clean the brake pipe unions and refit them to the master cylinder ports, tightening them to the specified torque.

14 Reconnect the clutch master cylinder supply pipe (where applicable), and level sensor wiring plug.

15 Connect the fluid supply pipe to the upper

10.6 Slacken the brake fluid pipes (arrowed)

10.7 Master cylinder securing nuts (arrowed)

10.8 Undo the retaining screw (arrowed) to remove the reservoir

11.1 Remove the trim (arrowed) from under the facia panel

11.2 Slide off the retaining clip (arrowed) from the clevis pin

11.3 Slacken and remove the pivot bolt and nut (arrowed)

reservoir, then fit the reservoir to the rear panel and tighten the retaining screws securely.

16 Refit the battery as described in Chapter 5A, Section 4.

17 Refit any other components removed to improve access then refill the master cylinder reservoir with new fluid. Bleed the complete hydraulic system as described in Section 2. **Note:** *A hydraulic clutch shares its fluid reservoir with the braking system, and may also need to be bled (see Chapter 6, Section 2).*

11 Brake pedal –
removal and refitting

Removal

1 Prise up the centre pins, prise out the complete expanding plastic rivets, and remove the driver's side lower facia panel above the pedals **(see illustration)**.

2 Slide off the retaining clip and withdraw the clevis pin securing the pedal crossover linkage pushrod to the pedal **(see illustration)**. Discard the clevis pin; Peugeot/Citroen recommend a new one is fitted.

3 Slacken and remove the pivot bolt and nut **(see illustration)**, and remove the brake pedal from the vehicle. Slide the spacer and washer (where fitted) out from the pedal pivot. Examine all components for signs of wear or damage, renewing them as necessary.

Refitting

4 Apply a smear of multipurpose grease to the spacer and washer, and insert it into the pedal pivot bore.

5 Manoeuvre the pedal into position, making sure it is correctly engaged with the pushrod, and then insert the pivot bolt. Refit the nut to the pivot bolt and tighten it securely.

6 Align the pedal with the pushrod and insert the new clevis pin, securing it in position with the retaining clip(s).

7 Refit the driver's side lower trim panel to the lower part of the facia.

12 Vacuum servo unit –
testing, removal and refitting

Testing

1 To test the operation of the servo unit, depress the footbrake several times to exhaust the vacuum, then start the engine whilst keeping the pedal firmly depressed. As the engine starts, there should be a noticeable 'give' in the brake pedal as the vacuum builds-up. Allow the engine to run for at least two minutes, and then switch it off. If the brake pedal is now depressed it should feel normal, but further applications should result in the pedal feeling firmer, with the pedal stroke decreasing with each application.

2 If the servo does not operate as described, first inspect the servo unit check valve as described in Section 13, also check the operation of the vacuum pump as described in Section 21.

3 If the servo unit still fails to operate satisfactorily, the fault lies within the unit itself. Repairs to the unit are not possible – if faulty, the servo unit must be renewed.

Removal

4 Remove the master cylinder as described in Section 10.

5 Release the wiring harness adjacent to the servo from its retaining clips, and move it to one side.

6 Release the retaining clip, and then disconnect the vacuum pipe from the servo unit check valve **(see illustration)**.

7 Working inside the vehicle, remove the trim panel from under the facia **(see illustration)**.

8 Undo the retaining nuts and remove the plastic trim cover from over the brake servo pushrod **(see illustration)**.

9 Remove the brake light switch from the servo mounting bracket with reference to Section 17.

10 Release the securing clips and then carefully disconnect the servo pushrod from the brake crossover shaft bracket.

11 Slacken and remove the securing nuts from the end of the brake crossover bar to the mounting bracket.

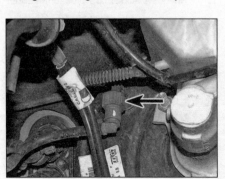

12.6 Depress the securing clip (arrowed)

12.7 Remove the trim panel

12.8 Remove plastic trim cover

12.12 Undo the four servo mounting nuts (arrowed)

12 Slacken and remove the four nuts securing the housing to the bulkhead **(see illustration)**.

13 Release the retaining clips, then ease the mounting bracket away from the bulkhead.

14 With the mounting bracket away from the bulkhead, release the retaining plate from the securing clips on the lower left and upper right servo studs. The retaining plate can then be withdrawn from between the bulkhead and the crossover bar mounting bracket. Take care not to damage the gaiter on the servo as the retaining plate is removed.

15 Working back in the engine compartment, manoeuvre the servo unit out of position, along with its gasket which is fitted between the servo and housing. Renew the gasket if it shows signs of damage.

Refitting

16 Refitting is the reverse of removal, noting the following points.

a) Lubricate all crossover linkage pivot points with multipurpose grease.

b) Refit the retaining plate between the bulkhead and the mounting bracket, taking care not to damage the gaiter on the servo pushrod.

c) Tighten the servo unit and mounting bracket nuts and bolts to their specified torque settings, where applicable.

d) Make sure the servo pushrod locates correctly with the brake crossover bar linkage.

e) Refit the master cylinder as described in Section 10 and bleed the complete

13.5 Vacuum pipe has an in-line valve (arrowed)

hydraulic system as described in Section 2.

f) Test the brakes and servo operation as described at the beginning of this Section.

13 Vacuum servo unit check valve – removal, testing and refitting

Removal

1 Release the retaining clip, and then disconnect the vacuum pipe from the servo unit check valve **(see illustration 12.6)**.

2 Withdraw the valve from its rubber sealing grommet in the servo, using a pulling and twisting motion. If required, remove the grommet from the servo and check its condition.

Testing

3 Examine the check valve for signs of damage, and renew if necessary. The valve may be tested by blowing through it in both directions. Air should flow through the valve in one direction only – when blown through from the servo unit end of the valve. Renew the valve if this is not the case.

4 Examine the rubber sealing grommet and flexible vacuum hose for signs of damage or deterioration, and renew as necessary.

5 There is also an in-line check valve fitted in the vacuum pipe from the pump to the servo **(see illustration)**. This can be tested in the same way as the check valve in the servo, see paragraph 3.

Refitting

6 Fit the sealing grommet into position in the servo unit.

7 Carefully ease the check valve into position, taking great care not to displace or damage the grommet. Reconnect the vacuum hose to the valve and, where necessary, securely tighten its retaining clip.

8 On completion, start the engine and check for air leaks from the check valve-to-servo unit connection.

14 Handbrake – adjustment

1 To check the handbrake adjustment, pull the handbrake lever to the fully applied position, applying normal moderate pressure, counting the number of clicks emitted from the handbrake ratchet mechanism. If adjustment is correct, there should be 2 clicks before the brakes begins to apply, and no more than 6 before the handbrake is fully applied. If this is not the case, adjust as follows.

2 Remove the centre console, as described in Chapter 11, Section 27.

3 Chock the front wheels, then jack up the rear of the vehicle and support it on axle stands (see Jacking and vehicle support). Check the handbrake cables are routed correctly and move freely. Also check the handbrake levers on the rear of the brake calipers operate correctly.

4 With the handbrake in the off position, press against the end of the locking button whilst moving the play compensation lever over to the left **(see illustrations)**. This will allow the integral play compensator to activate.

5 Release the locking button and the compensator will activate and take up the play in the cables.

Caution: DO NOT operate the handbrake more than one notch, whilst the play compensation activation lever is in the unlocked position, as the spring in the compensator may be damaged.

6 The play compensation lever can now be moved back to its original lock position to the right **(see illustration)**.

14.4a Keep pressure in the direction of the arrow...

14.4b ...whilst moving the lever over to the left

14.6 Move the lever back to the lock position

15.5 Disconnect the wiring connector from the switch

15.6 Disengage the cable end fittings (arrowed) from the equaliser plate

15.7 Undo the handbrake lever mounting nuts (arrowed)

7 Start the engine and depress the brake pedal approximately 10 times. Stop the engine.

8 Pull the handbrake lever on hard approximately 10 times.

9 Repeat the procedures once again for resetting the integral play compensation, as described in paragraphs 4 to 8.

10 Switch on the ignition and check that the handbrake warning light on the instrument panel operates correctly.

11 Release the lever and check by hand that the rear wheels rotate freely.

12 Refit the centre console and then lower the vehicle to the floor.

15 Handbrake lever and switch – removal and refitting

Removal

1 Chock the front wheels then jack up the rear of the vehicle and support it on axle stands (see *Jacking and vehicle support*).

2 Remove the centre console as described in Chapter 11, Section 27.

3 Referring to Section 14, release the handbrake lever to the off position and move the play compensation lever to the unlocked position.

Caution: DO NOT operate the handbrake more than one notch, whilst the play

compensation activation lever is in the unlocked position, as the spring in the compensator may be damaged.

4 Raise the handbrake lever to the first notch, then the play compensation lever can now be moved back to its original lock position to the right **(see illustration 14.6)**. The handbrake lever can now be released to the off position.

5 Disconnect the wiring connector from the handbrake warning light switch, and then if required unclip the switch from the handbrake mounting bracket **(see illustration)**.

6 Detach the two handbrake cables from the equaliser plate at the rear of the handbrake lever assembly **(see illustration)**.

7 Slacken and remove the lever mounting bracket retaining nuts, and remove the lever from the vehicle **(see illustration)**.

Refitting

8 Refitting is a reversal of removal. Tighten the lever retaining nuts, and adjust the handbrake (see Section 14).

16 Handbrake cables – removal and refitting

Removal

1 The handbrake cable consists of a left-hand section and a right-hand section connecting the rear brakes to the adjuster mechanism on

the handbrake lever rod. The cables can be removed separately.

2 Firmly chock the front wheels, slacken the relevant rear roadwheel bolts, and then jack up the rear of the vehicle and support it on axle stands (see *Jacking and vehicle support*).

3 Slacken the handbrake adjuster and disengage the relevant cable end fitting from the equaliser plate with reference to Section 14 and Section 15

4 Release the cable end fitting from the lever on the brake caliper, and remove the cable from the support bracket **(see illustrations)**.

5 Working underneath the vehicle, note its fitted location, then free the cable from the various retaining clips/brackets along its route.

6 Remove the rear seat cushions, as described in Chapter 11, Section 24. Then locate the front end of the cable and withdraw the cable through the opening in the floor panel.

Refitting

7 Refitting is a reversal of the removal procedure, adjusting the handbrake as described in Section 14.

17 Brake light switch – removal, refitting and adjustment

1 The brake light switch is located on the pedal crossover shaft bracket behind the passenger side of the facia. On models with cruise control there are two switches fitted to the bracket – the brake light switch is the left-hand of the two.

Removal

2 Working in the passenger's footwell, prise up the centre pins, lever out the complete plastic expanding rivets, and remove the trim beneath the passenger's glovebox (see illustration12.7).

3 Undo the retaining nuts and remove the plastic cover from over the brake light switch **(see illustration 12.8)**.

4 Disconnect the wiring, then rotate the

16.4a Disengage the inner cable from the lever…

16.4b …then squeeze the clips and pull the outer cable from the bracket

17.4a Disconnect the wiring connector from the switch

17.4b Rotate the brake light switch 90° anti-clockwise, and pull it from the bracket

17.5 Align the locking catch (arrowed) with the centering lug

switch 90° anti-clockwise and remove it from the bracket **(see illustrations)**.

Refitting and adjustment

5 Check that the red locking latch is in line with the locating lug on the side of the switch **(see illustration)**.

6 Refit the switch back into position in the mounting bracket, and turn it 90° clockwise to lock it in position.

7 Reconnect the wiring connector, and check that the switch plunger is up against the brake pedal lever bracket.

8 Check the operation of the brake lights and refit the trim cover and panel are refitted below the glovebox.

18 Anti-lock braking system (ABS) – general information

1 ABS is fitted to all models as standard; the system comprises a hydraulic valve block/ modulator unit and the four roadwheel sensors. The hydraulic/modulator unit contains the Electronic Control Module (ECM); the hydraulic solenoid valves and the electrically driven return pump. The purpose of the system is to prevent the wheel(s) locking during heavy braking. This is achieved by automatic release of the brake on the relevant wheel, followed by re-application of the brake.

2 The solenoid valves are controlled by the ECM, which itself receives signals from the four wheel speed sensors (front sensors are fitted to the swivel hubs, and the rear sensors are fitted to the rear hubs), which monitor the speed of rotation of each wheel. By comparing these signals, the ECM can determine the speed at which the vehicle is traveling. It can then use this speed to determine when a wheel is decelerating at an abnormal rate, compared to the speed of the vehicle, and therefore predicts when a wheel is about to lock. During normal operation, the system functions in the same way as a non-ABS braking system.

3 If the ECM senses that a wheel is about to lock, it closes the relevant outlet solenoid valves in the hydraulic unit, which then isolates the relevant brake(s) on the wheel(s) which is/ are about to lock from the master cylinder, effectively sealing-in the hydraulic pressure.

4 If the speed of rotation of the wheel continues to decrease at an abnormal rate, the ECM opens the inlet solenoid valves on the relevant brake(s), and operates the electrically-driven return pump which pumps the hydraulic fluid back into the master cylinder, releasing the brake. Once the speed of rotation of the wheel returns to an acceptable rate, the pump stops; the solenoid valves switch again, allowing the hydraulic master cylinder pressure to return to the caliper, which then re-applies the brake. This cycle can be carried out many times a second.

5 The action of the solenoid valves and return pump creates pulses in the hydraulic circuit. When the ABS system is functioning, these pulses can be felt through the brake pedal.

6 The operation of the ABS system is entirely dependent on electrical signals. To prevent the system responding to any inaccurate signals, a built-in safety circuit monitors all signals received by the ECM. If an inaccurate signal or low battery voltage is detected, the ABS system is automatically shut-down, and the warning light on the instrument panel is illuminated, to inform the driver that the ABS system is not operational. Normal braking should still be available, however.

7 Depending on model, it may also be equipped with additional safety features built around the ABS system. These systems are EBFD (electronic brake force distribution), which automatically apportions braking effort between the front and rear wheels, EBA (emergency brake assist) which guarantees full braking effort in the event of an emergency stop by monitoring the rate at

19.6 Remove the plastic weather cover from the unit

which the brake pedal is depressed, and ESP (electronic stability program) which monitors the vehicle's cornering forces and steering wheel angle, then applies the braking force to the appropriate roadwheel to enhance the stability of the vehicle.

8 If a fault does develop in the any of these systems, the vehicle must be taken to a Peugeot/Citroën dealer or suitably-equipped specialist for fault diagnosis and repair.

19 Anti-lock braking system (ABS) components – removal and refitting

Hydraulic valve block/modulator and ECM

Caution: Disconnect the battery before disconnecting the modulator hydraulic unions, and do not reconnect the battery until after the hydraulic system has been bled. Also ensure that the unit is stored upright (in the same position as it is fitted to the vehicle) and is not tipped onto its side or upside down. Failure to do this could lead to air entering the modulator unit, requiring the unit to be bled using special Peugeot/Citroën test equipment on refitting (see Section 2).

Note: *Before starting work, refer to the warning at the beginning of Section 2 concerning the dangers of hydraulic fluid.*

1 Disconnect the battery (see Chapter 5A, Section 1).

2 The hydraulic valve block assembly is located in the front left-hand corner of the engine compartment, behind the bumper, and below the left-hand headlight unit. Jack up the front of the vehicle and support it securely on axle stands (see *Jacking and vehicle support*).

3 Remove the front bumper as described in Chapter 11, Section 6.

4 Remove the left-hand front headlight unit as described in.

5 Use a brake pedal depressor tool, or length of wood jammed between the steering wheel and the brake pedal to firmly depress the brake pedal. This will prevent any flow of fluid when the brake pipes are disconnected.

6 Release the retaining clips and remove the plastic cover from around the hydraulic unit **(see illustration)**.

19.7a Unclip the plastic cover …

19.7b … and release the wiring plug locking lever (arrowed)

19.8 Mark the location of the various brake pipes before disconnecting them from the modulator

19.9 Undo the mounting bracket retaining bolts (arrowed)

19.10a Upper mounting securing nut (arrowed) …

19.10b … and two lower mounting securing nuts (arrowed)

7 Lift off the plastic cover, release the securing clip and disconnect the main wiring connector from the hydraulic valve block ECM **(see illustrations)**.

8 Mark the locations of the hydraulic fluid pipes to ensure correct refitting, then unscrew the union nuts, and disconnect the pipes from the modulator assembly **(see illustration)**. Be prepared for fluid spillage, and plug the open ends of the pipes and the modulator to prevent dirt ingress and further fluid loss.

9 Slacken and remove the modulator mounting bracket bolts and remove the assembly from the engine compartment **(see illustration)**.

10 If necessary, slacken the three mounting nuts on the hydraulic unit, and then it can be removed from the mounting bracket **(see**

illustrations). Renew the rubber mountings if they show signs of wear or damage.

11 Refitting is a reversal of removal, bearing in mind the following points:

a) *New valve blocks/modulator are supplied pre-filled with fluid – remove the plugs prior to connecting the fluid pipes.*

b) *New ECMs must be initialised and programmed using dedicated diagnostic equipment. Entrust this task to a Peugeot/Citroën dealer or suitably-equipped specialist.*

c) *Tighten the hydraulic pipes and mounting bolts to the specified torque, where applicable.*

d) *On completion, bleed the brake hydraulic system as described in Section 2.*

e) *Make sure the plastic cover is placed*

around the hydraulic unit, to prevent dirt and water ingress.

Electronic Control Module (ECM)

12 The ECM is integral with the hydraulic valve block assembly, and is not available separately. See paragraphs 1 to 11 for further information.

Front wheel sensor

13 Ensure the ignition is turned off.

14 Apply the handbrake, slacken the appropriate front roadwheel bolts, then jack up the front of the vehicle and support securely on axle stands (see *Jacking and vehicle support*). Remove the relevant front wheel.

15 Trace the wiring back from the sensor, releasing it from all the relevant clips and ties on the inner wing panel, whilst noting its correct routing, then disconnect the wiring connector **(see illustration)**. **Note:** *It may be necessary to remove the wheel arch inner liner to access the connector.*

16 Slacken and remove the retaining bolt and withdraw the sensor from the rear of the hub carrier **(see illustration)**.

17 Ensure that the mating faces of the sensor and the swivel hub are clean, and apply a little anti-seize grease to the swivel hub bore before refitting.

18 Make sure the sensor tip is clean and ease it into position in the swivel hub.

19 Clean the threads of the sensor bolt and apply a few drops of thread-locking

19.15 Disconnect the front sensor wiring connector (arrowed)

19.16 Undo the wheel speed sensor bolt (arrowed)

19.24 Disconnect the rear sensor wiring connector (arrowed)

19.25 Undo the speed sensor retaining bolt (arrowed)

19.32 Disconnect the sensor wiring plug connector (arrowed)

compound (Peugeot/Citroën recommend Loctite Frenetanch). Refit the retaining bolt and tighten it to the specified torque.

20 Work along the sensor wiring, making sure it is correctly routed, and securing it in position with all the relevant clips and ties. Reconnect the wiring connector.

21 Refit the roadwheel, lower the vehicle to the ground and tighten the wheel bolts to the specified torque.

Rear wheel sensor

22 Ensure the ignition is turned off.

23 Chock the front wheels, slacken the relevant rear roadwheel bolts, and then jack up the rear of the vehicle and support it on axle stands (see *Jacking and vehicle support*). Remove the relevant roadwheel.

24 Trace the wiring back from the sensor, releasing it from all the relevant clips and ties whilst noting its correct routing, and disconnect the wiring connector **(see illustration)**.

25 Working at the rear of the hub assembly, using an Allen key, slacken the retaining bolt and withdraw the sensor **(see illustration)**.

26 Ensure that the mating faces of the

sensor and the hub are clean, and apply a little anti-seize grease to the hub bore before refitting.

27 Make sure the sensor tip is clean and ease it into position in the rear of the hub.

28 Clean the threads of the sensor bolt and apply a few drops of thread-locking compound (Peugeot/Citroën recommend Loctite Frenetanch). Refit the retaining bolt and tighten it to the specified torque.

29 Work along the sensor wiring, making sure it is correctly routed, and securing it in position with all the relevant clips and ties. Reconnect the wiring connector.

30 Refit the roadwheel, lower the vehicle to the ground and tighten the wheel bolts to the specified torque.

Gyrometer/accelerometer sensor

31 Remove the centre console as described in Chapter 11, Section 27.

32 Release the retaining clip, and then disconnect the wiring plug **(see illustration)**.

33 Undo the two nuts and remove the sensor.

34 Refitting is a reversal of removal, ensuring the arrow on the top of the sensor points to the front of the vehicle.

20 Vacuum pump – removal and refitting

Removal

1 The pump is located at the left-hand end of the cylinder head.

2 To access the vacuum pump, remove the air cleaner ducting and pipes from the left-hand side of the cylinder head. Refer to Chapter 4A, Section 4 for further information.

3 Depress the retaining clip button and disconnect the vacuum hose from the pump **(see illustration)**.

4 Slacken and remove the retaining bolts/nut (as applicable) securing the pump to the left-hand end of the cylinder head, then remove the pump **(see illustration)**. Discard the sealing rings – new ones must be used on refitting. One of the pump retaining bolts acts as a locating stud for the air intake ducting.

Refitting

5 Fit new sealing ring(s) to the pump recess, then align the drive dog with the slot in the end of the camshaft, and refit the pump to the

20.3 Release the clip (arrowed) and disconnect the vacuum pipe

20.4 Vacuum pump mounting bolts (arrowed)

20.5a Renew the vacuum pump O-ring seals

20.5b Some pumps may have two O-ring seals (arrowed)

20.5c Ensure the pump drive dog engages with the slot in the end of the camshaft (arrowed)

cylinder head, ensuring that the sealing ring(s) remain correctly seated **(see illustrations)**.

6 Refit the pump mounting bolts/nut (as applicable) and tighten them securely.

7 Reconnect the vacuum hose to the pump, ensuring its retaining clip engages correctly, and (where necessary) refit the air cleaner ducting and pipes.

21 Vacuum pump – testing

1 The operation of the braking system vacuum pump can be checked using a vacuum gauge.

2 Start the engine and get it up to temperature, then allow it to idle.

3 Disconnect the vacuum pipe from the pump **(see illustration 20.3)**, and connect the gauge to the pump union using a suitable length of hose.

4 Measure the vacuum created by the pump; refer to specifications at the beginning of this Chapter. If the vacuum registered is significantly less than specified, it is likely that the pump is faulty. However, seek the advice of a Peugeot/Citroën dealer before condemning the pump.

5 Overhaul of the vacuum pump is not possible, since no components are available separately for it. If faulty, the complete pump assembly must be renewed.

Chapter 10
Suspension and steering

<hr>

Contents

Degrees of difficulty

Easy, suitable for novice with little experience	**Fairly easy,** suitable for beginner with some experience	**Fairly difficult,** suitable for competent DIY mechanic	**Difficult,** suitable for experienced DIY mechanic	**Very difficult,** suitable for expert DIY or professional

Specifications

Wheel alignment and steering angles

Front wheels:	
Tracking (toe setting)	-0°06' ± 0°04'
Camber:	
Left-hand wheel	0°01' (+ 0°40' – 0°20')
Right-hand wheel	0°01' (+ 0°20' – 0°40')
Castor:	
Car	+4°54' ± 0°30'
Van	+5°12' ± 0°30'
Pivot angle (king pin inclination – KPI):	
Left-hand wheel	11°42' (+ 0°20' – 0°40')
Right-hand wheel	11°42' (+ 0°40' – 0°20')
Rear wheels:	
Tracking (toe setting):	
Car	+0° 26' ± 0°04'
Van	+0° 28' ± 0°04'
Camber:	
Car	-1° 42' ± 0°30'
Van	-1° 44' ± 0°30'

Roadwheels

Type . . . .   Pressed-steel or aluminium alloy (depending on model)
Tyre pressures . . . .   See *Lubricants, fluids and tyre pressures*

Torque wrench settings

	Nm	lbf ft
Front suspension		
Anti-roll bar:		
Connecting link nuts*	50	37
Mounting clamp bolts:		
Rear bolt	104	77
Front nut	110	81
Driveshaft retaining nut	325	240
Hub carrier to strut*	90	66
Lower arm-to-subframe bolts	111	82
Lower balljoint:		
Balljoint to hub carrier	230	170
Retaining nut*	42	31
Lower crossmember mounting bolts:		
Vertical bolt	70	52
Horizontal bolt	51	38
Subframe mounting bolts	98	72
Suspension strut:		
Upper mounting plate nut	72	53
Upper spring seat nut	72	53
Rear suspension		
Axle hub nut: *		
Stage 1	70	52
Stage 2	Angle-tighten a further 45°	
Rear axle mounting bracket-to-body bolts	62	46
Rear axle-to-mounting bracket nut/bolt	76	56
Shock absorber:		
Lower mounting nut*	60	44
Upper mounting bolts	60	44
Stub axle bolts	63	46
Vibration damper (bolted on rear axle)	25	18
Steering		
High-pressure pipe-to-steering rack retaining bolt	20	15
High-pressure union on power steering pump	20	15
High-pressure union on steering rack/ram	10	7
Power steering pump mounting bolts:		
Lower mounting nut	22	16
Upper mounting nuts	23	17
Steering column mounting bolts	22	16
Steering column-to-steering rack pinch-bolt	22	16
Steering rack mounting nuts*	80	59
Steering rack mounting stud	10	7
Steering wheel housing to steering column nuts	22	16
Steering wheel retaining bolt	22	16
Track rod:		
Balljoint-to-hub carrier nut*	38	28
Balljoint locknut	55	41
Inner balljoint to steering rack	70	52
Roadwheels		
Wheel bolts	100	74

* *Do not re-use*

1.1 Front suspension

1 MacPherson strut
2 Anti-roll bar
3 Hub carrier
4 Lower balljoint
5 Subframe
6 Steering rack
  mounting nuts
7 Lower pivot arm
8 Anti-roll bar link
9 Track rod

H44697

1 General Information

1 The independent front suspension is of the MacPherson strut type, incorporating coil springs and integral telescopic shock absorbers. The MacPherson struts are located by transverse lower suspension arms, which utilise rubber inner mounting bushes. The front hub carriers, which carry the wheel bearings, the brake calipers, the hub/disc assemblies and the lower balljoints, are bolted to the MacPherson struts, and connected to the lower arms via the balljoints. A front anti-roll bar is fitted to all models. The anti-roll bar is rubber-mounted onto the subframe, and is connected to the front suspension struts by link rods **(see illustration)**.

2 The rear suspension has separate telescopic shock absorbers and coil springs fitted between the beam axle and the vehicle body. The rear beam axle has an integral anti-roll bar, and the axle pivots around rubber bushes that are bolted to the front mounting brackets.

3 The steering column has a universal joint fitted to its lower end, which is connected to the steering rack pinion by means of a clamp bolt.

4 The steering rack is mounted onto the front subframe, and is connected by two track rods, with balljoints at their outer ends, to the steering arms projecting rearwards from the hub carriers. The track rod ends are threaded, to facilitate adjustment.

5 A variable power steering system is fitted. The hydraulic pump alters the hydraulic pressure supplied to the steering rack to suit all conditions, ie, supplies high pressure when the vehicle is being driven slowly/parked and lower pressure when the vehicle is being driven at speed. The hydraulic steering

system is powered by an electrically operated pump, which is controlled by the engine management module (ECM).

2 Front hub carrier assembly – removal and refitting

Note: *A new track rod balljoint nut, lower balljoint nut, brake caliper mounting bracket bolts, and strut-to-hub carrier nuts will be required on refitting.*

Removal

1 Remove the wheel trim/hub cap (as applicable) then withdraw the R-clip and remove the locking cap from the driveshaft retaining nut. Slacken the driveshaft nut with the vehicle resting on its wheels **(see illustration)**. Also slacken the wheel bolts.

2 Chock the rear wheels of the car, firmly apply the handbrake, and then jack up the front of the car and support it on axle stands (see *Jacking and vehicle support*). Remove the appropriate front roadwheel.

3 Unbolt the wheel sensor and position it clear of the hub assembly (see Chapter 9,

Section 19). Note that there is no need to disconnect the wiring.

4 Slacken and remove the driveshaft retaining nut. If the nut was not slackened with the wheels on the ground (see paragraph 1), withdraw the R-clip and remove the locking cap. Refit at least two roadwheel bolts to the front hub, tightening them securely, then have an assistant firmly depress the brake pedal to prevent the front hub from rotating whilst you slacken and remove the driveshaft retaining nut. Alternatively, a tool can be fabricated to hold the hub stationary **(see illustration)**.

5 Slacken and remove the nut securing the steering rack track rod to the hub carrier then free the balljoint from the hub. If the balljoint is tight, use a universal balljoint separator to free it. Discard the nut; a new one should be used on refitting.

6 If the hub bearings are to be disturbed, remove the brake disc as described in Chapter 9, Section 6. If not, unscrew the two bolts securing the brake caliper mounting bracket assembly to the hub carrier, and slide the caliper assembly off the disc. Using a piece of wire or string, tie the caliper to the front suspension coil spring, to avoid placing any strain on the hydraulic brake hose.

2.1 Prise out the R-clip, remove the locking collar and slacken the driveshaft nut

2.4 Using a fabricated tool to hold the front hub stationary whilst the driveshaft nut is slackened.

2.7a Undo the lower balljoint retaining nut (arrowed) …

2.7b … use a Torx bit (arrowed) in the balljoint end to counterhold the nut

2.8 Undo the bolts (arrowed) noting their fitted position

7 Slacken and remove the lower balljoint nut and free the balljoint shank from the lower arm, if necessary, using a universal balljoint separator (see illustrations). Use a Torx bit in the end of the threaded part of the balljoint to counterhold the nut. Discard the nut and lift off the protector plate (if loose).

8 Undo the retaining nuts and withdraw the hub carrier-to-suspension strut bolts, noting that the bolts are inserted from the rear of the vehicle (see illustration).

9 Free the hub carrier assembly from the end of the strut, then release it from the outer constant velocity joint splines, and remove it from the vehicle. Suspend the driveshaft by string from the suspension strut to prevent any damage to the constant velocity joints.

Refitting

10 Ensure that the driveshaft outer constant velocity joint and hub splines are clean, and then slide the hub fully onto the driveshaft splines.

11 Slide the hub assembly fully into the suspension strut bracket and insert the bolts from the rear and fit the retaining nuts at the front.

12 Refit the protector plate (where removed) to the lower balljoint. Align the balljoint with the lower arm and fit the new retaining nut, tightening it to the specified torque.

13 Engage the track rod balljoint in the hub carrier, then fit the new retaining nut and tighten it to the specified torque.

14 Where necessary, refit the brake disc to the hub, referring to Chapter 9, Section 6

for further information. Slide the caliper into position, making sure the pads pass either side of the disc, and tighten the new caliper bracket bolts to the specified torque setting.

15 Refit the wheel sensor as described in Chapter 9, Section 19.

16 Lubricate the inner face and threads of the driveshaft retaining nut with clean engine oil, and refit it to the end of the driveshaft. Use the method employed on removal to prevent the hub from rotating (see paragraph 4), and tighten the driveshaft retaining nut to the specified torque. Check that the hub rotates freely then engage the locking cap with the driveshaft nut, so that one of its cut-outs is aligned with the driveshaft hole, and secure the cap in position with the R-clip. Alternatively, lightly tighten the nut at this stage and tighten it to the specified torque once the vehicle is resting on its wheels again.

17 Refit the roadwheel, then lower the vehicle to the ground and tighten the roadwheel bolts to the specified torque. If not already done, tighten the driveshaft retaining nut to the specified torque then refit the locking cap, aligning its cut-outs with the driveshaft hole, and secure it in position with the R-clip.

3 Front hub bearings – renewal

Note: The bearing is a sealed, pre-adjusted and pre-lubricated, double-row roller type, and is intended to last the car's entire service

life without maintenance or attention. Never overtighten the driveshaft nut beyond the specified torque wrench setting in an attempt to 'adjust' the bearing.

Note: A press will be required to dismantle and rebuild the assembly; if such a tool is not available, a large bench vice and spacers (such as large sockets) will serve as an adequate substitute. The bearing's inner races are an interference fit on the hub; if the inner race remains on the hub when it is pressed out of the hub carrier, a knife-edged bearing puller will be required to remove it. A new bearing retaining circlip must be used on refitting.

1 Remove the hub carrier assembly as described in Section 2.

2 Support the hub carrier securely on blocks or in a vice. Using a tubular spacer, which bears only on the inner end of the hub flange, press the hub flange out of the bearing (see illustration). If the bearing's outboard inner race remains on the hub, remove it using a bearing puller (see note above).

3 Extract the bearing retaining circlip from the inner end of the hub carrier assembly (see illustration).

4 Where necessary, refit the inner race back in position over the ball cage, and securely support the inner face of the hub carrier. Using a tubular spacer, which bears only on the inner race, press the complete bearing assembly out of the hub carrier.

5 Thoroughly clean the hub and hub carrier, removing all traces of dirt and grease, and polish away any burrs or raised edges that might hinder reassembly. Check both for cracks or any other signs of wear or damage, and renew them if necessary. Renew the circlip, regardless of its apparent condition.

6 On reassembly, apply a light film of oil (Peugeot/Citroën recommend Molykote 321R) to the bearing outer race and hub flange shaft, to aid installation of the bearing.

7 Securely support the hub carrier, and locate the bearing in the hub. Press the bearing fully into position, ensuring that it enters the hub squarely, using a tubular spacer which bears only on the bearing outer race. Note that the bearing is equipped with a magnetic encoder on its inboard face. When fitting the bearing, ensure this face is inboard adjacent to the ABS wheel speed sensor (see illustration).

3.2 Press the hub flange from the bearing

3.3 Extract the circlip from the inner side of the hub carrier

3.7 Take great care not to damage the seal in the bearing (arrowed) – it contains the encoder for the wheel speed sensor

4.2 Undo the anti-roll bar link upper nut (arrowed)

4.3 Remove the strut-to-hub carrier bolts – noting their fitted position

Take care not to damage this encoder, or place it adjacent to a magnetic source. Ensure the encoder face is clean.

8 Once the bearing is correctly seated, secure the bearing in position with the new circlip, ensuring that it is correctly located in the groove in the hub carrier. **Note:** *Align the gap between the ends of the circlip with the gap for the ABS wheel speed sensor.*

9 Securely support the outer face of the hub flange, and locate the hub carrier bearing inner race over the end of the hub flange. Press the bearing onto the hub, using a tubular spacer that bears only on the inner race of the hub bearing, until it seats against the hub shoulder. Check that the hub flange rotates freely, and wipe off any excess oil or grease.

10 Refit the hub carrier assembly as described in Section 2.

4 Front strut – removal and refitting

Note: *Always renew any self-locking nuts when working on the suspension/steering components.*

Removal

1 Chock the rear wheels, apply the handbrake, slacken the appropriate front roadwheel bolts, then jack up the front of the car and support on axle stands (see *Jacking*

and vehicle support). Remove the appropriate roadwheel.

2 Unclip the plastic wiring retaining clip and unscrew the nut securing the anti-roll bar connecting link to the strut **(see illustration)**. Position the link clear of the strut; if necessary, retain the balljoint shank with a Torx bit to prevent rotation whilst the nut is slackened. Refer to Section 9 for further information; discard the nut, a new one should be used on refitting.

3 Undo the bolts and pull the hub carrier away from the lower end of the strut **(see illustration)**, prevent the hub carrier assembly dropping whilst the strut is removed by supporting the lower arm. Take care not to strain the brake hose and the wiring attached to the brake caliper and the hub carrier.

4 Remove both wiper arms as described in Chapter 12 Section 13.

5 Undo the retaining bolts at each end then uclip the plastic scuttle panel from below the windscreen. Remove the rubber weather seal from the front edge and then pull up the ends of the scuttle panel to release it from the lower securing clips at the base of the windscreen **(see illustration)**.

6 Working in the scuttle aperture, slacken and remove the strut upper mounting nut, counterholding the strut rod with an Allen key located in the end of the rod. Support the strut, whilst removing the upper mounting nut, then withdraw it from under the wheel arch **(see illustrations)**.

Caution: As soon as the upper mounting nut is removed, the strut will be unsupported.

Refitting

7 Manoeuvre the strut assembly into position, ensuring that the end of the strut rod is correctly located in the corresponding hole in the inner wing. Fit the upper mounting nut and tighten it to the specified torque.

8 Engage the lower end of the strut with the hub carrier, insert the bolts from the rear and fit the retaining nuts.

9 Refit the scuttle plastic trim, and the wiper arms.

10 Reconnect the anti-roll bar connecting link to the strut. Do not forget the wiring support bracket. Tighten the nut to the specified torque.

11 Refit the roadwheel, then lower the vehicle to the ground and tighten the roadwheel bolts to the specified torque.

5 Front strut – overhaul

⚠️ *Warning: Before attempting to dismantle the front suspension strut, a suitable tool to hold the coil spring in compression must be obtained. Adjustable coil spring compressors are readily available, and are recommended for this operation. Any attempt to dismantle the strut without such a tool is likely to result in damage or personal injury.*

4.5 Remove the plastic scuttle panel

4.6a Undo the strut upper mounting nut ...

4.6b ... and use an Allen key in the end of the rod to counterhold whilst slackening the nut

5.1 Fit the coil compressors to the springs

5.2 Slacken the top nut whilst retaining the rod with an Allen key

5.3a Remove the nut …

5.3b … the thrust bearing …

5.3c … the spring seat …

5.4a … followed by the cap …

5.4b … the dust gaiter …

5.4c … and the bump stop

5.8 Ensure the lower end of the spring locates against the stop (arrowed)

Note: *Always renew any self-locking nuts when working on the suspension/steering components.*

1 With the strut removed from the car (as described in Section 4), clean away all external dirt, and then mount it upright in a vice. Fit the spring compressor and compress the coil spring until tension is relieved from the spring seats **(see illustration)**.

2 Slacken and remove the upper spring seat nut whilst retaining the shock absorber piston with a suitable Allen key **(see illustration)**.

3 Remove the nut then lift off the thrust bearing followed by the spring seat **(see illustrations)**.

4 Lift off the coil spring and remove the cap, dust gaiter and rubber bump stop from the shock absorber piston **(see illustrations)**.

5 Examine the shock absorber for signs of fluid leakage. Check the piston for signs

of pitting along its entire length, and check the shock body for signs of damage. While holding it in an upright position, test the operation of the shock absorber by moving the piston through a full stroke, and then through short strokes of 50 to 100 mm. In both cases, the resistance felt should be smooth and continuous. If the resistance is jerky, or uneven, or if there is any visible sign of wear or damage to the shock absorber, renewal is necessary.

6 Inspect all other components for signs of damage or deterioration, and renew any that are suspect.

7 Slide the rubber bump stop onto the piston. Fit the dust gaiter and cap, making sure the lower end of gaiter is correctly positioned over the shock absorber end.

8 Refit the coil spring; making sure its lower end is correctly seated against the spring

seat stop. Fit the upper spring seat, aligning its stop with the spring end, then the thrust bearing **(see illustration)**.

9 Fit the new nut. Retain the shock absorber piston and tighten the upper spring seat nut to the specified torque.

---

6 Front lower arm – removal, overhaul and refitting

Note: *Always renew any self-locking nuts when working on the suspension/steering components.*

Removal

1 Remove the relevant driveshaft as described in Chapter 8, Section 2.

2 Slacken and remove the nut, then free the lower balljoint shank from the lower arm, if necessary, using a universal balljoint separator. Discard the nut and lift off the protector plate (if loose). Use a Torx bit in the end of the balljoint shank to counterhold the nut.

3 Slacken and remove the lower arm front pivot bolt and nut **(see illustration)**.

4 Slacken and remove the rear pivot bolt and nut **(see illustration)**.

5 Manoeuvre the lower arm assembly out from underneath the vehicle.

Overhaul

6 Thoroughly clean the lower arm and the area around the arm mountings, removing all traces of dirt and underseal if necessary, then check carefully for cracks, distortion or any other signs of wear or damage, paying particular attention to the pivot bushes, and renew components as necessary.

7 Renewal of the front and rear pivot bushes will required the use of a hydraulic press, a bearing puller and several spacers, and should therefore be entrusted to a Peugeot/Citroën dealer or specialist with access to the necessary equipment. Depending how tight the bushes are in the lower arm, it may be possible, to remove and refit the bushes using an assortment of spacers and a threaded bar **(see illustrations)**.

Refitting

8 Manoeuvre the lower arm assembly into position, and refit the front pivot bolt and nut, tightening it finger-tight only.

9 Refit the rear pivot bolt and nut, and then tighten them to the specified torque.

10 Refit the protector plate (where removed) to the lower balljoint, and then locate the balljoint shank in the lower arm. Fit the new retaining nut and tighten it to the specified torque.

11 Refit the driveshaft (see Chapter 8, Section 2).

12 Refit the roadwheel, then lower the vehicle and tighten the roadwheel bolts to the specified torque. Rock the car to settle the disturbed components in position, and then tighten the lower arm front pivot bolt to the specified torque.

13 Check and, if necessary, adjust the front wheel alignment as described in Section 26.

7 Front lower balljoint –
removal and refitting

Removal

1 Remove the hub carrier assembly as described in Section 2.

2 Remove the protector plate from the balljoint and mount the assembly securely in a vice **(see illustration)**.

6.3 Undo the lower arm front pivot bolt (arrowed) …

6.7a Press the bushes into the lower arm …

7.2 Release the clips and remove the balljoint protector plate

3 Using a hammer and pointed-nose chisel, tap up the staking securing the balljoint in position **(see illustration)**.

4 Fit a deep socket to the balljoint, then unscrew it and remove it from the hub carrier.

Refitting

5 Screw the balljoint into the hub carrier assembly. Fit the special tool, taking care not to damage the balljoint gaiter, and tighten the balljoint to the specified torque. Secure the balljoint in position by firmly staking it into one of the hub carrier notches using a hammer and punch.

6 Fit the new protector plate to the balljoint and secure it in position by staking it into the one of the balljoint notches.

7 Refit the hub carrier (see Section 2).

6.4 … and rear pivot bolt (arrowed)

6.7b … by using spacers and a threaded rod

7.3 Use a chisel or a punch to unstake the balljoint

8 Front anti-roll bar –
removal and refitting

Note: *Always renew any self-locking nuts when working on the suspension/steering components.*

Removal

1 Chock the rear wheels, firmly apply the handbrake, slacken the front roadwheel bolts, then jack up the front of the vehicle and support on axle stands (see *Jacking and vehicle support*). Remove both front roadwheels.

2 Slacken and remove the nuts securing the left- and right-hand connecting links to the

8.2 Undo the anti-roll bar link lower nut (arrowed)

8.3 Undo the anti-roll bar clamp bolt/nut (one side shown)

anti-roll bar **(see illustration)**, and position the links clear of the bar. If necessary, retain the balljoint shank with a Torx bit to prevent rotation whilst the nut is slackened. Refer to Section 9 for further information; discard the nut, a new one should be used on refitting.

3 Slacken the two anti-roll bar mounting clamp retaining bolts and nuts, and remove both clamps from the top of the subframe **(see illustration)**.

4 Manoeuvre the anti-roll bar out from underneath the vehicle, and remove the mounting bushes from the bar.

5 Carefully examine the anti-roll bar components for signs of wear, damage or deterioration, paying particular attention to the mounting bushes. Renew worn components as necessary, noting the fitted position of the bushes if they are removed.

Refitting

6 Fit the rubber mounting bushes to the anti-roll bar. Position each bush so that the internal two flat surfaces are at the top and bottom and are correctly engaged with the flats on the anti-roll bar.

7 Offer up the anti-roll bar, and manoeuvre it into position on the subframe. Refit the mounting clamps, ensuring that their ends are correctly located in the hooks on the subframe, and refit the retaining bolts and nuts. Engage the connecting links with the ends of the bar then tighten the mounting clamp retaining bolts to the specified torque.

8 Fit the new retaining nuts to the connecting links and tighten them to the specified torque setting.

9 Refit the roadwheels then lower the vehicle to the ground and tighten the wheel bolts to the specified torque.

9.2a Undo the anti-roll bar link upper nut (arrowed) ...

9.3 Undo the anti-roll bar link lower nut (arrowed) ...

9.2b ... using a Torx bit to prevent rotation whilst the balljoint nut is undone

10.3 Undo the bolts (arrowed) securing the rear engine link rod

9 Front anti-roll bar connecting link – removal and refitting

Note: *New connecting link nuts will be required on refitting.*

Removal

1 Chock the rear wheels, firmly apply the handbrake, slacken the relevant roadwheel bolts, then jack up the front of the vehicle and support on axle stands (see *Jacking and vehicle support*). Remove the relevant roadwheel.

2 Unclip the plastic ABS wiring retaining clip from around the mounting bracket, and then undo the upper balljoint where it secures to the suspension strut **(see illustrations)**. If necessary, retain the balljoint shank with a Torx bit to prevent rotation whilst each nut is slackened.

3 Undo the lower balljoint where it secures to the end of the anti-roll bar **(see illustration)**; if necessary, retain the balljoint shank with a Torx bit to prevent rotation whilst each nut is slackened.

4 Inspect the link for signs of wear or damage and renew if necessary.

Refitting

5 Refitting is the reverse of removal, using new nuts and tightening them to the specified torque setting.

10 Front subframe – removal and refitting

Note: *Always renew any self-locking nuts when working on the suspension/steering components.*

Removal

1 Chock the rear wheels, firmly apply the handbrake, slacken the front roadwheel bolts, and then jack up the front of the vehicle and support it on axle stands (see *Jacking and vehicle support*). Remove both front roadwheels.

2 Remove the anti-roll bar as described in Section 8.

3 Slacken and remove the engine/ transmission rear lower mounting bolt and nut, then undo the nut and bolt securing the link rod to the subframe and remove the link **(see illustration)**.

4 Slacken and remove the left-hand lower balljoint nut and free the balljoint shank from the lower arm, if necessary, using a universal balljoint separator. Discard the nut. Repeat the procedure on the right-hand side.

5 Slacken and remove the steering rack mounting nuts and washers **(see illus-**

10.5 Steering rack mounting nuts (arrowed)

10.9a Undo the front subframe rear mounting bolts (arrowed) ...

10.9b ... and front mounting bolts (arrowed)

tration). Discard the nuts, as new ones must be fitted.

6 Unclip the heat shield from the steering rack, then (where applicable) undo the bolt securing the power steering pipe bracket to the subframe.

7 Make a final check that all control cables/ hoses that are attached to the subframe have been released and positioned clear so that they will not hinder the removal procedure.

8 Place a jack and a suitable block of wood under the subframe to support the subframe as it is lowered.

9 Slacken and remove the subframe mounting bolts then carefully lower the subframe assembly out of position and remove it from underneath the vehicle, taking great care to ensure that the subframe assembly does not catch the power steering pipes as it is lowered out of position. Recover the washers between the steering rack and the subframe **(see illustrations)**.

Refitting

10 Refitting is a reversal of the removal procedure, noting the following points:
a) Use new connecting link and lower balljoint nuts, and steering rack nuts.
b) Tighten all nuts and bolts to the specified torque settings (where given).
c) On completion check and, if necessary, adjust the front wheel alignment as described in Section 26.

11 Rear hub bearings –
checking and renewal

Note: *The bearing is a sealed, pre-adjusted and pre-lubricated, double-row ball type, and is intended to last the car's entire service life without maintenance or attention. Do not attempt to remove the bearing unless absolutely necessary, as it will be damaged during the removal operation. Never overtighten the hub nut in an attempt to 'adjust' the bearing. A press will be required to remove the bearing; if such a tool is not available, a large bench vice and suitable spacers (such as large sockets) will serve as an adequate substitute.*

Checking

1 Wear in the rear hub bearings can be checked for as described in or. However, the most common first symptom of bearing wear is a rumbling noise, noted at a particular roadspeed, or when the offending wheel is loaded-up during cornering. In this case, besides rocking the wheel, spin it and listen carefully to distinguish between the sound of the brake pads rubbing the disc, and the rumble of bearing wear. Compare the sound with the other rear wheel to confirm.

2 Wheel bearings do not have to be renewed in pairs. However, if the bearing on one side has worn, it may only be a short while before the other one needs renewal.

Removal

3 Remove the rear brake disc as described in Chapter 9, Section 7. **Note:** *New rear discs*

may come with new wheel bearings already fitted, but separate wheel bearing kits should also be available. Check for the availability of parts before stripping.

4 To remove the bearing, the retaining circlip must first be removed, which requires the use of a sturdy pair of circlip pliers **(see illustrations)**. A new circlip should be used when refitting – one is usually supplied in the bearing kits supplied.

5 Care must be taken during bearing renewal, as there is an ABS target ring fitted to the rear of the disc which must not be damaged. Mount the disc over the open jaws of a sturdy bench vice, with the target ring facing upwards **(see illustration)**.

6 After applying a generous amount of spray lubricant, we were able to pull the bearing out, using two blocks of wood, together with a large nut and bolt, and several washers/ spacers **(see illustration)**.

11.4a insert a pair of circlip pliers into the holes ...

11.4b ... then compress the circlip to remove

11.5 Mount the disc over the open jaws of a vice ...

11.6 ... then fit a large bolt, nut, spacers and two blocks of wood ...

11.7 … to extract the bearing

11.9a Offer the bearing into place …

11.9b … then tap it gently to start it into the hub

11.10a Fit the same nut, bolt and spacers used for removal …

11.10b … then tighten the nut/bolt to press the bearing into place

11.11 Fit the new bearing retaining clip

7 Tighten the nut and bolt to apply pressure to the bearing – this, and a few hammer blows, should be enough to get the bearing moving and extract it **(see illustration)**.

Refitting

8 Using emery paper, clean off any burrs or raised edges from the hub, which might stop the components going back together – take care not to damage the ABS target ring. Clean and lightly lubricate the bearing location in the hub.
9 Offer the bearing into position, and using a suitable spacer, tap it gently around its edge to start it squarely into the disc/hub **(see illustrations)**.
10 Using the same nut/bolt and spacers as for removal, tighten the nut and bolt to press the bearing into place **(see illustrations)**.

11 The bearing is fully seated when the circlip groove is visible. Fit the new circlip using suitable circlip pliers to retain the bearing **(see illustration)**.
12 Refit the brake disc/hub and wheel speed sensor as described in Chapter 9.

12 Rear shock absorber –
removal, testing and refitting

Note: *Always renew any self-locking nuts when working on the suspension/steering components.*

Removal

1 Chock the front wheels, slacken the relevant rear roadwheel bolts, and then jack up the rear of the vehicle and support it on axle stands (see *Jacking and vehicle support*). Remove the relevant rear roadwheel.
2 To remove the right-hand rear shock absorber, remove or lower the rear exhaust silencer to allow access to the upper mounting bracket. When working on the left-hand rear shock absorber remove the spare wheel from the carrier to make easier access to the upper mounting bracket.
3 Release the retaining clips and remove the plastic shields from the lower part of the rear axle assembly **(see illustration)**.
4 Using a trolley jack positioned under the axle, raise the lower arm until the rear suspension coil spring is slightly compressed **(see illustration)**.

12.3 Unclip the plastic shields

12.4 Place jack head under axle

12.5a Remove the lower shock absorber retaining nut...

12.5b ...and withdraw the mounting bolt

12.6 Remove the heat shield

Caution: DO NOT lower the jack with the shock absorber removed, as the spring may come away from between the axle and vehicle body.

5 Slacken and remove the lower mounting bolt and nut, then manoeuvre the shock absorber out of position **(see illustrations)**. Discard the nut; a new should be used on refitting.

6 To access the upper mounting bracket on the right-hand side of the vehicle, first undo the four retaining nuts and remove the heat shield **(see illustration)**.

7 Undo the upper mounting bracket securing bolts **(see illustrations)**, and then remove the shock absorber from under the vehicle

8 When renewing the shock absorber, undo the upper mounting bolt and remove the mounting bracket from the top of the shock absorber **(see illustration)**. Note the direction of the bolt before removal, as the threaded end of the bolt must point towards the spring on refitting.

Testing

9 Examine the shock absorber for signs of fluid leakage or damage. Test the operation of the shock absorber, while holding it in an upright position, by moving the piston through a full stroke and then through short strokes of 50 to 100 mm. In both cases, the resistance felt should be smooth and continuous. If the resistance is jerky, or uneven, or if there is any visible sign of wear or damage, renewal is

12.7a Undo the upper securing bolts...

12.7b ...and lower the assembly from under the vehicle

necessary. Also check the rubber mountings for damage and deterioration. Renew worn components as necessary. Inspect the shank of the mounting bolt for signs of wear or damage, and renew as necessary. The self-locking nuts should be renewed as a matter of course.

Refitting

10 Prior to refitting the shock absorber, mount it upright in the vice, and operate it fully through several strokes in order to prime it.

11 Refit the upper mounting bracket to the top of the shack absorber, and tighten the upper mounting bolt. Make sure the shock absorber is at 90° to the flats on the upper side of the mounting bracket before the upper bolt is fully tightened **(see illustration)**.

12 Manoeuvre the assembly into position and refit the upper mounting bracket bolts, and tighten them to the specified torque. Note some of the upper mountings have captivated nuts **(see illustration)** in the floor panel, make sure they are fitted correctly before refitting the upper mounting.

13 Align the shock absorber lower mounting with the lower arm and refit the mounting bolt. Fit the new nut, tightening it lightly only at this stage.

14 Refit the rear roadwheel then lower the vehicle to the ground and tighten the wheel bolts to the specified torque. Rock the vehicle to settle the shock absorber in position then tighten the shock absorber lower mounting to the specified torque setting.

12.8 Remove the upper mounting bolt

12.11 Shock absorber is at 90° to the flats on the mounting bracket

12.12 Make sure that the securing nuts are fitted correctly

13.7a Withdraw the upper part of the spring…

13 Rear coil spring – removal and refitting

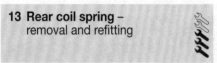

Note: *Always renew any self-locking nuts when working on the suspension/steering components.*

Removal

1 Chock the front wheels, slacken the rear roadwheel bolts, and then jack up the rear of the vehicle and support it on axle stands (see *Jacking and vehicle support*). Remove the rear roadwheels.
2 Release the retaining clips and remove the plastic shields from the lower part of the rear axle assembly **(see illustration 12.3)**.
3 Position a trolley jack underneath one of the lower arms of the rear axle **(see illustration 12.4)**, and then raise the arm until the rear suspension coil spring on that side is slightly compressed.
4 Unscrew the shock absorber lower mounting bolt/nut and withdraw the bolt **(see illustrations 12.5a and 12.5b)**. Discard the nut; a new should be used on refitting.
5 Slowly lower the jack as far as the lower arm will go, and remove the jack. At this point (unless the spring is broken) the spring should still stay in place between the axle and the vehicle body.
6 Now position the jack under the lower arm of the rear axle on the other side of the vehicle. Raise the arm until the coil spring on that side is slightly compressed, then

13.7b …and remove the spring complete with lower seat

slacken and remove the shock absorber lower mounting bolt. Again discard the nut as a new one will be required for refitting.
Caution: Check that there is no stress applied to any of the brake cables or hoses, as the axle is fully lowered.
7 Slowly lower the jack until all tension in the both springs are released, then remove the springs **(see illustrations)**. Note the fitted position of the upper and lower spring seat before removal.
8 Inspect the coil spring and its upper and lower seats for signs of wear or damage, then renew if necessary.

Refitting

9 Fit the lower plastic spring seat in position on the spring, and fit the upper rubber seat inside the top of the coil spring **(see illustrations)**.
10 Manoeuvre the springs into position and carefully raise one lower arm with the jack, ensuring that the coil spring lower seats are in the correct position. Align the shock absorber with the lower arm and refit its mounting bolt. Fit the new nut to the bolt, tightening it lightly only at this stage.
11 Remove the jack from underneath the lower arm, and position it under the rear axle lower arm on the remaining side. Raise the jack once again and align the lower mounting of the shock absorber with the arm. Insert the bolt, and fit a new nut, tightening it lightly only at this stage.
12 Refit the rear roadwheel then lower the vehicle to the ground and tighten the wheel

bolts to the specified torque. Rock the vehicle to settle the lower arm in position then tighten the shock absorber lower mounting bolts/nuts to their specified torque settings.

14 Rear stub axle – removal, overhaul and refitting

Note: *Always renew any self-locking nuts when working on the suspension/steering components.*

Removal

1 Chock the front wheels, slacken the relevant rear roadwheel bolts, and then jack up the rear of the vehicle and support it on axle stands (see *Jacking and vehicle support*). Remove the relevant roadwheel.
2 Unbolt the wheel sensor and position it clear of the stub axle (see Chapter 9, Section 19). Note that there is no need to disconnect the wiring.
3 Remove the disc/hub assembly as described in Chapter 9, Section 7. **Note:** *If the stub axle is to be renewed, there is no need to remove the disc/hub assembly, as the act of removal may destroy the bearing, necessitating its renewal.*
4 Undo the two rear brake caliper mounting bracket retaining bolts, and slide the caliper and bracket assembly from the disc. There is no need to disconnect the handbrake cable or caliper hose.
5 Undo the four bolts securing the stub axle to the lower arm and remove it, complete with disc backplate **(see illustration)**. **Note:** *The two upper bolts also secure the handbrake cable support bracket.*
6 Inspect the stub axle for signs of wear or damage. If the stub axle shaft is worn or damaged then the assembly must be renewed.

Refitting

7 Obtain all the new nuts required and lubricate the shanks of the pivot bolts and contact faces of the new nuts with multipurpose grease (Peugeot/Citroën recommend Molykote G Rapide Plus).
8 Offer up the stub axle and backplate, insert the bolts and tighten them to the specified torque.

13.9a Align the lower end of the spring seat…

13.9b …and refit the upper rubber seat

14.5 Stub axle securing bolts (arrowed)

15.2 Disconnect the ABS sensor wiring connector (arrowed)

15.3 Disconnect the brake hose union (arrowed)

15.5 Undo the four bolts each side (arrowed)

9 Fit the brake disc/hub assembly as described in Chapter 9, Section 7.
10 Refit the wheel speed sensor to the stub axle (see Chapter 9, Section 19).
11 Slide the brake caliper and bracket assembly over the edge of the disc, and tighten the mounting bracket bolts to the specified torque.
12 Refit the rear roadwheel then lower the vehicle to the ground and tighten the wheel bolts to the specified torque.

15 Rear beam axle – removal, overhaul and refitting

Note: *Always renew any self-locking nuts when working on the suspension/steering components.*

Removal

1 Remove the coil springs as described in Section 13.
2 Trace the ABS wheel speed sensor wiring back to its connector, and unplug it **(see illustration)**. Free the sensor harness from any retaining clips on the axle.
3 Clamp the flexible brake hose, and undo the hose union where the flexible hose connects to the rigid hose **(see illustration)**. Plug the end of the hose/pipe to prevent dirt ingress. Repeat this procedure on the remaining side.
4 Release the handbrake cables from the retaining clips along the axle, then release the ends of the cables from the caliper levers and support brackets (see Chapter 9, Section 16). Repeat the procedure on the remaining side.
5 Make alignment marks between the axle mounting brackets and the vehicle body to aid refitment. Undo the 4 bolts each side securing the mounting brackets to the vehicle body, and lower the axle to the floor **(see illustration)**. If the axle is to be renewed, remove the brake caliper (Chapter 9, Section 9), and the stub axle (Section 14).

Overhaul

6 Thoroughly clean the axle and the area around the axle mountings, removing all traces of dirt and underseal if necessary, then check carefully for cracks, distortion or any other signs of wear or damage, paying particular attention to the pivot bushes.

7 Renewal of the pivot bushes will require the use of a hydraulic press and several spacers, and should therefore be entrusted to a specialist with access to the necessary equipment.

Refitting

8 Lubricate the shanks of the axle mounting bracket bolts with multipurpose grease (Peugeot/Citroën recommend Molykote G Rapide Plus).
9 Offer up the axle and mounting brackets, aligning the previously-made marks, and insert the retaining bolts. Tighten them to the specified torque.
10 Refit the handbrake cables to their retaining clips on the axle, and reconnect the cable ends to the caliper levers (see Chapter 9, Section 16).
11 Reconnect the rear brake flexible hoses, tightening the hose/pipe unions securely. Remove the hose clamps.

16.2a Unclip the wiring block (arrowed) …

16.3a Undo the steering wheel retaining bolt …

12 Refit the coil spring with reference to Section 13. On completion bleed the brakes as described in Chapter 9, Section 2.

16 Steering wheel – removal and refitting

⚠ *Warning: Refer to the precautions given in before proceeding.*

Removal

1 Remove the airbag unit as described in Chapter 12 Section 22
2 Unclip the wiring block from the left-hand lower part of the steering wheel and disconnect **(see illustrations)**.
3 Slacken and remove the steering wheel retaining bolt, note the alignment mark on the steering wheel for alignment when refitting **(see illustrations)**. If no alignment marks are

16.2b … and disconnect

16.3b … noting the alignment marks (arrowed) for refitting

16.4 Withdraw the wiring through the steering wheel

obvious, then mark the steering wheel and steering column shaft in relation to each other.
4 Withdraw the steering wheel assembly off the top of the steering column. As the steering wheel is removed, withdraw the wiring through the aperture in the top of the steering wheel, releasing it from any retaining clips as it is withdrawn **(see illustration)**.

Refitting

5 Prior to refitting the steering wheel, ensure that the front wheels are still in the straight-ahead position.
6 Refitting is a reversal of removal, noting the following points:
a) On refitting, align the master spline or the marks made on removal, taking great care not to damage the wiring loom, then tighten the retaining bolt/nuts to the specified torque.
b) On completion, refit the airbag unit as described in Chapter 12 Section 22.

17.5a Remove the trim panel (arrowed)

17.5b Unclip the plastic cover from the lower part of the facia

17.3 Remove the column lower pinch-bolt/nut (arrowed)

17 Steering column – removal, inspection and refitting

Note: *As all models are equipped with a driver's airbag, refer to the precautions given in before proceeding.*
Note: *A new pinch-bolt nut will be needed on refitting.*

Removal

1 Remove the steering wheel as described in Section 16.
2 Move the driver's seat as far back as possible.
3 Working in the driver's footwell, make alignment marks between the universal joint and the steering rack pinion, release the retaining clip (where fitted), then undo and remove the pinch-bolt/nut from the joint at the base of the column **(see illustrations)**.
4 Remove the combination switches from the top of the steering column as described in Chapter 12 Section 4
5 Release the retaining clips and remove the lower facia panels above the driver's pedals **(see illustrations)**.
6 Disconnect the wiring connector at the rear of the ignition switch **(see illustration 18.5)**.
7 Note its fitted position, then release the wiring loom from its retaining clips and position it clear so that it does not hinder column removal.
8 Slacken and remove the four mounting bolts from the top of the column **(see illustration)**. Slide the column assembly upwards and free

17.8 Undo the mounting bolts (arrowed)

from the steering rack pinion, and remove it from the vehicle.

Inspection

9 Before refitting the steering column, examine the column and mountings for signs of damage and deformation, and renew as necessary. Check the steering shaft for signs of free play in the column bushes, and check the universal joints for signs of damage or roughness in the joint bearings. If any damage or wear is found on the steering column universal joint or shaft bushes, the column must be renewed as an assembly.

Refitting

10 Align the marks made prior to removal and engage the column universal joint with the steering rack pinion.
11 Slide the column assembly into position making sure its mounting bracket is correctly engaged with the facia bracket. Refit the column mounting bolts and tighten them to the specified torque setting.
12 Refit the universal joint pinch-bolt and nut, tighten them to the specified torque setting, and then refit the retaining clip.
13 The remainder of refitting is a reversal of the removal procedure, noting the following.
a) Ensure that all wiring is correctly routed and retained by all the necessary clips and ties.
b) Refit the steering wheel as described in Section 16.

18 Ignition switch/steering lock – removal and refitting

Removal

1 Disconnect the battery (refer to precautions in Chapter 5A, Section 1).
2 Undo the retaining screws securing the steering column lower shroud in position, then unclip the upper shroud, and release it from the retaining clips at its front edge **(see illustrations 30.1 and 30.2)**.
3 Trace the wiring back from the transponder and release the connector from the rear of the steering column combination switches **(see illustration)**.

18.3 Disconnect the transponder wiring connector (arrowed)

18.4 Unclip the transponder ring from the switch housing

18.5 Release the securing clip (arrowed)

18.6a Drill out the centre of the shear bolt ...

18.6b ... and use an extractor to remove the bolt

18.7 Depress the locating peg (arrowed) and slide the switch from the steering column

18.8 Fit the new shear bolt – tighten until the head shears off

4 Carefully lift the two plastic retaining clips and withdraw the transponder immobiliser unit to release it from the ignition switch housing **(see illustration)**. Take care not to damage the transponder assembly.
5 Release the securing clip and disconnect the wiring connector from the rear of the ignition switch **(see illustration)**.
6 Use a centre punch to mark the centre of the lock housing retaining screw (shear bolt), then using a drill and an extractor, remove the screw **(see illustrations)**. Obviously, a new screw will be required for refitting. **Note:** *It may be possible to use a hacksaw to cut a slot in the head of the bolt, and then use a large flat screwdriver to remove the old bolt.*
7 Insert the key into the steering lock and turn it to the first position, and then using a small screwdriver, depress the locating peg and slide the ignition switch from the steering column housing **(see illustration)**.

Refitting

8 Refitting is a reversal of removal, noting the following points:
a) *Ensure all wiring is correctly routed, and securely clipped back into its original positions.*
b) *Refit the steering lock housing with a new retaining/shear bolt* **(see illustration)**
c) *Tighten the bolt until the head shears off, leaving the threaded part securing the lock.*

19 Steering rack assembly – removal, overhaul and refitting

Note: *Always renew any self-locking nuts when working on the suspension/steering components.*

Removal

1 Firmly apply the handbrake, slacken the front roadwheel bolts, and then jack up the front of the vehicle and support it on axle stands (see *Jacking and vehicle support*). Remove both front roadwheels.
2 Slacken and remove the nuts securing the steering rack track rod balljoints to the hub carriers. Release the balljoint tapered shanks

using a universal balljoint separator, see Section 24. Discard the nuts; new ones will be needed on refitting.
3 Working underneath the vehicle, undo the remove the rack mounting nuts and studs **(see illustration)**. Recover the washers (where fitted) between the rack and the subframe, noting their positions. Discard the rack mounting studs and nuts, as new ones must be fitted.
4 Unclip the heat shield from the steering rack, then undo the bolt securing the steering rack pipe's bracket to the front of the subframe **(see illustration)**.
5 Position a jack under the centre of the front subframe. Remove the four subframe mounting bolts **(see illustrations 10.9a and 10.9b)**.

19.3 Steering rack mounting nuts (arrowed)

19.4 Steering rack pipe's bracket (arrowed)

19.6 Exhaust mounting retaining nuts (arrowed)

19.8 Undo the fluid pipes unions

6 Undo the retaining nuts and detach the exhaust rubber mountings from the rear of the subframe **(see illustration)**.

7 Undo the bolt and detach the rear engine-mounting link from the bracket on the rear of the cylinder block **(see illustration 10.3)**. Lower the subframe approximately 60 mm to allow for the steering rack to be removed.

8 Clean the area around the rack pinion housing, then undo the nuts securing the fluid pipes to the rack pinion housing **(see illustration)**, release the pipes from the retaining clamp, and drain the fluid into a container. To completely drain system, remove fluid reservoir cap and turn the steering wheel from lock-to-lock to assist the draining process; remember to recentre the steering wheel afterwards. Discard the pipes O-ring seals, new ones must be fitted. Plug the ends of the pipes to prevent dirt ingress.

9 Working in the driver's footwell, using paint or a suitable marker pen, make alignment marks between the steering column universal joint and the steering rack pinion, then slacken and remove the universal joint pinch-bolt, and release the retaining clip **(see illustration 17.3)**.

10 Still in the driver's footwell, undo the two retaining nuts and remove the seal around the steering rack pinion.

11 Free the steering rack pinion from the column universal joint and manoeuvre it out through the driver's side wheel arch aperture.

Overhaul

12 Examine the steering rack assembly for signs of wear or damage, and check that the rack moves freely throughout the full length of its travel, with no signs of roughness or excessive free play between the steering rack pinion and rack. Inspect all the steering rack fluid unions for signs of leakage, and check that all union nuts are securely tightened.

13 It is possible to overhaul the steering rack assembly housing components, but this task should be entrusted to a Peugeot/Citroën dealer or specialist. The only components that can be renewed easily by the home mechanic are the steering rack gaiters, the track rod balljoints and the track rods, which are covered elsewhere in this Chapter.

Refitting

14 Manoeuvre the steering rack into position and engage it with the column universal joint, aligning the marks made prior to removal.

15 Where applicable, slide the washer(s) into position between the subframe and steering rack. Insert the new mounting studs, and tighten the nuts to the specified torque.

16 The remainder of refitting is a reversal of removal, noting the following points:

a) *Top-up the fluid reservoir and bleed the hydraulic system as described in Section 21.*

b) *On completion check and, if necessary, adjust the front wheel alignment as described in Section 26.*

20 Steering rack rubber gaiters – renewal

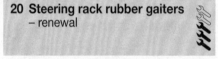

1 Remove the track rod balljoint as described in Section 24.

2 Disconnect the breather pipe from the gaiter **(see illustration)**.

3 Mark the correct fitted position of the gaiter on the track rod, then release the retaining clips and slide the gaiter off the steering rack housing and track rod end **(see illustration)**.

4 Thoroughly clean the track rod and the steering rack housing, using fine abrasive paper to polish off any corrosion, burrs or sharp edges which might damage the new gaiter's sealing lips on installation. Scrape off all the grease from the old gaiter, and apply it

20.2 Rack gaiter breather pipe and inner clip (arrowed)

to the track rod inner balljoint. (This assumes that grease has not been lost or contaminated as a result of damage to the old gaiter. Use fresh grease if in doubt.)

5 Carefully slide the new gaiter onto the track rod end, and locate it on the steering rack housing. Align the outer edge of the gaiter with the mark made on the track rod prior to removal, and then secure it in position with new retaining clips (where fitted).

6 Reconnect the breather pipe to the gaiter.

7 Refit the track rod balljoint as described in Section 24.

21 Power steering system – bleeding

1 This procedure will only be necessary when any of the hydraulic system has been disconnected.

2 Referring to *Weekly checks*, remove the fluid reservoir filler cap, and top-up with the specified fluid to the upper level mark.

3 With the engine stopped, slowly turn the steering from lock to lock approx 5 times to purge out any trapped air. Check the level and top up as necessary.

4 Start the engine and allow it to idle for 3 minutes without moving the steering wheel. Check the fluid level frequently during this period and top it up if necessary.

5 Slowly move the steering from lock-to-lock several times to purge out the trapped air, then top-up the level in the fluid reservoir. Repeat this procedure until the fluid level in the reservoir does not drop any further.

6 Turn the engine off and allow the system to cool. Once cool, check that fluid level is up to the upper mark on the power steering fluid reservoir, topping-up if necessary.

22 Power steering electro-pump – removal and refitting

Removal

1 Remove the windscreen washer fluid reservoir from inside the right-hand front wheel arch as described in Chapter 12 Section 16

20.3 Rack gaiter outer retaining clip (arrowed)

22.2 Disconnect the wiring connectors (arrowed)

22.3 Disconnect the fluid pipe and hose (arrowed) from the pump

22.4a Undo the upper pump mounting bolts (arrowed) ...

22.4b ... and lower mounting bolts (arrowed)

23.2 Remove the air intake hoses

2 Release the locking clips and disconnect the power steering pump wiring plug connectors **(see illustration)**. Unclip the wiring loom from the pump bracket and move it to one side.

3 Release the retaining clips and disconnect the fluid hose and fluid pipe from the power steering pump **(see illustration)**. Be prepared for fluid spillage, and plug the pump and pipe/ hose openings to prevent dirt ingress.

Caution: Do not bend the rigid power steering fluid pipe.

4 Undo the two upper and two lower pump mounting bolts, then remove the pump from the wheel arch **(see illustrations)**.

5 If the power steering pump is faulty it must be renewed. The pump is a sealed unit and cannot be overhauled.

Refitting

6 Manoeuvre the pump into position, then refit its mounting bolts and tighten them to the specified torque.

7 Reconnect the feed pipe to the pump and securely tighten the union bolt. Refit the supply pipe to the pump, and secure it with a new clip.

8 Refit the windscreen washer fluid reservoir as described in Chapter 12 Section 16.

9 On completion, bleed the hydraulic system as described in Section 21.

23 Power steering belt driven pump – removal and refitting

Removal

1 The power steering pump is mounted on the front facing side of the engine, and driven by the auxiliary belt.

2 Slacken the retaining clips and remove the air intake hoses from the front of the engine compartment **(see illustration)**.

3 Undo the two retaining bolts and remove the air intake ducting to the turbo **(see illustration)**.

4 Slacken the securing clips from the hoses, disconnect the wiring connectors from the sensors, then undo the retaining bolts and remove the air intake (doser) unit from above the power steering pump **(see illustration)**.

5 Undo the retaining bolts and remove the

23.3 Remove the air intake ducting

23.4 Remove the air intake (doser) unit

23.5 Remove the heat shield

23.7 Supply pipe support bracket bolt (arrowed)

heat shield from over the exhaust manifold/ turbo **(see illustration)**. This only needs to be removed to gain access the steering pump rear mounting bolt.

6 Remove the auxiliary drivebelt as described in Chapter 1, Section 16

7 Undo the bolt securing the fluid supply pipe to the support bracket located at the base of the pump **(see illustration)**.

8 Unscrew the power steering fluid reservoir filler cap and empty the hydraulic fluid from the reservoir by syphoning it out using a syringe or pipette. **Note:** *Do not syphon the fluid by mouth, as it is poisonous. Alternatively, the hose from the reservoir to the pump can be clamped off, to prevent any fluid loss.*

9 Place absorbent rags beneath the fluid supply and high pressure pipe and hose connections on the pump and be prepared for some fluid spillage.

10 Undo the union nut and disconnect the fluid high pressure pipe from the top of the pump **(see illustration)**. Move the pipe to one side and suitably cover the pipe end and the orifice in the pump to prevent dirt ingress.

11 Slacken the retaining clip, and disconnect the fluid supply hose from the pump **(see illustration 23.10)**. If the original crimped type clip is still fitted, cut the clip and discard it; use a standard worm-drive hose clip on refitting. Suitably cover the hose end and the orifice in the pump to prevent dirt ingress.

12 Undo the rear mounting bolt and the two front mounting bolts and withdraw the pump from the mounting bracket **(see illustrations)**. Access to the front mounting bolts can be gained through the holes in the pump pulley.

Refitting

13 Manoeuvre the pump into position, refit the pump mounting bolts and tighten them to the specified torque.

14 Reconnect the fluid high pressure pipe to the pump and securely tighten the union nut. Secure the pipe to the support bracket with the retaining bolt.

15 Refit the supply hose to the pump, and securely tighten its retaining clip.

16 Refit the heat shield, if removed.

17 Refit the turbocharger air intake hoses and ducting, making sure all the retaining clips are secure and the wiring connectors to the sensors are fitted securely.

18 Refit and tension the auxiliary drivebelt as described in Chapter 1, Section 16.

19 On completion, refill the system (if drained) and bleed the hydraulic system as described in Section 21.

23.10 Remove high pressure pipe (A) and supply hose (B)

23.12a Power steering pump rear mounting bolt (arrowed) …

24 Track rod balljoint – removal and refitting

Note: *A new balljoint retaining nut will be required on refitting.*

Removal

1 Apply the handbrake, slacken the appropriate front roadwheel bolts, then jack up the front of the vehicle and support it on axle stands (see *Jacking and vehicle support*). Remove the appropriate front roadwheel.

2 If the balljoint is to be re-used, use a straight-edge and a scriber, or similar, to mark its relationship to the track rod.

3 Hold the track rod, and unscrew the balljoint locknut by a quarter of a turn **(see illustration)**. Do not move the locknut from

23.12b … and front mounting bolts (arrowed)

24.3 Slacken the track rod end locknut (arrowed)

24.4a Undo the balljoint nut (arrowed) ...

24.4b ... then use a balljoint separator to release the tapered shank

this position, as it will serve as a handy reference mark on refitting.

4 Slacken and remove the nut securing the track rod balljoint to the hub carrier; discard the nut; a new one will be needed on refitting. Release the balljoint tapered shank using a universal balljoint separator **(see illustrations)**.

5 Counting the exact number of turns necessary to do so, unscrew the balljoint from the track rod end.

6 Count the number of exposed threads between the end of the balljoint and the locknut, and record this figure. If a new balljoint is to be fitted, unscrew the locknut from the old balljoint.

7 Carefully clean the balljoint and the threads. Renew the balljoint if its movement is sloppy or too stiff, if excessively worn, or if damaged in any way; carefully check the stud taper and threads. If the balljoint gaiter is damaged, the complete balljoint assembly must be renewed; it is not possible to obtain the gaiter separately.

Refitting

8 If a new balljoint is to be fitted, screw the locknut onto its threads, and position it so that the same number of exposed threads are visible, as was noted prior to removal.

9 Screw the balljoint into the track rod by the number of turns noted on removal. This should bring the balljoint locknut to within a quarter of a turn of the alignment marks that were made on removal (if applicable).

10 Ensure that the protector plate is in position then locate the balljoint shank in the hub carrier. Fit a new retaining nut and tighten it to the specified torque.

11 Refit the roadwheel, then lower the vehicle to the ground and tighten the roadwheel bolts to the specified torque.

12 Check and, if necessary, adjust the front wheel alignment as described in Section 26, then securely tighten the balljoint locknut.

25 Track rod arm – removal and refitting

Note: *A special wrench (Peugeot/Citroën number 0721-A) will be required to remove/refit the track rod inner balljoint from the end of the steering rack. Without the clamp, damage to the assembly is likely. The special wrench engages with the balljoint housing allowing the track rod to be easily slackened/tightened without the risk of damage. Note that without access to the special tool, track rod removal will be difficult, especially without causing damage.*
Note: *A new balljoint retaining nut will be required on refitting.*

Removal

1 Remove the relevant steering rack rubber gaiter as described in Section 20.

2 Using the special wrench (see note at the start of the Section), unscrew the track rod inner balljoint from the steering rack end. Take great care not to place excess strain on the rack, as the joint is unscrewed, if necessary, prevent the steering rack from turning by holding it carefully with a pair of grips. Take great care not to mark the surfaces of the rack and balljoint. To eliminate the possibility of damage, a Peugeot/Citroën special tool (0721-B) is available to prevent the rack from twisting.

3 Remove the track rod assembly. Examine the track rod inner balljoint for signs of slackness or tight spots, and check that the track rod itself is straight and free from damage. If necessary, renew the track rod; it is also recommended that the steering rack gaiter/dust cover is renewed.

Refitting

4 Screw the balljoint into the steering rack, and tighten it to the specified torque. If necessary, retain the steering rack with a pair of grips or the special tool, again taking great

care not to damage or mark the track rod balljoint or steering rack.

5 Carefully slide on the new gaiter, and locate it on the steering rack housing. Turn the steering fully from lock-to-lock, to check that the gaiter is correctly positioned on the track rod, then secure it in position with new retaining clips (where fitted).

6 Refit the track rod balljoint as described in Section 24.

26 Wheel alignment and steering angles – information, checking and adjustment

Definitions

1 A car's steering and suspension geometry is defined in four basic settings – all angles are expressed in degrees (toe settings are also expressed as a measurement); the steering axis is defined as an imaginary line drawn through the axis of the suspension strut, extended where necessary to contact the ground.

2 Camber is the angle between each roadwheel and a vertical line drawn through its centre and tyre contact patch, when viewed from the front or rear of the car. Positive camber is when the roadwheels are tilted outwards from the vertical at the top; negative camber is when they are tilted inwards. The camber angle is not adjustable.

3 Castor is the angle between the steering axis and a vertical line drawn through each roadwheel's centre and tyre contact patch, when viewed from the side of the car. Positive castor is when the steering axis is tilted so that it contacts the ground ahead of the vertical; negative castor is when it contacts the ground behind the vertical. The castor angle is not adjustable.

4 Toe is the difference, viewed from above, between lines drawn through the roadwheel centres and the car's centre-line. 'Toe-in' is when the roadwheels point inwards, towards each other at the front, while 'toe-out' is when they splay outwards from each other at the front.

5 The front wheel toe setting is adjusted by screwing the track rod in or out of its balljoints to alter the effective length of the track rod assembly.

6 Rear wheel toe setting is not adjustable.

Checking and adjustment

7 Due to the special measuring equipment necessary to check the wheel alignment and steering angles, and the skill required to use it properly, the checking and adjustment of these settings is best left to a Peugeot/Citroën dealer or similar expert. Note that most tyre-fitting shops now possess sophisticated checking equipment. The following is provided as a guide, should the owner decide to carry out a DIY check.

Front wheel toe setting

8 The front wheel toe setting (tracking) is checked by measuring the angle of the wheels in relation to the longitudinal axis of the vehicle. Proprietary toe measurement gauges are available from motor accessory shops.

9 Adjustment is made by screwing the balljoints in or out of their track rods, to alter the effective length of the track rod assemblies.

10 Before starting work, check first that the tyre sizes and types are as specified, then check the tyre pressures and tread wear, the roadwheel run-out, the condition of the hub bearings, the steering wheel free play, and the condition of the front suspension components (see *Weekly checks* and Chapter 1, Section 4. Correct any faults found.

11 Park the vehicle on level ground, check that the front roadwheels are in the straight-ahead position, then rock the rear and front ends to settle the suspension. Release the handbrake, and roll the vehicle backwards 1 metre, then forwards again, to relieve any stresses in the steering and suspension components.

12 Follow the tracking gauge manufacturer's instructions and measure the toe setting.

13 If adjustment is necessary, apply the handbrake, then jack up the front of the vehicle and support it securely on axle stands. Turn the steering wheel onto full-left lock, and record the number of exposed threads on the right-hand track rod end. Now turn the steering onto full-right lock, and record the number of threads on the left-hand side. If there are the same number of threads visible on both sides, then subsequent adjustment should be made equally on both sides. If there are more threads visible on one side than the other, it will be necessary to compensate for this during adjustment. **Note:** *It is most important that after adjustment, the same number of threads are visible on each track rod end.*

14 First clean the track rod threads; if they are corroded, apply penetrating fluid before starting adjustment. Release the rubber gaiter outboard clips (where necessary), and peel back the gaiters; apply a smear of grease to the inside of the gaiters, so that both are free, and will not be twisted or strained as their respective track rods are rotated.

15 Use a straight-edge and a scriber or similar to mark the relationship of each track rod to its balljoint then, holding each track rod in turn, unscrew its locknut fully.

16 Alter the length of the track rods, bearing in mind the note made in paragraph 13. Screw them into or out the balljoints, rotating the track rod using an open-ended spanner fitted to the flats provided on the track rod. Shortening the track rods (screwing them into their balljoints) will reduce toe-in/increase toe-out.

17 When the setting is correct, hold the track rods and tighten the balljoint locknuts to the specified torque setting. Check that the balljoints are seated correctly in their sockets, and count the exposed threads to check the length of both track rods. If they are not the same, then the adjustment has not been made equally, and problems will be encountered with tyre scrubbing in turns; also, the steering wheel spokes will no longer be horizontal when the wheels are in the straight-ahead position.

18 If the track rod lengths are the same, lower the vehicle to the ground and recheck the toe setting; re-adjust if necessary. When the setting is correct, tighten the track rod balljoint locknuts to the specified torque. Ensure that the rubber gaiters are seated correctly, and are not twisted or strained, and secure them in position with new retaining clips (where necessary).

Chapter 11
Bodywork and fittings

Contents

Degrees of difficulty

Easy, suitable for novice with little experience		Fairly easy, suitable for beginner with some experience		Fairly difficult, suitable for competent DIY mechanic		Difficult, suitable for experienced DIY mechanic		Very difficult, suitable for expert DIY or professional	

Specifications

Torque wrench setting	Nm	lbf ft
Seat belt mountings.	25	18
Sliding side door attachments:		
Lower carriage end stop.	8	6
Centre carriage bracket	20	15

1 General Information

1 The bodyshell is made of pressed-steel sections, and is available in Van or estate/ MPV format. Most components are welded together, but some use is made of structural adhesives.

2 The bonnet, doors and some other vulnerable panels are made of zinc-coated metal, and are further protected by being coated with an anti-chip primer prior to being sprayed.

3 Extensive use is made of plastic materials, mainly in the interior, but also in exterior components. The front and rear bumpers and the front grille are injection-moulded from a synthetic material which is very strong, yet light. Plastic components such as wheel arch liners are fitted to the underside of the vehicle, to improve the body's resistance to corrosion.

2 Maintenance – bodywork and underframe

1 The general condition of a vehicle's bodywork is the one thing that significantly affects its value. Maintenance is easy, but needs to be regular. Neglect, particularly after minor damage, can lead quickly to further deterioration and costly repair bills. It is important also to keep watch on those parts of the vehicle not immediately visible, for instance the underside, inside all the wheel arches, and the lower part of the engine compartment.

2 The basic maintenance routine for the bodywork is washing – preferably with a lot of water, from a hose. This will remove all the loose solids which may have stuck to the vehicle. It is important to flush these off in such a way as to prevent grit from scratching the finish. The wheel arches and underframe need washing in the same way, to remove any accumulated mud which will retain moisture and tend to encourage rust. Paradoxically enough, the best time to clean the underframe and wheel arches is in wet weather, when the mud is thoroughly wet and soft. In very wet weather, the underframe is usually cleaned of large accumulations automatically, and this is a good time for inspection.

3 Periodically, except on vehicles with a wax-based underbody protective coating, it is a good idea to have the whole of the underframe of the vehicle steam-cleaned, engine compartment included, so that a thorough inspection can be carried out to see what minor repairs and renovations are necessary. Steam-cleaning is available at many garages, and is necessary for the removal of the accumulation of oily grime, which sometimes is allowed to become thick in certain areas. If steam-cleaning facilities are not available, there are one or two excellent grease solvents available, which can be brush-applied; the dirt can then be simply hosed off. Note that these methods should not be used on vehicles with wax-based underbody protective coating, or the coating will be removed. Such vehicles should be inspected annually, preferably just prior to winter, when the underbody should be washed down, and any damage to the wax coating repaired using underseal. Ideally, a completely fresh coat should be applied. It would also be worth considering the use of wax-based protection for injection into door panels, sills, box sections, etc, as an additional safeguard against rust damage, where such protection is not provided by the vehicle manufacturer.

4 After washing paintwork, wipe off with a chamois leather to give an unspotted clear finish. A coat of clear protective wax polish will give added protection against chemical pollutants in the air. If the paintwork sheen has dulled or oxidised, use a cleaner/ polisher combination to restore the brilliance of the shine. This requires a little effort, but such dulling is usually caused because regular washing has been neglected. Care needs to be taken with metallic paintwork, as a special non-abrasive cleaner/polisher is required to avoid damage to the finish. Always check that the door and ventilator opening drain holes and pipes are completely clear, so that water can be drained out. Brightwork should be treated in the same way as paintwork. Windscreens and windows can be kept clear of the smeary film which often appears, by the use of proprietary glass cleaner. Never use any form of wax or other body or chromium polish on glass.

3 Maintenance – upholstery and carpets

1 Mats and carpets should be brushed or vacuum-cleaned regularly, to keep them free of grit. If they are badly stained, remove them from the vehicle for scrubbing or sponging, and make quite sure they are dry before refitting. Seats and interior trim panels can be kept clean by wiping with a damp cloth and a proprietary upholstery cleaner. If they do become stained (which can be more apparent on light-coloured upholstery), use a little liquid detergent and a soft nail brush to scour the grime out of the grain of the material. Do not forget to keep the headlining clean in the same way as the upholstery. When using liquid cleaners inside the vehicle, do not over-wet the surfaces being cleaned. Excessive damp could get into the seams and padded interior, causing stains, offensive odours or even rot. If the inside of the vehicle gets wet accidentally, it is worthwhile taking some trouble to dry it out properly, particularly where carpets are involved.

Caution: Do not leave oil or electric heaters inside the vehicle for this purpose.

4 Minor body damage – repair

Scratches

1 If the scratch is very superficial, and does not penetrate to the metal of the bodywork, repair is very simple. Lightly rub the area of the scratch with a paintwork renovator, or a very fine cutting paste, to remove loose paint from the scratch, and to clear the surrounding bodywork of wax polish. Rinse the area with clean water.

2 Apply touch-up paint to the scratch using a fine paint brush; continue to apply fine layers of paint until the surface of the paint in the scratch is level with the surrounding paintwork. Allow the new paint at least two weeks to harden, then blend it into the surrounding paintwork by rubbing the scratch area with a paintwork renovator or a very fine cutting paste. Finally apply wax polish.

3 Where the scratch has penetrated right through to the metal of the bodywork, causing the metal to rust, a different repair technique is required. Remove any loose rust from the bottom of the scratch with a penknife, then apply rust-inhibiting paint, to prevent the formation of rust in the future. Using a rubber or nylon applicator, fill the scratch with bodystopper paste. If required, this paste can be mixed with cellulose thinners, to provide a very thin paste which is ideal for filling narrow scratches. Before the stopper-paste in the scratch hardens, wrap a piece of smooth cotton rag around the top of a finger. Dip the finger in cellulose thinners, and quickly sweep it across the surface of the stopper-paste in the scratch; this will ensure that the surface of the stopper-paste is slightly hollowed. The scratch can now be painted over as described earlier in this Section.

Dents

4 When deep denting of the vehicle's bodywork has taken place, the first task is to pull the dent out, until the affected bodywork almost attains its original shape. There is little point in trying to restore the original shape completely, as the metal in the damaged area will have stretched on impact, and cannot be reshaped fully to its original contour. It is better to bring the level of the dent up to a point which is about 3 mm below the level of the surrounding bodywork. In cases where the dent is very shallow anyway, it is not worth trying to pull it out at all. If the underside of the dent is accessible, it can be hammered out gently from behind, using a mallet with a wooden or plastic head. Whilst doing this, hold a suitable block of wood firmly against the outside of the panel, to absorb the impact from the hammer blows and thus prevent a large area of the bodywork from being 'belled-out'.

5 Should the dent be in a section of the bodywork which has a double skin, or some

other factor making it inaccessible from behind, a different technique is called for. Drill several small holes through the metal inside the area – particularly in the deeper section. Then screw long self-tapping screws into the holes, just sufficiently for them to gain a good purchase in the metal. Now the dent can be pulled out by pulling on the protruding heads of the screws with a pair of pliers.

6 The next stage of the repair is the removal of the paint from the damaged area, and from an inch or so of the surrounding 'sound' bodywork. This is accomplished most easily by using a wire brush or abrasive pad on a power drill, although it can be done just as effectively by hand, using sheets of abrasive paper. To complete the preparation for filling, score the surface of the bare metal with a screwdriver or the tang of a file, or alternatively, drill small holes in the affected area. This will provide a really good 'key' for the filler paste.

7 To complete the repair, see the Section on filling and respraying.

Rust holes or gashes

8 Remove all paint from the affected area, and from an inch or so of the surrounding 'sound' bodywork, using an abrasive pad or a wire brush on a power drill. If these are not available, a few sheets of abrasive paper will do the job most effectively. With the paint removed, you will be able to judge the severity of the corrosion, and therefore decide whether to renew the whole panel (if this is possible) or to repair the affected area. New body panels are not as expensive as most people think, and it is often quicker and more satisfactory to fit a new panel than to attempt to repair large areas of corrosion.

9 Remove all fittings from the affected area, except those which will act as a guide to the original shape of the damaged bodywork (eg headlight shells etc). Then, using tin snips or a hacksaw blade, remove all loose metal and any other metal badly affected by corrosion. Hammer the edges of the hole inwards, in order to create a slight depression for the filler paste.

10 Wire-brush the affected area to remove the powdery rust from the surface of the remaining metal. Paint the affected area with rust-inhibiting paint; if the back of the rusted area is accessible, treat this also.

11 Before filling can take place, it will be necessary to block the hole in some way. This can be achieved by the use of aluminium or plastic mesh, or aluminium tape.

12 Aluminium or plastic mesh, or glass-fibre matting, is probably the best material to use for a large hole. Cut a piece to the approximate size and shape of the hole to be filled, then position it in the hole so that its edges are below the level of the surrounding bodywork. It can be retained in position by several blobs of filler paste around its periphery.

13 Aluminium tape should be used for small or very narrow holes. Pull a piece off the roll,

trim it to the approximate size and shape required, then pull off the backing paper (if used) and stick the tape over the hole; it can be overlapped if the thickness of one piece is insufficient. Burnish down the edges of the tape with the handle of a screwdriver or similar, to ensure that the tape is securely attached to the metal underneath.

Filling and respraying

14 Before using this Section, see the Sections on dent, minor scratch, rust holes and gash repairs.

15 Many types of bodyfiller are available, but generally speaking, those proprietary kits which contain a tin of filler paste and a tube of resin hardener are best for this type of repair; some can be used directly from the tube. A wide, flexible plastic or nylon applicator will be found invaluable for imparting a smooth and well-contoured finish to the surface of the filler.

16 Mix up a little filler on a clean piece of card or board – measure the hardener carefully (follow the maker's instructions on the pack), otherwise the filler will set too rapidly or too slowly. Using the applicator, apply the filler paste to the prepared area; draw the applicator across the surface of the filler to achieve the correct contour and to level the surface. As soon as a contour that approximates to the correct one is achieved, stop working the paste – if you carry on too long, the paste will become sticky and begin to 'pick-up' on the applicator. Continue to add thin layers of filler paste at 20-minute intervals, until the level of the filler is just proud of the surrounding bodywork.

17 Once the filler has hardened, the excess can be removed using a metal plane or file. From then on, progressively-finer grades of abrasive paper should be used, starting with a 40-grade production paper, and finishing with a 400-grade wet-and-dry paper. Always wrap the abrasive paper around a flat rubber, cork, or wooden block – otherwise the surface of the filler will not be completely flat. During the smoothing of the filler surface, the wet-and-dry paper should be periodically rinsed in water. This will ensure that a very smooth finish is imparted to the filler at the final stage.

18 At this stage, the 'dent' should be surrounded by a ring of bare metal, which in turn should be encircled by the finely 'feathered' edge of the good paintwork. Rinse the repair area with clean water, until all of the dust produced by the rubbing-down operation has gone.

19 Spray the whole area with a light coat of primer – this will show up any imperfections in the surface of the filler. Repair these imperfections with fresh filler paste or bodystopper, and once more smooth the surface with abrasive paper. If bodystopper is used, it can be mixed with cellulose thinners, to form a really thin paste which is ideal for filling small holes. Repeat this spray-and-

repair procedure until you are satisfied that the surface of the filler, and the feathered edge of the paintwork, are perfect. Clean the repair area with clean water, and allow to dry fully.

20 The repair area is now ready for final spraying. Paint spraying must be carried out in a warm, dry, windless and dust-free atmosphere. This condition can be created artificially if you have access to a large indoor working area, but if you are forced to work in the open, you will have to pick your day very carefully. If you are working indoors, dousing the floor in the work area with water will help to settle the dust which would otherwise be in the atmosphere. If the repair area is confined to one body panel, mask off the surrounding panels; this will help to minimise the effects of a slight mismatch in paint colours. Bodywork fittings (eg chrome strips, door handles etc) will also need to be masked off. Use genuine masking tape, and several thicknesses of newspaper, for the masking operations.

21 Before commencing to spray, agitate the aerosol can thoroughly, then spray a test area (an old tin, or similar) until the technique is mastered. Cover the repair area with a thick coat of primer; the thickness should be built up using several thin layers of paint, rather than one thick one. Using 400 grade wet-and-dry paper, rub down the surface of the primer until it is really smooth. While doing this, the work area should be thoroughly doused with water, and the wet-and-dry paper periodically rinsed in water. Allow to dry before spraying on more paint.

22 Spray on the top coat, again building up the thickness by using several thin layers of paint. Start spraying at the top of the repair area, and then, using a side-to-side motion, work downwards until the whole repair area and about 2 inches of the surrounding original paintwork is covered. Remove all masking material 10 to 15 minutes after spraying on the final coat of paint.

23 Allow the new paint at least two weeks to harden, then, using a paintwork renovator or a very fine cutting paste, blend the edges of the paint into the existing paintwork. Finally, apply wax polish.

Plastic components

24 With the use of more and more plastic body components by the vehicle manufacturers (eg bumpers. spoilers, and in some cases major body panels), rectification of more serious damage to such items has become a matter of either entrusting repair work to a specialist in this field, or renewing complete components. Repair of such damage by the DIY owner is not really feasible, owing to the cost of the equipment and materials required for effecting such repairs. The basic technique involves making a groove along the line of the crack in the plastic, using a rotary burr in a power drill. The damaged part is then welded back together, using a hot air gun to heat up and fuse a plastic filler rod into the groove.

Any excess plastic is then removed, and the area rubbed down to a smooth finish. It is important that a filler rod of the correct plastic is used, as body components can be made of a variety of different types (eg polycarbonate, ABS, polypropylene).

25 Damage of a less serious nature (abrasions, minor cracks etc) can be repaired by the DIY owner using a two-part epoxy filler repair material. Once mixed in equal proportions, this is used in similar fashion to the bodywork filler used on metal panels. The filler is usually cured in twenty to thirty minutes, ready for sanding and painting.

26 If the owner is renewing a complete component himself, or if he has repaired it with epoxy filler, he will be left with the problem of finding a suitable paint for finishing which is compatible with the type of plastic used. At one time, the use of a universal paint was not possible, owing to the complex range of plastics encountered in body component applications. Standard paints, generally speaking, will not bond to plastic or rubber satisfactorily. However, it is now possible to obtain a plastic body parts finishing kit which consists of a pre-primer treatment, a primer and coloured top coat. Full instructions are normally supplied with a kit, but basically, the method of use is to first apply the pre-primer to the component concerned, and allow it to dry for up to 30 minutes. Then the primer is applied, and left to dry for about an hour before finally applying the special-coloured top coat. The result is a correctly-coloured component, where the paint will flex with the plastic or rubber, a property that standard paint does not normally posses.

6.3 Disconnect the wiring connector – where applicable

5 Major body damage – repair

1 Where serious damage has occurred, or large areas need renewal due to neglect, it means that complete new panels will need welding-in, and this is best left to professionals. If the damage is due to impact, it will also be necessary to check completely the alignment of the bodyshell, and this can only be carried out accurately by a Peugeot/ Citroën dealer, or accident repair specialist, using special jigs. If the body is left misaligned, it is primarily dangerous, as the car will not handle properly, and secondly, uneven stresses will be imposed on the steering, suspension and possibly transmission, causing abnormal wear, or complete failure, particularly to such items as the tyres.

6.4 Undo the six upper fasteners (arrowed)

6 Front bumper – removal and refitting

Note: *The help of an assistant is useful to support the bumper during the removal and refitting procedure.*

Removal

1 Firmly apply the handbrake, then jack up the front of the vehicle and support it securely on axle stands (see *Jacking and vehicle support*).

2 To make access to the bumper fasteners, remove both front roadwheels, then release the fasteners from around the inner wheel arch liners and remove them from the vehicle.

3 Depending on model, working inside the front left-hand corner of the front bumper, disconnect the wiring connector for the day time running lights and fog lights **(see illustration)**.

4 Open the bonnet and remove the six fasteners from along the upper edge of the front bumper assembly **(see illustration)**.

5 Undo the three bolts securing the lower front part of the bumper to the radiator support platform **(see illustration)**.

6 Working under the wheel arch on each side, undo the four bolts securing each side of the bumper to the front wing panel **(see illustrations)**.

7 Carefully unclip the sides of the bumper from the wing panels **(see illustration)**.

8 With the help of an assistant, unclip the upper part of the bumper from the crossmember **(see illustration)**, and then

6.5 Undo the bolts (arrowed) securing the lower front part of the bumper

6.6a Remove the two upper bolts (arrowed)…

6.6b …and the two lower bolts (arrowed)

6.7 Unclip the sides of the bumper

6.8 Unclip the upper part of the bumper

7.2 Remove the wheel arch liner

7.5 Undo the bolts (arrowed)

7.6 Remove the lower securing screws (arrowed) – one side shown

7.7 Undo the bolt (arrowed) – with the rear light unit removed

7.8a Undo the upper bumper screws – car/estaste/MPV models

7.8b Undo the upper bumper screws – van models

carefully pull the bumper forwards from the vehicle.

Refitting

9 Refitting is a reversal of removal.

7 Rear bumper – removal and refitting

Note: *The help of an assistant is useful to support the bumper during the removal and refitting procedure.*

Removal

1 Chock the front wheels, then jack up the rear of the vehicle and support securely on axle stands (see *Jacking and vehicle support*).
2 To make access to the bumper fasteners, remove both rear roadwheels, then release the fasteners from around the inner wheel arch liners and remove them from the vehicle **(see illustration)**.
3 Depending on model, working inside the rear left-hand corner of the rear bumper, disconnect the wiring connector for the parking sensors.
4 On car/estate/MPV models with tailgate, remove the rear light units as described in
5 Undo the bolts at each side, securing the bumper to the wing panel **(see illustration)**.
6 Undo the two securing screws from the lower edge of the bumper to the rear crossmember **(see illustration)**.

7 On car/estate/MPV models with tailgate, undo the bumper securing bolt each side at the base of the rear light unit location **(see illustration)**.
8 Working your way along the upper edge of the bumper, remove the eight screws (car/estate/MPV models) and six screws (van models) securing the upper edge of the bumper **(see illustrations)**.
9 With the help of an assistant, unclip the bumper at each side from the wing panels **(see illustration)**, then carefully pull the bumper rearwards and off the car.
10 To remove the bumper metal bracket, undo the three bolts at each side **(see illustration)**, and then lift the bracket from its location.

Refitting

11 Refitting is a reversal of removal, ensuring that the retaining clips each side correctly engage with the rear wings as it is located in position. On car/estate/MPV models, refit the rear light unit with reference to

8 Bonnet – removal, refitting and adjustment

Removal

1 Open the bonnet and have an assistant support it then, using a pencil or felt tip pen, mark the outline of each bonnet hinge relative to the bonnet, to use as a guide on refitting.

7.9 Unclip the bumper at each side

7.10 Bumper bracket securing bolts

8.2 Washer tubing connector (arrowed)

8.3 Bonnet hinge retaining nuts

9.1 Bonnet lock retaining bolts (arrowed)

2 Release the washer jet supply tubing from the right-hand bonnet hinge and disconnect the tubing from the connector **(see illustration)**.

3 With an assistant supporting the other side of the bonnet, unscrew the bonnet-to-hinge retaining bolts each side **(see illustration)**. Carefully lift the bonnet from the vehicle and store it out of the way in a safe place.

4 Inspect the bonnet hinges for signs of wear and free play at the pivots, and if necessary renew. Each hinge is secured to the body by two bolts. On refitting, apply a smear of multi-purpose grease to the hinges.

Refitting and adjustment

5 With the aid of an assistant, offer up the bonnet, and engage the retaining bolts. Align the hinges with the marks made on removal, then tighten the retaining bolts securely. Reconnect the washer jet tubing.

6 Close the bonnet, and check for alignment with the adjacent panels. If necessary, slacken the hinge bolts and re-align the bonnet to suit. When correctly aligned, tighten the hinge bolts securely.

7 Once the bonnet is correctly aligned, check that the bonnet fastens and releases in a satisfactory manner. If adjustment is necessary, slacken the bonnet lock retaining bolts, and adjust the position of the lock to suit. Once the lock is operating correctly, securely tighten its retaining bolts.

9 Bonnet lock and release cable – removal and refitting

Removal

1 Undo the two bolts securing the bonnet lock to the radiator support frame **(see illustration)**. Unclip the cable from along the front of the crossmember, then withdraw the lock and disconnect the release cable.

2 Remove the battery and battery tray as described in Chapter 5A, Section 4

3 Work along the length of the cable in the engine compartment along the left-hand inner wing panel, note their fitted locations, and release the cable retaining clips.

4 Working inside the left-hand front footwell, release the securing clips and remove the trim panel from below the fascia **(see illustration)**.

5 Carefully pull back the door seal, along the front edge of the door aperture, next to the bonnet release lever **(see illustration)**.

6 Unclip the trim panel from the left-hand end of the facia panel **(see illustration)**.

7 Undo the retaining nut inside the rear of the panel and the screw at the outer top end of the release lever trim panel. The trim panel can then be withdrawn from over the release lever **(see illustrations)**.

9.4 Remove the lower trim panel

9.5 Pull back the door seal

9.6 Unclip the trim panel

9.7a Undo the inner retaining nut...

9.7b ...the outer screw...

9.7c ...then release the trim panel

9.8a Unclip the wiring and undo the nut (arrowed)...

9.8b ...then remove the lever assembly

9.9 Grommet (arrowed) for bonnet release cable

8 Unclip the wiring loom from the release lever mounting bracket, then undo the retaining nut and remove the release lever assembly from its location **(see illustrations)**.

9 Tie a length of string to the end of the cable in the engine compartment, note its routing, then carefully pull the cable through into the passenger compartment. Release the grommet from the bulkhead to withdraw the cable **(see illustration)**. Untie the string from the end of the cable, and leave it in position to aid refitting.

Refitting

10 Locate the cable in position in the passenger compartment.

11 Tie the end of the new cable to the string, and pull it through into the engine compartment.

12 Check that the bulkhead grommet is securely seated, then remove the string and connect the cable to the release lever.

13 Secure the release lever in place, tightening its retaining nut securely.

14 Reconnect the cable to the bonnet lock then refit the lock, tightening its retaining bolts securely.

15 Secure the cable in place with its retaining clips. Check the operation of the lock and, if necessary, adjust the position of the lock within the elongated bolt holes to achieve satisfactory operation prior to closing the bonnet.

16 Refit the radiator battery and tray with reference to Chapter 5A, Section 4.

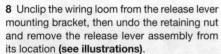

10 Door – removal and refitting

Front door

Removal

1 Disconnect the battery negative terminal (refer to the precautions in Chapter 5A, Section 1).

2 Open the door then pull back the rubber grommet **(see illustration)**, release the locking ring and disconnect the door wiring connector from inside the A-pillar.

3 Unscrew the securing bolt **(see illustration)**, and disconnect the door check strap from the door A-pillar.

4 Mark the position of the hinges on the door to aid refitting. Ensure that the door is adequately supported, then unscrew the

10.2 Unclip the wiring grommet from the A-pillar

upper and lower hinge pins. Carefully lift the door from the vehicle.

Refitting

5 Refitting is a reversal of removal, but on completion check the fit of the door in relation to the surrounding body panels. If adjustment is necessary, the door position can be altered by means of the elongated slots in the hinge plates attached to the door.

Sliding side door

Removal

6 Open the side door and unclip the trim panel from over the wiring loom to the sliding door. With the trim panel removed, undo the securing nut, unclip the wiring harness and disconnect the wiring connector **(see illustrations)**.

7 Undo the two retaining bolts from the upper door hinge/bracket **(see illustration)**.

10.3 Check strap securing bolt

10.6a Unclip the trim panel...

10.6b Undo retaining nut (A) and disconnect wiring connector (B)

10.7 Remove upper door hinge bolts

10.8 Remove the centre rail end stop

10.9 Undo the retaining screw arrowed

10.13 Unclip the rubber gaiter/grommet
from the rear pillar

10.14 Release the check strap with lever
(arrowed)

10.16a Undo the three upper bolts
(arrowed) …

10.16b … and three lower bolts (arrowed)

8 Undo the retaining screw and remove the end stop from the rear end of the centre guide rail **(see illustration)**.

9 Undo the retaining screw and remove the end stop from the rear end of the lower guide rail **(see illustration)**.

10 With the help of an assistant, the door can now be moved towards the rear of the vehicle, and then disengaged with the centre and lower guide rails. Carefully remove the door from the vehicle.

Refitting

11 Refitting is a reversal of removal, tightening the retaining bolts to the specified torque.

Hinged rear door (van models)

Note: *The following procedure is based on the equipment fitted to high-specification models. Some of the components listed may not be fitted to lower specification models.*

Removal

12 Disconnect the battery negative terminal (refer to Chapter 5A, Section 1).

13 When working on the left-hand rear door, first remove the inner trim panel from inside the luggage compartment on the left-hand side, to access the wiring connectors Section 26. Undo the retaining bolt to disconnect the earth cable, then disconnect the wiring block connector and withdraw it with the

rubber gaiter from the rear door pillar **(see illustration)**.

14 Disengage the door check strap from the bracket on the rear door, by lifting the release lever **(see illustration)**.

15 Release the wiring harness retaining clips from the door panel.

16 With the help of an assistant to support the door, undo the three upper bolts and three lower bolts securing the hinges to the door **(see illustrations)**. Carefully lift the door from the vehicle.

Refitting

17 Refitting is a reversal of removal, ensuring all wiring connectors are securely reconnected.

11 Door inner trim panel – removal and refitting

Front door

Note: *The securing clips that hold the trim panel in place are made of plastic, and can easily break on removal. It would be a good idea to purchase some new securing clips, before proceeding with this operation.*

Removal

1 Using a trim removal tool, carefully prise off the trim panel from around the door pull handle **(see illustrations)**.

11.1a Release the securing clips…

11.1b …and remove the trim panel

11.2 Undo the two screws (arrowed)

11.3 Unclip trim panel

11.4a Undo the upper front screw (arrowed)...

11.4b ...and the two rear screws (arrowed)

11.6 Carefully unclip the securing clips

11.10 Unclip the pull handle trim

2 Undo the two retaining screws from in the door pull handle **(see illustration)**.

3 Unclip the trim panel from the inside of the exterior mirror mounting plate **(see illustration)**.

4 Undo the three retaining screws from the door trim panel, one at the front upper part and two on the rear edge of the trim panel **(see illustrations)**.

5 Remove the loudspeaker from the door as described in Chapter 12 Section 18.

6 Using a suitable forked tool, work around the edge of the trim panel, and release the securing clips **(see illustration)**.

7 Carefully pull the panel outwards, then lift it up and remove it from the door.

Refitting

8 Before refitting, check whether any of the trim panel retaining studs were broken on removal. Renew the panel retaining studs as necessary, then refit the panel using a reversal of removal.

Sliding side door

Note: *The securing clips that hold the trim panel in place are made of plastic, and can easily break on removal. It would be a good idea to purchase some new securing clips, before proceeding with this operation.*

Removal

9 Peugeot/Citroen recommend removing the sliding side door as described in Section 10.
Note: *Although Peugeot/Citroen recommend*

that the door to be removed for this operation, we found that if the door is secured in a partially open position, the door trim panel can be removed. Always make sure the door is secure before proceeding, so as to prevent it closing and trapping any body parts, whilst working on the door.

10 Using a trim removal tool, carefully prise off the trim panel from around the door pull handle **(see illustration)**.

11 Carefully prise off the trim panel from around the door release handle and undo the three retaining screws **(see illustrations)**.

12 Undo the two screws securing the top of the panel to the door, one is at the upper front part and one is at the upper rear part of the door trim panel **(see illustration)**.

11.11a Remove the trim panel...

11.11b ...and undo the retaining screws

11.12 Removing the front upper screw

11.13 Remove lower trim panel

11.14 Release the securing clips and remove the trim panel

11.16a Release the fasteners...

11.16b ...and remove the trim panel

11.17 Using two fasteners to align the holes

12.2 Release the inner release handle from the door

13 Unclip the trim panel from the lower edge of the door **(see illustration)**.

14 Using a suitable forked tool, work around the edge of the trim panel, and release the securing clips. Then remove the door trim panel from the door **(see illustration)**.

Refitting

15 Refitting is a reversal of removal.

Hinged rear door

Removal

16 Release the centre pin of the fasteners, then unclip them from around the outside edge of the panel. Remove the trim panel from the door **(see illustrations)**.

Refitting

17 Refitting is a reversal of removal. Use

two of the fasteners through the trim panel to guide it into position on the door **(see illustration)**.

12 Front door handle and lock components – removal and refitting

Interior door release lever

1 Remove the door inner trim panel, as described in Section 11.

2 Remove the inner release lever by sliding the housing towards the rear edge of the door and then unclip it from the locating slots in the door **(see illustration)**.

3 Release the outer cable retaining clip from the housing and then disconnect the inner

cable from the back of the release lever **(see illustrations)**.

4 Refitting is a reversal of removal, but ensure that the operating cable is correctly fitted to the release lever. Refit the inner trim panel as described in Section 11.

Exterior door handle

5 Open the door and remove the rubber grommet/plastic blanking cover at the rear edge of the door to access the retaining screw **(see illustration)**.

6 Slacken the retaining screw until it cannot be turned no further and comes to a stop (DO NOT force the screw when it reaches the stop). The screw does not come completely out from the door panel. Carefully withdraw the push button/lock cylinder out from the

12.3a Release the retaining clip ...

12.3b ... and disconnect the operating cable

12.5 Remove the piece of tape covering the access hole

12.6 Slacken the retaining screw and withdraw the lock cylinder/push button

12.7 Slide the handle to the rear and pull it out to disengage it from the door

12.8 Make sure the handle hooks around the door lock lever (arrowed)

door handle assembly **(see illustration)**. Take care not to damage the paintwork as it is removed.

7 Detach the handle by sliding it to the rear of the door, and then pulling it out from the handle recess **(see illustration)**.

8 Refitting is a reversal of removal, but ensure that the handle locates securely inside the door lock housing. When fitting the rear of the door handle, make sure the leg on the rear of the handle is positioned behind the lever on the support bracket inside the door panel **(see illustration)**.

Door lock assembly

9 Make sure the window glass is in the fully closed position and remove the door trim panel, as described in Section 11.

10 Carefully cut around the edge of the inner sealing sheet, to release the sealer **(see illustration)**. Remove the sealing sheet and put it to one side for refitting.

11 Remove the interior door release lever as described previously in this Section.

12 Remove the exterior door handle as described previously in this Section, and then remove the seal and slacken the retaining screw (do not remove completely) for the door handle housing from the outside of the door **(see illustrations)**.

13 Undo the two screws securing the lock assembly to the rear edge of the door **(see illustration)**.

14 Reach inside the door to the rear of the

12.10 Removing the inner sealing sheet

12.12a Remove the seal from the door aperture ...

12.12b ... and undo the outer retaining screw from the handle support

12.13 Undo the two screws securing the lock to the edge of the door

lock assembly and disconnect the wiring plug from the lock assembly **(see illustration)**.

15 Release the interior handle operating cable from the grommet in the door panel,

then lower the lock assembly and manipulate it out through the door aperture **(see illustrations)**.

16 If required, unclip the lock operating outer

12.14 Disconnect the wiring from the lock assembly

12.15a Release the operating cable from the door panel ...

12.15b ... withdraw the lock assembly out from inside the door

12.16 Release the operating cable from the handle support

12.17 Release the outer cover and disconnect the cable

cable from the lever on the exterior handle support bracket **(see illustration)**.

17 To remove the operating cable from the door lock assembly, release the securing clips and open the plastic cover **(see illustration)**. Release the outer cable from the housing and then unclip the inner cable from the operating lever inside the lock assembly.

18 Refitting is a reversal of removal. Fit a new inner sealing sheet to the door if the original was damaged in any way during removal. On completion, refit the door inner trim panel as described in Section 11.

---

13 Sliding side door handle and lock components – removal and refitting

Note: *Although Peugeot/Citroen recommend that the door to be removed for this operation,* we found that if the door is secured in a partially open position, the door trim panel can be removed to access the lock components. Always make sure the door is secure before proceeding, so as to prevent it closing and trapping any body parts, whilst working on the door.

Interior door release lever

1 Remove the door inner trim panel, as described in Section 11.

2 Remove the inner release lever by sliding the housing towards the rear edge of the door and then unclip it from the locating slots in the door **(see illustration)**.

3 Release the outer cable retaining clip from the housing and then disconnect the inner cable from the back of the release lever **(see illustration)**.

4 Refitting is a reversal of removal, but ensure that the operating cable is correctly fitted to

the release lever. Refit the inner trim panel as described in Section 11.

Exterior door handle

5 Open the door and remove the rubber grommet/plastic blanking cover at the rear edge of the door to access the retaining screw **(see illustration 12.5)**.

6 Slacken the retaining screw until it cannot be turned no further and comes to a stop (DO NOT force the screw when it reaches the stop). The screw does not come completely out from the door panel. Carefully withdraw the push button out from the door handle assembly **(see illustrations)**. Take care not to damage the paintwork as it is removed.

7 Detach the handle by sliding it to the rear of the door, and then pulling it out from the handle recess **(see illustration)**.

8 Refitting is a reversal of removal, but ensure that the handle locates securely inside the door lock housing. When fitting the rear of the door handle, make sure the leg on the rear of the handle is positioned behind the lever on the support bracket inside the door panel **(see illustration 12.8)**.

Door lock assembly

9 Make sure the window glass is in the fully closed position and remove the door trim panel, as described in Section 11.

10 Carefully cut around the edge of the inner sealing sheet, to release the sealer **(see illustration)**. Remove the sealing sheet and put it to one side for refitting.

11 Remove the interior door release lever as described previously in this Section.

13.2 Release the inner release handle from the door

13.3 Release the retaining clip and disconnect the cable

13.6a Slacken the retaining screw...

13.6b ...and withdraw the push button

13.7 Slide the handle to the rear and pull it out to disengage it from the door

13.10 Remove the inner sealing sheet

13.12a Remove the seal from the door aperture …

13.12b … and undo the outer retaining screw from the handle support

13.13 Undo the two screws securing the lock to the edge of the door

12 Remove the exterior door handle as described previously in this Section, and then remove the seal and slacken the retaining screw (do not remove completely) for the door handle housing from the outside of the door **(see illustrations)**.
13 Undo the two screws securing the lock assembly to the rear edge of the door **(see illustration)**.
14 Reach inside the door to the rear of the lock assembly and disconnect the wiring plug from the lock assembly **(see illustration)**.
15 Release the interior handle operating cable from the grommet in the door panel, then lower the lock assembly and manipulate it out through the door aperture.
16 If required, unclip the lock operating outer cable from the lever on the exterior handle support bracket **(see illustration 12.16)**.
17 To remove the operating cable from the door lock assembly, release the securing clips and open the plastic cover **(see illustration 12.17)**. Release the outer cable from the housing and then unclip the inner cable from the operating lever inside the lock assembly.
18 Refitting is a reversal of removal. Fit a new inner sealing sheet to the door if the original was damaged in any way during removal. On completion, refit the door inner trim panel as described in Section 11.

13.14 Disconnect the wiring from the lock assembly

14.2 Undo the four retaining screws

14 Hinged rear door handle and lock components – removal and refitting

Door release lever – right-hand door

1 Remove the door inner trim panel, as described in Section 11.
2 Undo the four retaining screws, to release the release lever assembly from the door panel **(see illustration)**.
3 Note their fitted position, then release the

outer cables from the mounting bracket and the inner cables from the back of the release lever **(see illustrations)**.
4 Refitting is a reversal of removal, but ensure that the operating cables are correctly fitted to the release lever, as noted on removal. Refit the inner trim panel as described in Section 11.

Door upper and lower catches – right-hand door

5 Remove the door release lever as described previously in this Section.
6 Undo the three retaining bolts and withdraw

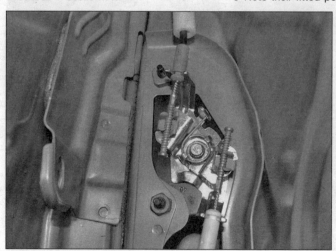

14.3a Disconnect the two operating cables…

14.3b …from the release lever

14.6 Unbolt the catch from the door panel

14.7a Unclip the outer cable...

14.7b ...and then the inner cable

the catch from the door panel complete with cable **(see illustration)**.

7 To remove the operating cable from the door catch, release the outer cable from the mounting bracket and then unclip the

14.9 Remove the piece of tape covering the access hole

inner cable from the operating lever **(see illustrations)**.

8 Refitting is a reversal of removal. Refit the release lever, as described earlier in this section. Refit the inner trim panel as described in Section 11.

Exterior door handle – left-hand door

9 Open the door and remove the rubber grommet/plastic blanking cover at the rear edge of the door to access the retaining screw **(see illustration)**.

10 Slacken the retaining screw until it cannot be turned no further and comes to a stop (DO NOT force the screw when it reaches the stop). The screw does not come completely out from the door panel. Carefully withdraw the push button/lock cylinder out from the door handle assembly **(see illustrations)**. Take care not to damage the paintwork as it is removed.

11 Detach the handle by sliding it to the rear of the door, and then pulling it out from the handle recess **(see illustration)**.

12 Refitting is a reversal of removal, but ensure that the handle locates securely inside the door lock housing. When fitting the rear of the door handle, make sure the leg on the rear of the handle is positioned behind the lever on the support bracket inside the door panel **(see illustration 12.8)**.

Door lock assembly

13 Remove the exterior door handle as described previously in this Section, and then remove the seal and slacken the retaining screw (do not remove completely) for the door handle housing from the outside of the door **(see illustrations)**.

14 Undo the two screws securing the lock assembly to the rear edge of the door **(see illustration)**.

14.10a Slacken the retaining screw...

14.10b ...and withdraw the lock cylinder/ push button

14.11 Slide the handle to the rear and pull it out to disengage it from the door

14.13a Remove the seal...

14.13b ... and undo the retaining screw (arrowed)

14.14 Undo the two screws securing the lock to the edge of the door

14.15 Disconnect the wiring from the lock assembly

14.16 Withdraw the lock assembly out from inside the door

14.17 Release the operating cable from the handle support

15.3 Carefully prise up the inner door seal

15 Front door window glass and regulator – removal and refitting

Door window glass

1 Position the window approximately three quarters of the way down.
2 Remove the door inner trim panel, as described in Section 11.
3 Unclip and remove the inner seal from the bottom of the window aperture (see illustration).
4 Carefully cut around the edge of the inner sealing sheet, to release the sealer (see illustration 12.8), and fold it back to access the window regulator.
5 Undo the two window glass clamp screws, and remove the window glass up through the aperture and out of the door (see illustrations).
6 Refitting is a reversal of removal, clean and check the fixings on the window glass (see illustration). Fit a new sealing sheet to the door if the original was damaged in any way during removal. On completion, refit the inner trim panel as described in Section 11.

15 Reach inside and manoeuvre the lock assembly from inside the door and disconnect the wiring plug connector (see illustration).
16 Release the exterior handle support from the door panel, then lower the lock assembly and remove the lock assembly out through the door aperture (see illustration).
17 If required, unclip the lock operating outer cable from the lever on the exterior handle support bracket (see illustration).

18 To remove the operating cable from the door lock assembly, release the securing clips and open the plastic cover. Release the outer cable from the housing and then unclip the inner cable from the operating lever inside the lock assembly. Note: On some models the cables are part of the lock assembly and cannot be renewed independently.
19 Refitting is a reversal of removal. On completion, refit the door inner trim panel as described in Section 11.

15.5a Remove the two window clamp screws (arrowed)...

15.5b ... and withdraw the window glass out from the door

15.6 Check the fixings for any damage

15.8 Disconnect the wiring connector

15.9a Undo the retaining bolts (arrowed)…

15.9b … and remove the motor/regulator from the door

Door window regulator

7 Remove the front door window glass, as described previously in this section.

8 Release the securing clip and disconnect the wiring plug connectors from the window motor **(see illustration)**.

9 Undo the three retaining bolts and manoeuvre the window motor/regulator assembly out from inside the door aperture **(see illustrations)**.

10 Refitting is a reversal of removal, but fit a new sealing sheet to the door if the original was damaged in any way during removal. On completion, refit the inner trim panel as described in Section 11.

16 Tailgate and support struts – removal and refitting

Tailgate

Removal

1 Open the glass window, then undo the retaining screw and unclip the trim panel from the mounting bracket **(see illustration)**.

2 Using a suitable forked tool, work around the edge of the trim panel, and release the securing clips **(see illustration)**.

3 Disconnect the wiring connectors from the following components with reference to the relevant Sections of this Chapter, and Chapter 12.

a) Rear window wiper motor.
b) Tailgate lock motor.
c) Rear window demister elements.
d) High-level stop-light.
e) Number plate lights.

4 Release the wiring harness retaining clips from the tailgate.

5 Check that all wiring connectors have been disconnected, then release the wiring harness grommet and withdraw the harness from the top of the tailgate. **Note:** *Tie a length of string to the ends of the wiring loom connectors inside the tailgate, note its routing, then carefully pull the wiring loom out through the top of the grommet in the tailgate. Untie the string from the end of the*

wiring loom, and leave it in position to aid refitting.

6 With the aid of an assistant to help support the tailgate, prise out the support strut spring clips, and pull the struts from the balljoints on the body **(see illustrations 16.12 and 16.13)**.

7 Unscrew the tailgate hinge retaining bolts (one at each side) and carefully lift the tailgate from the vehicle **(see illustration)**.

Refitting

8 If a new tailgate is to be fitted, transfer all serviceable components (lock mechanism, wiper motor, etc) to it, with reference to the relevant procedures in this Chapter, and in Chapter 12.

9 Refitting is a reversal of removal, bearing in mind the following points:

16.1 Undo screw and remove trim panel

16.7 Tailgate hinge retaining bolt (one side shown)

a) If necessary, adjust the rubber buffers to obtain a good fit when the tailgate is shut.
b) If necessary, adjust the position of the tailgate lock striker to achieve satisfactory lock operation.
c) On completion, refit the tailgate trim panel.

Support struts

Removal

10 Support the tailgate in the open position, with the help of an assistant.

11 Using a suitable flat-bladed screwdriver, release the spring clip, and pull the support strut from its balljoint on the body **(see illustration)**.

16.2 Unclip the trim panel

16.11 Release the spring clip, and pull the support strut from its balljoint on the body

12 Similarly, release the strut from the balljoint on the tailgate **(see illustration)**, and withdraw the strut from the vehicle.

Refitting

13 Refitting is a reversal of removal, but ensure the spring clips are correctly engaged.

17 Tailgate lock components – removal and refitting

Tailgate lock

Removal

1 Remove the tailgate trim panel as described in Section 16.
2 Undo the two bolts, at the lower edge of the tailgate, then withdraw the lock unit from inside the tailgate. As the it is withdrawn, disconnect the wiring connector **(see illustrations)**.

Refitting

3 Refitting is a reversal of removal. If necessary, adjust the position of the tailgate lock striker to achieve satisfactory lock operation. On completion, refit the tailgate trim panel as described in Section 16.

Tailgate lock striker

Removal

4 Carefully pull back the seal along the lower edge of the tailgate aperture **(see illustration)**.
5 Unclip the plastic trim panel from across the rear edge of the luggage compartment **(see illustration)**.
6 Mark the position of the striker on the body, for use when refitting. Unscrew the two securing bolts, and remove the striker from the body **(see illustration)**.

Refitting

7 Refitting is a reversal of removal. Before tightening the securing bolts, the position of the striker should be altered (the securing bolt holes are elongated) until satisfactory lock operation is obtained. Use the marks made prior to removal, if appropriate.

16.12 Upper balljoint securing clip (arrowed)

17.2b ...withdraw the lock...

17.4 Pull back the seal

17.2a Undo the two bolts...

17.2c ...and disconnect the wiring connector

17.5 Unclip the plastic trim panel

Tailgate exterior switch/handle

8 Remove the tailgate lower trim panel as described in Section 16.

9 Reach inside the tailgate and disconnect the wiring connector from the rear of the switch **(see illustration)**.

17.6 Striker plate securing bolts

17.9 Disconnect the wiring plug connector ...

10 Undo the six retaining nuts, then from outside the tailgate remove the trim panel from above the number plate **(see illustrations)**.

11 Release the securing clips and remove the switch from the trim panel **(see illustrations)**.

12 Refitting is a reversal of removal. On completion, refit the tailgate trim panel as described in Section 16.

18 Central locking components – removal and refitting

17.10a Undo the retaining nuts (three one one side shown)…

17.10b …and remove the trim panel

Control unit

1 The central locking system is controlled by the Built-in Systems Interface (BSI) which is the vehicle central computer controlling the main body electrical system functions. The unit is located under the facia on the left-hand side. Refer to for further information.

2 Should any problems be experienced with the operation of the central locking system or any of the other functions controlled by the BSI, the vehicle should be taken to a Peugeot/Citroën dealer for diagnostic investigation.

Front door lock motor

3 The motor is integral with the door lock assembly. Removal and refitting of the lock assembly is described in Section 12.

17.11a Release the securing clips…

17.11b …and remove the switch from the panel

Sliding side door lock motor

4 The motor is integral with the door lock assembly. Removal and refitting of the lock assembly is described in Section 13.

Hinged rear door lock motor

5 The motor is integral with the door lock assembly. Removal and refitting of the lock assembly is described in Section 14.

Tailgate lock motor

6 The motor is integral with the door lock assembly. Removal and refitting of the lock assembly is described in Section 17.

Remote control transmitter

Battery renewal

7 When the remote control transmitter battery is nearing the end of its life, an audible signal will be emitted from within the vehicle, accompanied by a message on the instrument panel multifunction screen. The battery should then be renewed with a type CR 1620 (3 volt) battery.

8 Using a small coin in the slot at the upper end of the key, carefully prise the two halves of the transmitter apart **(see illustrations)**.

9 Remove the printed circuit board and slide the battery out from its location in the circuit board, noting its fitted position **(see illustrations)**.

10 Fit the new battery and reassemble the transmitter.

Initialisation

11 To initialise the unit after renewing the battery, put the key in the ignition and leave it in the off position. Then switch on the ignition (without starting) and immediately press the locking button on the key for 10 seconds. Then switch off the ignition and remove the key from the ignition lock. The key remote should now be fully operational.

18.8a Twist the coin in the slot provided …

18.8b … and unclip the cover from the key

18.9a Remove the circuit board from the cover

18.9b Slide the new battery into its location on the circuit board

19.3 Disconnect the mirror wiring connector

19.4 Undo the three retaining screws

19.6 Carefully lever the outer edge of the mirror glass

19 Mirrors and mirror glass – removal and refitting

Exterior mirror assembly

Removal

1 Ensure the ignition is turned off.
2 Remove the door inner trim panel as described in Section 11.
3 Disconnect the mirror wiring connectors **(see illustration)**.
4 Whilst supporting the weight of the mirror, undo the three retaining screws and remove the mirror from the door frame **(see illustration)**.

Refitting

5 Refitting is a reversal of removal.

Exterior mirror glass

Removal

6 Carefully press the mirror glass in at the inner edge, and then working through the gap at the outside edge of the mirror glass, use a lever to release the clips that secure the mirror glass to the mirror body **(see illustration)**.
7 Withdraw the glass, and where applicable, disconnect the wiring connectors for the heater element.

Refitting

8 Where applicable, reconnect the wiring connectors, then push the mirror glass into the mirror until it locks into position.

Exterior mirror shell

9 Remove the mirror glass as described previously in this Section.
10 Working from inside the mirror housing, release the retaining clips that secure the mirror shell to the mirror body **(see illustration)**.
11 Fold the mirror inwards, and unclip the outer shell from the mirror **(see illustration)**.
12 To refit, carefully push the mirror shell onto the mirror body until the securing clips lock into position. Refit mirror glass, as described previously in this section.

Interior mirror

13 The mirror can be twisted and pulled

sharply downwards, to release it from the mounting base on the windscreen **(see illustration)**.
14 To refit the interior mirror to the base, offer it up to the mounting base at about 60° degrees offset from its final position. Push the retaining clip onto the mounting base, then twist the mirror, to secure it in the correct position **(see illustration)**.

20 Windscreen, tailgate and rear door window glass – general information

1 These areas of glass are secured by the tight fit of the weatherstrip in the body aperture, and are bonded in position with a special adhesive. Renewal of such fixed glass is a difficult, messy and time-consuming task, which is considered beyond the scope of the home mechanic. It is difficult, unless one has plenty of practice, to obtain a secure,

19.10 Release the retaining clips (arrowed)

19.13 Twist and pull down to remove

waterproof fit. Furthermore, the task carries a high risk of breakage; this applies especially to the laminated glass windscreen. In view of this, owners are strongly advised to have this sort of work carried out by one of the many specialist windscreen fitters.

21 Sunroof – general information

1 The factory-fitted sunroof is of the electric tilt/slide type.
2 Due to the complexity of the sunroof mechanism, considerable expertise is required to repair, renew or adjust the sunroof components successfully. Removal of the roof first requires the headlining to be removed, which is a tedious operation, and not a task to be undertaken lightly. Any problems with the sunroof should be referred to a Peugeot/ Citroën dealer.

19.11 Unclip outer shell

19.14 Refit the mirror by twisting into place

22.2 Release the centre part (arrowed)

22.3 Removing the left-hand rear liner

23.1 Remove the weather seal

22 Body exterior fittings – removal and refitting

Wheel arch liners

1 Firmly apply the handbrake, then jack up the front of the car and support it securely on axle stands (see *Jacking and vehicle support*). Remove the relevant front roadwheel.
2 The wheel arch liners are secured by a number of push-fit clips **(see illustration)**. Release the centre pin and then withdraw the plastic clips from the liner.
3 Once all the clips have been removed, withdraw the liner from under the wheel arch **(see illustration)**.

Body trim strips and badges

4 The various body trim strips and badges are held in position with a special adhesive membrane. Removal requires the trim/badge to be heated, to soften the adhesive, and then cut away from the surface. Due to the high risk of damage to the vehicle paintwork during this operation, it is recommended that this task should be entrusted to a Peugeot/Citroën dealer.

23 Scuttle grille panel – removal and refitting

Removal

1 Open and support the bonnet, then remove the weather seal from along the front edge of the scuttle panel **(see illustration)**.
2 Remove the windscreen wiper arms as described in Chapter 12 Section 13.

3 Unclip the moulded foam packing pieces from each end of the scuttle panel **(see illustration)**.
4 Undo the retaining screw securing the centre of the scuttle panel in position **(see illustration)**.
5 Undo the two bolts at each end of the scuttle panel **(see illustration)**.
6 Undo the two retaining screws and remove the brake/clutch fluid reservoir from the crossmember **(see illustration)**. Move the reservoir to one side, taking care not to spill any fluid.
7 Release the fasteners from along the front edge of the scuttle crossmember and pull the sound proofing away from the crossmember **(see illustrations)**.
8 Remove the rubber grommets from around the wiper spindles and lift the scuttle panel from the rear of the engine compartment **(see illustrations)**.

23.3 Remove the moulded foam corner piece

23.4 Undo the retaining screw

23.5 Undo the two bolts (arrowed) – one side shown

23.6 Remove reservoir from crossmember

23.7a Release the fasteners…

23.7b …and pull away the soundproofing

23.8a Unclip the rubber grommets…

23.8b …and remove the scuttle panel

23.9 Remove the rear crossmember

9 Unclip the wiper motor wiring loom from the securing clip and then remove the crossmember from the rear of the engine compartment **(see illustration)**.

Refitting

10 Refitting is a reversal of removal. Refit the wiper arms with reference to Chapter 12 Section 13

24 Seats – removal and refitting

Front seats

⚠ *Warning: Depending on model, the front seats may be equipped with seat belt pretensioners, and side*

airbags may be built into the outer sides of the seats. Where side airbags are fitted, refer to for the precautions which should be observed when dealing with an airbag system. Do not tamper with the seat belt pretensioner unit in any way, and do not attempt to test the unit. Note that the unit is triggered if the mechanism is supplied with an electrical current (including via an ohmmeter), or if the assembly is subjected to a temperature of greater than 100°C.

Removal

Single sliding seat

1 Where applicable, de-activate the airbag system (see Chapter 12) before attempting to remove the seat.
2 Move the seat fully forwards and remove the bolts (one on each side) securing the rear

of the seat rails to the floor mounted seat brackets **(see illustration)**.
3 Move the seat fully rearwards, the remove the bolts (one bolt on each side) securing the front of the seat frame to the floor mounted brackets **(see illustration)**.
4 Tip the seat backwards and disconnect the seat wiring connectors, then release the wiring harness from the retaining clip on the seat frame **(see illustrations)**. Carefully manoeuvre the seat out from the passenger compartment, taking care not to damage the paintwork on the way out through the door aperture.

Double fixed passenger seat

5 Lift up the seat cushion, then slide the plastic storage compartment under the centre seat towards the rear and remove it from under the seat **(see illustrations)**.
6 Undo the securing bolt and disconnect

24.2 Undo the rear seat bolts (arrowed)

24.3 Undo the front seat bolts (arrowed)

24.4a Disconnect the wiring connectors…

24.4b …and release the wiring loom retaining clips

24.5a Push the storage compartment to the rear…

24.5b …to disengage the securing clips (arrowed)

24.6 Undo the seat belt securing bolt (arrowed)

25.1a Release the securing clip (arrowed)…

25.1b …and remove the trim cover

the centre seat belt anchorage bracket from the right-hand side of the seat frame **(see illustration)**.

7 Remove the bolts securing the seat frame to the floor panel. Carefully manoeuvre the seat out from the passenger compartment, taking care not to damage the paintwork on the way out through the door aperture.

Refitting

8 Refitting is a reversal of removal. Where applicable, reactivate the airbag system as described in Chapter 12 before reconnecting the battery.

Rear seats

9 Make sure the headrest is in its lowest position. Release the seat catch on the upper part of the seat back, and then fold the seat back forwards and down onto the seat cushion. **Note:** *If the headrest fouls the back of the front seat, then slide the front seat forward on its runners.*

25.2 Remove the upper seat belt anchor bolt

25.5 Unclip seat belt guide

10 Release the seat control bar under the rear of the seat cushion and tilt the complete seat forwards and up to the vertical position.
11 The seat can now be lifted upwards and out from the anchor plates in the floor panel. Carefully manoeuvre the seat out from the passenger compartment, taking care not to damage the paintwork on the way out through the door aperture.

Refitting

12 Refitting is a reversal of removal.

25 Seat belt components – removal and refitting

⚠️ *Warning: Depending on model, the front seats may be equipped with seat belt pretensioners, and side airbags may be built into the*

25.3 Remove cap to access lower bolt

25.6 Disconnect the wiring connector (arrowed)

outer sides of the seats. Where side airbags are fitted, refer to for the precautions which should be observed when dealing with an airbag system. Do not tamper with the seat belt pretensioner unit in any way, and do not attempt to test the unit. Note that the unit is triggered if the mechanism is supplied with an electrical current (including via an ohmmeter), or if the assembly is subjected to a temperature of greater than 100°C.
Note: *Record the positions of the washers and spacers on the seat belt anchors, and ensure they are refitted in their original positions.*

Front seat belt

Removal

1 Release the two securing clips (one at each side) and slide the trim cover upwards, to disengage it from the seat height adjustment bracket **(see illustrations)**.
2 Undo the seat belt upper anchor bolt, and recover the washer/spacer **(see illustration)**.
3 Prise off the trim cap, then undo the seat belt lower anchor bolt, and recover the washer/spacer **(see illustration)**.
4 Remove the centre 'B-pillar' trim panels as described in Section 26.
5 Unclip the seat belt guide from the pillar **(see illustration)**.
6 Release the locking clip and disconnect the wiring connector from the inertia reel seat belt **(see illustration)**.
7 Pull back the carpet and undo the inertia reel mounting bolt **(see illustration)**.

25.7 Inertia reel mounting bolt

25.11a Disconnect the wiring connector...

25.11b ...and undo the seat belt stalk securing bolt (arrowed)

25.13a Unclip the trim cap...

25.13b ...and remove the upper anchor bolt

25.14a Unclip the trim cap...

25.14b ...and remove the lower anchor bolt

8 Withdraw the inertia reel from the lower part of the door pillar, then withdraw the seat belt assembly from the vehicle.

Refitting

9 Refitting is a reversal of removal. Ensure that all washers and/or spacers are positioned as noted before removal, and tighten all mounting bolts to the specified torque.

Front seat belt stalk

Removal

10 To make access easier, remove the front seat as described in Section 24.

11 Disconnect the wiring connector from under the seat, and the undo the bolt securing the seat belt stalk to the seat frame **(see illustrations)**.

25.16 Inertia reel retaining bolt

Refitting

12 Refitting is a reversal of removal. Ensure that all washers and/or spacers are positioned as noted before removal, and tighten all mounting bolts to the specified torque.

Rear seat belt

Removal

13 Prise off the trim cap, then undo the seat belt upper anchor bolt, and recover the washer/spacer **(see illustrations)**.

14 Prise off the trim cap, then undo the seat belt lower anchor bolt, and recover the washer/spacer**(see illustrations)**.

15 Remove the 'C-pillar' and luggage compartment side trim panel as described in Section 26.

16 Undo the anchor bolt securing the seat

26.2 Pull seal away from trim panel

belt inertia reel to the vehicle body and remove the reel and seat belt from the car **(see illustration)**.

17 To remove the seat belt buckles, fold forward the rear seats forward and undo the bolt securing the buckles to the rear seat mounting.

18 To remove the centre seat belt inertia reel, the seat must be partially dismantled. This work should be entrusted to a Peugeot/ Citroën dealer.

Refitting

19 Refitting is a reversal of removal. Tighten the seat belt mounting bolts to the specified torque.

26 Interior trim – removal and refitting

Note: *There are numerous combinations of interior trim layout according to model year, vehicle type and whether or not sliding side doors are fitted. The following information is a guide to the most common arrangements.*

Door inner trim panels

1 Refer to Section 11.

Front A-pillar trim panel

2 Prise the weather seal from the front door aperture in the vicinity of the pillar trim **(see illustration)**. Take care not to damage the seal as it is being removed.

26.3 Unclip the trim panel

26.7 Lift trim upwards to release the lower pegs (arrowed)

26.8 Release the clips (arrowed) and unclip the trim panel

26.9 Upper trim locating lug

26.11a Undo the retaining screw…

26.11b..and unclip the trim panel

3 Pull the trim away from the pillar starting at the top, then work down the trim panel and release it from behind the facia panel **(see illustration)**. Note that when removing the trim panel, the wiring loom or aerial lead may travel up the pillar (depending on which side is removed) and can make it awkward to disengage the bottom of the A-pillar trim panel from the facia, take care not to damage the wiring loom.
4 Refitting is a reversal of removal, but ensure that all retaining clips are fully engaged, and that the weatherstrip is fully seated.

Centre B-pillar trim panels
Removal
5 Disconnect the seat belt upper anchorage

point from the B-pillar, as described in Section 25.
6 Prise the weatherstrip from the front door aperture in the vicinity of the door pillar.
7 Carefully pull the upper part of the lower trim from the pillar to release the securing clips, then lift it upwards to disengage from the lower bracket **(see illustration)**.
8 Unclip the locking pegs, then release the retaining clips to disengage the lower part of the upper trim from the pillar **(see illustration)**.
9 Carefully pull the upper trim downwards and away from the pillar to release the upper locating lug from the roof panel **(see illustration)**.
Refitting
10 Refitting is a reversal of removal, but

ensure that all retaining clips are fully engaged and that the weatherstrip is fully seated.

Side trim panel – MPV models
Removal
11 Undo the retaining screw and unclip the upper trim panel from the rear D-pillar **(see illustrations)**.
12 Disconnect the seat belt upper anchorage point from the C-pillar, as described in Section 25.
13 Undo the retaining screw and unclip the upper trim panel from the rear C-pillar **(see illustrations)**. Unclip the upper part of the trim panel from the slot in the top of the pillar.
14 Unclip the trim panel from over the

26.13a Undo the retaining screw…

26.13b …unclip the trim panel…

26.13c …and release the upper part from the top of the pillar

26.14 Unclip wiring loom cover trim

26.16a Unclip the trim panel

26.16b Release the seat belt from the trim panel

26.18 Unclip the trim panel

26.19a Undo the retaining screws (arrowed)…

26.19b …and remove the trim panel

wiring loom going to the sliding door **(see illustration)**.

15 Disconnect the seat belt lower anchorage point from the C-pillar, as described in Section 25.

16 Unclip the lower trim panel from the side of the luggage compartment. As the panel is removed release the seat belt from the top of the trim panel **(see illustrations)**.

Refitting

17 Refitting is a reversal of removal, but ensure that all retaining clips are fully engaged and that the weatherstrip is fully seated.

Luggage compartment side trim panel – van models

Removal

18 Unclip the trim panel from the lower

right-hand side of the luggage compartment **(see illustration)**.

19 Undo the retaining screws and remove the floor trim panel from the right-hand side of the luggage compartment **(see illustrations)**.

20 Carefully prise the side panel away from the body, to release the internal clips, then remove the trim panel **(see illustrations)**. Depending on model, and which side panel is removed, disconnect the wiring connectors from the 12-volt auxiliary supply.

Refitting

21 Refitting is a reversal of removal, but ensure that all retaining clips are fully engaged.

Headlining

Note: *Headlining removal requires considerable skill and experience if it is to be carried out without damage, and is therefore best entrusted*

to a Peugeot/Citroën dealer or bodywork specialist. A general overview of the procedure is given below for those with the expertise to attempt the operation on a DIY basis.

22 The headlining is clipped and glued to the roof, and can be withdrawn only once all fittings such as the grab handles, courtesy lights, sunvisors, sunroof (if fitted), pillar trim panels, and associated additional panels have been removed. The door, tailgate and sunroof aperture weatherstrips will also have to be prised clear and any additional screws and clips removed. Once the headlining attachments are released, the adhesive bonding in the centre panels must be broken using a hot air gun and spatula, starting at the front and working rearwards.

23 When refitting, a coat of neoprene adhesive (available from Peugeot/Citroën dealers) must be applied to the centre panels in the locations noted during removal. Position the headlining carefully and refit all components disturbed during removal. Clean the headlining with soap and water or white spirit on completion.

27 Centre console – removal and refitting

Removal

1 On vehicles fitted with a double passenger seat, it will be necessary to remove the complete seat, as described in Section 24.

26.20a Unclip the trim panel

26.20b Disconnect the wiring connector – where applicable

27.3 Unclip the handbrake lever trims

27.4 Undo the two retaining nuts (arrowed)

27.5 Undo the two bolts at the rear of the console

2 On models with a storage compartment fitted to the top of the centre console. First release the handle at the rear of the upper storage compartment, then lift it upwards and remove it from the lower part of the centre console. With the storage compartment removed, lift out the centre console carpet by pulling it to the rear of the console.

3 Unclip the two parts of the handbrake lever trim to remove them from the lever (see illustration).

4 At the front of the console, remove the carpet from inside the cup holders, then undo the two retaining nuts (see illustration).

5 Undo the two bolts, at the rear of the centre console (see illustration).

6 Pull the rear of the console upwards, then slide it up and over the handbrake lever to remove it from the car.

Refitting

7 Refitting is a reversal of removal.

28 Facia panel components – removal and refitting

Steering column shrouds

1 Undo the two screws securing the lower shroud in position (see illustration).

2 Unclip the upper shroud from the lower shroud, then remove the lower shroud. Release the lug at the lower end of the shroud from the slot in the steering column bracket (see illustrations).

3 To remove the upper shroud, first unclip the plastic surround from around the instrument panel (see illustrations). The both panels can then be removed from the top of the facia. Note: *The upper shroud and the instrument panel surround are attached together by a piece of material. If required the both panels can be separated once they have been removed.*

4 Refitting is a reversal of removal, making sure the lug on the lower shroud locates correctly in the slot on the steering column shroud.

28.1 Undo the two screws (arrowed)

28.2a Unclip the upper shroud from the lower shroud...

28.2b ...and remove the lower shroud...

28.2c ...releasing lug (A) from slot (B)

28.3a Unclip the small centre trim...

28.3b ...and then remove the instrument surround complete with upper shroud

28.5 Unclip and remove the lower trim panel

28.6a Release the securing clips (arrowed)...

28.6b ...and remove the trim panel

Lower facia panels

5 Carefully unclip the lower part of the facia panel on the driver's side below the steering column, pulling it free from its retaining clips **(see illustration)**.

6 The trim panels above the driver's pedals and passenger footwell are secured by expanding plastic rivets. Prise out the centre pins, and then lever the complete rivets from place **(see illustrations)**. Disconnect the wiring connector (where fitted) from the footwell light as the trim is removed. When refitting, ensure the front edge of the panel engages with the support bracket.

7 Refitting is a reversal of removal.

Drivers side switch panel

8 Unclip the facia lower trim panel as described earlier in this section **(see illustration 28.5)**.

9 Unclip the instrument panel surround trim as described earlier in this section **(see illustration 28.3)**.

10 The switch trim panel to the right of the steering column can now be released from the facia. Unclip the trim panel from the facia and disconnect the wiring connectors from the switches **(see illustrations)**.

11 Refitting is a reversal of removal, making sure all wiring connectors are fitted correctly.

Centre switch panel

12 Remove the gear lever centre console, as described later on in this section.

13 Carefully unclip the small trim panel from below the heater control panel and undo the two switch panel securing screws **(see illustration)**.

14 Withdraw the switch panel from the facia and disconnect the wiring connectors from the switches **(see illustration)**.

15 Refitting is a reversal of removal, making sure all wiring connectors are fitted correctly.

Footwell trim panels

16 The trim panels at each side of the front footwells, in front of the centre console, are secured by screws. Undo the retaining screws and remove the trim panels from the front footwells **(see illustrations)**.

28.10a Unclip the switch panel...

28.10b ... and disconnect the wiring

28.13 Unclip trim panel and undo the screws (arrowed)

28.14 Remove the switch panel

28.16a Undo the retaining screw (arrowed)...

28.16b ...and remove the trim panel

28.19a Unclip the trim from the right-hand end of the facia...

28.19b ...and disconnect the airbag switch wiring connector

28.19c Unclip the trim from the left-hand end of the facia

17 To remove the outer footwell side panels, refer to Section 9.
18 Refitting is a reversal of removal.

Facia end panels

19 Carefully unclip the trim panels from each end of the facia, pulling them free from their retaining clips **(see illustrations)**. Disconnect the wiring connector from the airbag switch on the right-hand side trim panel, as it is removed.
20 Refitting is a reversal of removal.

Passenger side glovebox

21 Release the three clips, and remove the trim beneath the facia **(see illustrations)**. Where applicable, disconnect the wiring connector from the footwell light as the trim is removed.
22 Open the glovebox, then release the

28.21a Release the securing clips...

28.21b ...and remove the trim panel

securing clips and push the diagnostic plug inwards to release it from glovebox **(see illustration)**.

28.22 Disengage diagnostic plug from glovebox

28.23 Unclip fusebox cover

23 Unclip the fusebox cover from inside the glovebox **(see illustration)**.
24 Release the centre pin and remove the fastener from the left-hand side of the glovebox **(see illustration)**.
25 Working inside the glovebox, undo all the screws securing the glovebox to the facia **(see illustration)**.
26 Release the retaining clips on the outer edge of the glovebox and slide the assembly out from the facia. Disconnect any wiring loom retaining clips attached to the rear of the glovebox as it is removed **(see illustration)**.
27 Refitting is a reversal of removal.

Drivers side upper glovebox

28 Unclip the instrument panel surround trim as described earlier in this section **(see illustration 28.3)**.

28.24 Remove the fastener

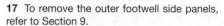

28.25 Undo the retaining screws (arrowed)

28.26 Withdraw the glovebox from the facia

28.29a Undo the two upper screws (arrowed)...

28.29b ...and the one inside the compartment

28.30a Unclip the trim panel...

29 Open the glovebox, then undo the two upper retaining screws and the one from inside the bottom of the compartment **(see illustrations)**.
30 Unclip the small panel from the bottom of the compartment, then unclip and remove the upper part of the compartment from inside the glovebox **(see illustrations)**.
31 The complete upper glovebox can now be unclipped from the top of the facia and removed **(see illustration)**.
32 Refitting is a reversal of removal.

Gear lever centre console

33 Unclip the front footwell side panels, as described earlier in this section **(see illustration 28.10a and 28.10b)**.
34 With the side panels removed, undo the two screws (one each side) from the front lower end of the gear lever centre console **(see illustrations)**.
35 Carefully unclip the trim from around the gear lever by releasing it upwards and away from the facia **(see illustration)**.
36 Undo the three retaining screws and lift the centre console from over the gear lever assembly **(see illustrations)**.
37 Refitting is a reversal of removal.

Instrument panel

38 Refer to Chapter 12 Section 9.

Multifunction display

39 Refer Chapter 12 Section 10.

Complete facia assembly

Note: *This is an involved operation entailing*

28.30b ...then unclip the inner compartment

28.31 Remove the drivers side upper glovebox

the removal of numerous components and assemblies, and the disconnection of a multitude of wiring connectors. Make notes or take pictures of the location of all

disconnected wiring, or attach labels to the connectors, to avoid confusion when refitting.
40 Disconnect the battery (refer to precautions in Chapter 5A Section 1).

28.34a Remove the screw (arrowed) from the right-hand side...

28.34b ...and the lower left-hand side

28.35 Unclip the trim from around the gear lever

28.36a Undo the retaining screw (arrowed)...

28.36b ...and lift off the centre console

28.49 Aerial lead connection (arrowed)

28.52 Disconnect the wiring connectors

28.54 Undo the centre retaining bolts (arrowed)

28.55 Left-hand mounting bolts (arrowed)

41 Move the front seats as far back as possible. Set the steering wheel in the straight-ahead position, and engage the steering lock.

42 Remove the following facia panels as described previously in this Section:

a) *Steering column shrouds.*
b) *Lower facia panels – driver's side.*
c) *Drivers side switch panel*
d) *Centre switch panel*
e) *Front footwell trim panels*
f) *Passenger side glovebox.*

g) *Drivers side upper glovebox*
h) *Facia end panels.*
i) *Gear lever centre console*

43 Remove the steering wheel and steering column, as described in Chapter 10 Section 16 and Chapter 10 Section 17.

44 Remove the instrument panel and multifunction display, as described in Chapter 12.

45 Remove the audio unit from the facia, as described in Chapter 12 Section 17.

46 Remove the heater/climate control panel, as described in Chapter 3 Section 10.

47 Remove the passenger airbag, as described Chapter 12.

48 Remove the gear lever assembly, as described in Chapter 7 Section 3.

49 Disconnect the aerial lead connection from inside the right-hand side of the facia **(see illustration)**.

50 Remove the centre console, as described in Section 27.

51 Disconnect the wiring connector from the airbag control unit under the centre console and also undo the retaining nut and disconnect the earth cable. Pull back the wiring loom from under the carpet.

52 Follow the facia wiring loom and disconnect the wiring connectors going to the BSI unit, noting their fitted position **(see illustration)**. When the facia/dashboard is removed the wiring loom will stay attached to the crossbar and be removed with the facia.

53 Undo the retaining bolt from inside the drivers side, upper glovebox aperture.

54 Undo the two retaining screws from inside the centre part of the facia **(see illustration)**.

55 Working through the apertures at each end of the facia, unscrew the two bolts each side securing the facia crossmember **(see illustration)**.

56 Note their fitted positions and harness routing, then disconnect any facia wiring retaining clips. Take note of the location of the various wiring harness retaining clips, to aid refitment.

57 Check around the facia for any other fixings and then with the help of an assistant, lift the facia complete with bulkhead crossmember from place, and remove it from the vehicle.

58 Refitting is a reversal of removal ensuring that all wiring is correctly reconnected and all mountings securely tightened.

Chapter 12
Body electrical systems

Contents

Degrees of difficulty

Easy, suitable for novice with little experience	**Fairly easy,** suitable for beginner with some experience	**Fairly difficult,** suitable for competent DIY mechanic	**Difficult,** suitable for experienced DIY mechanic	**Very difficult,** suitable for expert DIY or professional

Specifications

General
System type . . . . 12 volt negative earth

Bulbs

	Type	Wattage
Brake/tail light	P21/5W Bayonet	21/5
Direction indicator light (amber)	PY21W Bayonet	21
Direction indicator side repeater (amber)	WY5W Push-fit	5
Foglight:		
Front	H1	55
Rear	P21W Bayonet	21
Front sidelights.	W5W Push-fit	5
Glovebox light	Push-fit	5
Headlights (Halogen)	H4	55
High-level brake light	W16W Push fit	16
Interior/courtesy lights	Push-fit	5
Luggage compartment light.	Push-fit	5
Number plate light	W5W Push-fit	5
Reversing light	P21W Bayonet	21

Torque wrench setting

	Nm	lbf ft
Airbag control unit retaining nuts	8	6
Accelerometer sensor retaining bolts.	8	6

1 General Information

Warning: Before carrying out any work on the electrical system, read through the precautions given in Safety first! at the beginning of this manual, and in Chapter 5A Section 1.

1 The electrical system is of 12 volt negative earth type. Power for the lights and all electrical accessories is supplied by a lead-acid type battery, which is charged by the alternator.

2 Many of the body electrical systems are controlled by individual electronic control modules (ECMs), these are in turn controlled by a main ECM known as a built-in systems interface (BSI). The various ECMs and the BSI exchange data with each other via a multiplex network. The multiplex network is a two-wire system linking the BSI with the system ECMs and is termed by Peugeot/Citroën as CAN (controlled area network) and VAN (vehicle area network). Essentially this means that the BSI and the ECMs controlling the 'comfort' systems, safety systems, security systems, and entertainment systems in the vehicle, are all interconnected via vehicle area networks.

3 An ECM connected to the multiplex network only receives some of the data needed for it to operate directly, with the remaining data being supplied by the other ECMs on the network. Because the ECMs share information via the network, several ECMs can control the operation of the same system. Also, one ECM can control several systems in an autonomous manner. The BSI is the manager of this information interchange as well as also being responsible for the control of certain vehicle systems itself. The BSI has a full diagnostic capability whereby any fault in any of the ECMs on the multiplex network can be traced using diagnostic equipment connected to the vehicle diagnostic connector, located inside the passenger glovebox **(see illustration)**. Should any fault develop with a system on the network, have the self-diagnosis facility interrogated by a Peugeot/Citroën dealer or suitably-equipped specialist.

4 This Chapter covers repair and service

1.3 Vehicle diagnostic plug connector (arrowed)

procedures for the various electrical components not associated with the engine. Information on the battery, alternator and starter motor can be found in Chapter 5A.

5 It should be noted that, prior to working on any component in the electrical system, the battery should first be disconnected; to prevent the possibility of electrical short-circuits (see Chapter 5A Section 1).

2 Electrical fault finding – general information

Note: Refer to the precautions given in Safety first! and in Chapter 5A Section 1 before starting work. The following tests relate to testing of the main electrical circuits, and should not be used to test delicate electronic circuits (such as anti-lock braking systems), particularly where an electronic control unit (ECM) or multiplexing is used (see Section 1).

General

1 A typical electrical circuit consists of an electrical component; any switches, relays, motors, fuses, fusible links or circuit breakers related to that component, and the wiring and connectors which link the component to both the battery and the chassis. To help to pinpoint a problem in an electrical circuit, wiring diagrams are included at the end of this Chapter.

2 Before attempting to diagnose an electrical fault, first study the appropriate wiring diagram, to obtain a more complete understanding of the components included in the particular circuit concerned. The possible sources of a fault can be narrowed down, by noting whether other components related to the circuit are operating properly. If several components or circuits fail at one time, the problem is likely to be related to a shared fuse or earth connection.

3 Electrical problems usually stem from simple causes, such as loose or corroded connections, a faulty earth connection, a blown fuse, a melted fusible link, or a faulty relay (refer to Section 3 for details of testing relays). Visually inspect the condition of all fuses, wires and connections in a problem circuit before testing the components. Use the wiring diagrams to determine which terminal connections will need to be checked, in order to pinpoint the trouble spot.

4 The basic tools required for electrical fault finding include a circuit tester or voltmeter; an ohmmeter (to measure resistance); a battery and set of test leads; and a jumper wire, preferably with a circuit breaker or fuse incorporated, which can be used to bypass suspect wires or electrical components. Before attempting to locate a problem with test instruments, use the wiring diagram to determine where to make the connections.

5 To find the source of an intermittent wiring fault (usually due to a poor or dirty connection,

or damaged wiring insulation), a 'wiggle' test can be performed on the wiring. This involves wiggling the wiring by hand, to see if the fault occurs as the wiring is moved. It should be possible to narrow down the source of the fault to a particular section of wiring. This method of testing can be used in conjunction with any of the tests described in the following sub-Sections.

6 Apart from problems due to poor connections, two basic types of fault can occur in an electrical circuit – open-circuit, or short-circuit.

7 Open-circuit faults are caused by a break somewhere in the circuit, which prevents current from flowing. An open-circuit fault will prevent a component from working, but will not cause the relevant circuit fuse to blow.

8 Short-circuit faults are caused by a 'short' somewhere in the circuit, which allows the current flowing in the circuit to 'escape' along an alternative route, usually to earth. Short-circuit faults are normally caused by a breakdown in wiring insulation, which allows a feed wire to touch either another wire, or an earthed component such as the bodyshell. A short-circuit fault will normally cause the relevant circuit fuse to blow. **Note:** *As an aid to economy and to prevent battery discharge, certain functions of the electrical system can only be used for 30 minutes after the engine has been stopped. Bear this in mind when tracing power supply faults on these systems. After this period the BSI (built-in systems interface) cuts the power to these circuits. To restore power, start the engine. It is also possible for the BSI to turn off certain functions (heater blower, heated rear window) depending on the state of charge of the battery. When tracing a fault, ensure the battery is in a good state of charge.*

Functions affected

- Windscreen wipers.
- Electric windows.
- Sunroof.
- Courtesy lights.
- Audio equipment.

Finding an open-circuit

9 To check for an open-circuit, connect one lead of a voltmeter to either the negative battery terminal or a known good earth.

10 Connect the other lead to a connector in the circuit being tested, preferably nearest to the battery or fuse.

11 Switch on the circuit, bearing in mind that some circuits are live only when the ignition switch is moved to a particular position.

12 If voltage is present (indicated either by the tester bulb lighting or a voltmeter reading, as applicable), this means that the section of the circuit between the relevant connector and the battery is problem-free.

13 Continue to check the remainder of the circuit in the same fashion.

14 When a point is reached at which no voltage is present, the problem must lie

2.20a Earth connection inside passenger compartment ...

2.20b ... on the top of the transmission (arrowed)

3.3 Unclip the fusebox cover

between that point and the previous test point with voltage. Most problems can be traced to a broken, corroded or loose connection.

Finding a short-circuit

15 To check for a short-circuit; first disconnect the load(s) from the circuit (loads are the components which draw current from a circuit, such as bulbs, motors, heating elements, etc).
16 Remove the relevant fuse from the circuit, and connect a circuit tester or voltmeter to the fuse connections.
17 Switch on the circuit, bearing in mind that some circuits are live only when the ignition switch is moved to a particular position.
18 If voltage is present (indicated either by the tester bulb lighting or a voltmeter reading, as applicable), this means that there is a short-circuit.
19 If no voltage is present, but the fuse still blows with the load(s) connected, this indicates an internal fault in the load(s).

Finding an earth fault

20 The battery negative terminal is connected to 'earth' – the metal of the engine/ transmission and the car body – and most systems are wired so that they only receive a positive feed, the current returning via the metal of the car body. This means that the component mounting and the body form part of that circuit. Loose or corroded mountings can therefore cause a range of electrical faults, ranging from total failure of a circuit,

to a puzzling partial fault. In particular, lights may shine dimly (especially when another circuit sharing the same earth point is in operation), motors (eg, wiper motors or the radiator cooling fan motor) may run slowly, and the operation of one circuit may have an apparently unrelated effect on another. Note that on many vehicles, earth straps are used between certain components, such as the engine/transmission and the body, usually where there is no metal-to-metal contact between components, due to flexible rubber mountings, etc (see illustrations).
21 To check whether a component is properly earthed, disconnect the battery, and connect one lead of an ohmmeter to a known good earth point. Connect the other lead to the wire or earth connection being tested. The resistance reading should be zero; if not, check the connection as follows.
22 If an earth connection is thought to be faulty, dismantle the connection, and clean back to bare metal both the bodyshell and the wire terminal or the component earth connection mating surface. Be careful to remove all traces of dirt and corrosion, and then use a knife to trim away any paint, so that a clean metal-to-metal joint is made. On reassembly, tighten the joint fasteners securely; if a wire terminal is being refitted, use serrated washers between the terminal and the bodyshell, to ensure a clean and secure connection. When the connection is remade, prevent the onset of corrosion in the future by applying a coat of petroleum jelly or

silicone-based grease, or by spraying on (at regular intervals) a proprietary ignition sealer or water-dispersant lubricant.

3 Fuses and relays – general information

Fuses

1 Fuses are designed to break a circuit when a predetermined current is reached, in order to protect the components and wiring, which could be damaged by excessive current flow. Any excessive current flow will be due to a fault in the circuit, usually a short-circuit (see Section 2).
2 The majority of fuses are located behind the glovebox lid on the passenger's side of the facia. Additional fuses (including the larger, higher-rated fuses) are located in the fuse/ relay box on the left-hand side of the engine compartment.
3 To gain access to the facia fuses, open the glovebox then unclip the cover from the facia (see illustration).
4 To gain access to the fuses in the engine compartment, simply unclip the cover from the fuse/relay box (see illustrations). There are also additional fuses are under the red cover on top of the battery cover.
5 To remove a fuse, first switch off the circuit concerned (or the ignition), and then pull the

3.4a Lift up the plastic cover ...

3.4b ... to access the fuses and relays ...

3.4c ... additional fused links on top of battery

3.5a Pull the fuse from its position in the fusebox

3.5b Using a pair of long-nose pliers to remove the fuses

3.8 The ABS relay (A) and the diesel pre/ post-heating relay (B) located in front of fusebox

fuse out of its terminals **(see illustrations)**. The wire within the fuse should be visible; if the fuse has blown it will be broken or melted.
6 Always renew a fuse with one of the correct rating; never use a fuse with a different rating from that specified. The fuse rating is stamped on the top of the fuse; the fuses are also colour-coded as follows. Refer to the wiring diagrams for details of the fuse ratings and the circuits protected.

COLOUR	RATING
Orange	5A
Red	10A
Blue	15A
Yellow	20A
White/Clear	25A
Green	30A

7 Never renew a fuse more than once without tracing the source of the trouble. If the new fuse blows immediately, find the cause before renewing it again; a short to earth as a result of faulty insulation is most likely. Where a fuse protects more than one circuit, try to isolate the fault by switching on each circuit in turn (where possible) until the fuse blows again. Always carry a supply of spare fuses of each relevant rating on the vehicle; a spare of each rating should be clipped into the fusebox.

Relays

Note: *The BSI unit is located on the passenger's side of the facia where it is situated directly behind the glovebox (see Section 23).*
8 The majority of relay functions are incorporated into the built-in system interface (BSI) unit (see Section 23). Other relays are located in the fuse/relay box in the engine compartment and the ABS and pre/ post-heating system (diesel models) relays are located in front of the engine compartment fusebox housing **(see illustration)**.
9 If a circuit or system controlled by a relay develops a fault and the relay is suspect, operate the system. If the relay is functioning, it should be possible to hear it 'click' as it is energised. If this is the case, the fault lies with the components or wiring of the system.

If the relay is not being energised, then either the relay is not receiving a main supply or a switching voltage, or the relay itself is faulty. Testing is by the substitution of a known good unit, but be careful – while some relays are identical in appearance and in operation, others look similar but perform different functions.
10 To remove a relay, first ensure that the relevant circuit is switched off. The relay can then simply be pulled out from the socket, and pushed back into position.

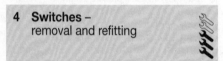

4 Switches – removal and refitting

Note: *Disconnect the battery before removing any switch, and reconnect the lead after refitting the switch (see Chapter 5A Section 4).*

Ignition switch

1 Refer to Chapter 10 Section 18.

Steering column switches

2 Remove the driver's airbag as described in Section 22.
3 Remove the steering wheel as described in Chapter 10 Section 16.
4 Remove the steering column lower and upper shrouds as described in Chapter 11 Section 28.
5 Disconnect the wiring plugs from the rear of the switch assembly **(see illustration 4.6a)**.
6 If the switch assembly is to be refitted,

4.6a Slacken the retaining clamp bolt (arrowed) ...

immobilise the airbag rotary contact disc with adhesive tape. Note that as long as the wheels are in the straight-ahead position, the contact disc should lock in position. Slacken the switch assembly retaining clamp, then using a small screwdriver, carefully prise the retaining catches away from the lug on the column and lift the switch assembly from place **(see illustrations)**.
Caution: Take great care not to damage the switch assembly retaining catches.
7 If required, the cruise control switch and remote radio control switch can be unclipped from the combination switch assembly as described in paragraphs 13 to 15.
8 Although refitting is a reversal of removal, the airbag contact unit built into the switch assembly must be set in the correct position as follows:
9 Ensure the wheels are in the straight-ahead position.
10 If refitting the existing switch assembly, simply remove the adhesive tape applied during removal.
11 If the new switch assemblies are manufactured by Delphi or Valeo a setting-up procedure must be carried out. Units supplied by other manufacturers are supplied with the contact ring immobilised in the correct position by a self-adhesive label, which should be removed just prior to steering wheel refitment.
12 The following procedure applies to new or used Delphi or Valeo units. Press in the centre collar of the rotary contact unit, then gently

4.6b ... then carefully lift the retaining catch (arrowed)

4.12 Align the index peg (arrowed) with the notch in the outer edge of the rotary switch

4.14a Release the securing clip...

4.14b ... and slide out the switch

4.18a Release the securing clips...

4.18b ... and unclip the switch from the panel

rotate the collar clockwise until it comes to a stop (DO NOT force it any further). Turn the collar 2.5 revolutions anti-clockwise until the red index peg is aligned with the notch in the outside edge of the rotary switch (see illustration). If the steering wheel is not to be fitted immediately, immobilise the contact in this position with adhesive tape.

Caution: Do not turn the collar anti-clockwise until the 'stop' has been reached, otherwise the unit will be irreparably damaged.

Note: If a new switch assembly if fitted to a vehicle with ESP (electronic stability programme) the unit must be initialised using dedicated test equipment. Entrust this task to a Peugeot dealer or suitably-equipped specialist.

Audio unit control/cruise control

13 Remove the steering column lower and upper shrouds as described in Chapter 11 Section 28.

14 Release the securing clip and slide the switch from its position in the side of the steering column switch assembly (see illustrations).

15 Refitting is the reversal of removal.

Headlight height, exterior mirror, ESP, parking assist and alarm switches

16 The switch trim panel to the right of the steering column houses the headlight height adjustment, exterior mirror adjustment, ESP, parking assistance and anti-intrusion alarm

switches. Depending on model and trim level, not all these switches will be fitted.

17 Remove the switch panel as described in Chapter 11 Section 28.

18 Disconnect the wiring connector from the relevant switch and then release the securing clips and press the switch out from the trim panel (see illustrations).

19 Refitting is the reversal of removal.

Hazard warning, central locking and electric window switches

20 Remove the switch panel from above the gear lever centre console, as described in Chapter 11 Section 28.

21 Disconnect the wiring connector from the relevant switch, and then release the securing clips and press the switch out from the switch panel (see illustration).

22 Refitting is the reversal of removal.

Passenger airbag on/off switch

23 Unclip the trim panel from the right-hand end of the facia (see illustration).

24 Using a small screwdriver, carefully unclip the wiring connector from the rear of the switch (see illustration). Then release the securing clips to remove the switch from the trim panel.

25 Refitting is the reverse of removal.

Heating/ventilation control and heated rear window switch

26 The switches are an integral part of the heater/ventilation control panel, and cannot be renewed separately. If any switch is faulty, the complete control panel must be renewed – refer to Chapter 3 Section 10 for details.

Brake light switch

27 Refer to Chapter 9 Section 17.

4.21 Disconnect the wiring connector from relevant switch

4.23 Remove the trim panel

4.24 Release the wiring connector securing clip

Handbrake warning light switch

28 Remove the centre console as described in Chapter 11 Section 27.

29 Pull the handbrake fully on and disconnect the switch wiring connector **(see illustration)**.

30 Release the retaining clips and remove the switch downwards and out from the handbrake mounting bracket **(see illustration)**.

31 Refitting is the reverse of removal.

Courtesy light switch

32 The courtesy light switches are an integral part of the door lock assemblies. Refer to Chapter 11 Section 12 for door lock removal and refitting details.

Luggage area light switch

33 The luggage compartment light switch function is integral with the tailgate lock assembly. For tailgate lock removal, refer to Chapter 11 Section 17.

Rain/sunlight sensor

34 The rain/sunlight sensor is covered in the heater/ventilation control system; refer to Chapter 3 Section 10, for the removal and refitting procedure.

Caution: Do not touch the rain sensor lens or the windscreen glass in the area of the sensor. These areas must be kept spotlessly clean if the sensor is to function correctly.

4.29 Disconnect the wiring connector …

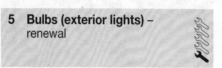

5 Bulbs (exterior lights) – renewal

General

1 Whenever a bulb is renewed, note the following points:

a) *Remember that, if the light has just been in use, the bulb may be extremely hot.*

b) *Always check the bulb contacts and holder, ensuring that there is clean metal-to-metal contact between the bulb and its live(s) and earth. Clean off any corrosion or dirt before fitting a new bulb.*

c) *Wherever bayonet-type bulbs are fitted (see Specifications), ensure that the live*

4.30 … and unclip the switch from the handbrake bracket

contact(s) bear firmly against the bulb contact.

d) *Always ensure that the new bulb is of the correct rating, and that it is completely clean before fitting it; this applies particularly to headlight/foglight bulbs (see below)*

Headlight

Note: *When handling the new bulb, use a tissue or clean cloth to avoid touching the glass with the fingers; moisture and grease from the skin can cause blackening and rapid failure of this type of bulb. If the glass is accidentally touched, wipe it clean using methylated spirit.*

2 Reach behind the headlamp unit, and unclip the headlight bulb protective cover and remove it **(see illustration)**.

3 Disconnect the wiring plug from the bulb **(see illustration)**.

4 Release the bulb retaining clip, and withdraw the bulb **(see illustrations)**.

5 Install the new bulb, ensuring that its locating tabs are correctly seated in the light cut-outs, and secure it in position with the retaining clip.

6 Reconnect the wiring plug, and refit the protective cover.

Sidelight

7 Reach behind the headlamp and unclip the headlight bulb protective cover and remove it **(see illustration)**.

5.2 Unclip the headlight bulb protective cover

5.3 Disconnect the headlight bulb wiring plug

5.4a Release the retaining clip …

5.4b … and remove the bulb

5.7 Unclip the sidelight bulb protective cover

5.8 Pull the bulbholder to remove…

5.9 … then pull the bulb from its holder

5.12 Disconnect the foglight wiring plug

5.13 Rotate the bulbholder anti-clockwise to remove

5.16 Unclip the sidelight bulb protective cover

5.17 Rotate the bulbholder anti-clockwise to remove …

8 Pull the bulb holder from the rear of the light unit **(see illustration)**.

9 The bulb is a capless (push-fit) type, and can easily be removed by pulling it out of the bulbholder **(see illustration)**.

10 Refitting is the reverse of the removal procedure.

Front foglight

11 The front foglights are located in the front bumper. Chock the rear wheels then jack up the front of the vehicle and support it on axle stands (see *Jacking and vehicle support*). For access to the foglight, it is necessary to release the front of the wheel arch liner by removing the fasteners.

12 Reach up under the front bumper and disconnect the wiring from the foglight bulbholder **(see illustration)**.

13 Turn the bulbholder 60° anti-clockwise and withdraw it from the rear of the foglight, then remove the bulb **(see illustration)**.

14 When handling the new bulb, use a tissue or clean cloth to avoid touching the glass with the fingers; moisture and grease from the skin can cause blackening and rapid failure of this type of bulb. If the glass is accidentally touched, wipe it clean using methylated spirit.

15 Fit the new bulb using a reversal of the removal procedure.

Front direction indicator

16 Reach behind the headlamp and unclip

the headlight bulb protective cover and remove it **(see illustration)**.

17 Rotate the bulbholder 60° and free it from the rear of the headlight unit **(see illustration)**.

18 The bulb is a bayonet-fit in the holder, and can be removed by pressing it in and rotating it anti-clockwise **(see illustration)**.

19 Refitting is the reverse of the removal procedure, ensuring that the bulbholder seal is in good condition.

Side repeater

20 Push the side repeater towards the rearwards to free its retaining clip, then ease it out from the wing panel **(see illustrations)**.

21 Disconnect the wiring connector from the

5.18 … then press in the bulb and rotate it anti-clockwise to remove it

5.20a Push the light unit to the rear…

5.20b …and unclip it from the wing

5.21 ... and disconnect the wiring connector

5.24a Release the retaining clips (van model)...

5.24b ...and pull the bulbholder from the light unit (van model)

5.24c Release the retaining clips (MPV model)...

5.24d ...and pull the bulbholder from the light unit (MPV model)

light unit **(see illustration)**. The bulb is part of the light unit; the side repeater will need to be renewed as a complete unit.

22 Refitting is a reversal of the removal procedure.

Rear light cluster

23 Remove the relevant rear light unit as described in Section 7.

24 Release the retaining tabs and remove the bulbholder assembly, from the rear of the light unit **(see illustrations)**.

25 All the bulbs have bayonet fittings. The relevant bulb can be removed by pressing it in and rotating it anti-clockwise **(see illustrations)**.

26 Refitting is the reverse of removal, ensuring the light unit and bulbholder seals are in good condition.

High-level brake light

27 Remove the high level light unit as described in Section 7.

28 Release the retaining clip and hinge the bulb holder away from the light unit, the bulb is of the capless (push-fit) type, and can easily be removed by pulling it out of the bulbholder **(see illustrations)**.

29 Refitting is the reverse of removal.

5.25a Press in the bulb and rotate it anti-clockwise to remove it (van model)

5.25b Press in the bulb and rotate it anti-clockwise to remove it (MPV model)

5.28a Carefully prise the light lens from place ...

5.28b ... and pull the bulb from the holder

5.30a Carefully prise the light lens from place ...

5.30b ... then pull the bulb from the holder

5.32 Remove the trim panel

5.33a Pull the bulbholder from the light unit...

5.33b ...and pull the bulb from the bulbholder

Number plate light

MPV models

30 Using a small flat-bladed screwdriver, carefully prise out the lens and remove it. The bulb is of the capless (push-fit) type, and can be removed by simply pulling it out of the light unit (see illustrations).

31 Refitting is the reverse of the removal procedure, ensuring that the lens is securely clipped in position.

Van models

32 Release the securing clips and remove the trim panel from inside the rear door (see illustration).

33 Pull the bulb holder out of the light unit, the bulb is of the capless (push-fit) type, and

can easily be removed by pulling it out of the bulbholder (see illustrations).

34 Refitting is the reverse of the removal procedure.

Front day time running lights

Note: *The front day time running light units have LED's fitted and can only be renewed as a complete unit.*

35 Remove the front day time running light units, as described in Section 7.

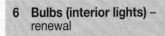

6 Bulbs (interior lights) – renewal

General

1 Refer to Section 5, paragraph 1.

Passenger compartment lights

2 Using a flat bladed-screwdriver, carefully unclip the plastic lens cover from the light unit (see illustration).

3 The bulbs are of the capless (push-fit) type, and can be removed by simply pulling it out of the bulbholder (see illustration).

4 If required, release the securing clips and carefully remove the light unit from the headlining (see illustration). Disconnect the wiring from the rear of the unit as it is removed.

5 Refitting is the reverse of the removal procedure

Instrument panel lights

6 The instrument panel and warning lights are illuminated by integral LEDs. It is not possible to renew them independently of the panel. Instrument panel renewal is described in Section 9.

Heating/ventilation control illumination

Note: *The following procedure is for models with manually operated heater controls. On models with automatic climate control, the heater control panel is illuminated by integral LEDs. It is not possible to renew them independently of the panel.*

7 Remove the heater control panel as described in Chapter 3 Section 10.

8 Using a pair of long-nose pliers, twist the bulbholder and remove it from the rear of the

6.2 Carefully unclip the light lens

6.3 Pull the bulb from the front light unit

6.4 Disconnect the wiring plug

6.8 Rotate the bulbholder to remove

6.9 Pull the bulb from the bulb holder

heater control panel **(see illustration)**. There are two bulbs fitted the rear of the heater control panel.

9 The bulbs are of the capless (push-fit) type, and can be removed by simply pulling it out of the bulbholder **(see illustration)**.

10 Refitting is the reverse of the removal procedure

Multifunction display illumination

11 The multifunction display is illuminated by integral LEDs. It is not possible to renew them independently of the display. Remove the multifunction display as described in Section 10.

Switch illumination

12 All of the switches that are illuminated are done so by LEDs. These LEDs are an integral part of the switch and cannot be renewed separately. Renewal will therefore require renewal of the complete switch assembly (see Section 4).

---

7 Exterior light units –
removal and refitting

Headlight

1 Remove the front bumper (see Chapter 11 Section 6).

2 Undo the retaining bolts and remove the crossmember from along the top of the radiator panel **(see illustration)**.

3 When removing the right-hand headlight unit, unclip the filler neck of the washer reservoir from the rear of the light unit **(see illustration)**.

4 Reach behind the headlight, release the locking clip and disconnect the wiring connector from the rear of the headlight unit **(see illustration)**.

5 Slacken and remove the three mounting bolts and free the headlight unit from its mounting. Unclip the headlight from the surrounding panels, then manoeuvre the unit out of position **(see illustrations)**.

6 When refitting, offer up the headlight unit making sure it is clipped into the surrounding panels correctly.

7 Position the headlight in its aperture, and then refit and tighten the headlight mounting bolts.

8 Reconnect the wiring connector to the rear of the light unit and check the operation of the headlight, then refit the front bumper. On right-hand headlights, refit the washer reservoir filler neck to the retaining clip on the rear of the light unit.

9 Check the headlight beam alignment using the information given in Section 8.

Front indicator side repeater

10 Remove the indicator side repeater from the wing panel, as described in Section 5.

Rear light unit

MPV models

11 Open the tailgate, then undo the two retaining screws, one from the top and the

7.2 Remove the upper crossmember

7.3 Unclip the washer reservoir – right-hand headlight

7.4 Disconnect the wiring connector

7.5a Undo the two lower headlamp mounting bolts (arrowed) …

7.5b … and upper mounting bolt (arrowed)…

7.5c …and remove the light unit

7.11a Undo the upper...

7.11b ...and lower retaining screw

7.12 Disconnect the wiring connector

other inner lower part of the rear light unit **(see illustrations)**.

12 Disconnect the wiring connector from the light unit as it is removed from the vehicle **(see illustration)**.

13 Refitting is the reverse of removal, ensuring the light unit locating pegs are located in the rear panel correctly **(see illustrations)**.

Van models

14 Open the hinged rear doors, then undo the two retaining screws, one from the top and the other from the lower part of the rear light unit **(see illustrations)**.

15 Carefully pull back on the light unit to disengage the locating peg. Disconnect the wiring connector from the light unit as it is removed from the vehicle **(see illustration)**.

16 Refitting is the reverse of removal, ensuring the light unit locating peg locates in the rear panel correctly **(see illustration)**.

High-level brake light

MPV models

17 Open the tailgate and remove the two fasteners at the upper inside edge of the tailgate **(see illustration)**.

18 Disconnect the washer tube and the

7.13a Align the upper and lower pegs (arrowed)...

7.13b ...with the holes (arrowed) in the rear panel

7.14a Undo the upper screw (arrowed)...

7.14b ...and lower screw (arrowed)

7.15 Disconnect the wiring connector

7.16 Align the locating peg (arrowed)

7.17 Remove the two fasteners

7.18a Disconnect the washer tube…

7.18b …and the wiring connector

7.21a Undo the two fasteners…

7.21b … and unclip the light unit from the rear door

wiring connector from the light unit, as it is removed **(see illustrations)**.

19 If required, the washer jet can be removed from the end of the light unit, as described in Section 16.

20 Refitting is the reverse of removal.

Van models

21 Open the left-hand side rear hinged door, then undo the two fasteners and remove the

light unit from the upper edge of the door **(see illustrations)**.

22 Refitting is the reverse of removal.

Number plate light

MPV models

23 Remove the tailgate lower trim panel as described in Chapter 11 Section 16.

24 Reach inside the tailgate and disconnect the wiring connectors from the rear of the two switches **(see illustration)**.

25 Undo the six retaining nuts, then from outside the tailgate remove the trim panel from above the number plate **(see illustrations)**.

26 Disconnect the wiring connector, release the securing clips and remove the number plate light unit from the tailgate panel **(see illustration)**.

27 Refitting is a reversal of removal. On completion, refit the tailgate trim panel as described in Chapter 11 Section 16.

Van models

28 Remove the number plate light bulb, as described in Section 5.

29 Release the securing clip and remove the number plate light unit from the rear door **(see illustration)**.

30 Refitting is the reverse of the removal procedure.

Front foglights

31 Remove the front fog light bulb as described in Section 5.

32 Undo the two mounting screws and

7.24 Disconnect the wiring plug connector (one shown)

7.25a Undo the retaining nuts (three one one side shown)…

7.25b …and remove the trim panel

7.26 Remove the number plate light

7.29a Release the securing clip (arrowed)…

7.29b …and unclip the light unit

7.32a Undo the retaining screws (arrowed)...

7.32b ...and remove the fog light unit

7.35a Undo the mounting screws (arrowed)...

withdraw the foglight unit from the rear of the bumper **(see illustrations)**.

33 Refitting is a reversal of removal.

Front day time running lights

Note: *The front day time running light units have LED's fitted and can only be renewed as a complete unit.*

34 Remove the front bumper, as described in Chapter 11 Section 6.

35 Undo the two mounting screws and withdraw the light unit from the rear of the bumper **(see illustrations)**.

36 Release the securing clip and disconnect the wiring connector from the light unit **(see illustration)**.

37 Refitting is a reversal of removal.

7.35b ...and remove the light unit

7.36 Disconnect the wiring connector

8 Headlight beam alignment – general information

1 Accurate adjustment of the headlight beam is only possible using optical beam-setting equipment, and this work should therefore be carried out by a Peugeot/Citroën dealer or suitably-equipped workshop.

2 For reference, the vertical and horizontal alignment of the headlights can be adjusted by rotating the adjuster assemblies, which are accessible at the rear of the headlight casing **(see illustration)**.

3 On models equipped with headlight leveling, ensure the adjuster switch on the facia panel inside the vehicle is set to position 0 before the headlights are adjusted.

4 The adjuster should be positioned as follows according to the load being carried in the vehicle:

0	No load
1	Partial load
2	Average load
3	Maximum load

5 On models with front foglights, these can be adjusted by using an Allen key at the rear of the light unit. Reach up behind the wheel arch liner to gain access **(see illustration)**.

9 Instrument panel – removal and refitting

Removal

1 Disconnect the battery (refer to precautions in Chapter 5A Section 1).

2 Remove the instrument panel surround trim, as described in Chapter 11 Section 28.

8.2 Vertical adjusters (A) horizontal adjuster (B)

8.5 Using an Allen key to adjust the front foglight alignment

9.3a Undo the retaining screw (arrowed)…

9.3b …and lift out the instrument panel

9.4 Disconnect the wiring connector

3 Undo the retaining screw at the upper centre part of the instrument panel, then pull it out at the top and lift it upwards from the lower locating pegs **(see illustrations)**.
4 Release the locking clip and disconnect the wiring plug(s) as the unit is withdrawn **(see illustration)**.
5 Should the instrument panel develop a fault, have the vehicle's self-diagnosis facility interrogated by a Peugeot/Citroën dealer or suitably-equipped specialist. No parts are available separately for the instrument panel, if faulty, the complete assembly must be renewed.

Refitting

6 Refitting is a reversal of removal, ensuring that the wiring connectors are securely fitted and the retaining clips engage correctly when the instrument panel is pressed into position in the top of the facia. Refit the instrument

panel surround trim, with reference to Chapter 11 Section 28.

10 Multifunction display unit – removal and refitting

1 On higher specification models, the display unit is built into the Audio unit, see Section 17.

Removal

2 Ensure the ignition is switched off.
3 Carefully unclip the display unit from the top of the facia panel, release the securing clip and disconnect the wiring plug connector, as it is removed **(see illustrations)**.
4 if required the display unit can be removed from the surround trim panel by releasing the retaining clips **(see illustration)**.

Refitting

5 Refitting is a reversal of removal.

11 Cigarette lighter/accessory socket – removal and refitting

Removal

1 Remove the centre switch panel assembly, as described in Section 4.
2 Where illumination is fitted to the socket, carefully release the retaining clips and slide the light assembly off the base of the socket, taking great care not to break its electrical contacts.
3 Pull out the lighter element then release the tangs and push out the metal insert/accessory socket. The plastic outer section can then be removed from the console.

Refitting

4 Align the plastic outer section tab with the cut-out then insert it into the console.
5 Align the bulbholder contact on the metal insert with the holder tangs on the plastic outer then clip the insert into position.
6 Slide the illumination light assembly onto the metal insert and clip it securely onto the plastic outer.
7 Ensure the cigarette lighter is correctly assembled then refit the centre console and/or trim panels.

12 Horn – removal and refitting

10.3a Unclip the display unit…

10.3b …and disconnect the wiring connector

10.4 Unclip the display unit from the trim panel

12.1 Location of the horn (arrowed)

Removal

1 The horn(s) are located behind the front bumper, on the left-hand side **(see illustration)**.
2 Unclip the inner wheel arch liner in front of the left-hand side front wheel, and then reach in to access the horns. If required, to make access easier, remove the front bumper as described in Chapter 11 Section 6.
3 Disconnect the wiring connector, then slacken the mounting bracket bolt and remove the horn from under the front crossmember.

Refitting

4 Refitting is a reversal of removal.

13.1 Wiper blade alignment mark on screen

13.2 Undo the wiper arm spindle nuts (arrowed)

13.3a Remove the wiper arm ...

13 Wiper arm – removal and refitting

Note: *The wiper arms can be a very tight fit on their spindles, a puller may be needed to remove them safely and without damage.*

Front wiper

1 There are alignment marks provided on the windscreen to aid refitting **(see illustration)**.
2 Lift up the wiper arm spindle nut cover (where fitted) then slacken and remove the spindle nut **(see illustration)**.
3 Lift the blade off the glass, and move the wiper arms carefully side to side to release them from the spindle. If the arm is very tight, free it from the spindle using a suitable puller **(see illustrations)**.
4 Ensure that the wiper arm and spindle splines are clean and dry, then refit the arm to the spindle, aligning the wiper blade with the alignment marks provided.
5 Refit the spindle nuts and tightening them securely.

Rear wiper

6 Operate the wiper motor, then switch it off so that the wiper arm returns to the at-rest position. Stick tape to the screen alongside the wiper blade to ensure the correct position for refitting.
7 Unclip the centre cap from the wiper arm spindle nut, then slacken and remove the spindle nut **(see illustration)**.

13.3b ... if it is tight on the spindle, use a puller

8 Remove the wiper arm spindle nut, lift the blade off the glass, and pull the wiper arm off its spindle. If the arm is very tight, free it from the spindle using a suitable puller **(see illustration 13.3b)**.
9 Ensure that the wiper arm and spindle splines are clean and dry, then refit the arm to the spindle, aligning the wiper blade with the tape fitted on removal.
10 Refit the spindle nut, tightening it securely, and clip cover back into position.

14 Windscreen wiper motor and linkage – removal and refitting

Removal

1 Remove the wiper arms (see Section 13).

13.7 Unclip the trim cover to access the wiper arm spindle nut

2 Remove the scuttle panel lower grille panel as described in Chapter 11 Section 23.
3 Release the retaining clip and disconnect the wiring connector from the wiper motor **(see illustration)**.
4 The wiper motor/linkage assembly is secured by a bolt at each end of the linkage, and a locating peg in the bulkhead at the centre **(see illustrations)**. Undo the bolts, and then lift the assembly from the locating peg on the bulkhead, then manoeuvre it from the engine compartment
5 If required, disconnect the linkage rods from the wiper motor spindle arm by levering them from their balljoints. Undo the retaining nut to remove the arm from the wiper spindle, noting its fitted position. To remove the wiper motor from the linkage bracket,

14.3 Disconnect the wiper motor wiring plug

14.4a undo the bolts (arrowed) ...

14.4b ... and remove the wiper motor/ linkage

14.5a Remove the wiper linkage rods and arm retaining nut ...

14.5b ... then undo the three retaining screws to remove the motor

14.6 Locating peg aligned with grommet in bulkhead

undo the three retaining screws **(see illustrations)**.

Refitting

6 Refitting is a reversal of removal, ensuring all fasteners are securely tightened. Note that before tightening the linkage mounting bolts, ensure the assembly is correctly fitted over the locating peg on the bulkhead **(see illustration)**.

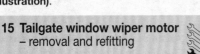

15 Tailgate window wiper motor – removal and refitting

Removal

1 Ensure the ignition is turned off.
2 Remove the tailgate inner trim panel as described in Chapter 11 Section 17.
3 Remove the wiper arm (see Section 13).
4 Disconnect the wiring connector from the wiper motor **(see illustration)**.
5 Undo the three retaining nuts securing the wiper motor to the tailgate **(see illustration)**. Remove the wiper motor from inside the tailgate.

Refitting

6 Make sure that any rubber mountings and collars (where fitted) are correctly positioned in the wiper motor mounting bracket.

7 Manoeuvre the wiper motor into position and secure it in position with the retaining nuts.
8 Reconnect the wiring connector to the motor then refit the trim panel to the tailgate. Turn on the ignition, then operate the wiper and allow it to stop in the park position.
9 Refit the wiper arm as described in Section 13.

16 Washer system components – removal and refitting

Note: *Before working on the reservoir or pump, it is advisable to drain as much fluid*

15.4 Disconnect the wiring plug connector

out of the reservoir as possible, to prevent any spillage.
1 The washer reservoir is located behind the right-hand side of the front bumper **(see illustration)** and supplies both the windscreen and tailgate washers via the same pump. On models equipped with headlight washers, the reservoir also supplies the headlight washer jets via an additional pump.

Washer fluid reservoir

2 Remove the front bumper as described in Chapter 11 Section 6.
3 Unclip the top of the reservoir filler neck from the bracket behind the headlight **(see illustration)**.

15.5 Undo the three retaining nuts

16.1 Location of washer reservoir behind right-hand side of bumper

16.3 Unclip the top of the filler neck from the securing clip

16.6a Undo the retaining nut (arrowed) …

16.6b …and release the two locating points (arrowed)

16.12 Disconnect hoses from the washer pump (arrowed)

4 Note the correct fitted location of the washer hoses (if necessary, mark them for identification purposes) then disconnect the hoses from the washer pump(s). Position a container beneath the reservoir to catch any washer fluid from the pump and hoses.

5 Disconnect the wiring connector(s) from the washer pump(s).

6 Slacken and remove the retaining nut from the upper rear part of the reservoir, then slide the reservoir backwards to release it from the upper mounting brackets **(see illustrations)**.

7 Manoeuvre the reservoir out of position, releasing any wiring or hoses from locating clips in the side of the reservoir. If required the filler neck can be unscrewed from the reservoir, noting the sealing washer fitted between the two.

8 Refitting is the reverse of removal, ensuring that the hoses are securely reconnected. Refill the reservoir and check for leaks.

Washer pump

9 Slacken the right-hand front roadwheel bolts. Jack up the front of the vehicle, and support it securely on axle stands (see *Jacking and vehicle support*). Remove the right-hand roadwheel.

10 Remove the front right-hand wheel arch liner. The liner is secured by several expanding plastic rivets. Release the centre pins, then prise the complete rivets from place, and manoeuvre the front section of the liner out from underneath the wing.

11 Position a container beneath the reservoir to catch the washer fluid as the pump is removed.

12 Disconnect the washer fluid hoses and wiring connector from the washer pump **(see illustration)**.

13 Carefully ease the pump out from the reservoir, and recover its sealing grommet. Wash off any spilt fluid with cold water.

14 Refitting is the reverse of removal, using a new sealing grommet if the original shows signs of damage or deterioration. Refill reservoir and check the pump grommet for leaks on completion.

Windscreen washer jet

15 Open the bonnet and disconnect the washer hose(s) from the relevant jet. Depress the retaining clips and release the jet out of position from the rear edge of the bonnet.

16 On refitting, clip the jet into the bonnet and make sure the hose is reconnected securely; check the operation of the washer jet.

Tailgate washer jet

17 Remove the high-level brake light unit as described in Section 7.

18 Disconnect the washer hose from the jet, then carefully release the retaining clips and unclip the washer jet from the end of the light unit **(see illustration)**. Where applicable, recover the jet O-ring.

19 Refitting is the reverse of removal. Make sure the hose is reconnected securely and check the operation of the washer jet.

Headlight washer jet

20 Carefully prise the jet cover from the bumper, and pull the assembly out to its

full extent. To prevent any damage to the paintwork around the washer jet, use masking tape on the front bumper.

21 Have an assistant grip the washer jet tube with a pair of grips, then depress the retaining clips and pull the jet from the tube.

22 To remove the washer cylinders, remove the front bumper as described in Chapter 11 Section 6, then disconnect the washer tubing, and unclip the cylinders.

23 Refitting is the reverse of removal.

17 Audio unit – removal and refitting

Note: *The following procedures show a basic and a higher range Audio unit, which are typical for the range of equipment fitted by Peugeot/Citroën. There are many types of audio unit fitted depending on model; the type of removal clips (radio keys) will vary also.*

Removal

1 Ensure the audio unit and ignition is switched off.

Basic range audio unit

2 Insert the removal clips (radio keys) into the holes at the sides of the unit until they release the retaining clips. Push the clips outwards to release the unit from the facia **(see illustration)**. If the removal clips are not available, insert a small screwdriver/punch into the holes on each side of the unit to release the clips.

16.18 Release the clips and remove the washer jet

17.2a Insert two pins into each side of the audio unit…

17.2b …to release the clips, then pull the unit from place

17.3 Disconnect the wiring plug connectors

17.4a Unclip the trim panel...

17.4b ...undo the retaining screws...

17.4c ...and remove the upper trim cover

17.5a Disconnect the wiring connectors...

17.5b ...and carefully unclip the trim surround

3 Once both retaining clips have been released, slide the audio unit out of position. Disconnect the wiring connections and aerial lead, then remove the unit from the vehicle **(see illustration)**.

Higher range audio unit

4 Unclip the small trim panel from the top of the unit, then undo the two retaining screws and remove the upper trim cover **(see illustrations)**.
5 Disconnect the wiring connectors from the rear of the switches, then carefully unclip the plastic trim from around the audio unit screen **(see illustrations)**.
6 Insert the removal clips (radio keys) into the holes at the sides of the unit until they release the securing clips. Push the clips outwards to release the unit from the facia **(see illustration)**. If the removal clips are not available, insert a small screwdriver/punch into the holes on each side of the unit to release the clips.
7 Once the retaining clips have been released, slide the audio unit out of position. Disconnect the wiring connections and aerial lead, then remove the unit from the vehicle **(see illustration)**.

Refitting

8 Prior to refitting, reset the unit retaining clips.
9 Securely reconnect the aerial lead and wiring connectors, then slide the unit back into position, taking care not to trap any wiring.

17.6 Insert the removal clips to release the securing clips

17.7 Disconnect the wiring

18.2a Undo the four screws and remove the speaker …

18.2b … then disconnect the wiring connector

18.4a Disconnect the wiring connector…

18.4b …and undo the speaker retaining screws

18.5 Carefully prise the tweeter/speaker from the facia

19.1 Unscrew the aerial mast from the base

18 Loudspeakers – removal and refitting

Removal

Door speakers

1 Remove the door inner trim panel as described in Chapter 11 Section 11.
2 Undo the four screws and remove the speaker from the door (see illustrations), disconnecting the wiring plug as it becomes accessible.

Rear speakers

3 Remove the rear side trim panel, as described in Chapter 11 Section 26.
4 Disconnect the wiring connector from the speaker, then undo the retaining screws and remove the speaker from the side trim panel (see illustrations).

Front tweeter

5 Carefully prise the tweeter from the upper corner of the facia (see illustration).
6 Disconnect the wiring plug connector from the tweeter is withdrawn. Secure the wiring connector to the top of the facia, to prevent losing the wiring inside the facia.

Refitting

7 Refitting is a reversal of removal. Making sure that all wiring connectors are secure and the trim panels are clipped securely in position, with reference to Chapter 11.

19 Radio aerial – removal and refitting

Removal

1 The aerial mast is a screw-fit in its base and is easily removed (see illustration).
2 Remove the interior light unit from the front of the headlining.
3 Undo the retaining nut, disconnect the aerial cable and remove the aerial base out from the roof panel.
4 To remove the aerial cable, trace it back through the headlining and behind the trim panels, then disconnect the wiring plug connector from the control box on the rear pillar. Refer to Chapter 11 Section 26 for information on removal of trim panels.

Refitting

5 Refitting is the reverse of removal.

20 Engine immobiliser and anti-theft alarm system – general information

Note: *This information is applicable only to the systems fitted by Citroën as standard equipment.*

Engine immobiliser

1 An engine immobiliser system is fitted as standard to all models and the system is operated automatically every time the ignition key is inserted/removed.
2 The immobiliser system ensures the vehicle can only be started using the original Peugeot/Citroën ignition key. The key contains an electronic chip (transponder), which is programmed with a code. When the key is inserted into the ignition switch it uses the current present in the sensor ring (which is fitted to the ignition switch housing) to send a signal to the immobiliser electronic control module (ECM). The ECM is incorporated into the built-in systems interface (BSI) unit (see Section 23). The ECM checks this code every time the ignition is switched on. If the key code does not match the ECM code, the ECM will disable the starter, fuel and ignition (as applicable) to prevent the engine being started.
3 When the vehicle is new, a confidential security card is supplied along with the other vehicle documentation. This card contains the security code which your Peugeot/Citroën dealer requires when carrying out any work on the immobiliser system. Keep this card in a safe place at home; never store it in the vehicle. If the ignition key is lost, a new one can be obtained from a Peugeot/Citroën dealer. Take the confidential security card and all the existing keys along to your Peugeot/ Citroën dealer who will supply a new key and reprogramme all the keys with a new security code; this will render the lost key useless.
Caution: Without the confidential security card, it will not be possible to have the keys and immobiliser system reprogrammed.

4 Any problems with the engine immobiliser system should be referred to a Peugeot/Citroën dealer.

Anti-theft alarm system

5 Most models covered in this were also equipped with an anti-theft alarm system as standard equipment. The system was available as an option on all other models. The alarm is automatically armed when the deadlocking is set using the remote central locking transmitter and is disarmed when the doors are unlocked using the remote transmitter. The alarm system has switches on the bonnet, tailgate and each of the doors, and also has ultrasonic sensing, which detects movement inside the vehicle via sensors mounted on either side of the vehicle interior.

6 When the system is activated, the direction indicators will flash continuously for two seconds. **Note:** *If the bonnet, tailgate or one of the doors are not properly closed when the alarm is set, the siren will sound briefly. If the bonnet/tailgate/door (as applicable) is properly closed within 45 seconds the alarm will be armed. If not the alarm will remain disarmed.*

7 If for some reason the remote central locking transmitter fails whilst the alarm is armed, the alarm can be disarmed using the key. To do this, open the door with the key, and then enter the vehicle, noting that the alarm will sound as the door is opened. Insert the key and switch on the ignition, the immobiliser will recognise the key and will switch off the alarm.

8 Depending on model, the ultrasonic sensing facility of the alarm can be switched off, whilst retaining the switched side of the system. With the ignition switched off, depress the alarm switch (mounted on the driver's side of the facia) until the alarm indicator light on the switch is continuously lit. Get out of the vehicle and operate the deadlocking function using the remote transmitter to arm the alarm. The direction indicators will flash as normal but only the switched (door, tailgate and bonnet) side of the alarm system will be operational. This facility is useful as it allows you to leave the windows/sunroof open, and still arm the alarm. If the windows/sunroof are left open with the ultrasonic sensing not switched off, the alarm may be falsely triggered by a gust of wind.

9 Prior to Disconnecting the battery, the alarm system should be disabled; this will prevent the alarm sounding when the battery is disconnected/reconnected. To do this, switch on the ignition then immediately depress and hold the alarm switch for two seconds; the indicator light on the switch should then flash rapidly for approximately three seconds indicating the alarm has been disabled. Switch off the ignition and disconnect the battery.

10 Once the battery has been reconnected, operate the deadlocking with the remote transmitter then unlock the vehicle. The alarm will be set as normal; the next time the deadlocking is set.

11 Should the alarm system become faulty, the vehicle should be taken to a Peugeot/Citroën dealer for examination.

21 Airbag system – general information and precautions

1 The airbag system is triggered in the event of a heavy frontal impact above a predetermined force, depending on the point of impact. The airbag is then inflated within milliseconds, and forms a safety cushion between the cabin occupants and the vehicle interior. This prevents contact between the upper body and vehicle interior, and therefore greatly reduces the risk of injury. The airbag then deflates almost immediately. The control unit also operates the front seat belt tensioner mechanisms at the same time.

2 There is a gyrometer/accelerometer sensor fitted to the floor panel between the two front seats, under the centre console.

3 The side airbags are fitted to the seat back of each front seat. The curtain airbags are fitted behind the windscreen pillars and headlining on each side of the passenger cabin.

4 Every time the ignition is switched on, the airbag control unit performs a self-test. The self-test takes approximately six seconds and during this time the warning light in the instrument panel will be illuminated. After the self-test is complete, the warning light will go out (unless the passenger airbag unit has been deactivated – see paragraph 5). If the warning light fails to come on, remains illuminated after the self-test period, or comes on at any time when the vehicle is being driven, there is a fault in the airbag system. The vehicle should be taken to a Peugeot/Citroën dealer for examination at the earliest possible opportunity.

5 Most vehicles with a passenger airbag are equipped with a disabling switch fitted inside the right-hand side of the glovebox **(see illustration)**. The switch is operated using the ignition key and switches off the passenger

21.5 Location of passenger airbag disabling switch (arrowed)

airbag (it is not possible to disable the driver's or side/curtain airbags) to enable a rear-facing child seat to be installed in the passenger seat. Whilst the passenger airbag is disabled, the airbag warning light on the instrument panel will remain illuminated all the time.

 Warning: Before carrying out any operations on the airbag system, disconnect the battery (see Chapter 5A Section 1) and wait at least five minutes. Remove the centre console (see Chapter 11 Section 27), and then release the retaining clip and disconnect the wiring connector(s) from the airbag control unit. When the operations are complete, securely reconnect the control unit then refit the centre console. Make sure no one is inside the vehicle when the battery is reconnected then, with the driver's door open, switch the ignition on from outside vehicle and check the operation of the airbag warning light.

 Warning: Do not subject the area of the body around the control unit to any form of shock, which could trigger the system.

 Warning: Note that the airbags must not be subjected to temperatures in excess of 100°C. When the airbag is removed, ensure that it is stored the correct way up (padded surface uppermost) to prevent possible inflation.

 Warning: Do not allow any solvents or cleaning agents to contact the airbag assemblies. They must be cleaned using only a damp cloth.

 Warning: The airbags and control unit are both sensitive to impact. If either is dropped or damaged they should be renewed.

 Warning: Disconnect the airbag control unit wiring connector prior to using arc-welding equipment on the vehicle.

 Warning: Never fit a rear-facing child seat to the front passenger seat unless the passenger airbag has been disabled (paragraph 5).

 Warning: Peugeot/Citroën recommend that the airbag units be renewed every ten years.

22 Airbag system components – removal and refitting

 Warning: Refer to the precautions given in Section 21 before carrying out the following operations.

Driver's airbag

1 Disconnect the battery (see Chapter 5A Section 4) and wait at least five minutes.

2 With the wheel in the straight-ahead position and the steering lock engaged, insert

22.2a Insert a thin screwdriver/punch ...

22.2b ... to release the retaining clip
(arrowed) which secures the airbag

22.3a Remove the airbag ...

a screwdriver (or round punch) into the hole in
the lower part of the steering wheel boss, and
push it upwards to release the retaining clips
(see illustrations).
3 Carefully lift the airbag unit away from the
wheel, disconnecting the wiring connectors as
they become accessible **(see illustrations)**.

> ⚠ *Warning: Do not knock or drop the
> airbag unit and store it with its
> padded surface uppermost.*

4 Securely reconnect the wiring connectors
then seat the airbag unit in the steering
wheel, ensuring the wiring does not become
trapped.
5 Fit the airbag unit; press it into place in the
steering wheel until the retaining clips engage.
6 Make sure no one is inside the vehicle then
reconnect the battery. With the driver's door
open, switch the ignition on from outside
vehicle and check the operation of the
warning light.

Passenger's airbag

7 Disconnect the battery and wait at least five
minutes.
8 Remove the passenger side glovebox
assembly, as described in Chapter 11 Section
28.
9 Unclip the small trim panel from below the
heater control panel **(see illustration)**.
10 Working up inside the glovebox aperture,
under the facia panel, undo the four retaining
bolts **(see illustration)**, that are securing the
airbag unit to the vehicle crossmember.
11 Follow the wiring down from the

22.3b ... lift up the locking clip ...

22.3c ... and disconnect the wiring
connector from the airbag

22.3d Disconnect the earth wire

22.9 Unclip the trim panel

passenger airbag unit and disconnect the
wiring connector **(see illustration)**.
12 Carefully unclip the passenger side facia

trim panel, complete with airbag from the
main facia panel **(see illustration)**.
13 With the trim panel and airbag removed,

22.10 Undo the four bolts (arrowed)

22.11 Disconnect the wiring connector for
the passenger airbag

22.12 Unclip the trim panel and airbag from
the facia

22.13a Disconnect the wiring connector

22.13b Unclip the airbag from the trim panel

22.18 Release the locking catch to disconnect the wiring

22.20 Make sure the arrow on the top of the unit is facing forwards

22.24 Location of gyrometer/ accelerometer sensor

22.30 Disconnect the wiring connector and undo the sensor retaining bolt

disconnect the wiring connector from the rear of the airbag and if required unclip the passenger airbag from the facia trim panel **(see illustrations)**.

14 Refitting is the reversal of removal, noting the following points:

15 If removed refit the airbag unit to the rear of the facia trim panel.

16 Ensure the wiring is correctly connected and routed, and the nuts/bolts are securely tightened.

17 The remainder of refitting is the reverse of removal. On completion, make sure no one is inside the vehicle then reconnect the battery. With the door open, switch the ignition on from outside vehicle and check the operation of the warning light.

Airbag control unit

18 Disconnect the battery (see Chapter 5A Section 4) and wait at least five minutes. Remove the centre console (see Chapter 11 Section 27) then release the retaining clip and disconnect the wiring connectors from the airbag control unit **(see illustration)**.

19 Unscrew the control unit retaining nuts, and then remove the control unit from the floor of the vehicle.

20 Refit the control unit, making sure the arrow on the top of the unit is pointing towards the front of the vehicle **(see illustration)**. Refit the control unit retaining nuts and tighten them to the specified torque.

21 Securely reconnect the airbag control unit wiring connectors.

22 Refit the centre console (see Chapter 11

Section 27). Make sure no one is inside the vehicle then reconnect the battery. With the driver's door open, switch the ignition on from outside vehicle and check the operation of the warning light.

Gyrometer/accelerometer sensor

23 The sensor (where fitted) is located under the centre console in front of the handbrake assembly. Remove the centre console as described in Chapter 11 Section 27.

24 Release the retaining clip, and then disconnect the wiring plug **(see illustration)**.

25 Undo the two nuts and remove the sensor.

26 Refitting is a reversal of removal, ensuring the arrow on the top of the sensor points to the front of the vehicle.

Lateral accelerometer sensor

27 Remove the relevant front seat, as described in Chapter 11 Section 24.

28 Remove the B-pillar lower trim panel, as described in Chapter 11 Section 26.

29 Pull back the carpet to gain access to the side airbag sensor (where fitted).

30 Disconnect the wiring connector then undo the retaining bolt and remove the sensor from the inner sill panel **(see illustration)**.

31 Refitting is a reversal of removal, ensuring the bolt is tightened to the specified torque.

Side airbag

32 Removal and refitting of the side airbag units should be entrusted to a Peugeot/ Citroën dealer. The seat must be dismantled to enable the airbag unit to removed/refitted.

Curtain airbag

33 Removal and refitting of the curtain airbag units should be entrusted to a Peugeot/Citroën dealer. The headlining must be partially removed to enable the airbag unit to removed/refitted.

23 Built-in systems interface (BSI) unit/fusebox – general, removal and refitting

General information

1 The built-in systems interface (BSI) unit is an electronic control unit which controls a variety of functions normally controlled by individual control units and relays. The BSI unit is located behind the facia panel on the passenger's side of the facia where it is situated directly behind the glovebox **(see illustration)**. The

23.1 Built in system interface (BSI) unit (arrowed), behind glovebox

23.6 Disconnect the wiring connectors

23.7 Snap off the two retaining clips (arrowed)

23.8 Slide the BSI unit downwards (arrow)

BSI unit controls the following functions (not all functions are fitted to all models).
a) *Direction indicator/hazard warning lights.*
b) *Windscreen/tailgate wiper motors.*
c) *Rear window heating element.*
d) *Immobiliser system.*
e) *Anti-theft alarm system.*
f) *Lights-on/ignition key warning buzzer.*
g) *Central locking/deadlocking, including the remote central locking receiver.*
h) *Door open indicator.*
i) *Courtesy light delay timer.*
j) *Automatic transmission audible warning system.*

2 Should any of the above functions become faulty, first check the condition of the fuses. If this fails to locate the problem, take the vehicle to a Peugeot/Citroën dealer for testing. The only satisfactory way to test the BSI unit is by substitution with another unit that is known to be functioning correctly.

3 There are three levels of BSI unit fitted, depending on specification of vehicle. On the label attached to the BSI unit, there will be two capital letters stamped in the bottom right-hand corner:

BG	Lower range
MG	Mid-range
HG	Upper range

Removal

4 Disconnect the battery (see Chapter 5A Section 4).
5 Remove the passenger side glovebox as described in Chapter 11 Section 28.
6 Release the securing clips and disconnect all of the wiring block connectors from the BSI unit **(see illustration)**. Most of the connectors are colour coded and can only be refitted in one position. Always make a note (or take a picture), as some of the connectors may be the same. Take your time to study the wiring connectors, and release them without using excessive force as they are easily damaged.
7 Fold down the two plastic retaining clips at the lower part of the unit and snap them off **(see illustration)**. Replacement metal spring clips can be purchased from you local Peugeot/Citroen dealer for refitting.
8 Pull the lower part of the BSI unit outwards, and then slide it downwards out from its position in the white plastic housing **(see illustration)**.

Refitting

9 Refitting is the reverse of removal, ensuring the wiring connectors are all securely reconnected and the BSI unit is secured. Secure the lower part of the BSI unit in position using two new metal spring clips, see your local Peugeot/Citroen dealer.

BUILT-IN SYSTEM INTERFACE(BSI1)

FUSE/RELAY	VALUE	DESCRIPTION
F1	15 A	Rear wiper
F2	30 A	Front/Rear locking, unlocking and deadlocking
F3	5 A	Airbag control unit
F4	10 A	Diagnostic socket, Headlight adjusment, Rear-view mirror diming control, Additional fuel pump, control panel, Traction control switch
F5	30 A	Front power windows
F6	30 A	Luggage compartment opening relay
F7	5 A	Interior lights,
F8	20 A	Radio, Tyre pressure monitor control unit, Multifunction display, Control panel, Interior protection control unit, Alarm siren, Trailer control unit, Body control unit
F9	30 A	Front 12v socket, Cigarette lighter, Interior lights, Map reading light
F10	15 A	Upper steering column
F11	15 A	Immobiliser
F12	15 A	Rain and light sensor, Airbag control unit, Trailer control unit
F13	5 A	Fuse and relay bos in engine compartment, Control panel
F14	15 A	parking assistance, hands-free car kit
F15	30 A	Deadlock
F16	-	Not used
F17	40 A	Heated rear windscreen, Heated mirrors

Fuses and relays

NO LOCATION INFORMATION IS AVAILABLE FOR THE FOLLOWING RELAYS

FUSE/RELAY	VALUE	DESCRIPTION
R1	-	Front power windows
R2	-	Rear wiper
R3	-	ACC+
R4A	-	Door unlock relay
R4B	-	Door lock relay
R5A	-	Deadlock relay
R5B	-	Door lock relay
R6	-	Deadlock relay
R7	-	Engine control unit, main relay
R8	-	Heated rear windscreen, Heated mirrors

ENGINE COMPARTMENT FUSEBOX PANEL

Fuses and relays (continued)

FUSE/RELAY	VALUE	DESCRIPTION
F1	20 A	Engine control unit, Cooling fan control unit
F2	15 A	Horns
F3	10 A	Front and rear windscreen washer
F4	20 A	Headlight washer
F5	15 A	Diesel fuel preheater
F6	10 A	ABS/ESP control unit, Double relay, Power steering unit, ESP accelerometer gyroscope, Power steering pump
F7	10 A	Stop switch, Clutch switch
F8	25 A	Starter relay
F9	10 A	Relay 3 protection switch unit, Headlight adjustment
F10	30 A	Injection pump
F11	40 A	Blower control relay
F12	30 A	Front wiper control
F13	40 A	Fuses on the BSI
F14	30 A	Exhaust heat exchanger pump
F15	10 A	Right main beam
F16	10 A	Left main beam
F17	15 A	Left dipped beam
F18	15 A	Right dipped beam
F19	15 A	Air heating
F20	10 A	Charge pressure control solenoid, Water separator sensor, Exhaust heat exchanger solenoid valve, Turbocharger valve
F21	5 A	Cooling fan control unit, Mass airflow meter
MF1	40 A	Blower relay
MF2	40 A/50 A	Trailer relay, Air-conditioning relay
MF3	50 A	Cooling fan
MF4	80 A	Fuses on the BSI
MF5	80 A	Fuses on the BSI
MF6	50 A	ABS motor relay or ESP relay
MF7	40 A	Fuse box in passenger compartment
MF8	30 A	ABS motor relay or ESP relay

NO LOCATION INFORMATION IS AVAILABLE FOR THE FOLLOWING RELAYS

FUSE/RELAY	VALUE	DESCRIPTION
R1	-	Engine control unit, main relay
R2	-	Engine control unit power
R3	-	Air-conditioning relay
R4	-	Windscreen wiper relay(s)
R5	-	Windscreen wiper relay
R6	-	Ignition control
R7	-	Blower
R8	-	Starter relay
R9	-	Windscreen washer front
R10	-	Windscreen washer rear

Fuses and relays (continued)

R11	-	Headlight washer relay
R12	-	Horn relay

SUPPLY CONTROL UNIT

FUSE/RELAY	VALUE	DESCRIPTION
F1	5 A	Battery sensor or Brake light switch
F2	15 A	Diagnostic socket
F3	15 A	Brake light switch or not used
F4	-	Not used
F5	80 A	Power steering pump
F6	70 A	Pre-post heating
F7	100 A	Relat 3 protection switch unit
F8	-	Not used
F9	-	Not used
F10	30 A	Engine management relay or not used

Fuses and relays (continued)

CABIN FUSEBOX

FUSE/RELAY	VALUE	DESCRIPTION
F1	-	Not used
F2	20 A	Heated seats
F3	-	Not used
F4	10 A	Folding mirror
F5	15 A	Accessory socket

RELAY 3 PROTECTION SWITCH UNIT

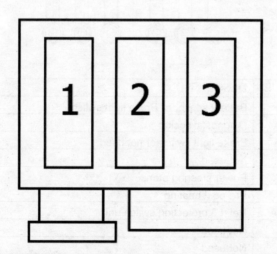

FUSE/RELAY	VALUE	DESCRIPTION
F1	40 A	Blower
F2	40 A	Blower
F3	40 A	Blower

Fuses and relays (continued)

Starting & Charging 1 of 2

Starting & Charging 2 of 2

AC Heating & Cooling

AC Heating & Cooling Automatic Air Conditioning

AC Heating & Cooling Manual Air Conditioning

CAN

ENGINE ECU

9001R 9001R 33
42 42 26 8093 8092N
70V BK 10 8094N 8094 8093 BK 3
3V BK

REFRIGERANT PRESSURE SENSOR

9000F 9001F

AIR BLOWER RELAY
8048 8020

AIR BLOWER MOTOR

IC26 6V BK

EM46D

IC85 6V BK

9000J 9001J

MC4AA
MC46B

MCBSI

REAR AIR BLOWER

BLOWER SPEED CONTROL (IF SEPARATE)
M1A M1B M8098

MC46A

AE809 AE809
IC85 6V BK
ICP9 2V BK

ADDITIONAL AIR CONDITIONING SWITCH

M8098
ICP9 2V BK

8V BK BM01
2V BK 8049

19 MEBSM ME46
MCBSM MEBSI
MC10A
16V GN 6 40V BK 21 24
16V GN 8

AE809 16V GN 8
17,10V BK 4 IC91B
AE809 8051 2 10V GN 7
M

ENGINE COMPARTMENT CONNECTION BOARD-FUSE BOX

MF1

12 15V YE 4 5 28V GY 26 M8060
9018A 8058
2V BK 1
AIR CONDITIONING COMPRESSOR
35

28V GY 11
9017A

8052 IC26 6V BK 1
Z

EVAPORATOR TEMPERATURE SENSOR

BUILT-IN SYSTEM INTERFACE

MF4

DIAGNOSTIC SOCKET
3 8 9029
9028 9028 9031
40V BK 33

16 8052 16 1

CE80

VE01E VE01E

AIR INLET FLAP REDUCTION MOTOR
3 G L2 R
6V BK 4 B2 6V BK 1 C

F9

AIR CONDITIONING CONTROL PANEL (IF SEPARATE)
7 9 808
13 8037 8053
15 9025A
14 9024B 9025B
16 Z01A
IC91A 35V BK
18V WH 16

AIR BLOWER SPEED RESISTOR (IF SEPARATE)
N1

F11

BM04 BM08
16V GY 1 5 2V GY 2
10V BK 1
10V VWH 4
1065A
10V VWH

INSTRUMENTATION CONNECTOR
Z01A

INSTRUMENT PANEL
3 8 8101 8110
12V BN 5 5V VWH 3 2 B1
RG B1 L1 3
M0004 ME51C 12V BN 2
18V VWH 18 ME51C

MF5

8V BK 5
IGNITION SWITCH
1065A
1065B

BB01A 1V

BATTERY TAKE-OFF FUSE BOX
BB02A
MMP
MCP
BATTERY

F7

BF7 3 RELAY SWITCHING AND PROTECTION UNIT
CM00A 28V BN
CM00B
6V BK 4
1V BK 1

F3
F2
F3

8066
8067 8068
M806C M806B

ADDITIONAL AIR CONDITIONING AIR BLOWER RESISTOR
M806C M806B

6V BK 1

AC Heating & Cooling Seat Heating

Power Windows

Power Door locks

*1 Available just for deadlock and automatic locking
*2 Available just for simple central locking

Wiper Washer - Headlamp wash

Wiper Washer - Screen wash

Exterior Lights

*1 With tailgate
*2 Without tailgate

Interior Lights

*1 Left hand drive
*2 Right hand drive

Sound System

Sound System – Telematics

Fuel pump

*1 For engine code: DV6FC, DV6FD, DV6FE
*2 For engine code: DV6AUTED4, DV6BUTED4, DV6BUTED, DV6DTED, DV6DU, DV6ETED, DV6EU, DV6TED4, DV6TED4BU, DV6ATED4, DV6B, DV6C

Notes

Dimensions and weights

Note: *All figures are approximate, and may vary according to model. Refer to manufacturer's data for exact figures.*

Dimensions	MPV	Van
Overall length	4380 mm	4380 mm (short) 4628 mm (long)
Overall height	1801 – 1862 mm	1805 – 1834 mm
#Excluding mirrors	1810 mm	1810 mm
#Including mirrors.	2112 mm	2112 mm
Wheelbase	2728 mm	2728 mm

Weights

Kerb weight :	
MPV	1472 – 1504 kg
Van (short).	1411 – 1430 kg
Van (long)	1459 – 1476 kg
Maximum gross vehicle weight*:	
MPV	1960 – 2205 kg
Van (short).	1960 – 2205 kg
Van (long)	2130 kg
Maximum gross train (vehicle and trailer) weight*:	
MPV	2925 – 3065 kg
Van (short).	2935 – 3135 kg
Van (long)	3100 – 3130 kg

* Refer to the Vehicle Identification Plate for the exact figure for your vehicle – see 'Vehicle Identification Numbers'.

Fuel economy

Although depreciation is still the biggest part of the cost of motoring for most car owners, the cost of fuel is more immediately noticeable. These pages give some tips on how to get the best fuel economy.

Working it out

Manufacturer's figures

Car manufacturers are required by law to provide fuel consumption information on all new vehicles sold. These 'official' figures are obtained by simulating various driving conditions on a rolling road or a test track. Real life conditions are different, so the fuel consumption actually achieved may not bear much resemblance to the quoted figures.

How to calculate it

Many cars now have trip computers which will

display fuel consumption, both instantaneous and average. Refer to the owner's handbook for details of how to use these.

To calculate consumption yourself (and maybe to check that the trip computer is accurate), proceed as follows.

1. Fill up with fuel and note the mileage, or zero the trip recorder.
2. Drive as usual until you need to fill up again.
3. Note the amount of fuel required to refill the tank, and the mileage covered since the previous fill-up.
4. Divide the mileage by the amount of fuel used to obtain the consumption figure.

For example:

Mileage at first fill-up (a) = 27,903
Mileage at second fill-up (b) = 28,346
Mileage covered (b - a) = 443
Fuel required at second fill-up = 48.6 litres

The half-completed changeover to metric units in the UK means that we buy our fuel

in litres, measure distances in miles and talk about fuel consumption in miles per gallon. There are two ways round this: the first is to convert the litres to gallons before doing the calculation (by dividing by 4.546, or see Table 1). So in the example:

48.6 litres ÷ 4.546 = 10.69 gallons
443 miles ÷ 10.69 gallons = 41.4 mpg

The second way is to calculate the consumption in miles per litre, then multiply that figure by 4.546 (or see Table 2).

So in the example, fuel consumption is:

443 miles ÷ 48.6 litres = 9.1 mpl
9.1 mpl x 4.546 = 41.4 mpg

The rest of Europe expresses fuel consumption in litres of fuel required to travel 100 km (l/100 km). For interest, the conversions are given in Table 3. In practice it doesn't matter what units you use, provided you know what your normal consumption is and can spot if it's getting better or worse.

Table 1: conversion of litres to Imperial gallons

litres	1	2	3	4	5	10	20	30	40	50	60	70
gallons	0.22	0.44	0.66	0.88	1.10	2.24	4.49	6.73	8.98	11.22	13.47	15.71

Table 2: conversion of miles per litre to miles per gallon

miles per litre	5	6	7	8	9	10	11	12	13	14
miles per gallon	23	27	32	36	41	46	50	55	59	64

Table 3: conversion of litres per 100 km to miles per gallon

litres per 100 km	4	4.5	5	5.5	6	6.5	7	8	9	10
miles per gallon	71	63	56	51	47	43	40	35	31	28

Maintenance

A well-maintained car uses less fuel and creates less pollution. In particular:

Filters

Change air and fuel filters at the specified intervals.

Oil

Use a good quality oil of the lowest viscosity specified by the vehicle manufacturer (see *Lubricants and fluids*). Check the level often and be careful not to overfill.

Spark plugs

When applicable, renew at the specified intervals.

Tyres

Check tyre pressures regularly. Under-inflated tyres have an increased rolling resistance. It is generally safe to use the higher pressures specified for full load conditions even when not fully laden, but keep an eye on the centre band of tread for signs of wear due to over-inflation.

When buying new tyres, consider the 'fuel saving' models which most manufacturers include in their ranges.

Driving style

Acceleration

Acceleration uses more fuel than driving at a steady speed. The best technique with modern cars is to accelerate reasonably briskly to the desired speed, changing up through the gears as soon as possible without making the engine labour.

Air conditioning

Air conditioning absorbs quite a bit of energy from the engine – typically 3 kW (4 hp) or so. The effect on fuel consumption is at its worst in slow traffic. Switch it off when not required.

Anticipation

Drive smoothly and try to read the traffic flow so as to avoid unnecessary acceleration and braking.

Automatic transmission

When accelerating in an automatic, avoid depressing the throttle so far as to make the transmission hold onto lower gears at higher speeds. Don't use the 'Sport' setting, if applicable.

When stationary with the engine running, select 'N' or 'P'. When moving, keep your left foot away from the brake.

Braking

Braking converts the car's energy of motion into heat – essentially, it is wasted. Obviously some braking is always going to be necessary, but with good anticipation it is surprising how much can be avoided, especially on routes that you know well.

Carshare

Consider sharing lifts to work or to the shops. Even once a week will make a difference.

Electrical loads

Electricity is 'fuel' too; the alternator which charges the battery does so by converting some of the engine's energy of motion into electrical energy. The more electrical accessories are in use, the greater the load on the alternator. Switch off big consumers like the heated rear window when not required.

Freewheeling

Freewheeling (coasting) in neutral with the engine switched off is dangerous. The effort required to operate power-assisted brakes and steering increases when the engine is not running, with a potential lack of control in emergency situations.

In any case, modern fuel injection systems automatically cut off the engine's fuel supply on the overrun (moving and in gear, but with the accelerator pedal released).

Gadgets

Bolt-on devices claiming to save fuel have been around for nearly as long as the motor car itself. Those which worked were rapidly adopted as standard equipment by the vehicle manufacturers. Others worked only in certain situations, or saved fuel only at the expense of unacceptable effects on performance, driveability or the life of engine components.

The most effective fuel saving gadget is the driver's right foot.

Journey planning

Combine (eg) a trip to the supermarket with a visit to the recycling centre and the DIY store, rather than making separate journeys.

When possible choose a travelling time outside rush hours.

Load

The more heavily a car is laden, the greater the energy required to accelerate it to a given speed. Remove heavy items which you don't need to carry.

One load which is often overlooked is the contents of the fuel tank. A tankful of fuel (55 litres / 12 gallons) weighs 45 kg (100 lb) or so. Just half filling it may be worthwhile.

Lost?

At the risk of stating the obvious, if you're going somewhere new, have details of the route to hand. There's not much point in

achieving record mpg if you also go miles out of your way.

Parking

If possible, carry out any reversing or turning manoeuvres when you arrive at a parking space so that you can drive straight out when you leave. Manoeuvering when the engine is cold uses a lot more fuel.

Driving around looking for free on-street parking may cost more in fuel than buying a car park ticket.

Premium fuel

Most major oil companies (and some supermarkets) have premium grades of fuel which are several pence a litre dearer than the standard grades. Reports vary, but the consensus seems to be that if these fuels improve economy at all, they do not do so by enough to justify their extra cost.

Roof rack

When loading a roof rack, try to produce a wedge shape with the narrow end at the front. Any cover should be securely fastened – if it flaps it's creating turbulence and absorbing energy.

Remove roof racks and boxes when not in use – they increase air resistance and can create a surprising amount of noise.

Short journeys

The engine is at its least efficient, and wear is highest, during the first few miles after a cold start. Consider walking, cycling or using public transport.

Speed

The engine is at its most efficient when running at a steady speed and load at the rpm where it develops maximum torque. (You can find this figure in the car's handbook.) For most cars this corresponds to between 55 and 65 mph in top gear.

Above the optimum cruising speed, fuel consumption starts to rise quite sharply. A car travelling at 80 mph will typically be using 30% more fuel than at 60 mph.

Supermarket fuel

It may be cheap but is it any good? In the UK all supermarket fuel must meet the relevant British Standard. The major oil companies will say that their branded fuels have better additive packages which may stop carbon and other deposits building up. A reasonable compromise might be to use one tank of branded fuel to three or four from the supermarket.

Switch off when stationary

Switch off the engine if you look like being stationary for more than 30 seconds or so. This is good for the environment as well as for your pocket. Be aware though that frequent restarts are hard on the battery and the starter motor.

Windows

Driving with the windows open increases air turbulence around the vehicle. Closing the windows promotes smooth airflow and

reduced resistance. The faster you go, the more significant this is.

And finally . . .

Driving techniques associated with good fuel economy tend to involve moderate acceleration and low top speeds. Be considerate to the needs of other road users who may need to make brisker progress; even if you do not agree with them this is not an excuse to be obstructive.

Safety must always take precedence over economy, whether it is a question of accelerating hard to complete an overtaking manoeuvre, killing your speed when confronted with a potential hazard or switching the lights on when it starts to get dark.

Conversion factors

Length (distance)

Inches (in)	x 25.4	= Millimetres (mm)	x 0.0394	= Inches (in)
Feet (ft)	x 0.305	= Metres (m)	x 3.281	= Feet (ft)
Miles	x 1.609	= Kilometres (km)	x 0.621	= Miles

Volume (capacity)

Cubic inches (cu in; in^3)	x 16.387	= Cubic centimetres (cc; cm^3)	x 0.061	= Cubic inches (cu in; in^3)
Imperial pints (Imp pt)	x 0.568	= Litres (l)	x 1.76	= Imperial pints (Imp pt)
Imperial quarts (Imp qt)	x 1.137	= Litres (l)	x 0.88	= Imperial quarts (Imp qt)
Imperial quarts (Imp qt)	x 1.201	= US quarts (US qt)	x 0.833	= Imperial quarts (Imp qt)
US quarts (US qt)	x 0.946	= Litres (l)	x 1.057	= US quarts (US qt)
Imperial gallons (Imp gal)	x 4.546	= Litres (l)	x 0.22	= Imperial gallons (Imp gal)
Imperial gallons (Imp gal)	x 1.201	= US gallons (US gal)	x 0.833	= Imperial gallons (Imp gal)
US gallons (US gal)	x 3.785	= Litres (l)	x 0.264	= US gallons (US gal)

Mass (weight)

Ounces (oz)	x 28.35	= Grams (g)	x 0.035	= Ounces (oz)
Pounds (lb)	x 0.454	= Kilograms (kg)	x 2.205	= Pounds (lb)

Force

Ounces-force (ozf; oz)	x 0.278	= Newtons (N)	x 3.6	= Ounces-force (ozf; oz)
Pounds-force (lbf; lb)	x 4.448	= Newtons (N)	x 0.225	= Pounds-force (lbf; lb)
Newtons (N)	x 0.1	= Kilograms-force (kgf; kg)	x 9.81	= Newtons (N)

Pressure

Pounds-force per square inch (psi; lbf/in^2; lb/in^2)	x 0.070	= Kilograms-force per square centimetre (kgf/cm^2; kg/cm^2)	x 14.223	= Pounds-force per square inch (psi; lbf/in^2; lb/in^2)
Pounds-force per square inch (psi; lbf/in^2; lb/in^2)	x 0.068	= Atmospheres (atm)	x 14.696	= Pounds-force per square inch (psi; lbf/in^2; lb/in^2)
Pounds-force per square inch (psi; lbf/in^2; lb/in^2)	x 0.069	= Bars	x 14.5	= Pounds-force per square inch (psi; lbf/in^2; lb/in^2)
Pounds-force per square inch (psi; lbf/in^2; lb/in^2)	x 6.895	= Kilopascals (kPa)	x 0.145	= Pounds-force per square inch (psi; lbf/in^2; lb/in^2)
Kilopascals (kPa)	x 0.01	= Kilograms-force per square centimetre (kgf/cm^2; kg/cm^2)	x 98.1	= Kilopascals (kPa)
Millibar (mbar)	x 100	= Pascals (Pa)	x 0.01	= Millibar (mbar)
Millibar (mbar)	x 0.0145	= Pounds-force per square inch (psi; lbf/in^2; lb/in^2)	x 68.947	= Millibar (mbar)
Millibar (mbar)	x 0.75	= Millimetres of mercury (mmHg)	x 1.333	= Millibar (mbar)
Millibar (mbar)	x 0.401	= Inches of water (inH$_2$O)	x 2.491	= Millibar (mbar)
Millimetres of mercury (mmHg)	x 0.535	= Inches of water (inH$_2$O)	x 1.868	= Millimetres of mercury (mmHg)
Inches of water (inH$_2$O)	x 0.036	= Pounds-force per square inch (psi; lbf/in^2; lb/in^2)	x 27.68	= Inches of water (inH$_2$O)

Torque (moment of force)

Pounds-force inches (lbf in; lb in)	x 1.152	= Kilograms-force centimetre (kgf cm; kg cm)	x 0.868	= Pounds-force inches (lbf in; lb in)
Pounds-force inches (lbf in; lb in)	x 0.113	= Newton metres (Nm)	x 8.85	= Pounds-force inches (lbf in; lb in)
Pounds-force inches (lbf in; lb in)	x 0.083	= Pounds-force feet (lbf ft; lb ft)	x 12	= Pounds-force inches (lbf in; lb in)
Pounds-force feet (lbf ft; lb ft)	x 0.138	= Kilograms-force metres (kgf m; kg m)	x 7.233	= Pounds-force feet (lbf ft; lb ft)
Pounds-force feet (lbf ft; lb ft)	x 1.356	= Newton metres (Nm)	x 0.738	= Pounds-force feet (lbf ft; lb ft)
Newton metres (Nm)	x 0.102	= Kilograms-force metres (kgf m; kg m)	x 9.804	= Newton metres (Nm)

Power

Horsepower (hp)	x 745.7	= Watts (W)	x 0.0013	= Horsepower (hp)

Velocity (speed)

Miles per hour (miles/hr; mph)	x 1.609	= Kilometres per hour (km/hr; kph)	x 0.621	= Miles per hour (miles/hr; mph)

Fuel consumption*

Miles per gallon, Imperial (mpg)	x 0.354	= Kilometres per litre (km/l)	x 2.825	= Miles per gallon, Imperial (mpg)
Miles per gallon, US (mpg)	x 0.425	= Kilometres per litre (km/l)	x 2.352	= Miles per gallon, US (mpg)

Temperature

Degrees Fahrenheit = (°C x 1.8) + 32   Degrees Celsius (Degrees Centigrade; °C) = (°F - 32) x 0.56

It is common practice to convert from miles per gallon (mpg) to litres/100 kilometres (l/100km), where mpg x l/100 km = 282

Spare parts are available from many sources, including maker's appointed garages, accessory shops, and motor factors. To be sure of obtaining the correct parts, it will sometimes be necessary to quote the vehicle identification number. If possible, it can also be useful to take the old parts along for positive identification. Items such as starter motors and alternators may be available under a service exchange scheme – any parts returned should be clean.

Our advice regarding spare parts is as follows.

Officially appointed garages

This is the best source of parts which are peculiar to your car, and which are not otherwise generally available (eg, badges, interior trim, certain body panels, etc). It is also the only place at which you should buy parts if the car is still under warranty.

Accessory shops

These are very good places to buy materials and components needed for the maintenance of your car (oil, air and fuel filters, light bulbs, drivebelts, greases, brake pads, touch-up paint, etc). Components of this nature sold by a reputable shop are usually of the same standard as those used by the car manufacturer.

Besides components, these shops also sell tools and general accessories, usually have convenient opening hours, charge lower prices, and can often be found close to home. Some accessory shops have parts counters where components needed for almost any repair job can be purchased or ordered.

Motor factors

Good factors will stock all the more important components which wear out comparatively quickly, and can sometimes supply individual components needed for the overhaul of a larger assembly (eg, brake seals and hydraulic parts, bearing shells, pistons, valves). They may also handle work such as cylinder block reboring, crankshaft regrinding, etc.

Engine reconditioners

These specialise in engine overhaul and can also supply components. It is recommended that the establishment is a member of the Federation of Engine Re-Manufacturers, or a similar society.

Tyre and exhaust specialists

These outlets may be independent, or members of a local or national chain. They frequently offer competitive prices when compared with a main dealer or local garage, but it will pay to obtain several quotes before making a decision. When researching prices, also ask what extras may be added – for instance fitting a new valve, balancing the wheel and tyre disposal all both commonly charged on top of the price of a new tyre.

Other sources

Beware of parts or materials obtained from market stalls, car boot sales, on-line auctions or similar outlets. Such items are not invariably sub-standard, but there is little chance of compensation if they do prove unsatisfactory. In the case of safety-critical components such as brake pads, there is the risk not only of financial loss, but also of an accident causing injury or death.

Second-hand components or assemblies obtained from a car breaker can be a good buy in some circumstances, but this sort of purchase is best made by the experienced DIY mechanic.

Vehicle identification

Modifications are a continuing and unpublicised process in vehicle manufacture, quite apart from major model changes. Spare parts manuals and lists are compiled upon a numerical basis, the individual vehicle identification numbers being essential for correct identification of the part concerned.

When ordering spare parts, always give as much information as possible. Quote the car model, year of manufacture, body and engine numbers, but most importantly, the after sales replacement parts number (referred to as RPO number: Replacement Parts Organisation number).

The vehicle production code number is on a label on the driver's door B-pillar **(see illustration)**. The code provides peugeot/Citroën dealers with details of the exact build date, model and where it was made. The first five numbers are the RPO number and then the next two letters/numbers are the factory code (eg, 88 is Mulhouse factory). The vehicle paint code is also given here (eg, EZR is Arctic Steel), along with the tyre pressures.

The vehicle identification number (VIN) is stamped onto right-hand upper strut inner wing panel, in the engine compartment **(see illustration)**.

The vehicle identification number (VIN) is also on a plate/label on the right-hand inner wing engine mounting bracket on early models. The plate carries the VIN and vehicle weight information **(see illustration)**. The vehicle identification number is also stamped onto a plate visible through the base of the windscreen **(see illustration)**.

The engine number is stamped on the base of the cylinder block at the front, it is on the flat surface located on the right-hand side of the oil filter/cooler.

Vehicle parts and production code (A) and paint code (B) on driver's A-pillar

On early models, the vehicle identification number (VIN) is also on a label on the right-hand engine mounting bracket …

The vehicle identification number (VIN) is stamped on the right-hand inner wing panel

… and on a plate visible through the base of the windscreen

Whenever servicing, repair or overhaul work is carried out on the car or its components, observe the following procedures and instructions. This will assist in carrying out the operation efficiently and to a professional standard of workmanship.

Joint mating faces and gaskets

When separating components at their mating faces, never insert screwdrivers or similar implements into the joint between the faces in order to prise them apart. This can cause severe damage which results in oil leaks, coolant leaks, etc upon reassembly. Separation is usually achieved by tapping along the joint with a soft-faced hammer in order to break the seal. However, note that this method may not be suitable where dowels are used for component location.

Where a gasket is used between the mating faces of two components, a new one must be fitted on reassembly; fit it dry unless otherwise stated in the repair procedure. Make sure that the mating faces are clean and dry, with all traces of old gasket removed. When cleaning a joint face, use a tool which is unlikely to score or damage the face, and remove any burrs or nicks with an oilstone or fine file.

Make sure that tapped holes are cleaned with a pipe cleaner, and keep them free of jointing compound, if this is being used, unless specifically instructed otherwise.

Ensure that all orifices, channels or pipes are clear, and blow through them, preferably using compressed air.

Oil seals

Oil seals can be removed by levering them out with a wide flat-bladed screwdriver or similar implement. Alternatively, a number of self-tapping screws may be screwed into the seal, and these used as a purchase for pliers or some similar device in order to pull the seal free.

Whenever an oil seal is removed from its working location, either individually or as part of an assembly, it should be renewed.

The very fine sealing lip of the seal is easily damaged, and will not seal if the surface it contacts is not completely clean and free from scratches, nicks or grooves. If the original sealing surface of the component cannot be restored, and the manufacturer has not made provision for slight relocation of the seal relative to the sealing surface, the component should be renewed.

Protect the lips of the seal from any surface which may damage them in the course of fitting. Use tape or a conical sleeve where possible. Where indicated, lubricate the seal lips with oil before fitting and, on dual-lipped seals, fill the space between the lips with grease.

Unless otherwise stated, oil seals must be fitted with their sealing lips toward the lubricant to be sealed.

Use a tubular drift or block of wood of the appropriate size to install the seal and, if the seal housing is shouldered, drive the seal down to the shoulder. If the seal housing is unshouldered, the seal should be fitted with its face flush with the housing top face (unless otherwise instructed).

Screw threads and fastenings

Seized nuts, bolts and screws are quite a common occurrence where corrosion has set in, and the use of penetrating oil or releasing fluid will often overcome this problem if the offending item is soaked for a while before attempting to release it. The use of an impact driver may also provide a means of releasing such stubborn fastening devices, when used in conjunction with the appropriate screwdriver bit or socket. If none of these methods works, it may be necessary to resort to the careful application of heat, or the use of a hacksaw or nut splitter device. Before resorting to extreme methods, check that you are not dealing with a left-hand thread!

Studs are usually removed by locking two nuts together on the threaded part, and then using a spanner on the lower nut to unscrew the stud. Studs or bolts which have broken off below the surface of the component in which they are mounted can sometimes be removed using a stud extractor.

Always ensure that a blind tapped hole is completely free from oil, grease, water or other fluid before installing the bolt or stud. Failure to do this could cause the housing to crack due to the hydraulic action of the bolt or stud as it is screwed in.

For some screw fastenings, notably cylinder head bolts or nuts, torque wrench settings are no longer specified for the latter stages of tightening, "angle-tightening" being called up instead. Typically, a fairly low torque wrench setting will be applied to the bolts/nuts in the correct sequence, followed by one or more stages of tightening through specified angles.

When checking or retightening a nut or bolt to a specified torque setting, slacken the nut or bolt by a quarter of a turn, and then retighten to the specified setting. However, this should not be attempted where angular tightening has been used.

Locknuts, locktabs and washers

Any fastening which will rotate against a component or housing during tightening should always have a washer between it and the relevant component or housing.

Spring or split washers should always be renewed when they are used to lock a critical component such as a big-end bearing retaining bolt or nut. Locktabs which are folded over to retain a nut or bolt should always be renewed.

Self-locking nuts can be re-used in non-critical areas, providing resistance can be felt when the locking portion passes over the bolt or stud thread. However, it should be noted that self-locking stiffnuts tend to lose their effectiveness after long periods of use, and should then be renewed as a matter of course.

Split pins must always be replaced with new ones of the correct size for the hole.

When thread-locking compound is found on the threads of a fastener which is to be re-used, it should be cleaned off with a wire brush and solvent, and fresh compound applied on reassembly.

Special tools

Some repair procedures in this manual entail the use of special tools such as a press, two or three-legged pullers, spring compressors, etc. Wherever possible, suitable readily-available alternatives to the manufacturer's special tools are described, and are shown in use. In some instances, where no alternative is possible, it has been necessary to resort to the use of a manufacturer's tool, and this has been done for reasons of safety as well as the efficient completion of the repair operation. Unless you are highly-skilled and have a thorough understanding of the procedures described, never attempt to bypass the use of any special tool when the procedure described specifies its use. Not only is there a very great risk of personal injury, but expensive damage could be caused to the components involved.

Environmental considerations

When disposing of used engine oil, brake fluid, antifreeze, etc, give due consideration to any detrimental environmental effects. Do not, for instance, pour any of the above liquids down drains into the general sewage system, or onto the ground to soak away, as this is likely to pollute your local environment. Many local council refuse tips provide a facility for waste oil disposal, as do some garages. You can find your nearest disposal point by calling the Environment Agency on 03708 506 506 or by visiting www.oilbankline.org.uk.

Note: It is illegal and anti-social to dump oil down the drain. To find the location of your local oil recycling bank, call 03708 506 506 or visit www.oilbankline.org.uk.

The jack supplied with the vehicle should only be used for changing the roadwheels – see Wheel changing at the front of this manual. When carrying out any other kind of work, raise the vehicle using a hydraulic (or 'trolley') jack, and always supplement the jack with axle stands at the vehicle jacking points.

When using a hydraulic jack or axle stands, always position the jack head or axle stand head under one of the relevant jacking points; the jacking point is the area below the slot in the sill **(see illustration)**.

Do not attempt to jack the vehicle under the front crossmember, rear axle, engine, transmission or any of the suspension components.

The jack supplied with the vehicle locates at the jacking points on the underside of the sills – see Wheel changing. Ensure that the jack head is correctly engaged before attempting to raise the vehicle.

Never work under, around, or near a raised vehicle, unless it is adequately supported in at least two places.

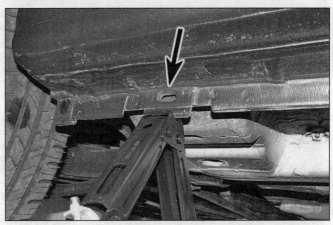

The jacking point is below the slot in the side of the sill

Introduction

A selection of good tools is a fundamental requirement for anyone contemplating the maintenance and repair of a motor vehicle. For the owner who does not possess any, their purchase will prove a considerable expense, offsetting some of the savings made by doing-it-yourself. However, provided that the tools purchased meet the relevant national safety standards and are of good quality, they will last for many years and prove an extremely worthwhile investment.

To help the average owner to decide which tools are needed to carry out the various tasks detailed in this manual, we have compiled three lists of tools under the following headings: *Maintenance and minor repair*, *Repair and overhaul*, and *Special*. Newcomers to practical mechanics should start off with the *Maintenance and minor repair* tool kit, and confine themselves to the simpler jobs around the vehicle. Then, as confidence and experience grow, more difficult tasks can be undertaken, with extra tools being purchased as, and when, they are needed. In this way, a *Maintenance and minor repair* tool kit can be built up into a *Repair and overhaul* tool kit over a considerable period of time, without any major cash outlays. The experienced do-it-yourselfer will have a tool kit good enough for most repair and overhaul procedures, and will add tools from the *Special* category when it is felt that the expense is justified by the amount of use to which these tools will be put.

Maintenance and minor repair tool kit

The tools given in this list should be considered as a minimum requirement if routine maintenance, servicing and minor repair operations are to be undertaken. We recommend the purchase of combination spanners (ring one end, open-ended the other); although more expensive than open-ended ones, they do give the advantages of both types of spanner.

☐ *Combination spanners:*
  Metric - 8 to 19 mm inclusive
☐ *Adjustable spanner - 35 mm jaw (approx.)*
☐ *Spark plug spanner (with rubber insert) - petrol models*
☐ *Spark plug gap adjustment tool - petrol models*
☐ *Set of feeler gauges*
☐ *Brake bleed nipple spanner*
☐ *Screwdrivers:*
  Flat blade - 100 mm long x 6 mm dia
  Cross blade - 100 mm long x 6 mm dia
  Torx - various sizes (not all vehicles)
☐ *Combination pliers*
☐ *Hacksaw (junior)*
☐ *Tyre pump*
☐ *Tyre pressure gauge*
☐ *Oil can*
☐ *Oil filter removal tool (if applicable)*
☐ *Fine emery cloth*
☐ *Wire brush (small)*
☐ *Funnel (medium size)*
☐ *Sump drain plug key (not all vehicles)*

Repair and overhaul tool kit

These tools are virtually essential for anyone undertaking any major repairs to a motor vehicle, and are additional to those given in the *Maintenance and minor repair* list. Included in this list is a comprehensive set of sockets. Although these are expensive, they will be found invaluable as they are so versatile - particularly if various drives are included in the set. We recommend the half-inch square-drive type, as this can be used with most proprietary torque wrenches.

The tools in this list will sometimes need to be supplemented by tools from the *Special* list:

☐ *Sockets to cover range in previous list (including Torx sockets)*
☐ *Reversible ratchet drive (for use with sockets)*
☐ *Extension piece, 250 mm (for use with sockets)*
☐ *Universal joint (for use with sockets)*
☐ *Flexible handle or sliding T "breaker bar" (for use with sockets)*
☐ *Torque wrench (for use with sockets)*
☐ *Self-locking grips*
☐ *Ball pein hammer*
☐ *Soft-faced mallet (plastic or rubber)*
☐ *Screwdrivers:*
  Flat blade - long & sturdy, short (chubby), and narrow (electrician's) types
  Cross blade – long & sturdy, and short (chubby) types
☐ *Pliers:*
  Long-nosed
  Side cutters (electrician's)
  Circlip (internal and external)
☐ *Cold chisel - 25 mm*
☐ *Scriber*
☐ *Scraper*
☐ *Centre-punch*
☐ *Pin punch*
☐ *Hacksaw*
☐ *Brake hose clamp*
☐ *Brake/clutch bleeding kit*
☐ *Selection of twist drills*
☐ *Steel rule/straight-edge*
☐ *Allen keys (inc. splined/Torx type)*
☐ *Selection of files*
☐ *Wire brush*
☐ *Axle stands*
☐ *Jack (strong trolley or hydraulic type)*
☐ *Light with extension lead*
☐ *Universal electrical multi-meter*

Sockets and reversible ratchet drive

Brake bleeding kit

Torx key, socket and bit

Hose clamp

Angular-tightening gauge

Special tools

The tools in this list are those which are not used regularly, are expensive to buy, or which need to be used in accordance with their manufacturers' instructions. Unless relatively difficult mechanical jobs are undertaken frequently, it will not be economic to buy many of these tools. Where this is the case, you could consider clubbing together with friends (or joining a motorists' club) to make a joint purchase, or borrowing the tools against a deposit from a local garage or tool hire specialist.

The following list contains only those tools and instruments freely available to the public, and not those special tools produced by the vehicle manufacturer specifically for its dealer network. You will find occasional references to these manufacturers' special tools in the text of this manual. Generally, an alternative method of doing the job without the vehicle manufacturers' special tool is given. However, sometimes there is no alternative to using them. Where this is the case and the relevant tool cannot be bought or borrowed, you will have to entrust the work to a dealer.

- [ ] *Angular-tightening gauge*
- [ ] *Valve spring compressor*
- [ ] *Valve grinding tool*
- [ ] *Piston ring compressor*
- [ ] *Piston ring removal/installation tool*
- [ ] *Cylinder bore hone*
- [ ] *Balljoint separator*
- [ ] *Coil spring compressors (where applicable)*
- [ ] *Two/three-legged hub and bearing puller*
- [ ] *Impact screwdriver*
- [ ] *Micrometer and/or vernier calipers*
- [ ] *Dial gauge*
- [ ] *Tachometer*
- [ ] *Fault code reader*
- [ ] *Cylinder compression gauge*
- [ ] *Hand-operated vacuum pump and gauge*
- [ ] *Clutch plate alignment set*
- [ ] *Brake shoe steady spring cup removal tool*
- [ ] *Bush and bearing removal/installation set*
- [ ] *Stud extractors*
- [ ] *Tap and die set*
- [ ] *Lifting tackle*

Buying tools

Reputable motor accessory shops and superstores often offer excellent quality tools at discount prices, so it pays to shop around.

Remember, you don't have to buy the most expensive items on the shelf, but it is always advisable to steer clear of the very cheap tools. Beware of 'bargains' offered on market stalls, on-line or at car boot sales. There are plenty of good tools around at reasonable prices, but always aim to purchase items which meet the relevant national safety standards. If in doubt, ask the proprietor or manager of the shop for advice before making a purchase.

Care and maintenance of tools

Having purchased a reasonable tool kit, it is necessary to keep the tools in a clean and serviceable condition. After use, always wipe off any dirt, grease and metal particles using a clean, dry cloth, before putting the tools away. Never leave them lying around after they have been used. A simple tool rack on the garage or workshop wall for items such as screwdrivers and pliers is a good idea. Store all normal spanners and sockets in a metal box. Any measuring instruments, gauges, meters, etc, must be carefully stored where they cannot be damaged or become rusty.

Take a little care when tools are used. Hammer heads inevitably become marked, and screwdrivers lose the keen edge on their blades from time to time. A little timely attention with emery cloth or a file will soon restore items like this to a good finish.

Working facilities

Not to be forgotten when discussing tools is the workshop itself. If anything more than routine maintenance is to be carried out, a suitable working area becomes essential.

It is appreciated that many an owner-mechanic is forced by circumstances to remove an engine or similar item without the benefit of a garage or workshop. Having done this, any repairs should always be done under the cover of a roof.

Wherever possible, any dismantling should be done on a clean, flat workbench or table at a suitable working height.

Any workbench needs a vice; one with a jaw opening of 100 mm is suitable for most jobs. As mentioned previously, some clean dry storage space is also required for tools, as well as for any lubricants, cleaning fluids, touch-up paints etc, which become necessary.

Another item which may be required, and which has a much more general usage, is an electric drill with a chuck capacity of at least 8 mm. This, together with a good range of twist drills, is virtually essential for fitting accessories.

Last, but not least, always keep a supply of old newspapers and clean, lint-free rags available, and try to keep any working area as clean as possible.

Micrometers

Dial test indicator ("dial gauge")

Oil filter removal tool (strap wrench type)

Compression tester

Bearing puller

This is a guide to getting your vehicle through the MOT test. Obviously it will not be possible to examine the vehicle to the same standard as the professional MOT tester. However, working through the following checks will enable you to identify any problem areas before submitting the vehicle for the test.

It has only been possible to summarise the test requirements here, based on the regulations in force at the time of printing. Test standards are becoming increasingly stringent, although there are some exemptions for older vehicles.

An assistant will be needed to help carry out some of these checks.

The checks have been sub-divided into four categories, as follows:

1 Checks carried out **FROM THE DRIVER'S SEAT**

2 Checks carried out **WITH THE VEHICLE ON THE GROUND**

3 Checks carried out **WITH THE VEHICLE RAISED AND THE WHEELS FREE TO TURN**

4 Checks carried out on **YOUR VEHICLE'S EXHAUST EMISSION SYSTEM**

---

1 Checks carried out **FROM THE DRIVER'S SEAT**

Handbrake (parking brake)

☐ Test the operation of the handbrake. Excessive travel (too many clicks) indicates incorrect brake or cable adjustment.
☐ Check that the handbrake cannot be released by tapping the lever sideways. Check the security of the lever mountings.

☐ If the parking brake is foot-operated, check that the pedal is secure and without excessive travel, and that the release mechanism operates correctly.
☐ Where applicable, test the operation of the electronic handbrake. The brake should engage and disengage without excessive delay. If the warning light does not extinguish when the brake is disengaged, this could indicate a fault which will need further investigation.

Footbrake

☐ Depress the brake pedal and check that it does not creep down to the floor, indicating a master cylinder fault. Release the pedal, wait a few seconds, then depress it again. If the pedal travels nearly to the floor before firm resistance is felt, brake adjustment or repair is necessary. If the pedal feels spongy, there is air in the hydraulic system which must be removed by bleeding.

☐ Check that the brake pedal is secure and in good condition. Check also for signs of fluid leaks on the pedal, floor or carpets, which would indicate failed seals in the brake master cylinder.
☐ Check the servo unit (when applicable) by operating the brake pedal several times, then keeping the pedal depressed and starting the engine. As the engine starts, the pedal will move down slightly. If not, the vacuum hose or the servo itself may be faulty.

Steering wheel and column

☐ Examine the steering wheel for fractures or looseness of the hub, spokes or rim.
☐ Move the steering wheel from side to side and then up and down. Check that the steering wheel is not loose on the column, indicating wear or a loose retaining nut. Continue moving the steering wheel as before, but also turn it slightly from left to right.

☐ Check that the steering wheel is not loose on the column, and that there is no abnormal movement of the steering wheel, indicating wear in the column support bearings or couplings.
☐ Check that the ignition lock (where fitted) engages and disengages correctly.
☐ Steering column adjustment mechanisms (where fitted) must be able to lock the column securely in place with no play evident.

Windscreen, mirrors and sunvisor

☐ The windscreen must be free of cracks or other significant damage within the driver's field of view. (Small stone chips are acceptable.) Rear view mirrors must be secure, intact, and capable of being adjusted.

☐ The driver's sunvisor must be capable of being stored in the "up" position.

Seat belts and seats

Note: *The following checks are applicable to all seat belts, front and rear.*

☐ Examine the webbing of all the belts (including rear belts if fitted) for cuts, serious fraying or deterioration. Fasten and unfasten each belt to check the buckles. If applicable, check the retracting mechanism. Check the security of all seat belt mountings accessible from inside the vehicle, ensuring any height adjustable mountings lock securely in place.

☐ Seat belts with pre-tensioners, once activated, have a "flag" or similar showing on the seat belt stalk. This, in itself, is not a reason for test failure.

☐ The front seats themselves must be securely attached and the backrests must lock in the upright position.

Doors

☐ Both front doors must be able to be opened and closed from outside and inside, and must latch securely when closed.

Bonnet and boot/tailgate

☐ The bonnet and boot/tailgate must latch securely when closed.

2 Checks carried out WITH THE VEHICLE ON THE GROUND

Vehicle identification

☐ Number plates must be in good condition, secure and legible, with letters and numbers correctly spaced – spacing at (**A**) should be 33 mm and at (**B**) 11 mm. At the front, digits must be black on a white background and at the rear black on a yellow background. Other background designs (such as honeycomb) are not permitted.

☐ The VIN plate and/or homologation plate must be permanently displayed and legible.

Electrical equipment

☐ Switch on the ignition and check the operation of the horn.

☐ Check the windscreen washers and wipers, examining the wiper blades; renew damaged or perished blades. Also check the operation of the stop-lights.

☐ Check the operation of the sidelights and number plate lights. The lenses and reflectors must be secure, clean and undamaged.

☐ Check the operation and alignment of the headlights. The headlight reflectors must not be tarnished and the lenses must be undamaged.

☐ Switch on the ignition and check the operation of the direction indicators (including the instrument panel tell-tale) and the hazard warning lights. Operation of the sidelights and stop-lights must not affect the indicators - if it does, the cause is usually a bad earth at the rear light cluster. Indicators should flash at a rate of between 60 and 120 times per minute – faster or slower than this could indicate a fault with the flasher unit or a bad earth at one of the light units.

☐ Check the operation of the rear foglight(s), including the warning light on the instrument panel or in the switch.

☐ The warning lights must illuminate in accordance with the manufacturer's design. For most vehicles, the ABS and other warning lights should illuminate when the ignition is switched on, and (if the system is operating properly) extinguish after a few seconds. Refer to the owner's handbook.

Footbrake

☐ Examine the master cylinder, brake pipes and servo unit for leaks, loose mountings, corrosion or other damage. If ABS is fitted, this unit should also be examined for signs of leaks or corrosion.

☐ The fluid reservoir must be secure and the fluid level must be between the upper (**A**) and lower (**B**) markings.

☐ Inspect both front brake flexible hoses for cracks or deterioration of the rubber. Turn the steering from lock to lock, and ensure that the hoses do not contact the wheel, tyre, or any part of the steering or suspension mechanism. With the brake pedal firmly depressed, check the hoses for bulges or leaks under pressure.

Steering and suspension

☐ Have your assistant turn the steering wheel from side to side slightly, up to the point where the steering gear just begins to transmit this movement to the roadwheels. Check for excessive free play between the steering wheel and the steering gear, indicating wear or insecurity of the steering column joints, the column-to-steering gear coupling, or the steering gear itself.

☐ Have your assistant turn the steering wheel more vigorously in each direction, so that the roadwheels just begin to turn. As this is done, examine all the steering joints, linkages, fittings and attachments. Renew any component that shows signs of wear or damage. On vehicles with power steering, check the security and condition of the steering pump, drivebelt and hoses.

☐ Check that the vehicle is standing level, and at approximately the correct ride height.

Shock absorbers

☐ Depress each corner of the vehicle in turn, then release it. The vehicle should rise and then settle in its normal position. If the vehicle continues to rise and fall, the shock absorber is defective. A shock absorber which has seized will also cause the vehicle to fail.

Exhaust system

☐ Start the engine. With your assistant holding a rag over the tailpipe, check the entire system for leaks. Repair or renew leaking sections.

3 Checks carried out **WITH THE VEHICLE RAISED AND THE WHEELS FREE TO TURN**

Jack up the front and rear of the vehicle, and securely support it on axle stands. Position the stands clear of the suspension assemblies. Ensure that the wheels are clear of the ground and that the steering can be turned from lock to lock.

Steering mechanism

☐ Have your assistant turn the steering from lock to lock. Check that the steering turns smoothly, and that no part of the steering mechanism, including a wheel or tyre, fouls any brake hose or pipe or any part of the body structure.

☐ Examine the steering rack rubber gaiters for damage or insecurity of the retaining clips. If power steering is fitted, check for signs of damage or leakage of the fluid hoses, pipes or connections. Also check for excessive stiffness or binding of the steering, a missing split pin or locking device, or severe corrosion of the body structure within 30 cm of any steering component attachment point.

Front and rear suspension and wheel bearings

☐ Starting at the front right-hand side, grasp the roadwheel at the 3 o'clock and 9 o'clock positions and rock gently but firmly. Check for free play or insecurity at the wheel bearings, suspension balljoints, or suspension mount-ings, pivots and attachments.

☐ Now grasp the wheel at the 12 o'clock and 6 o'clock positions and repeat the previous inspection. Spin the wheel, and check for roughness or tightness of the front wheel bearing.

☐ If excess free play is suspected at a component pivot point, this can be confirmed by using a large screwdriver or similar tool and levering between the mounting and the component attachment. This will confirm whether the wear is in the pivot bush, its retaining bolt, or in the mounting itself (the bolt holes can often become elongated).

☐ Carry out all the above checks at the other front wheel, and then at both rear wheels.

Springs and shock absorbers

☐ Examine the suspension struts (when applicable) for serious fluid leakage, corrosion, or damage to the casing. Also check the security of the mounting points.

☐ If coil springs are fitted, check that the spring ends locate in their seats, and that the spring is not corroded, cracked or broken.

☐ If leaf springs are fitted, check that all leaves are intact, that the axle is securely attached to each spring, and that there is no deterioration of the spring eye mountings, bushes, and shackles.

☐ The same general checks apply to vehicles fitted with other suspension types, such as torsion bars, hydraulic displacer units, etc. Ensure that all mountings and attachments are secure, that there are no signs of excessive wear, corrosion or damage, and (on hydraulic types) that there are no fluid leaks or damaged pipes.

☐ Inspect the shock absorbers for signs of serious fluid leakage. Check for wear of the mounting bushes or attachments, or damage to the body of the unit.

Driveshafts (fwd vehicles only)

☐ Rotate each front wheel in turn and inspect the constant velocity joint gaiters for splits or damage. Also check that each driveshaft is straight and undamaged.

Braking system

☐ If possible without dismantling, check brake pad wear and disc condition. Ensure that the friction lining material has not worn excessively, (A) and that the discs are not fractured, pitted, scored or badly worn (B).

☐ Examine all the rigid brake pipes underneath the vehicle, and the flexible hose(s) at the rear. Look for corrosion, chafing or insecurity of the pipes, and for signs of bulging under pressure, chafing, splits or deterioration of the flexible hoses.

☐ Look for signs of fluid leaks at the brake calipers or on the brake backplates. Repair or renew leaking components.

☐ Slowly spin each wheel, while your assistant depresses and releases the footbrake. Ensure that each brake is operating and does not bind when the pedal is released.

□ Examine the handbrake mechanism, checking for frayed or broken cables, excessive corrosion, or wear or insecurity of the linkage. Check that the mechanism works on each relevant wheel, and releases fully, without binding.

□ It is not possible to test brake efficiency without special equipment, but a road test can be carried out later to check that the vehicle pulls up in a straight line.

Fuel and exhaust systems

□ Inspect the fuel tank (including the filler cap), fuel pipes, hoses and unions. All components must be secure and free from leaks. Locking fuel caps must lock securely and the key must be provided for the MOT test.

□ Examine the exhaust system over its entire length, checking for any damaged, broken or missing mountings, security of the retaining clamps and rust or corrosion.

Wheels and tyres

□ Examine the sidewalls and tread area of each tyre in turn. Check for cuts, tears, lumps, bulges, separation of the tread, and exposure of the ply or cord due to wear or damage. Check that the tyre bead is correctly seated on the wheel rim, that the valve is sound and properly seated, and that the wheel is not distorted or damaged.

□ Check that the tyres are of the correct size for the vehicle, that they are of the same size and type on each axle, and that the pressures are correct.

□ Check the tyre tread depth. The legal minimum at the time of writing is 1.6 mm over the central three-quarters of the tread width. Abnormal tread wear may indicate incorrect front wheel alignment or wear in steering or suspension components.

□ If the spare wheel is fitted externally or in a separate carrier beneath the vehicle, check that mountings are secure and free of excessive corrosion.

Body corrosion

□ Check the condition of the entire vehicle structure for signs of corrosion in load-bearing areas. (These include chassis box sections, side sills, cross-members, pillars, and all suspension, steering, braking system and seat belt mountings and anchorages.) Any corrosion which has seriously reduced the thickness of a load-bearing area (or is within 30 cm of safety-related components such as steering or suspension) is likely to cause the vehicle to fail. In this case professional repairs are likely to be needed.

□ Damage or corrosion which causes sharp or otherwise dangerous edges to be exposed will also cause the vehicle to fail.

Towbars

□ Check the condition of mounting points (both beneath the vehicle and within boot/hatchback areas) for signs of corrosion, ensuring that all fixings are secure and not worn or damaged. There must be no excessive play in detachable tow ball arms or quick-release mechanisms.

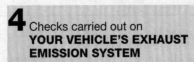

4 Checks carried out on **YOUR VEHICLE'S EXHAUST EMISSION SYSTEM**

Petrol models

□ The engine should be warmed up, and running well (ignition system in good order, air filter element clean, etc).

□ Before testing, run the engine at around 2500 rpm for 20 seconds. Let the engine drop to idle, and watch for smoke from the exhaust. If the idle speed is too high, or if dense blue or black smoke emerges for more than 5 seconds, the vehicle will fail. Typically, blue smoke signifies oil burning (engine wear);

black smoke means unburnt fuel (dirty air cleaner element, or other fuel system fault).

□ An exhaust gas analyser for measuring carbon monoxide (CO) and hydrocarbons (HC) is now needed. If one cannot be hired or borrowed, have a local garage perform the check.

CO emissions (mixture)

□ The MOT tester has access to the CO limits for all vehicles. The CO level is measured at idle speed, and at 'fast idle' (2500 to 3000 rpm). The following limits are given as a general guide:

At idle speed – Less than 0.5% CO
At 'fast idle' – Less than 0.3% CO
Lambda reading – 0.97 to 1.03

□ If the CO level is too high, this may point to poor maintenance, a fuel injection system problem, faulty lambda (oxygen) sensor or catalytic converter. Try an injector cleaning treatment, and check the vehicle's ECU for fault codes.

HC emissions

□ The MOT tester has access to HC limits for all vehicles. The HC level is measured at 'fast idle' (2500 to 3000 rpm). The following limits are given as a general guide:

At 'fast idle' – Less then 200 ppm

□ Excessive HC emissions are typically caused by oil being burnt (worn engine), or by a blocked crankcase ventilation system ('breather'). If the engine oil is old and thin, an oil change may help. If the engine is running badly, check the vehicle's ECU for fault codes.

Diesel models

□ The only emission test for diesel engines is measuring exhaust smoke density, using a calibrated smoke meter. The test involves accelerating the engine at least 3 times to its maximum unloaded speed.

Note: *On engines with a timing belt, it is VITAL that the belt is in good condition before the test is carried out.*

□ With the engine warmed up, it is first purged by running at around 2500 rpm for 20 seconds. A governor check is then carried out, by slowly accelerating the engine to its maximum speed. After this, the smoke meter is connected, and the engine is accelerated quickly to maximum speed three times. If the smoke density is less than the limits given below, the vehicle will pass:

Non-turbo vehicles: 2.5m-1
Turbocharged vehicles: 3.0m-1

□ If excess smoke is produced, try fitting a new air cleaner element, or using an injector cleaning treatment. If the engine is running badly, where applicable, check the vehicle's ECU for fault codes. Also check the vehicle's EGR system, where applicable. At high mileages, the injectors may require professional attention.

Engine

- ☐ Engine fails to rotate when attempting to start
- ☐ Engine rotates, but will not start
- ☐ Engine difficult to start when cold
- ☐ Engine difficult to start when hot
- ☐ Starter motor noisy or excessively rough in engagement
- ☐ Engine starts, but stops immediately
- ☐ Engine idles erratically
- ☐ Engine misfires at idle speed
- ☐ Engine misfires throughout the driving speed range
- ☐ Engine hesitates on acceleration
- ☐ Engine stalls
- ☐ Engine lacks power
- ☐ Engine backfires
- ☐ Engine runs-on after switching off
- ☐ Engine noises

Cooling system

- ☐ Overheating
- ☐ Overcooling
- ☐ External coolant leakage
- ☐ Internal coolant leakage
- ☐ Corrosion

Fuel and exhaust systems

- ☐ Excessive fuel consumption
- ☐ Fuel leakage and/or fuel odour
- ☐ Excessive noise or fumes from exhaust system

Clutch

- ☐ Pedal travels to floor – no pressure or very little resistance
- ☐ Clutch fails to disengage (unable to select gears)
- ☐ Clutch slips (engine speed rises, with no increase in vehicle speed)
- ☐ Judder as clutch is engaged
- ☐ Noise when depressing or releasing clutch pedal

Manual transmission

- ☐ Noisy in neutral with engine running
- ☐ Noisy in one particular gear
- ☐ Difficulty engaging gears
- ☐ Jumps out of gear
- ☐ Vibration
- ☐ Lubricant leaks

Driveshafts

- ☐ Clicking or knocking noise on turns (at slow speed on full-lock)
- ☐ Vibration when accelerating or decelerating

Braking system

- ☐ Vehicle pulls to one side under braking
- ☐ Noise (grinding or high-pitched squeal) when brakes applied
- ☐ Excessive brake pedal travel
- ☐ Brake pedal feels spongy when depressed
- ☐ Excessive brake pedal effort required to stop vehicle
- ☐ Judder felt through brake pedal or steering wheel when braking
- ☐ Brakes binding
- ☐ Rear wheels locking under normal braking

Suspension and steering

- ☐ Vehicle pulls to one side
- ☐ Wheel wobble and vibration
- ☐ Excessive pitching and/or rolling around corners, or during braking
- ☐ Wandering or general instability
- ☐ Excessively-stiff steering
- ☐ Excessive play in steering
- ☐ Lack of power assistance
- ☐ Tyre wear excessive

Electrical system

- ☐ Battery won't hold a charge for more than a few days
- ☐ Ignition/no-charge warning light stays on with engine running
- ☐ Ignition/no-charge warning light fails to come on
- ☐ Lights inoperative
- ☐ Instrument readings inaccurate or erratic
- ☐ Horn inoperative, or unsatisfactory in operation
- ☐ Windscreen/tailgate wipers failed, or unsatisfactory in operation
- ☐ Windscreen/tailgate washers failed, or unsatisfactory in operation
- ☐ Electric windows inoperative, or unsatisfactory in operation
- ☐ Central locking system inoperative, or unsatisfactory in operation

Introduction

The vehicle owner who does his or her own maintenance according to the recommended service schedules should not have to use this section of the manual very often. Modern component reliability is such that, provided those items subject to wear or deterioration are inspected or renewed at the specified intervals, sudden failure is comparatively rare. Faults do not usually just happen as a result of sudden failure, but develop over a period of time. Major mechanical failures in particular are usually preceded by characteristic symptoms over hundreds or even thousands of miles. Those components that do occasionally fail without warning are often small and easily carried in the vehicle.

With any fault-finding, the first step is to decide where to begin investigations. Sometimes this is obvious, but on other occasions, a little detective work will be necessary. The owner who makes half a dozen haphazard adjustments or replacements may be successful in curing a fault (or its symptoms), but will be none the wiser if the fault recurs, and ultimately may have spent more time and money than was necessary. A calm and logical approach will be found to be more satisfactory in the long run. Always take into account any warning signs or abnormalities that may have been noticed in the period preceding the fault – power loss, high or low gauge readings, unusual smells, etc – and remember that failure of components such as fuses or spark plugs may only be pointers to some underlying fault.

The pages that follow provide an easy-reference guide to the more common problems, which may occur during the operation of the vehicle. These problems and their possible causes are grouped under headings denoting various components or systems, such as Engine, Cooling system, etc. The general Chapter that deals with the problem is also shown in brackets; refer to the relevant part of that Chapter for system-specific information. Whatever the fault, certain basic principles apply. These are as follows:

Verify the fault. This is simply a matter of being sure that you know what the symptoms are before starting work. This is particularly important if you are investigating a fault for someone else, who may not have described it very accurately.

Don't overlook the obvious. For example, if the vehicle won't start, is there fuel in the tank? (Don't take anyone else's word on this particular point, and don't trust the fuel gauge either!) If an electrical fault is indicated, look for loose or broken wires before digging out the test gear.

Cure the disease, not the symptom. Substituting a flat battery with a fully charged one will get you off the hard shoulder, but if the underlying cause is not attended to, the new battery will go the same way. Similarly, changing oil-fouled spark plugs (petrol models) for a new set will get you moving again, but remember that the reason for the fouling (if it wasn't simply an incorrect grade of plug) will have to be found and corrected.

Don't take anything for granted. Particularly, don't forget that a 'new' component may itself be defective (especially if it's been rattling around in the boot for months), and don't leave components out of a fault diagnosis sequence just because they are new or recently fitted. When you do finally diagnose a difficult fault, you'll probably realise that all the evidence was there from the start.

Engine

Engine fails to rotate when attempting to start
- [ ] Battery terminal connections loose or corroded (Weekly checks).
- [ ] Battery discharged or faulty (Chapter 5A).
- [ ] Broken, loose or disconnected wiring in the starting circuit (Chapter 5A).
- [ ] Defective starter motor (Chapter 5A Section 9).
- [ ] Starter pinion or flywheel/driveplate ring gear teeth loose or broken (Chapter 2A or Chapter 2B and chapter 5A).
- [ ] Engine earth strap broken or disconnected (Chapter 5A).

Engine rotates, but will not start
- [ ] Fuel tank empty.
- [ ] Battery discharged (engine rotates slowly) (Chapter 5A).
- [ ] Battery terminal connections loose or corroded (See Weekly checks).
- [ ] Preheating system faulty (Chapter 5B).
- [ ] Air in fuel system (Chapter 4A).
- [ ] Fuel injector/injection pump fault (Chapter 4A).
- [ ] Low cylinder compressions (Chapter 2A or Chapter 2B).
- [ ] Major mechanical failure (eg, camshaft drive) (Chapter 2A orChapter 2B).

Engine difficult to start when cold
- [ ] Battery discharged (Chapter 5A).
- [ ] Battery terminal connections loose or corroded (See Weekly checks).
- [ ] Preheating system faulty (Chapter 5B).
- [ ] Fuel injector/injection pump fault (Chapter 4A).

Engine difficult to start when hot
- [ ] Fuel injector/injection pump fault (Chapter 4A).
- [ ] Low cylinder compressions (Chapter 2A or Chapter 2B).

Starter motor noisy or excessively rough in engagement
- [ ] Starter pinion or flywheel/driveplate ring gear teeth loose or broken (Chapter 2A or Chapter 2B and Chapter 5A).
- [ ] Starter motor mounting bolts loose or missing (Chapter 5A Section 10).
- [ ] Defective starter motor (Chapter 5A).

Engine starts, but stops immediately
- [ ] Air in fuel system (Chapter 4A).
- [ ] Fuel injector/injection pump fault (Chapter 4A).

Engine idles erratically
- [ ] Air in fuel system (Chapter 4A).
- [ ] Fuel injector/injection pump fault (Chapter 4A).
- [ ] Uneven or low cylinder compressions (Chapter 2A or Chapter 2B).
- [ ] Timing belt/chain incorrectly fitted (Chapter 2A or Chapter 2B).

- [ ] Camshaft lobes worn (Chapter 2A or Chapter 2B).
- [ ] Timing belt/chain incorrectly fitted (Chapter 2A or Chapter 2B).

Engine misfires at idle speed
- [ ] Faulty injector(s) (Chapter 4A).
- [ ] Uneven or low cylinder compressions (Chapter 2A or Chapter 2B).
- [ ] Timing belt/chain incorrectly fitted (Chapter 2A or Chapter 2B).
- [ ] Disconnected, leaking, or perished crankcase ventilation hoses (Chapter 4B).

Engine misfires throughout the driving speed range
- [ ] Fuel filter blocked (Chapter 1 Section 7).
- [ ] Fuel pump faulty (Chapter 4A).
- [ ] Fuel tank vent blocked, or fuel pipes restricted (Chapter 4A).
- [ ] Fuel injector/injection pump fault (Chapter 4A).
- [ ] Uneven or low cylinder compressions (Chapter 2A or Chapter 2B).

Engine hesitates on acceleration
- [ ] Fuel injector/injection pump fault (Chapter 4A).

Engine stalls
- [ ] Fuel filter blocked (Chapter 1 Section 7).
- [ ] Fuel pump faulty (Chapter 4A).
- [ ] Fuel tank vent blocked, or fuel pipes restricted (Chapter 4A).
- [ ] Fuel injector/injection pump fault (Chapter 4A).

Engine lacks power
- [ ] Timing belt/chain incorrectly fitted (Chapter 2A or Chapter 2B).
- [ ] Fuel filter blocked (Chapter 1 Section 7).
- [ ] Fuel pump faulty (Chapter 4A).
- [ ] Uneven or low cylinder compressions (Chapter 2A or Chapter 2B).
- [ ] Fuel injector/injection pump fault (Chapter 4A).
- [ ] Brakes binding (Chapter 1 or Chapter 9).
- [ ] Clutch slipping (Chapter 6).

Engine backfires
- [ ] Timing belt/chain incorrectly fitted (Chapter 2A or Chapter 2B).
- [ ] ◇ pressure warning light on with engine running
- [ ] Low oil level, or incorrect oil grade (See Weekly checks).
- [ ] Faulty oil pressure warning light switch (Chapter 5A).
- [ ] Worn engine bearings and/or oil pump (Chapter 2C).
- [ ] High engine operating temperature (Chapter 3).
- [ ] Oil pressure relief valve defective (Chapter 2A or Chapter 2B).
- [ ] Oil pick-up strainer clogged (Chapter 2A or Chapter 2B).

Engine runs-on after switching off
- [ ] Excessive carbon build-up in engine (Chapter 2C).
- [ ] High engine operating temperature (Chapter 3).
- [ ] Fuel injection pump fault (Chapter 4A).

Engine (continued)

Engine noises

Pre-ignition (pinking) or knocking during acceleration or under load

☐ Excessive carbon build-up in engine (Chapter 2C).

Whistling or wheezing noises

☐ Leaking vacuum hose (Chapter 4A or Chapter 9).
☐ Blowing cylinder head gasket (Chapter 2A orChapter 2B).

Tapping or rattling noises

☐ Worn valve gear or camshaft (Chapter 2A orChapter 2B).
☐ Ancillary component fault (coolant pump, alternator, etc) (Chapter 3 or Chapter 5A etc).

Knocking or thumping noises

☐ Worn big-end bearings (regular heavy knocking, perhaps less under load) (Chapter 2C).
☐ Worn main bearings (rumbling and knocking, perhaps worsening under load) (Chapter 2C).
☐ Piston slap (most noticeable when cold) (Chapter 2C).
☐ Ancillary component fault (coolant pump, alternator, etc) (Chapter 3 or Chapter 5A etc).

Cooling system

Overheating

☐ Insufficient coolant in system (See Weekly checks).
☐ Thermostat faulty (stuck closed) (Chapter 3).
☐ Radiator core blocked, or grille restricted (Chapter 3).
☐ Electric cooling fan or sensor faulty (Chapter 3).
☐ Pressure cap faulty (Chapter 3).
☐ Inaccurate temperature gauge/sensor (Chapter 3).
☐ Airlock in cooling system (Chapter 1 Section 19).
☐ Engine management system fault (Chapter 4A).

Overcooling

☐ Thermostat faulty (stuck open) (Chapter 3).
☐ Inaccurate temperature gauge/sensor (Chapter 3).

External coolant leakage

☐ Deteriorated or damaged hoses or hose clips (Chapter 1 Section 3).

☐ Radiator core or heater matrix leaking (Chapter 3).
☐ Pressure cap faulty (Chapter 3).
☐ Coolant pump leaking (Chapter 3).
☐ Boiling due to overheating (Chapter 3).
☐ Core plug leaking (Chapter 2C).

Internal coolant leakage

☐ Leaking cylinder head gasket (Chapter 2A or Chapter 2B).
☐ Cracked cylinder head or cylinder bore (Chapter 2A, Chapter 2B or Chapter 2C).

Corrosion

☐ Infrequent draining and flushing (Chapter 1 Section 19).
☐ Incorrect coolant mixture or inappropriate coolant type (Chapter 1 Section 19).

Fuel and exhaust systems

Excessive fuel consumption

☐ Air filter element dirty or clogged (Chapter 1 Section 20).
☐ Engine management system fault (Chapter 4A).
☐ Faulty injector(s) (Chapter 4A).
☐ Tyres under-inflated (See Weekly checks).
☐ Brakes binding (Chapter 1 and Chapter 9).

Fuel leakage and/or fuel odour

☐ Damaged or corroded fuel tank, pipes or connections (Chapter 4A).

Excessive noise or fumes from exhaust system

☐ Leaking exhaust system or manifold joints (Chapter 1 or Chapter 4A).
☐ Leaking, corroded or damaged silencers or pipe (Chapter 1 or Chapter 4A).
☐ Broken mountings causing body or suspension contact (Chapter 1 or Chapter 4A).

Clutch

Pedal travels to floor – no pressure or very little resistance

- ☐ Air in hydraulic system/faulty master or slave cylinder (Chapter 6).
- ☐ Broken clutch release bearing or fork (Chapter 6).
- ☐ Broken diaphragm spring in clutch pressure plate (Chapter 6).

Clutch fails to disengage (unable to select gears)

- ☐ Air in hydraulic system/faulty master or slave cylinder (Chapter 6).
- ☐ Clutch disc sticking on gearbox input shaft splines (Chapter 6).
- ☐ Clutch disc sticking to flywheel or pressure plate (Chapter 6).
- ☐ Faulty pressure plate assembly (Chapter 6).
- ☐ Clutch release mechanism worn or incorrectly assembled (Chapter 6).

Clutch slips (engine speed rises, with no increase in vehicle speed)

- ☐ Faulty hydraulic release system (Chapter 6).
- ☐ Clutch disc linings excessively worn (Chapter 6).
- ☐ Clutch disc linings contaminated with oil or grease (Chapter 6).
- ☐ Faulty pressure plate or weak diaphragm spring (Chapter 6).

Judder as clutch is engaged

- ☐ Clutch disc linings contaminated with oil or grease (Chapter 6).
- ☐ Clutch disc linings excessively worn (Chapter 6).
- ☐ Faulty or distorted pressure plate or diaphragm spring (Chapter 6).
- ☐ Worn or loose engine or gearbox mountings (Chapter 2A or Chapter 2B).
- ☐ Clutch disc hub or gearbox input shaft splines worn (Chapter 6).

Noise when depressing or releasing clutch pedal

- ☐ Worn clutch release bearing (Chapter 6).
- ☐ Worn or dry clutch pedal bushes (Chapter 6).
- ☐ Faulty pressure plate assembly (Chapter 6).
- ☐ Pressure plate diaphragm spring broken (Chapter 6).
- ☐ Broken clutch disc cushioning springs (Chapter 6).

Manual transmission

Noisy in neutral with engine running

- ☐ Input shaft bearings worn (noise apparent with clutch pedal released, but not when depressed) (Chapter 7).*
- ☐ Clutch release bearing worn (noise apparent with clutch pedal depressed, possibly less when released) (Chapter 6).

Noisy in one particular gear

- ☐ Worn, damaged or chipped gear teeth (Chapter 7).*

Difficulty engaging gears

- ☐ Clutch fault (Chapter 6).
- ☐ Worn or damaged gear selection cables (Chapter 7).
- ☐ Worn synchroniser units (Chapter 7).*

Jumps out of gear

- ☐ Worn or damaged gear selection cables (Chapter 7).

- ☐ Worn synchroniser units (Chapter 7).*
- ☐ Worn selector forks (Chapter 7).*

Vibration

- ☐ Lack of oil (Chapter 1 and Chapter 7).
- ☐ Worn bearings (Chapter 7).*

Lubricant leaks

- ☐ Leaking differential output oil seal (Chapter 7).
- ☐ Leaking housing joint (Chapter 7).*
- ☐ Leaking input shaft oil seal (Chapter 7).

Although the corrective action necessary to remedy the symptoms described is beyond the scope of the home mechanic, the above information should be helpful in isolating the cause of the condition, so that the owner can communicate clearly with a professional mechanic.

Driveshafts

Clicking or knocking noise on turns (at slow speed on full-lock)

☐ Lack of constant velocity joint lubricant, possibly due to damaged gaiter (Chapter 8).
☐ Worn outer constant velocity joint (Chapter 8).

Vibration when accelerating or decelerating

☐ Worn inner constant velocity joint (Chapter 8).
☐ Bent or distorted driveshaft (Chapter 8).
☐ Worn intermediate bearing (Chapter 8).

Braking system

Vehicle pulls to one side under braking

Note: *Before assuming that a brake problem exists, make sure that the tyres are in good condition and correctly inflated, that the front wheel alignment is correct, and that the vehicle is not loaded with weight in an unequal manner.*

☐ Apart from checking the condition of all pipe and hose connections, any faults occurring on the anti-lock braking system should be referred to a Citroën dealer for diagnosis.
☐ Worn, defective, damaged or contaminated brake pads on one side (Chapter 9).
☐ Seized or partially-seized front brake caliper (Chapter 9).
☐ A mixture of brake pad materials fitted between sides (Chapter 9).
☐ Brake caliper mounting bolts loose (Chapter 9).
☐ Worn or damaged steering or suspension components (Chapter 1 or Chapter 10).

Noise (grinding or high-pitched squeal) when brakes applied

☐ Brake pad material worn down to metal backing (Chapter 1 or Chapter 9).
☐ Excessive corrosion of brake disc.
☐ May be apparent after the vehicle has been standing for some time (Chapter 9).
☐ Foreign object (stone chipping, etc) trapped between brake disc and shield (Chapter 9).

Excessive brake pedal travel

☐ Faulty master cylinder (Chapter 9).
☐ Air in hydraulic system (Chapter 9).
☐ Faulty vacuum servo unit (Chapter 9).

Brake pedal feels spongy when depressed

☐ Air in hydraulic system (Chapter 9).
☐ Deteriorated flexible rubber brake hoses (Chapter 1 or Chapter 9).
☐ Master cylinder mounting nuts loose (Chapter 9).
☐ Faulty master cylinder (Chapter 9).

Excessive brake pedal effort required to stop vehicle

☐ Faulty vacuum servo unit (Chapter 9).
☐ Disconnected, damaged or insecure brake servo vacuum hose (Chapter 9).
☐ Primary or secondary hydraulic circuit failure (Chapter 9).
☐ Seized brake caliper (Chapter 9).
☐ Brake pads incorrectly fitted (Chapter 9).
☐ Incorrect grade of brake pads fitted (Chapter 9).
☐ Brake pads contaminated (Chapter 9).

Judder felt through brake pedal or steering wheel when braking

☐ Excessive run-out or distortion of discs (Chapter 9).
☐ Brake pads worn (Chapter 1 or Chapter 9).
☐ Brake caliper mounting bolts loose (Chapter 9).
☐ Wear in suspension or steering components or mountings (Chapter 1 or Chapter 10).

Brakes binding

☐ Seized brake caliper (Chapter 9).
☐ Incorrectly-adjusted handbrake mechanism (Chapter 9).
☐ Faulty master cylinder (Chapter 9).

Rear wheels locking under normal braking

☐ Rear brake pads contaminated (Chapter 1 or Chapter 9).
☐ ABS system fault (Chapter 9).

Suspension and steering

Vehicle pulls to one side

☐ Note: Before diagnosing suspension or steering faults, be sure that the trouble is not due to incorrect tyre pressures, mixtures of tyre types, or binding brakes.
☐ Defective tyre (See Weekly checks).
☐ Excessive wear in suspension or steering components (Chapter 1 or Chapter 10).
☐ Incorrect front wheel alignment (Chapter 10 Section 26).
☐ Damage to steering or suspension components (Chapter 1 Section 9 or Chapter 10).

Wheel wobble and vibration

☐ Front roadwheels out of balance (vibration felt mainly through the steering wheel) (Chapter 1 or Chapter 10).
☐ Rear roadwheels out of balance (vibration felt throughout the vehicle) (Chapter 1 or Chapter 10).
☐ Roadwheels damaged or distorted (Chapter 1 or Chapter 10).
☐ Faulty or damaged tyre (See Weekly checks).
☐ Worn steering or suspension joints, bushes or components (Chapter 1 Section 9 or Chapter 10).
☐ Wheel bolts loose (Chapter 1 or Chapter 10).

Excessive pitching and/or rolling around corners, or during braking

☐ Defective shock absorbers (Chapter 1 or Chapter 10).
☐ Broken or weak spring and/or suspension part (Chapter 1 or Chapter 10).
☐ Worn or damaged anti-roll bar or mountings (Chapter 10 Section 8).

Wandering or general instability

☐ Incorrect front wheel alignment (Chapter 10 Section 26).
☐ Worn steering or suspension joints, bushes or components (Chapter 1 or Chapter 10).
☐ Roadwheels out of balance (Chapter 1 or Chapter 10).
☐ Faulty or damaged tyre (See Weekly checks).
☐ Wheel bolts loose (Chapter 1 or Chapter 10).
☐ Defective shock absorbers (Chapter 1 or Chapter 10).

Excessively-stiff steering

☐ Lack of power steering fluid (Chapter 10).

☐ Seized track rod end balljoint or suspension balljoint (Chapter 1 or Chapter 10).
☐ Incorrect front wheel alignment (Chapter 10).
☐ Steering rack or column bent or damaged (Chapter 10).
☐ Power steering pump fault (Chapter 10).

Excessive play in steering

☐ Worn steering column universal joint (Chapter 10).
☐ Worn steering track rod end balljoints (Chapter 1 or Chapter 10).
☐ Worn steering rack (Chapter 10 Section 19).
☐ Worn steering or suspension joints, bushes or components (Chapter 1 or Chapter 10).

Lack of power assistance

☐ Incorrect power steering fluid level (See Weekly checks).
☐ Restriction in power steering fluid hoses (Chapter 1).
☐ Faulty power steering pump (Chapter 10 Section 22, 23).
☐ Faulty steering rack (Chapter 10 Section 19).

Tyre wear excessive

Tyre treads exhibit feathered edges

☐ Incorrect toe setting (Chapter 10 Section 26).

Tyres worn in centre of tread

☐ Tyres over-inflated (See Weekly checks).

Tyres worn on inside and outside edges

☐ Tyres under-inflated (See Weekly checks).

Tyres worn on inside or outside edges

☐ Incorrect camber/castor angles (wear on one edge only) (Chapter 10 Section 26).
☐ Worn steering or suspension joints, bushes or components (Chapter 1 or Chapter 10).
☐ Excessively-hard cornering.
☐ Accident damage.

Tyres worn unevenly

☐ Tyres/wheels out of balance (See Weekly checks).
☐ Excessive wheel or tyre run-out (Chapter 10 Section 26).
☐ Worn shock absorbers (Chapter 1 or Chapter 10).
☐ Faulty tyre (See Weekly checks).

Electrical system

Battery won't hold a charge for more than a few days

- [ ] Note: For problems associated with the starting system, refer to the faults listed under 'Engine' earlier in this Section.
- [ ] Battery defective internally (Chapter 5A).
- [ ] Battery terminal connections loose or corroded (See Weekly checks).
- [ ] Auxiliary drivebelt broken, worn or incorrectly adjusted (Chapter 1 Section 16).
- [ ] Alternator not charging at correct output (Chapter 5A Section 5).
- [ ] Alternator or voltage regulator faulty (Chapter 5A Section 5).
- [ ] Short-circuit causing continual battery drain (Chapter 5A and Chapter 12).

Ignition/no-charge warning light stays on with engine running

- [ ] Auxiliary drivebelt broken, worn, or incorrectly adjusted (Chapter 1 Section 16).
- [ ] Internal fault in alternator or voltage regulator (Chapter 5A Section 5).
- [ ] Broken, disconnected, or loose wiring in charging circuit (Chapter 5A Section 5).

Ignition/no-charge warning light fails to come on

- [ ] Warning light bulb blown (Chapter 12).
- [ ] Broken, disconnected, or loose wiring in warning light circuit (Chapter 12).
- [ ] Alternator faulty (Chapter 5A Section 5, 7).

Lights inoperative

- [ ] Bulb blown (Chapter 12).
- [ ] Corrosion of bulb or bulbholder contacts (Chapter 12 Section 5, 6).
- [ ] Blown fuse (Chapter 12 Section 3).
- [ ] Faulty relay (Chapter 12 Section 3).
- [ ] Broken, loose, or disconnected wiring (Chapter 12).
- [ ] Faulty switch (Chapter 12 Section 2, 4).

Instrument readings inaccurate or erratic

Fuel or temperature gauges give no reading

- [ ] Faulty gauge sensor unit (Chapter 3 or Chapter 4A).
- [ ] Wiring open-circuit (Chapter 12 Section 2).
- [ ] Faulty gauge (Chapter 12).

Fuel or temperature gauges give continuous maximum reading

- [ ] Faulty gauge sensor unit (Chapter 3 or Chapter 4A).
- [ ] Wiring short-circuit (Chapter 12 Section 2).
- [ ] Faulty gauge (Chapter 12).

Horn inoperative, or unsatisfactory in operation

Horn operates all the time

- [ ] Horn push either earthed or stuck down (Chapter 12).
- [ ] Horn cable-to-horn push earthed (Chapter 12).

Horn fails to operate

- [ ] Blown fuse (Chapter 12 Section 3).
- [ ] Cable or cable connections loose, broken or disconnected (Chapter 12 Section 2).
- [ ] Faulty horn (Chapter 12 Section 12).

Horn emits intermittent or unsatisfactory sound

- [ ] Cable connections loose (Chapter 12 Section 2).
- [ ] Horn mountings loose (Chapter 12 Section 12).
- [ ] Faulty horn (Chapter 12 Section 12).

Windscreen/tailgate wipers failed, or unsatisfactory in operation

Wipers fail to operate, or operate very slowly

- [ ] Wiper blades stuck to screen, or linkage seized or binding (Chapter 12 Section 14).
- [ ] Blown fuse (Chapter 12 Section 3).
- [ ] Cable or cable connections loose, broken or disconnected (Chapter 12 Section 2).
- [ ] Faulty built-in system interface (BSI) unit (Chapter 12 Section 23).
- [ ] Faulty wiper motor (Chapter 12 Section 14).

Wiper blades sweep over too large or too small an area of the glass

- [ ] Wiper arms incorrectly positioned on spindles (Chapter 12 Section 13).
- [ ] Excessive wear of wiper linkage (Chapter 12 Section 14).
- [ ] Wiper motor or linkage mountings loose or insecure (Chapter 12 Section 14).

Wiper blades fail to clean the glass effectively

- [ ] Wiper blade rubbers worn or perished (See Weekly checks).
- [ ] Wiper arm tension springs broken, or arm pivots seized (Chapter 12 Section 13).
- [ ] Insufficient windscreen washer additive to adequately remove road film (See Weekly checks).

Windscreen/tailgate washers failed, or unsatisfactory in operation

One or more washer jets inoperative

- [ ] Blocked washer jet (See Weekly checks).
- [ ] Disconnected, kinked or restricted fluid hose (Chapter 12 Section 16).
- [ ] Insufficient fluid in washer reservoir (See Weekly checks).

Washer pump fails to operate

- [ ] Broken or disconnected wiring or connections (Chapter 12 Section 16).
- [ ] Blown fuse (Chapter 12 Section 3).
- [ ] Faulty washer switch (Chapter 12 Section 4).
- [ ] Faulty washer pump (Chapter 12 Section 16).

Electrical system (continued)

Electric windows inoperative, or unsatisfactory in operation

Window glass will only move in one direction
- [ ] Faulty switch (Chapter 12 Section 4).

Window glass slow to move
- [ ] Regulator seized or damaged, or in need of lubricant (Chapter 11 Section 15).
- [ ] Door internal components or trim fouling regulator (Chapter 11 Section 15).
- [ ] Faulty motor (Chapter 11 Section 15).

Window glass fails to move
- [ ] Blown fuse (Chapter 12 Section 3).
- [ ] Broken or disconnected wiring or connections (Chapter 12 Section 2).
- [ ] Faulty motor (Chapter 11 Section 15).
- [ ] Faulty built-in systems interface (BSI) unit (Chapter 12 Section 23).

Central locking system inoperative, or unsatisfactory in operation

Complete system failure
- [ ] Blown fuse (Chapter 12 Section 3).
- [ ] Broken or disconnected wiring or connections (Chapter 12 Section 2).
- [ ] Faulty built-in system interface (BSI) unit (Chapter 12 Section 23).

Door/tailgate locks but will not unlock, or unlocks but will not lock
- [ ] Broken or disconnected link rod(s) (Chapter 11 Section 12, 13, 14).
- [ ] Faulty lock motor (Chapter 11 Section 12, 13, 14).
- [ ] lock fails to operate
- [ ] Broken or disconnected wiring or connections (Chapter 12 Section 2).
- [ ] Faulty lock motor (Chapter 11 Section 12, 13, 14).
- [ ] Broken, binding or disconnected link rod(s) (Chapter 11 Section 12, 13, 14).

A

ABS (Anti-lock brake system) A system, usually electronically controlled, that senses incipient wheel lockup during braking and relieves hydraulic pressure at wheels that are about to skid.

Air bag An inflatable bag hidden in the steering wheel (driver's side) or the dash or glovebox (passenger side). In a head-on collision, the bags inflate, preventing the driver and front passenger from being thrown forward into the steering wheel or windscreen.

Air cleaner A metal or plastic housing, containing a filter element, which removes dust and dirt from the air being drawn into the engine.

Air filter element The actual filter in an air cleaner system, usually manufactured from pleated paper and requiring renewal at regular intervals.

Air filter

Allen key A hexagonal wrench which fits into a recessed hexagonal hole.

Alligator clip A long-nosed spring-loaded metal clip with meshing teeth. Used to make temporary electrical connections.

Alternator A component in the electrical system which converts mechanical energy from a drivebelt into electrical energy to charge the battery and to operate the starting system, ignition system and electrical accessories.

Ampere (amp) A unit of measurement for the flow of electric current. One amp is the amount of current produced by one volt acting through a resistance of one ohm.

Anaerobic sealer A substance used to prevent bolts and screws from loosening. Anaerobic means that it does not require oxygen for activation. The Loctite brand is widely used.

Antifreeze A substance (usually ethylene glycol) mixed with water, and added to a vehicle's cooling system, to prevent freezing of the coolant in winter. Antifreeze also contains chemicals to inhibit corrosion and the formation of rust and other deposits that would tend to clog the radiator and coolant passages and reduce cooling efficiency.

Anti-seize compound A coating that reduces the risk of seizing on fasteners that are subjected to high temperatures, such as exhaust manifold bolts and nuts.

Asbestos A natural fibrous mineral with great heat resistance, commonly used in the composition of brake friction materials.

Asbestos is a health hazard and the dust created by brake systems should never be inhaled or ingested.

Axle A shaft on which a wheel revolves, or which revolves with a wheel. Also, a solid beam that connects the two wheels at one end of the vehicle. An axle which also transmits power to the wheels is known as a live axle.

Axleshaft A single rotating shaft, on either side of the differential, which delivers power from the final drive assembly to the drive wheels. Also called a driveshaft or a halfshaft.

B

Ball bearing An anti-friction bearing consisting of a hardened inner and outer race with hardened steel balls between two races.

Bearing The curved surface on a shaft or in a bore, or the part assembled into either, that permits relative motion between them with minimum wear and friction.

Bearing

Big-end bearing The bearing in the end of the connecting rod that's attached to the crankshaft.

Bleed nipple A valve on a brake wheel cylinder, caliper or other hydraulic component that is opened to purge the hydraulic system of air. Also called a bleed screw.

Brake bleeding Procedure for removing air from lines of a hydraulic brake system.

Brake bleeding

Brake disc The component of a disc brake that rotates with the wheels.

Brake drum The component of a drum brake that rotates with the wheels.

Brake linings The friction material which contacts the brake disc or drum to retard the vehicle's speed. The linings are bonded or riveted to the brake pads or shoes.

Brake pads The replaceable friction pads that pinch the brake disc when the brakes are applied. Brake pads consist of a friction material bonded or riveted to a rigid backing plate.

Brake shoe The crescent-shaped carrier to which the brake linings are mounted and which forces the lining against the rotating drum during braking.

Braking systems For more information on braking systems, consult the *Haynes Automotive Brake Manual*.

Breaker bar A long socket wrench handle providing greater leverage.

Bulkhead The insulated partition between the engine and the passenger compartment.

C

Caliper The non-rotating part of a disc-brake assembly that straddles the disc and carries the brake pads. The caliper also contains the hydraulic components that cause the pads to pinch the disc when the brakes are applied. A caliper is also a measuring tool that can be set to measure inside or outside dimensions of an object.

Camshaft A rotating shaft on which a series of cam lobes operate the valve mechanisms. The camshaft may be driven by gears, by sprockets and chain or by sprockets and a belt.

Canister A container in an evaporative emission control system; contains activated charcoal granules to trap vapours from the fuel system.

Canister

Carburettor A device which mixes fuel with air in the proper proportions to provide a desired power output from a spark ignition internal combustion engine.

Castellated Resembling the parapets along the top of a castle wall. For example, a castellated balljoint stud nut.

Castor In wheel alignment, the backward or forward tilt of the steering axis. Castor is positive when the steering axis is inclined rearward at the top.

Catalytic converter A silencer-like device in the exhaust system which converts certain pollutants in the exhaust gases into less harmful substances.

Catalytic converter

Circlip A ring-shaped clip used to prevent endwise movement of cylindrical parts and shafts. An internal circlip is installed in a groove in a housing; an external circlip fits into a groove on the outside of a cylindrical piece such as a shaft.

Clearance The amount of space between two parts. For example, between a piston and a cylinder, between a bearing and a journal, etc.

Coil spring A spiral of elastic steel found in various sizes throughout a vehicle, for example as a springing medium in the suspension and in the valve train.

Compression Reduction in volume, and increase in pressure and temperature, of a gas, caused by squeezing it into a smaller space.

Compression ratio The relationship between cylinder volume when the piston is at top dead centre and cylinder volume when the piston is at bottom dead centre.

Constant velocity (CV) joint A type of universal joint that cancels out vibrations caused by driving power being transmitted through an angle.

Core plug A disc or cup-shaped metal device inserted in a hole in a casting through which core was removed when the casting was formed. Also known as a freeze plug or expansion plug.

Crankcase The lower part of the engine block in which the crankshaft rotates.

Crankshaft The main rotating member, or shaft, running the length of the crankcase, with offset "throws" to which the connecting rods are attached.

Crankshaft assembly

Crocodile clip See Alligator clip

D

Diagnostic code Code numbers obtained by accessing the diagnostic mode of an engine management computer. This code can be used to determine the area in the system where a malfunction may be located.

Disc brake A brake design incorporating a rotating disc onto which brake pads are squeezed. The resulting friction converts the energy of a moving vehicle into heat.

Double-overhead cam (DOHC) An engine that uses two overhead camshafts, usually one for the intake valves and one for the exhaust valves.

Drivebelt(s) The belt(s) used to drive accessories such as the alternator, water pump, power steering pump, air conditioning compressor, etc. off the crankshaft pulley.

Accessory drivebelts

Driveshaft Any shaft used to transmit motion. Commonly used when referring to the axleshafts on a front wheel drive vehicle.

Drum brake A type of brake using a drum-shaped metal cylinder attached to the inner surface of the wheel. When the brake pedal is pressed, curved brake shoes with friction linings press against the inside of the drum to slow or stop the vehicle.

E

EGR valve A valve used to introduce exhaust gases into the intake air stream.

Electronic control unit (ECU) A computer which controls (for instance) ignition and fuel injection systems, or an anti-lock braking system. For more information refer to the *Haynes Automotive Electrical and Electronic Systems Manual*.

Electronic Fuel Injection (EFI) A computer controlled fuel system that distributes fuel through an injector located in each intake port of the engine.

Emergency brake A braking system, independent of the main hydraulic system, that can be used to slow or stop the vehicle if the primary brakes fail, or to hold the vehicle stationary even though the brake pedal isn't depressed. It usually consists of a hand lever that actuates either front or rear brakes mechanically through a series of cables and linkages. Also known as a handbrake or parking brake.

Endfloat The amount of lengthwise movement between two parts. As applied to a crankshaft, the distance that the crankshaft can move forward and back in the cylinder block.

Engine management system (EMS) A computer controlled system which manages the fuel injection and the ignition systems in an integrated fashion.

Exhaust manifold A part with several passages through which exhaust gases leave the engine combustion chambers and enter the exhaust pipe.

F

Fan clutch A viscous (fluid) drive coupling device which permits variable engine fan speeds in relation to engine speeds.

Feeler blade A thin strip or blade of hardened steel, ground to an exact thickness, used to check or measure clearances between parts.

Feeler blade

Firing order The order in which the engine cylinders fire, or deliver their power strokes, beginning with the number one cylinder.

Flywheel A heavy spinning wheel in which energy is absorbed and stored by means of momentum. On cars, the flywheel is attached to the crankshaft to smooth out firing impulses.

Free play The amount of travel before any action takes place. The "looseness" in a linkage, or an assembly of parts, between the initial application of force and actual movement. For example, the distance the brake pedal moves before the pistons in the master cylinder are actuated.

Fuse An electrical device which protects a circuit against accidental overload. The typical fuse contains a soft piece of metal which is calibrated to melt at a predetermined current flow (expressed as amps) and break the circuit.

Fusible link A circuit protection device consisting of a conductor surrounded by heat-resistant insulation. The conductor is smaller than the wire it protects, so it acts as the weakest link in the circuit. Unlike a blown fuse, a failed fusible link must frequently be cut from the wire for replacement.

G

Gap The distance the spark must travel in jumping from the centre electrode to the side electrode in a spark plug. Also refers to the spacing between the points in a contact breaker assembly in a conventional points-type ignition, or to the distance between the reluctor or rotor and the pickup coil in an electronic ignition.

Adjusting spark plug gap

Gasket Any thin, soft material - usually cork, cardboard, asbestos or soft metal - installed between two metal surfaces to ensure a good seal. For instance, the cylinder head gasket seals the joint between the block and the cylinder head.

Gasket

Gauge An instrument panel display used to monitor engine conditions. A gauge with a movable pointer on a dial or a fixed scale is an analogue gauge. A gauge with a numerical readout is called a digital gauge.

H

Halfshaft A rotating shaft that transmits power from the final drive unit to a drive wheel, usually when referring to a live rear axle.
Harmonic balancer A device designed to reduce torsion or twisting vibration in the crankshaft. May be incorporated in the crankshaft pulley. Also known as a vibration damper.
Hone An abrasive tool for correcting small irregularities or differences in diameter in an engine cylinder, brake cylinder, etc.
Hydraulic tappet A tappet that utilises hydraulic pressure from the engine's lubrication system to maintain zero clearance (constant contact with both camshaft and valve stem). Automatically adjusts to variation in valve stem length. Hydraulic tappets also reduce valve noise.

I

Ignition timing The moment at which the spark plug fires, usually expressed in the number of crankshaft degrees before the piston reaches the top of its stroke.
Inlet manifold A tube or housing with passages through which flows the air-fuel mixture (carburettor vehicles and vehicles with throttle body injection) or air only (port fuel-injected vehicles) to the port openings in the cylinder head.

J

Jump start Starting the engine of a vehicle with a discharged or weak battery by attaching jump leads from the weak battery to a charged or helper battery.

L

Load Sensing Proportioning Valve (LSPV) A brake hydraulic system control valve that works like a proportioning valve, but also takes into consideration the amount of weight carried by the rear axle.
Locknut A nut used to lock an adjustment nut, or other threaded component, in place. For example, a locknut is employed to keep the adjusting nut on the rocker arm in position.
Lockwasher A form of washer designed to prevent an attaching nut from working loose.

M

MacPherson strut A type of front suspension system devised by Earle MacPherson at Ford of England. In its original form, a simple lateral link with the anti-roll bar creates the lower control arm. A long strut - an integral coil spring and shock absorber - is mounted between the body and the steering knuckle. Many modern so-called MacPherson strut systems use a conventional lower A-arm and don't rely on the anti-roll bar for location.
Multimeter An electrical test instrument with the capability to measure voltage, current and resistance.

N

NOx Oxides of Nitrogen. A common toxic pollutant emitted by petrol and diesel engines at higher temperatures.

O

Ohm The unit of electrical resistance. One volt applied to a resistance of one ohm will produce a current of one amp.
Ohmmeter An instrument for measuring electrical resistance.
O-ring A type of sealing ring made of a special rubber-like material; in use, the O-ring is compressed into a groove to provide the sealing action.
Overhead cam (ohc) engine An engine with the camshaft(s) located on top of the cylinder head(s).

Overhead valve (ohv) engine An engine with the valves located in the cylinder head, but with the camshaft located in the engine block.
Oxygen sensor A device installed in the engine exhaust manifold, which senses the oxygen content in the exhaust and converts this information into an electric current. Also called a Lambda sensor.

P

Phillips screw A type of screw head having a cross instead of a slot for a corresponding type of screwdriver.
Plastigage A thin strip of plastic thread, available in different sizes, used for measuring clearances. For example, a strip of Plastigage is laid across a bearing journal. The parts are assembled and dismantled; the width of the crushed strip indicates the clearance between journal and bearing.

Plastigage

Propeller shaft The long hollow tube with universal joints at both ends that carries power from the transmission to the differential on front-engined rear wheel drive vehicles.
Proportioning valve A hydraulic control valve which limits the amount of pressure to the rear brakes during panic stops to prevent wheel lock-up.

R

Rack-and-pinion steering A steering system with a pinion gear on the end of the steering shaft that mates with a rack (think of a geared wheel opened up and laid flat). When the steering wheel is turned, the pinion turns, moving the rack to the left or right. This movement is transmitted through the track rods to the steering arms at the wheels.
Radiator A liquid-to-air heat transfer device designed to reduce the temperature of the coolant in an internal combustion engine cooling system.
Refrigerant Any substance used as a heat transfer agent in an air-conditioning system. R-12 has been the principle refrigerant for many years; recently, however, manufacturers have begun using R-134a, a non-CFC substance that is considered less harmful to the ozone in the upper atmosphere.
Rocker arm A lever arm that rocks on a shaft or pivots on a stud. In an overhead valve engine, the rocker arm converts the upward movement of the pushrod into a downward movement to open a valve.

Rotor In a distributor, the rotating device inside the cap that connects the centre electrode and the outer terminals as it turns, distributing the high voltage from the coil secondary winding to the proper spark plug. Also, that part of an alternator which rotates inside the stator. Also, the rotating assembly of a turbocharger, including the compressor wheel, shaft and turbine wheel.

Runout The amount of wobble (in-and-out movement) of a gear or wheel as it's rotated. The amount a shaft rotates "out-of-true." The out-of-round condition of a rotating part.

S

Sealant A liquid or paste used to prevent leakage at a joint. Sometimes used in conjunction with a gasket.

Sealed beam lamp An older headlight design which integrates the reflector, lens and filaments into a hermetically-sealed one-piece unit. When a filament burns out or the lens cracks, the entire unit is simply replaced.

Serpentine drivebelt A single, long, wide accessory drivebelt that's used on some newer vehicles to drive all the accessories, instead of a series of smaller, shorter belts. Serpentine drivebelts are usually tensioned by an automatic tensioner.

Serpentine drivebelt

Shim Thin spacer, commonly used to adjust the clearance or relative positions between two parts. For example, shims inserted into or under bucket tappets control valve clearances. Clearance is adjusted by changing the thickness of the shim.

Slide hammer A special puller that screws into or hooks onto a component such as a shaft or bearing; a heavy sliding handle on the shaft bottoms against the end of the shaft to knock the component free.

Sprocket A tooth or projection on the periphery of a wheel, shaped to engage with a chain or drivebelt. Commonly used to refer to the sprocket wheel itself.

Starter inhibitor switch On vehicles with an automatic transmission, a switch that prevents starting if the vehicle is not in Neutral or Park.

Strut See MacPherson strut.

T

Tappet A cylindrical component which transmits motion from the cam to the valve stem, either directly or via a pushrod and rocker arm. Also called a cam follower.

Thermostat A heat-controlled valve that regulates the flow of coolant between the cylinder block and the radiator, so maintaining optimum engine operating temperature. A thermostat is also used in some air cleaners in which the temperature is regulated.

Thrust bearing The bearing in the clutch assembly that is moved in to the release levers by clutch pedal action to disengage the clutch. Also referred to as a release bearing.

Timing belt A toothed belt which drives the camshaft. Serious engine damage may result if it breaks in service.

Timing chain A chain which drives the camshaft.

Toe-in The amount the front wheels are closer together at the front than at the rear. On rear wheel drive vehicles, a slight amount of toe-in is usually specified to keep the front wheels running parallel on the road by offsetting other forces that tend to spread the wheels apart.

Toe-out The amount the front wheels are closer together at the rear than at the front. On front wheel drive vehicles, a slight amount of toe-out is usually specified.

Tools For full information on choosing and using tools, refer to the *Haynes Automotive Tools Manual*.

Tracer A stripe of a second colour applied to a wire insulator to distinguish that wire from another one with the same colour insulator.

Tune-up A process of accurate and careful adjustments and parts replacement to obtain the best possible engine performance.

Turbocharger A centrifugal device, driven by exhaust gases, that pressurises the intake air. Normally used to increase the power output from a given engine displacement, but can also be used primarily to reduce exhaust emissions (as on VW's "Umwelt" Diesel engine).

U

Universal joint or U-joint A double-pivoted connection for transmitting power from a driving to a driven shaft through an angle. A U-joint consists of two Y-shaped yokes and a cross-shaped member called the spider.

V

Valve A device through which the flow of liquid, gas, vacuum, or loose material in bulk may be started, stopped, or regulated by a movable part that opens, shuts, or partially obstructs one or more ports or passageways. A valve is also the movable part of such a device.

Valve clearance The clearance between the valve tip (the end of the valve stem) and the rocker arm or tappet. The valve clearance is measured when the valve is closed.

Vernier caliper A precision measuring instrument that measures inside and outside dimensions. Not quite as accurate as a micrometer, but more convenient.

Viscosity The thickness of a liquid or its resistance to flow.

Volt A unit for expressing electrical "pressure" in a circuit. One volt that will produce a current of one ampere through a resistance of one ohm.

W

Welding Various processes used to join metal items by heating the areas to be joined to a molten state and fusing them together. For more information refer to the *Haynes Automotive Welding Manual*.

Wiring diagram A drawing portraying the components and wires in a vehicle's electrical system, using standardised symbols. For more information refer to the *Haynes Automotive Electrical and Electronic Systems Manual*.

Note: *References throughout this index are in the form* **"Chapter number"** • **"Page number"**. *So, for example, 2C•15 refers to page 15 of Chapter 2C.*

Note: *References throughout this index are in the form* "**Chapter number**" • "**Page number**". *So, for example, 2C•15 refers to page 15 of Chapter 2C.*